BIBLICAL LOGIC
IN THEORY & PRACTICE

Biblical Logic
In theory & Practice

Refuting the Fallacies of Humanism, Darwinism,
Atheism, and Just Plain Stupidity

Joel McDurmon

American Vision Press
Powder Springs, Georgia

Biblical Logic
In Theory and Practice

by Joel McDurmon

Copyright © 2009 *The American Vision, Inc*

The American Vision, Inc.
3150 Florence Road
Powder Springs, Georgia 30127-5385
www.AmericanVision.org
1-800-628-9460

No part of this publication may be reproduced, stored in a retrieval system, or transmitted in any form by any means, electronic, mechanical, photocopy, recording, or otherwise, without the prior written permission of the publisher, except for brief quotations in critical reviews or articles. Such quotations must be in context.

Printed in the United States of America.

Jacket design by Luis Lovelace
Typesetting by Adam Stiles

ISBN10: 0-9840641-1-7
ISBN13: 978-0-9840641-1-3

CONTENTS

PART ONE: A BIBLICAL STUDY OF LOGIC

INTRODUCTION: *Five Points of Truth and Fallacy* 9
1 THE BIBLICAL MANDATE FOR LOGICAL THINKING 19
2 THEOLOGICAL FOUNDATIONS OF LOGIC 27
3 THE TEN COMMANDMENTS AND LOGIC 41
4 THE BIBLE AND CRITICAL THINKING 53
5 SOPHISTRY, REFUTATION, AND FALLACY 61

PART TWO: BIBLICAL LOGIC APPLIED

Fallacies of Worldview:

6 "LEAKY BUCKETS": *Fallacies of Worldview* 77

Fallacies of Representation:

7 "TOO SIMPLE": *Fallacies of Oversimplification* 103
    FALSE DILEMMA
    GENERALIZATIONS *(Sweeping and Hasty)*
    REDUCTIONISM

8 "NOT CLEAR": *Fallacies of Ambiguity* 123
    AMPHIBOLY
    EQUIVOCATION
    HYPOSTIZATION/REIFICATION
    ACCENT

9 "HIDDEN PRESUMPTIONS": *Fallacies of Plain Deceit* 149
    BEGGING THE QUESTION
    EPITHET/EUPHEMISM
    COMPLEX "TRICK" QUESTION
    DOUBLE STANDARD
    THE BIG "IF"

10 "STRETCHING THE FACTS": *Fallacies of Distortion* — 185
   FALSE ANALOGY
   COMPOSITION/DIVISION
   STRAW MAN
   INCREMENTS/CONTINUUM *(Beards)*

Fallacies of Property:

11 "BREAKING BOUNDARIES": *Fallacies of Property* — 223
   "IS" AND "OUGHT"
   CATEGORY MISTAKES

Fallacies of Relevance:

12 "DOESN'T MATTER": *Fallacies of Dogmatism* — 245
   APPEAL TO AUTHORITY *(one, many, elite)*
   APPEAL TO IGNORANCE
   ARGUMENT FROM SILENCE

13 "NO SWEAT": *Fallacies of Emotion* — 271
   APPEAL TO FORCE/FEAR
   APPEAL TO PITY
   PEER PRESSURE/MOB
   POISONING THE WELL

14 "WRONG ROAD": *Fallacies of Diversion* — 315
   AD HOMINEM
   RED-HERRING

Fallacies of Time:

15 "OUT OF TOUCH": *Fallacies of Time* — 337
   FALLACIES OF CAUSE
   GAMBLER'S FALLACY
   SLIPPERY SLOPE

16 "ANCIENTS VS. MODERNS": *Fallacies of the Age* — 367
   APPEAL TO PROGRESS
   APPEAL TO ANTIQUITY

APPENDIX: *Augustine and Calvin vs. Rationalism* — 385
INDEX — 399

PART ONE

A BIBLICAL STUDY OF LOGIC

Introduction:
Five Points of Truth and Fallacy

Like all things that exist before the face of God, we can only fully understand truth and logic from within God's covenantal plan for man. God's covenants always include five points: God, Man, Law, Consequences, and Inheritance.[1] We must consider how truth and logic relate to each area—how they affect each area, and how each area affects our understanding of them. We can easily develop such an understanding by posing related questions about truth. Once we have done so for each covenantal point, we can easily see how ignoring the role of truth and logic in any particular area creates specific, understandable types of fallacies. A brief introduction to these five crucial perspectives on truth and critical thinking follows below.

What is truth?

The first point addresses ultimacy: God. From a covenant perspective believers must ask, "Who's in charge here?" "Where does the buck stop?" "What is ultimate, really?" In relation to truth and logic we must ask, "What is true, ultimately?" and, "What guarantees the certainty of our laws of thinking"?

Pontius Pilate's interrogation of Christ has always interested me for the great irony it presents. The King of Kings stands before the inquisition and judgment of the Roman ruler of Judea, one of the least respected Roman provinces. When Pilate asked Jesus if He was a king, Jesus responded, *You say that I am a king. For this purpose I was born and for this purpose I have come into the world—to bear witness to the truth. Everyone who is of the truth listens to my voice* (John 18:37). Pilate gave the classic response of a skeptic: "What is truth?" There stood Jesus, the personal embodiment of Truth; Pilate stood looking Him in the face, and Pilate could not see Him. This scene, to me, perhaps portrays most clearly the effects of human depravity on the mind. Pilate, an educated man, looked Truth Himself in the face and asked, "What is truth?"

From this story, among other things, we learn that the existence of truth, and even the stark clarity of truth staring someone in the face, does not guarantee that anyone will accept it. Even with impeccable truth and logic, people may still call you a phony and refuse to accept the truth you offer. Truth may exist while people reject it; and people may in turn create all types of falsehoods and call them truth. These activities represent fallen man's desperate attempts to impute his own truth instead of God's.

In the long run, however, everyone must answer the question of ultimate truth—in fact they do answer it, even if they cannot articulate it—and how they answer the question in turn has far-reaching effects for the rest of their worldview. The first part of this book lays out the case for a distinctly biblical view of logic and critical thinking. Apart from this, I would argue, no sound worldview can stand. The following two chapters deal with what I call Worldview Fallacies, including how the unbiblical assumptions people can make about ultimate reality fail, and in failing they destroy all further foundations of knowledge, morality, and peace.

Working from the biblical view of reasoning, I will continue on to the next major point: man, or representation.

Speaking for Truth

After God comes the second major point, Man; but this refers to man as the Image of God, and thus God's representative on earth. Representation plays a central role in a biblical worldview, as Adam represented all mankind in his fall, and Christ represents all believers in His death, burial, resurrection, and glorification. As the Image of God, we should act as faithful representatives of His character. Adam failed in this (and we do too), but through Christ we aim for a higher standard: God's commandments.

One of the most pressing concerns for scholars, students, debaters, and everyone actually, involves the question of representing the truth. By this I mean both how we present our own arguments to the public, and how we represent the arguments of those we disagree with. Representation play a vital role the Christian faith, and we must make every effort to treat God and others fairly and faithfully in what we speak and write.

Never forget that intellectual endeavors always involve at least two parties: each one involves at least you and God, but more often than not they involve or you, God, and other people. Either way, this means that your claims, arguments, and propositions will always fall under scrutiny—the judgment of God and of others. As the proverb says, *The first to plead his case seems right, until another comes and examines him* (Prov. 18:17). We should, therefore, endeavor to present a case so impeccably clear and unassailable that our cross-examiners (whether they be casual listeners, or critical analysts) can do nothing but submit to our reasoning or fall into fallacy themselves.

This means presenting our opponents' arguments in their fullest, strongest, and most positive light possible. The Reformed scholar Loraine Boettner speaks strongly to this point. As he criticizes some enthusiastic prophecy writers for presenting their own theories with an authoritative air while they ignore competing views Boettner writes, "True scholars do not hesitate to state the position of an opponent, and then expose the errors, if there are any." In fact, he adds, "It has often been said that a person really does not know either side of a question until he knows both sides."[2] Many have noted of the influential medieval theologian Thomas Aquinas that he presented his opponents' arguments better than they themselves did.[3] Part of his success and fame certainly derives from this fact, and no doubt he earned the respect of many of his opponents for it, even if they disagreed with his conclusions.

Part of achieving the ability to represent others fairly requires us to overcome fears and dysfunctions in our own souls. Fallacies arise quite often from the hidden sins and prejudices of the heart, and chief among these prejudices—perhaps subsuming them all—lurks *pride*. As C. S. Lewis explains, the great sin of all sins is that of spiritual pride or self-conceit: unduly exalting ourselves above others, even before God himself. He writes, "[I]t was through Pride that the devil became the devil: Pride leads to every other vice: it is the complete anti-God state of mind."[4]

Pride will move us to miss truth simply because we already dearly hold certain perceptions and will not open up to other possibilities. Proud Naaman almost missed being healed of leprosy because he did not like the way the truth came to him. Through the suggestion of a servant girl he traveled to Elisha's house. Instead of meeting the soldier directly, Elisha sent a messenger to tell him what to do: go dip in the muddy Jordan river. Naaman grew angry. "I thought the prophet would speak to important me directly! And why the Jordan? Why not one of the *clean* rivers in Syria?!" Were it not for the persuading efforts of his servants, he would have missed God's blessing (2 Kings 5:1–14). Were it not for a servant girl, a prophet's messenger servant, and Naaman's personal servants, the truth would not have prevailed. Like Naaman, if we let our preconceptions about the world and our own sense of importance about ourselves drive our worldview and view of God, then we risk missing the truth altogether. We must listen to everyone, and enter the muddy trenches of intellectual discourse in faith that God's truth will prevail.

Jesus taught that the things which defile a man come from the heart (Matt. 15:1–20). Out of the fallen human heart comes *murders, adulteries, fornications, thefts, false witness, slanders*. These hidden, spiritual forces drive us to hedge, overstate, ignore, or otherwise misrepresent views and opinions that conflict with our own. Jesus gave this teaching purposefully to correct the misrepresentation of godliness promoted by the Pharisees. They condemned the disciples for not washing their hands according to *the tradition of the elders* (Matt. 15:2). Jesus pointed out that parts of their beloved tradition ignored *the commandment of God* (15:3). Thus they attempted to enforce a piety not revealed by God while simultaneously breaking some of what God had revealed. Thus they honored God in speech, but their hearts ignored Him (15:8). Such power does the heart have to trample God's law in the name of God, and predispose a person against God in the name of righteousness.

Even the famous atheistic philosopher Antony Flew recognized the power that prejudices and preconceptions have in leading us to distort our arguments. He recognized this, keenly, in the careless use of the word "prejudice" itself:

> Often it is treated as roughly equivalent to 'opinion' or 'conviction', albeit with powerful pejorative overtones. In this all too common abusage I have my opinions and convictions, but you and he merely have prejudices—so called for no better reason than that they are yours or his and not mine....
>
> It is obscurantist and demoralizing to apply the word in order to abuse other people's opinions, or even all strong convictions simply as such.... What is obnoxious, and what merits all the abuse in the stockpile, is the willful maintaining of preconceptions against the weight of the evidence. But to do that is not an always incurable feature of the human condition. Nor is it the exclusive prerogative of other people.[5]

Overcoming the fears and prejudices that distort our argumentation imposes a difficult and sometimes painful process, but we have good reasons to endure it. First, it is the nature of *learning* that we are often proven wrong. The process of learning means by definition that we don't know everything already. When a rival argument confronts us, we can best address it by first representing that argument *in its full force* so that it may have its full impact upon us. If it contains any element of truth, then that truth will prevail upon examination. Otherwise, we have nothing to fear from the argument.

Secondly, in the end, the Christian intellectual position and your personal faith can only grow stronger through your practice of patient, humble honesty. If we set up our opponents' arguments as weak (as Straw Men) and then defeat them, what have we accomplished? Not much. If we aim at the weakest parts of our opponent's case, and bring that part down, how far have we progressed? On the contrary, if we present our opponent in his *best* light, and allow him his *strongest* case, and then defeat that case, we have not only made much progress, but we have dealt the other side the greatest possible blow. If we aim at the most impenetrable part of his armor and still break through, then we have achieved a triumph, and we leave the enemy with little defense, if any.

The section of this book that covers Fallacies of Representation will include explanations and examples of many ways of *misrepresenting* the truth. This section covers four fallacies that oversimplify matters, four that obscure language, five that hide loaded assumptions into positions, and four that stretch and distort the facts.

Rules of Truth

The question of law simply asks, in any given covenant or organization, "What are the rules?" Perhaps no field of learning other than mathematics adheres more strictly to rules than logic. The "laws of logic" determine the forms which valid or invalid arguments can take. The same God who created the world also decrees the order of the world. He determines truth and error as well as the paths of arriving at truth or error. He determines the boundaries of truth, and thus the "laws of logic."

Informal fallacies that transgress these God-decreed boundaries rest on the simple denial of reality as we know it. These fallacies closely resemble worldview fallacies in that they rely on faulty assumptions about reality. In this section of fallacies I will deal will the humanistic attempt to derive ethical values from nature, and also the confusion of "categories" (groups for classification and understanding of reality) on which many humanists rely for denying God's revelation. In both cases, fallacious thinkers deny the boundaries of reality.

The Relevance of Truth

The fourth question asks, "What happens if someone keeps or breaks the rules?" In other words, it inquires about force, power, consequences, or *influence*. In truth and logic this point looks at *relevance*, and expects to find conclusions or refutations that have a direct connection to the argument or issue at hand. How does the argument relate to the issue? Does it necessarily affect it? Does the conclusion lay a burden of *necessity* up its audience? Does an alleged refutation actually address the issue? If none of these conditions appears, then a Fallacy of Relevance comes into view.

Unlike fallacies of representation, where truth itself gets distorted, obscured, or baited, Fallacies of Relevance often present very real and true claims. The fallacy with these lies in the fact that the claim or argument has no bearing on the real issue, misses the point, or diverts attention to another issue in some way.

Under this heading, this book will cover variations of arguments that rely on the influence of man instead of truth, some that attempt to hide behind the power of silence, four that attempt to gain assent through mere emotional appeals, and two others that attack the wrong target completely.

Truth and Time

Perhaps the trickiest category to grasp, Time asks questions that relate to development and continuity over time. "Who shall inherit?" or "Who shall receive damnation?" present theological questions in this regard. For truth and logic, here, we must inquire, "Does timing or age affect truth?"

Time provides opportunity for many instances of fallacies, though only a few actual types. The section on Fallacies of Time will expose three ways in which people mistake time or probability for causation (one in which opens people to very risky decisions), and two that describe generational or ideological prejudice in relation to something's age or development. Despite its trickiness to grasp totally, the reader will find that the fallacies described in this section touch on some of the most important issues of today, namely politics and evolution.

CONCLUSION

The aforementioned Antony Flew, who spent most of his life writing as an atheist, devoted much time to the subject of *Thinking Straight*, often employing logic as a tool with which to attack Christianity. Despite his anti-Christian stance, one of his metaphors provides a running theme for this book. He described fallacious arguments as leaky buckets: they don't hold water.[6] I will mention this theme several times, and also show how Flew's (and his more recent atheist clones') skeptical worldview itself holds no water.

God not only equates fallacious thinking with idolatry, but speaks of idolatry in terms of our working metaphor (long before Flew): a leaky bucket. Jeremiah records, *For my people have committed two evils; they have forsaken me the fountain of living waters, and hewed them out cisterns, broken cisterns, that can hold no water* (Jer. 2:13). This book will return to that fountain of living water to find the source of logic; it will also point out the leaky buckets by the dozen, and show the holes in each one.

Most books on fallacies admit that the field lacks any good system of categorization.[7] This lack, I think, exists because most attempt to work within the vacuum of autonomous human reason, unconnected to its necessary source, the Trinitarian God. In short, most books on the subject ignore that truth and logic operate within a larger worldview in which essential questions and assumptions must factor. Putting logic within the framework of God's covenant forces us to recognize that 1) human reason does not operate autonomously, 2) human reason must reckon with human nature, other people, and the rest of creation, 3) logical laws exist, and people break them in many ways, 4) good logic must lead to necessary and relevant conclusions (truth has consequences), and 5) time can pose certain obstacles to discerning truth. The failures of human reason that we call "fallacies" also fall within these five main points, and represent distinct failures in each area.

The rest of this book works within this system of categorization. Readers may feel that certain fallacies in Part 2 belong here or there in a different category; I have scratched my head over a few myself. In each case, however, I feel confident that any move would merely take the subject to another place in the same comprehensive system. In other words, the system itself suffices to catch all one way or another. Memorize these points—God (worldview), Man (representation), Law (Boundaries), Consequences (relevance), and Future (time)—and you will have a handy system in which to evaluate the truth and falsity of nearly every possible argument out there. Part 1 presents positively the biblical view of logic. Then, with that doctrine in place, Part 2 examines and discerns fallacies in dozens of ways.

May God, through His Word and Spirit, help us all to think, reason, and discern more faithfully. *May the words of our mouths and the meditations of our hearts be acceptable in Thy sight, O Lord, our rock and our Redeemer* (Ps. 19:14).

NOTES

1. Many readers will notice this as the five-point covenant model developed by Ray Sutton, *That You May Prosper: Dominion by Covenant* (Tyler, TX: Institute for Christian Economics, 1987). Those not familiar will recognize that the five points line up generally with the standard loci of systematic theology—Theology proper, Anthropology/Christology, Soteriology (law and sanctions), and Eschatology—and thus lie implicitly in traditional theology. I find great encouragement in the fact that John Frame sees "some merit" in this five point model as well, though he retains a three-point model for his own use. While affirming nothing different in substance, he simply differs in "perspective and structure." Whichever route we take, the value of each lies the fact that we move toward a distinctly biblical system, not a rationalistic system imposed from without onto Scripture. See John Frame, *The Doctrine of God* (Phillipsburg, NJ: Presbyterian and Reformed, 2002), 42n19.

2. Loraine Boettner, *The Millenium* (Phillipsburg, NJ: Presbyterian and Reformed, 1984) 371.

3. Noted in James V. Schall, *Jacques Maritain: The Philosopher in Society*, 4th Ed. (Lanham, MD: Rowman and Littlefield, 1998), xiii.

4. C. S. Lewis, *Mere Christianity* (New York: Collier Books and MacMillan Publishing Co., 1984 [1952]), 94.

5. Antony Flew, *Thinking Straight* (Buffalo, NY: Prometheus Books, 1977), 29–30.

6. Antony Flew, *God and Philosophy* (New York: Harcourt, Brace and World, Inc., 1966), 63.

7. See the note by one of the standard textbooks of logic, Irving M. Copi, *Introduction to Logic*, 7th Ed. (New York: MacMillan Publishing Co., and London: Collier MacMillan Publishers, 1986), 89, stating, "There is no universally accepted classification of fallacies." Copi quotes the classic work of De Morgan: "There *is* no such thing as a classification of the ways in which men arrive at an error: it is much to be doubted whether there ever *can be*."

CHAPTER 1

THE BIBLICAL MANDATE FOR LOGICAL THINKING

In the so-called "marketplace of ideas," Christians face countless attacks on and challenges to their faith, many of which attempt to undermine the whole counsel of God by subverting rhetoric and logic. Whether coming from skeptics, atheist, leftists, cults, or even other Christians, poor logic and dubious reasoning deserve exposure and correction. Likewise, no matter how allegedly prestigious the medium—whether mainstream news media, major newspapers or magazines, major publishers, cable TV shows, successful businessmen, university professors, etc.—all people bear the fallen nature of man and thus all are prone to both intellectual folly and even the devious tactics of covering that folly.

New material bombards us from every outlet every day; a new batch of fallacies passes under an editor's eye or across a producer's screen and into the public every minute. Much of what authors and editors should have tossed in a waste bin, and what news producers should have left on the cutting room floor nevertheless gets published, leaving your mind and your critical thinking ability as the last filter of your soul. You, as an honest Jane or Joe, responsible before God, must discern truth from error, fact from fallacy.

One philosopher describes the task in mundane but pertinent terms: "[T]he task of exposing fallacious reasoning is much like garbage collecting: neither task can ever be completed, since new material to be treated arrives all the time. However, in neither case does the perpetuity of the task make it any less urgent."[1] Someone has to take the intellectual garbage out around here! But in order to do so, we need to decide what to keep and what to throw away. We need a standard of good reasoning versus bad reasoning—a standard suited to the average person, for the average person, especially the average Christian, suffers the bombardment more acutely than most. The time has come for them to equip their minds with biblical logic and fight back.

But is Christian *faith* the place to turn for *logic*? Is not logic the domain of scholars and philosophers? The British philosopher John Locke condemns this common misconception: "God has not been so sparing to men to make them barely two-legged creatures, and left it to Aristotle to make them rational."[2] In other words, Locke recognized that logic existed and people reasoned and used the critical faculties of their minds before any philosopher came along to teach about it. God created logic and reasoning as he created man, and he created it for man, and therefore we should find it reasonable that the God's Word has something to say—if not a lot to say—about logic, rationality, and good judgment.

The Bible presents simple and broad demands for sound reasoning—demands that apply to everyone and shall be exacted of everyone. They are much simpler to remember and obey than the complex beast logic has become (or has been ever since Aristotle). Locke continues to explain that God has not left critical thinking to

> those few of them that he could get so to examine the grounds of syllogisms, as to see that, in above three score ways, that three propositions may be laid together, there are but about fourteen wherein one may be sure that the conclusion is right; and upon what grounds it is, that, in these few, the conclusion is certain, and in the other not.[3]

No, God has not left proper thinking and reasoning to the elite, the universities, the select few who receive intellectual accolades, or to the few who learn how to unthread the tangled wig of institutionalized logic. "God has been far more bountiful to mankind than so." In fact, the critical-thinking mind is God's gift to all men: "He has given them a mind that can reason, without being instructed in the methods of syllogizing: the understanding is not taught to reason by these rules; it has a native faculty to perceive the coherence or incoherence of its ideas, and can range the right, without any such perplexing repetitions."[4] Recent scientific studies have confirmed that, at least with regard to some fallacies of reasoning, average people consistently detect illegitimate logic.[5] The study concludes,

> In their reasonableness judgments ordinary arguers consistently make a sharp distinction between discussion moves with and discussion moves without a fallacy: discussion moves with a fallacy are regarded as much more unreasonable than discussion moves without a fallacy.[6]

In short, you do not need a Ph.D. in philosophy or law in order to engage in logical thinking. God has given us an innate ability to do so. Learning may sharpen this ability, but it does not produce it. God gives it, and we have it.

Now of course this essentially biblical teaching carries with it a double requirement: 1) True, we do not have to remain content with the monopoly of "reason" by elites and philosophers, but this at the same time means that 2) *we must learn to think critically* for ourselves. The biblical command to exercise good judgment *requires* us to think for ourselves, and *forbids* us to throw the burden of reasoning onto someone else. The biblical view of logic, therefore, protects us from the tyranny of professed elites, but also demands the training and exercise of our own minds. Intellectual freedom comes at the price of intellectual responsibility.

For now, the proper emphasis should remain on the fact that God created logic. In approaching the question "What is logic?" we must begin at the same point as we begin in understanding anything about man or the universe: we must begin with God's word. The same God who created man and man's mind has incorporated in that mind the "native faculty" of judgment that Locke mentions. The proper understanding of human thinking and reasoning then, must begin with a proper understanding of creation, and therefore of the Creator. In other words, the proper understanding of logic requires a proper understanding of theology. The following study will assume that the reader possesses a basic knowledge of Christian doctrine, including the existence of the Sovereign Triune God of the Bible, the distinction between this Creator and His creation, the special creation of man in the image of this God, and the authority of God's revelation as found in the Bible and the person of

Jesus Christ. We could add more to this list, but the basics will suffice for developing the biblical doctrine of logic and reasoning which follows.

THE BIBLE AND LOGIC

We normally think of logic as a set of abstract rules that apply to reasoning, and since the study of logic suffers from the hyperactivity of philosophers and scholars and thus runs into numerous complexities of expression and analysis, most people ignore logic as an "ivory tower" subject. We must remedy this scholarly affliction by returning to the simplicity of what the Bible teaches about human reasoning. Logic is, indeed, the science of human reasoning, or the study of the rules, laws, means, and ways humans should think. Of course, the word "should" implies ethics, and this means that logic has a strong ethical basis.[7] Put simply, the ethical biblical basis for *all of logic* is the ninth commandment: *You shall not bear false witness against your neighbor* (Ex. 20:16). This command presupposes a few things—which I will discuss momentarily—but for now simplifies our understanding of logic. *Logic is the systematic study and practice of discerning and telling the truth.*

This definition includes both the rules *and* practice of logic—the knowing *and* telling of the truth—in order to emphasize that logic, like all of Christian life, involves more than an intellectual endeavor. *It is an ethical matter* which we should approach as seriously as any other ethical matter. To the extent that things like murder, rape, theft, abortion, and blasphemy concern us as ethical issues, to that same degree we should condemn bearing false witness. The fact that this command subsumes everything we think or say should clearly impress the ethical heart of the knowledge and practice of logic, and therefore why we should study its biblical basis and theory.

Other biblical teaching highlights both the simplicity and power of the ninth commandment as a basis for human thinking. Jesus taught, *let your statement be, "Yes, yes" or "No, no"; anything beyond these is of evil* (Matt. 5:37). Jesus did not mean by this that we should never say anything but the words "yes" or "no," but rather that in all that we say we should communicate in plain and simple terms faithful to the truth. He speaks here as in a courtroom setting (recalling many of the Old Testament laws pertaining to witness, oaths, and judgment). He says, *make no oath at all, either by heaven, for it is the throne of God, or by the earth, for it is the footstool of His feet, or by Jerusalem, for it is the city of the great king. Nor shall you make an oath by your head, for you cannot make one hair white or black* (Matt. 5:34–36). How do these statements relate to truth-telling? They point out what I have already mentioned above. We should not try to add weight to what we say by "swearing" on "my mama's grave" or "a stack of Bibles"—to mention a couple from popular speech—or any other superfluous authority (I will discuss many more grievous examples of this fallacy later under Appeal to Authority), or any other subversion (which includes all of the other fallacies this book will cover). Our duty is to report the truth faithfully, in black and white "yes or no" terms, without using any rhetorical measures or extra religious-talk to persuade or intimidate our listeners as to the truth of what we say.

The objective, "yes" and "no" character of truth lays at the root of God's creation and man's thinking (of which I will have more to say in the next chapter). This primitive objectivity appears in the most fundamental accounting device in the created world—a computer. At its most fundamental level, a computer chip simply interprets a series of "one" and "zero"—a digital version of "yes" and "no," "positive" and "negative." This "binary" (allowing only two answers) language (processed at billions of "yes" and "no" per second) can code and process everything you see happening on your computer screen. In this system, there is no "maybe," "possibly," "probably," or the like. When it comes down to it, therefore, everything from games and graphics to the most complex mathematics and engineering boils down to a series of "yes" and "no." (And one improper answer can lock up the entire system!). Of course, computers do not make a perfect analogy to the human mind, and certainly not to human experience in total, but the fact that the fundamental level of data processing equates to simple honesty shows us that at its root level, creation functions according to an objective order that is both very simple and inescapable.

Jesus' teaching gives us good reasons for this understanding. The duty of simple honesty calls because God is God and we are not, God determines how the world operates and we do not. Only God creates reality, man must submit to God's creation and report his witness honestly. God rules as the sovereign Judge; we stand as witnesses in His universal courtroom. Jesus simply explains that we can go nowhere to escape God's court, and we can find nothing higher than God by which to swear (as even God Himself could not; Heb. 6:13). Not *heaven*, for God rules even that; not the *earth*, for God rules that; not the great sacred city Jerusalem, for God rules her; and certainly not by our own heads, for man does not even have the power to determine the natural color of the hairs on his head. No matter where you turn, what you might look to as a source of "swearing," you will find God sovereign over it. You cannot escape God's courtroom. God—who numbers *every* hair on *every* head (Matt. 10:29–31; Luke 12:6–7)—is both all-knowing and all-powerful. Therefore, submit to His rule and simply report your witness of reality in simple "yes" or "no" terms. This order simply reflects the terms of community between a Creator and His people.

Paul teaches this covenantal (God as sovereign, giving laws to His people) view of human communication. He recognizes that God alone is the foundation for truth: *let God be found true, though every man be found a liar* (Rom. 3:4). In this the apostle echoes the Psalmist singing to God, *Men of low degree are only vanity and men of rank are a lie... Against You, You only, I have sinned and done what is evil in Your sight, So that You are justified when You speak And blameless when You judge* (Ps. 62:9; 51:4). Christ is truth, and even if we refuse to believe, He remains the self-consistent standard of truth, and therefore *must be* true: *If we are faithless, He remains faithful, for He cannot deny Himself* (2 Tim. 2:13; see also Tit. 1:2). Again Paul echoes the Old Testament: *God is not a man, that He should lie, Nor a son of man, that He should repent; Has He said, and will He not do it? Or has He spoken, and will He not make it good?* (Num 23:19; see also 1 Sam. 15:29; Ezek. 24:14; Mal. 3:6).

Paul warns those who seek to base knowledge on anything other than God's revelation in Christ: *See to it that no one takes you captive through philosophy and empty deception, according to the tradition of men, according to the elementary principles of the world, rather than according to Christ... in whom are hidden all the treasures of wisdom and knowledge* (Col. 2:8, 3). Paul does not here condemn philosophy (and thus the study of logic) in general, but rather philosophy *according to the tradition of men... rather than according to Christ*. Christ is the only guarantor of truth and wisdom, *For in Him all the fullness of Deity dwells in bodily form, and in Him you have been made complete, and He is the head over all rule and authority* (Col. 2:9–10).

Since Christ "completes" us as believers, we should therefore strive to live according to the image of this New Man. This includes the *renewing of your mind* (Rom. 12:2). We should obey God's revelation in all things, including how we think and speak. The standard we pursue involves *speaking the truth in love* that we may *grow up in all aspects into Him who is the* head, even Christ (Eph. 4:15). This includes *that you be renewed in the spirit of your mind, and put on the new self, which in the likeness of God has been created in righteousness and holiness of the truth* (Eph. 4:23–24). This renewed mind means corrected, righteous thinking, and will thus mean faithful, honest behavior: *Therefore, laying aside falsehood, speak truth each one of you with his neighbor, for we are members of one another* (Eph. 4:25). For Paul, truth-telling ranks prominently on the list of behaviors involved in Christian life: *Let no unwholesome* [literally "rotten"] *word proceed from your mouth* (Eph. 4:25), but rather, *Let your speech always be with grace, as though seasoned with salt, so that you will know how you should respond to each person* (Col. 4:6).

James commends the same standards. God is the self-consistent, unchanging standard of truth and goodness who gives us the gift of wisdom and understanding: *Do not be deceived, my beloved brethren. Every good thing given and every perfect gift is from above, coming down from the Father of lights, with whom there is no variation or shifting shadow. In the exercise of His will He brought us forth by the word of truth* (James 1:16–18). James repeats the teaching of Christ: *But above all, my brethren, do not swear, either by heaven or by earth or with any other oath; but your yes is to be yes, and your no, no, so that you may not fall under judgment* (James 5:12). As with Jesus and the other apostles, James sees truth as a life and death matter. Therefore, the pursuit of truth and engagement in debate with others has a vital aspect: *My brethren, if any among you strays from the truth and one turns him back, let him know that he who turns a sinner from the error of his way will save his soul from death and will cover a multitude of sins* (James 5:19–20).

Conclusion

The Bible clearly teaches a supernatural foundation for truth, and a divine mandate for us to act and speak truthfully. This means logic and reason derive from God and can only function properly in a God-created and God-governed world. If man pretends that logic and reason begin with his own mind, the entire system will break down (I discuss at least one instance of this under Worldview Fallacies). What we call "logic," therefore, is the detailed study of methods to think and communicate faithfully within God's world-order, as well as discerning and refuting the myriad of ways in which man attempts to skirt the simple rule against bearing false witness. As Solomon said, *God made men upright, but they have sought out many devices* (Eccl. 7:29). This rings true in every area of life, including the broad range of intellectual dialogue subject to logical scrutiny. The Bible gives us the tools to engage correctly in proper thinking and to correct the errors of poor argumentation.

NOTES

1. Sven Ove Hansson, "Fallacies of Risk," *Journal of Risk Research* 7/3 (April 2004): 360.

2. John Locke, "An Essay Concerning Human Understanding," IV.XVII.4, in *The Works of John Locke*, 2 Vols. (Freeport, NY: Books for Libraries Press, [1877] 1969), 2:285. This is quoted in Greg Bahnsen, *Always Ready: Directions for Defending the Faith*, ed. Robert R. Booth (Atlanta, GA: American Vision, and Texarkana, AR: Covenant Media Press, 1996), 133.

3. John Locke, "An Essay Concerning Human Understanding," IV.XVII.4, in *The Works of John* Locke, 2:285.

4. John Locke, "An Essay Concerning Human Understanding," IV.XVII.4, in *The Works of John* Locke, 2:285.

5. Frans H. van Eemeren, Bart Garssen, and Bert Meuffels, "The Unreasonableness of the *Ad Baculum* Fallacy," *Arguing Community and Culture, Selected Papers from the Twelfth NCA/AFA Conference on Argumentation*, ed. G. Thomas Goodnight, et al (Washington, D.C.: National Communication Association, 2002), 343–350.

6. Frans H. van Eemeren, Bart Garssen, and Bert Meuffels, "The Unreasonableness of the *Ad Baculum* Fallacy," *Arguing Community and Culture, Selected Papers from the Twelfth NCA/AFA Conference on Argumentation*, 349.

7. John Robbins, late disciple of Gordon H. Clark, notices the ethical import of logic: "Logic is not psychology. It does not describe what people think about or how they usually reach conclusion; it describes how they *ought* to think if they wish to reason correctly" (John Robbins, "Why Study Logic?" in Gordon H. Clark, *Logic*, vi). Robbins notes a necessary connection between morality and logic, but seems to think that logic comes first in the order of things ("Why Study Logic," viii–x). I believe logic itself is an ethical endeavor *at its root*, and thus logic and morality presuppose each other, and both exist simultaneously and as analogous to the ordering and holy character of God who created them.

CHAPTER 2

THEOLOGICAL FOUNDATIONS OF LOGIC

The ability to study and employ logic presupposes a few things, as I mentioned. Firstly, it presupposes that our thoughts correspond to reality, and this requires that reality be *objective*. Reality and truth must stand as true or false irrespective of who looks at it, how he looks at it, or whether he likes how it looks or not. Reality, in other words, must stand true independently of *man*, and cannot depend on man for its true meaning. These requirements presuppose an objective world-order. This in turn requires some Source of objectivity, which we find in the self-consistency of the Creator *who upholds all things by the word of His power* (Heb. 1:3), who Himself does not change (James 1:12, 17; Heb. 13:8; Num. 23:19), and who creates an orderly creation (Ps. 19:1–6; Prov. 8:22–31; Eccl. 1:4–10; 3:1–8).

This Creator-God exists as the sole self-attesting and self-consistent Source of all order, wisdom, knowledge, and power in time and eternity. He exists separately from creation and no part of creation can move Him or improve upon Him (Ps. 33:10–11; Is. 43:10–13; 46:5–11). This invariable God reveals Himself to mankind by His word, by which He created the world (Gen. 1; Ps. 19; 33:6–11; John 1:1–5; Col. 1:16), and by which He orders the world (Gen. 8:22–9:7; Ps. 33:6–22; 147:15–20; Jer. 33:25; Heb. 1:3). By this we learn that the universe is not governed by its own independent, abstract laws, but by the decrees of God.[1] The order that God wills for His creation to display originates from His own perfection, certainty, righteousness, purity, eternity, and truth (Ps. 19:7–9). Creation's order is imputed from without, not self-originating—dependent on God, not autonomous.

The works of God exhibit these attributes. In Him we find the Source of all being (Ex. 3:14; Acts 17:28; Rom. 11:36; Col. 1:17). In this same self-consistent Being we have the Source of personality and intelligence: the self-identifying, self-naming "I AM" (Ex. 3:14; John 8:58). He exists, orders, and rules as self-authoritative: beyond Him no higher source of "swearing" (guaranteeing of truth) exists:

> *For when God made the promise to Abraham, since He could swear by no one greater, He swore by Himself, saying, "I will surely bless you, and I will surely multiply you." And thus, having patiently waited, he obtained the promise. For men swear by one greater than themselves, and with them an oath given as confirmation is an end of every dispute. In the same way God, desiring even more to show to the heirs of the promise the unchangeableness of His purpose, interposed with an oath, in order that by two unchangeable things, in which it is impossible for God to lie, we may have strong encouragement, we who have fled for refuge in laying hold of the hope set before us* (Heb. 6:13).

Truth, notice, only needs such a guarantee when a community of persons exists. The passage above even refers to an oath ending a "dispute"—something that only happens between at least two persons (or a divided personality!). In God Himself we find community (three persons), who as a Unity enters into covenant (an ordered community) with men and promises to bless and *multiply* them. The objective world-order, then, is a reflection, through His decree, of the Creator's own self-order—an order that exhibits His unity and diversity, and His unchangeable faithfulness and authority.

At the same time, however, man's thinking, knowledge, and communication must comport with the facts of this objective world in order for such a thing as truth in human communication to exist. Else, we have no guarantee that human experience faithfully expresses reality, or that one man can relate his experience to another man reliably and intelligibly. Again, we find this guarantee in the Creator who has created mankind in His image. Just as God names, communicates, creates, governs, improves, and rests all according to His perfect, self-ordered nature, so does His image (Gen 1:26–30; 2:7) engage in orderly identity, naming, and communing (Gen. 2:18–25), governing (Gen. 1:28, Ps. 8:4–8), "creating" and improving (Gen. 2:15), and resting (Gen. 2:2; Ex. 20:11). As God's image, then, man experiences the order God has imputed to His creation; God provides the order, He provides our inherent ability to witness, identify, understand, and communicate that order, and He guarantees the normal continuity of the order.

Thus, in the Christian doctrine of God (and only in this God) we possess the only guarantee that human ordered-thought (logic), and therefore the arts and sciences, have meaning, coherence, and can actually describe the world around us faithfully:

> The sciences find their unity in the personal wisdom of God (Ps. 104:24). "He is before all things, and in him all things hold together" (Col. 1:17). This is why mathematics [and/or logic] applies to physics. This is why the fundamental laws of physics have such simple form. We trust that mathematics will continue to find application to physics, not because of blind faith…, but out of the conviction that the laws of physics and mathematics are simply two diverse ways in which Christ comprehensively rules the universe.[2]

Man comprehends and engages these God-decreed facts and laws only because of his relationship of bearing their (and his) Creator's image. This image exists in man prior to (*a priori*) his experience of the creation, and yet works together with God's revelation of nature to man, thus creating coherence between man's nature and nature's nature. Thus, "The *a priori* capability of man's created nature really corresponds to the *a posteriori* of what is 'out there,' because man is in the *image* of the One who ordained what is 'out there.'"[3] Only through the ultimate Unity and Diversity of the Creator-God do we rest secure in the human understanding of His creation: the unity of what we call the "laws of logic" actually correspond to the diversity of facts of God's creation.

Yet we must bear in mind that we "image" God, we do not replicate Him. All of our identifying and communicating reflect our Creator's activity, but within the limits of creation. Our ordering is not an extension of God's own, but a reflection of it. We think analogously to God, not identical to Him. To the extent that the creation exists distinctly from its Creator (completely), so does a divide exist between our thought and God's (Is. 55:8–9). I will expand on this further below.

Secondly, the *imperative* to tell the truth must come from a truly authoritative source in order to have genuine meaning. Even in an objective universe, for example, without some overarching system of ethics, people have no pressing need to tell the truth unless it somehow benefits them. Even then they would have no ethical *requirement* to do so. Under the Creator and Sovereign God of the Bible, we have the guarantee of an objective world-order necessary for logic, knowledge, and science, the assurance that other people bear the image of God as we do and thus can engage knowledge as well as we, *and* we also have the clearly revealed command to communicate honestly. This command comes as part of God's law (Ex. 20:16), which further expresses that God originally intended His creation to behave according to order, and that He still wills for it to do so.

Further, in such a Christian universe, the Creator determines reality, and man's report of what he sees (his witness) should faithfully express God's thoughts after Him. Man either affirms the Creator's works, or denies them (or worse yet, purposefully slanders them). He need not say anything directly about the Creator for this to remain true. When an individual speaks truly, he affirms implicitly that the world is the way it is, that God is sovereign in the world, and that other people should see the world in the same way. The ninth commandment, therefore, does not call us merely to blind submission, but rather it integrates with the total endeavor of knowing God, loving God, living in a God-created world, and loving your neighbor.

Creation and Logic

From a biblical point of view we learn that God makes orderly experience possible because of His own self-consistent, self-authoritative, and faithful nature, which He imputes in a creaturely way to his creation, and particularly to his image, man. The God of orderly creation *planted a garden* and then set His image, man, in that garden *to cultivate it and keep it* (Gen 2:8, 15)—in other words, to image God's acts of orderly productive work. Man must think God's thoughts after Him, and as well should work God's works after Him, although man does both at the level of a creature and not Creator.

Theologian Dr. Morton H. Smith summarizes the importance of the biblical doctrine of creation for human experience. His teaching helps us understand the biblical worldview which makes logical study possible. He writes:

> The Biblical doctrine of creation thus gives man the basis for the developing of a metaphysics or a theory of reality. The opening verse of the Bible indicates that reality is two-layered in nature. The upper layer is the uncreated, self-contained, independent, living God of the Bible. He is the God who sovereignly determines to create a universe that is dependent upon him. Thus we have the Creator-creation distinction in the area of metaphysics that describes all of reality.
>
> Along with this kind of metaphysics the Christian recognizes that there must also be a two-layered view of epistemology or of knowledge. God, who is the source of all truth has all knowledge in and of himself. He preinterprets all the truth and all the facts that he places in the created universe, so that as man learns more and more of this universe, he is rethinking God's thoughts after him. In the area of epistemology, God thinks originally, and creatively, whereas man thinks analogically, thinking God's thoughts after him. He does not think originally, but derivatively and recreatively. From this two-layered view of metaphysics and of epistemology the area of ethics is two-layered, with God as Lord, and the creature as the servant, who must obey his Maker.[4]

This means that man's thinking depends upon the God of the Bible. It depends upon Him for its being and its order: God both creates the human mind and determines the laws and conditions that govern man's thinking. Thus, God makes logical reasoning possible, meaningful, and reliable.

Smith's summary exhibits the revolutionary theological insights of Cornelius Van Til, whose contributions to apologetics and philosophy direct the Christian to Scripture *first* in order to develop a worldview. This includes the concepts of knowledge and logic. Van Til writes,

> Christianity holds that God existed alone before any time existence was brought forth. He existed as the self-

> conscious and self-consistent being. The [logical] *law of contradiction, therefore, as we know it, is but the expression on a created level of the internal coherence of God's nature.* Christians should therefore never appeal to the law of contradiction as something that, as such, determines what can or cannot be true.[5]

Logic, being part of creation, cannot act as the standard for judging all of reality, especially not truth about God Himself. Logic has limits. Does this mean it has no place in Christian life? Certainly not. In fact, only the nature (including the omniscience and omnipotence) of the Creator God can guarantee that logic works and correlates with reality, as I have already shown. Logical laws (such as the law of contradiction) are therefore good, invaluable, and necessary tools:

> Christians should employ the law of contradiction, whether positively or negatively, as means by which to systematize the facts of revelation. Whether these facts are found in the universe at large or in the Scripture. The law of contradiction cannot be thought of as operating anywhere except against the background of the nature of God.... [T]he facts of the universe, if they are to be rationally intelligible, are not ultimately dependent upon the law of contradiction as man knows it, but upon God's internal coherence that lies behind the law of contradiction.[6]

Logic and Revelation

Van Til sees logic as a gift from God—a gift which we must use in accordance with God's laws and the limits of our creatureliness:

> The gift of logical reason was given by God to man in order that he might order the revelation of God for himself. It was not given him that he might by means of it legislate as to what is possible and what is actual. When man makes a "system" for himself of the content of revelation given him in Scripture, this system is subject to, not independent of, Scripture.[7]

This means that the possibility, nature, and practice of logic depend upon God alone and not man. Without God, any talk of logical rules, instances of logical or illogical statements (logical judgments), facts of reality, or logical relations between facts of reality, would have no meaning whatsoever—neither for the individual nor anyone with which he desired to communicate. For Van Til,

> Identification of fact or truth in history by human reason must be frankly based upon identification by God. Only if the authority of God's self-identification and of his self-authenticated revelation to man in history is assumed can there be any intelligible predication by man. But such self-identification of God cannot be obtained if it be allowed that God may reveal anything at all. God can reveal only that which is consistent with his nature as a self-identified being. The law of identity in human logic must be seen to be resting upon the character of God and therefore upon the authoritative revelation of God.... [I]dentification of any fact or truth in the phenomenal realm is possible to man in history only because all things in history are controlled by God back of history....[8]

The God of the Bible, therefore, alone makes truth and logic possible. Yet we must recognize that the Creator-creature distinction means that human logic, being part of the created order, can achieve only so much as God has intended. God has set its boundaries—boundaries between His though and our thought, and perhaps even boundaries between our thought and the unknown (to us) extents of creation. God has designed logic as a tool of man's discernment within the created order. As Dr. John Frame notes, God "both vindicates and limits the competence of human logic."[9] Frame elaborates on the relationship: "The *validity of the laws of logic* derives from the *character of God*. God is not subject to some source of (logical or other) possibility more ultimate than himself. Rather, He *himself alone determines ultimately what is possible.*"[10] This fact has certain implications for man's use of logic: "We cannot reason any way we want to. We must reason in full awareness of the fact that God is the foundation of logic. Logic itself does not determine what is possible or probable; only God does that. Logic does not give to man exhaustive knowledge; only God has that."[11]

Frame here summarizes the view of Van Til, who had earlier explained,

> *God alone knows himself and all the things of the created universe exhaustively.* He has revealed himself to man. But he did not reveal himself exhaustively to man. Neither the created universe nor the Bible exhaustively reveals God to man. Nor has man the capacity to receive such an exhaustive revelation. *All revelation is anthropomorphic* [given in man's language using forms man has the capacity to understand]. Neither by logical reasoning nor by intuition can man do more than take to himself the revelation of God on the authority of God.... God reveals to man in Scripture a system of truth. But this system is not an exhaustive replica of the truth as it is in God himself. It is a system that is adapted to human understanding.[12]

This simply parallels the biblical teaching: *"For My thoughts are not your thoughts, Nor are your ways My ways," declares the Lord. "For as the heavens are higher than the earth, So are My ways higher than your ways And My thoughts than your thoughts"* (Is. 55:8–9).

We must draw at least two conclusions from this biblical understanding. First, since human logic is creaturely logic, we stand incapable of understanding everything about God. Human reason simply cannot totally comprehend God. In making deductions about God—about what God may be, act, or desire—beyond what Scripture reveals risks creating a idol. Worse yet, any system of theology or philosophy—or any "application" made in preaching or studying—that derives from such deductions risks initiating an idolatrous lifestyle. God has given us His revelation adapted to human understanding. This does not mean that human reason determines God's will. Human understanding *receives* God's revelation, it does not determine it.

The subject of idolatry leads us to a second conclusion. Many people today see the anthropomorphic nature of the Bible, have therefore concluded that it does not merely adapt to man, but derives from man alone. Humanists, atheists, and unbelievers of all sorts follow this route, essentially taking the former error to its logical conclusion. They follow the error of believing that human reason determines God's will to the point of "realizing" that God's will does not exist, human reason determines everything. Humanism is the ultimate idolatry, setting up man—the image of God—as the ultimate graven image in place of the true God. At this point they unhinge their entire worldview from rationality in the name of rationality. I will cover this error more fully in the chapter on Worldview Fallacies.

We cannot fully comprehend God's thoughts, but we can trust the certainty of what He has given us. *"For as the rain and the snow come down from heaven, And do not return there without watering the earth and making it bear and sprout, and furnishing seed to the sower and bread to the eater; So will My word be which goes forth from My mouth; It will not return to Me empty, Without accomplishing what I desire, and without succeeding in the matter for which I sent it"* (Is. 55:10–11).

The certain truth God gives is not abstract ideas, but active, personal, and *redemptive* truth. It calls the erring thinker—whether Christian or non-Christian—to repentance and faithfulness of witness. The same passage from Isaiah that speaks of the certainty of God's word accomplishing His purpose, reveals that purpose as restorative and redemptive: *"Instead of the thorn bush the cypress will come up, and instead of the nettle the myrtle will come up, and it will be a memorial to the Lord, for an everlasting sign which will not be cut off"* (Is. 55:13). By this promise He calls His people to Himself: *Seek the Lord while He may be found; Call upon Him while He is near. Let the wicked forsake his way And the unrighteous man his thoughts; And let him return to the Lord, And He will have compassion on him, And to our God, For He will abundantly pardon* (Is. 55:6–7).

Van Til notes the same thrust of confrontation for the erring reasoner:

> God requires of men that they love and obey him. He made them perfect in his image. They rebelled against him. Now he is, in grace, calling them to repentance through his Son. He tells them about his call to repentance and love in the Bible. So, Christ, the Redeemer, the Son of God, speaks directly to us in the words of Scripture.
>
> It follows that those who take the Bible to be what it says it is, must present this Bible as conveying a challenge of Christ to men. They must use it always as a means with which to send forth a clarion of surrender to those who are rebels against God. To be sure, it is the grace

> of God that is offered to men. Just as Jesus wept over Jerusalem and her children, desiring that they might repent, so those who are believers must be filled with deep concern and love for the lost. But in their love for the lost they must, none the less, not lower the claims of God revealed in Christ who calls upon "all men everywhere" to repent (Acts 17:30). This call to repentance everywhere has application for the whole of human life and for all the activities of men.[13]

He quotes theologian Herman Bavinck: "The authority of Scripture extends itself over the whole man and over the whole of humanity. It stands above mind and will, above heart and conscience; it cannot be compared to any other authority."[14] Van Til adds, "Men must therefore be asked to repent for the way they have carried on their scientific enterprises, no less than for the way they have worshipped idols."[15] Bavinck again:

> If Christianity is in the full sense of the term a religion of redemption and therefore wants to redeem men from the error of his intellect as well as from the iniquity of his heart, if it wants to save man from the death of his soul as well as from that of his body, then it can in the nature of the case not subject itself to the criticism of man, but must subject man to the criticism of itself.[16]

This redemptive word "is not only normative but also causative. It fights for its own triumph. It conquers for itself the hearts of men. It makes itself irresistible."[17]

Logic and Christology

Since logic derives from the Creator, comes by revelation, and infuses human communication, we should expect to find a strong biblical connection between Christ (as both Creator and Redeemer) and logic. We, in fact, do find this. To begin with, the well-known prologue to the Gospel of John specifically refers to Christ as "the Word," translating the broader Greek term *logos* (John 1:1–5). We must take care at this point to avoid committing any fundamental "word-study" fallacies,[18] but the fact that John calls Christ the *logos* (the root of our word "logic") begs for closer examination. At least some connection exists between Christ and the principal order of creation, and Christians should acknowledge it if not learn as much about it as possible.

Whatever the exact translation of the word *logos*, it certainly involves something to do with ordered, purposeful speech. We need not go to the extreme of some writers and say *logos* literally means "logic," as if John meant to narrow our understanding of Jesus to an abstract philosophical concept.[19] We should, however, recognize John's direct connection between the Greek word for "word" and the person of Jesus himself, whom John also reveals as the creator of *all things*. John also presents Him using the very language of creation itself: *In the beginning* this Word existed *with God*, sharing the very (unchanging) nature of God, and having in Himself *life, and the life was the light of men*. Further, *the Light shines in the darkness* (John 1:4–5). This language recalls Genesis 1:1–3, and thus makes direct connections between God, Christ the Word, and God's creation of the world via His spoken word. This includes the direct reference to God's first act of creation: the creation of light via His word. It also includes the broader concept of creation: that of God creating *life* (Gen. 1:20–28; 2:7). John brings these ideas together in Christ: He is *life*, and that life is the *light* of men. In Christ we have everything—our being, life, environment, community, communication, "light" or understanding—and this certainly includes an orderly, intelligible universe that derives its order from the order of its Creator.

Paul teaches the same clear connection between Christ and creation. He writes: *For by Him all things were created, both in the heavens and on earth, visible and invisible, whether thrones or dominions or rulers or authorities—all things have been created through Him and for Him. He is before all things, and in Him all things hold together* (Col. 1:15–17). Paul later attributes to this same Creator-Christ *all the treasures of wisdom and knowledge* (Col. 2:3) as mentioned earlier.

Furthermore, in the dual nature of Christ—fully man and fully God—we see the Creator-creation distinction formed and upheld by divine power (Heb. 1:3). In our Creator and representative before God we see divine wisdom operating in the created realm as a model of how God created us to think, and thus how we *ought* to think. While we cannot follow Christ in as far as He is very God, we absolutely must image Him as far as He reveals to us perfect humanity. The distinction holds as far as the two natures of Christ remain (to follow the Confession of Chalcedon) "without confusion, change, division, or separation." Yet the mandate for us comes in the fact that Christ, "perfect in humanity," who is "composed of a rational soul and body," thus reveals to us the perfect human reasoner (among other things) as a human image of the Father (John 1:14–18). Further, in the myserious fusion of divine and human nature rests the incomprehensible "point of contact" in the analogous symmetry between God's thought and ours.

All of this means that we must consider everything about the doctrine of Christ if we hope to fully understand human logic: Divinity, Humanity, Law, Sin, *and* Redemption. Dr. Vern Poythress explains the importance of Christ in relation to human logic:

> Human reasoning and human use of logic are dependent on knowledge of God and are guided by it. This truth should be obvious from the very character of human thought, which should "think God's thoughts after him." But this dependence becomes more obvious when we root logic in the Trinitarian character of God. God in his Triunity decisively reveals himself through the redemptive work of Christ in the New Testament. The full revelation of the character of God, the being of God, and the logical self-consistency of God comes in the form of a climax of redemption in the person and work of Christ....
>
> The fullness of logical understanding requires a fullness in development of redemptive history. Human logic is redemptive-historically conditioned. It is not the same before and after the coming of Christ. Redemption in Christ includes the redemptive reformation of human logic. That reform takes place once and for all in the resurrection of Christ. As the last Adam, the spiritual man (1 Cor 15:45–49), seated at God's right hand, he is the human pattern and exemplar for all redeemed human logic. On the basis of this one climactic event, reformation of human logic takes place in the church through the progressive renewal of our minds (Rom 12:2).[20]

Jesus Christ, the perfect man, reveals to us the standard of human wisdom, thought, analysis, judgment, discernment, and honesty. The more we think like Christ, the more we approach a biblical standard of logic—that is, the more we conform to the simple "yes" or "no" standard of truth, and the penetrating standard of judgment that God requires of us. The efforts and progress we make toward this goal falls within the duty of Christian life to renew our minds and conform to the image of God's Son (Rom. 8:29; 12:1–2). It is part of Christian life as we struggle to shed sinful habits and embrace the law of God—a law which represents the perfect order of *life* (Deut. 30:19).

Once again, we understand that God gives us a logical world, a logical mind, and a command to think, act, and speak logically. We add to this understanding the role of Christ in creating this order, in Redeeming it in the New Covenant, and Renewing it in us as we are submitted to Him. Furthermore, with Christ being both fully man and fully God, we have in Christ *both* the Creator of logic *and* the perfect exemplar of a logical life.

A biblical understanding of logic, therefore, will observe the doctrines of Trinity, Creation, Revelation, and Redemption as bases for understanding human intellectual (and all other) experience. In short, God created the world and man, including logic. Each of these things integrates together in the system of God's creation. Man employs logic in the process of ordering the revelation God has provided us in Scripture and in nature. Thus he uses logic in order to understand his Maker, himself, his neighbor, and the world around him. God has made Scripture and creation intelligible as much as need be for life and godliness (2 Peter 1:3–4). Logic is therefore, the ordering of human experience in a way that faithfully reports the work of God. Logic involves nothing less than faithfulness in witnessing the truth of God. Thus we arrive at my original definition: *Logic is the systematic study and practice of discerning and telling the truth.*

NOTES

1. Vern Poythress, "A Biblical View of Mathematics," *Foundations of Christian Scholarship: Essays in the Van Til Perspective*, ed. Gary North (Vallecito, CA: Ross House Books, 1976), 177. I draw from Poythress' article for some points through the next few paragraphs.

2. Vern Poythress, "A Biblical View of Mathematics," *Foundations of Christian Scholarship: Essays in the Van Til Perspective*, 183.

3. Vern Poythress, "A Biblical View of Mathematics," *Foundations of Christian Scholarship: Essays in the Van Til Perspective*, 185.

4. Morton H. Smith, "The Theological Significance of the Doctrine of Creation," *Did God Create in Six Days?*, eds. Joseph A. Pipa and David W. Hall (Greenville, SC: Southern Presbyterian Press, and Oak Ridge, TN: The Covenant Foundation, 1999), 244.

5. Cornelius Van Til, *An Introduction to Systematic Theology* (Phillipsburg, NJ: Presbyterian and Reformed, 1978), 11.

6. Cornelius Van Til, *An Introduction to Systematic Theology*, 11, 37.

7. Cornelius Van Til, *An Introduction to Systematic Theology*, 256.

8. Cornelius Van Til, *A Christian Theory of Knowledge* (Grand Rapids, MI: Baker Book House, 1969), 202.

9. John M. Frame, "The Problem of Theological Paradox," *Foundations of Christian Scholarship: Essays in the Van Til Perspective*, 322.

10. John M. Frame, "The Problem of Theological Paradox," *Foundations of Christian Scholarship: Essays in the Van Til Perspective*, 323.

11. John M. Frame, "The Problem of Theological Paradox," *Foundations of Christian Scholarship: Essays in the Van Til Perspective*, 323.

12. Cornelius Van Til, *A Christian Theory of Knowledge*, 37–38.

13. Cornelius Van Til, *A Christian Theory of Knowledge*, 39.

14. Quoted in Cornelius Van Til, *A Christian Theory of Knowledge*, 39.

15. Cornelius Van Til, *A Christian Theory of Knowledge*, 39.

16. Quoted in Cornelius Van Til, *A Christian Theory of Knowledge*, 40.

17. Herman Bavinck, quoted in Cornelius Van Til, *A Christian Theory of Knowledge*, 40.

18. D. A. Carson, *Exegetical Fallacies*, 2nd Ed. (Grand rapids, MI: Baker Books, 1996), 27–64.

19. See my treatment of such a translation under the Fallacy of Equivocation.

20. Vern S. Poythress, "Reforming Ontology and Logic in the Light of the Trinity: An Application of Van Til's Idea of Analogy," *Westminster Theological Journal* 57/1 (1995):187–219; http://www.frame-poythress.org/poythress_articles/1995Reforming.htm (accessed April 10, 2009).

CHAPTER 3

THE TEN COMMANDMENTS AND LOGIC

The previous chapters have established that what we commonly call "logic," when fully understood within the framework of God's revelation, involves pursuing, discerning, and confessing truth in every area of life. This process expands upon the ninth commandment—forbidding false witness—throughout the covenantal themes of God, Man, Law, Consequences, and Time. To further illuminate this way of intellectual life, I wish to exhibit how each of the Ten Commandments relates to logical and critical thinking.

The construction of this exhibit requires some groundwork. The introduction to this book explains the "Five Points of Logic and Fallacy." I did not pull these five points out of the air; they come directly from the Bible's own self-organization. The five points show up throughout Scripture: the five books of Moses follow this pattern, as does the book of Deuteronomy itself, the Psalms, the Gospel of Matthew, Romans, Revelation, and much more.[1]

Most importantly, the Ten Commandments follow these five points. Not two-by-two, as the math might suggest at first, but certainly in each of the God-given division of the *two tables* of the law—five-by-five. Not ironically, God gave Moses the commandments in the form of two tablets (Ex. 24:12; 32:15–16; 34:4, 29), and not ironically again, Jesus summarized the whole law (including the prophets' proclamation of it) in the form of *two* greatest commandments: *"You shall love the Lord your God with all your heart, and with all your soul, and with all your mind." This is the great and foremost commandment. The second is like it, "You shall love your neighbor as yourself." On these two commandments depend the whole Law and the Prophets* (Matt. 22:37–40). The two commandments reflect our double-duty as both priests and kings (Ex. 19:5–6; 1 Peter 2:5; Rev. 1:6; 5:10). The first table/great commandment contains our priestly duty, the second our kingly duty. This biblical division falls out naturally within the commandments, each table following the five points of the covenant. Ray Sutton and others (myself included) have accepted this model not because it "fits" onto the commandments, but because it arises so naturally from them, and accords with so much throughout the rest of Scripture.

So before I get to a brief discussion of how each of the commandments relates to logic and critical thinking, let us look at the five points as they arise from the ten. Some of these will require a little explanation, but with just a little the "ah hah!" sets in. The layout looks like this:

First Table

Commandment	Covenantal Point
1) I am the Lord your God, who brought you out of the land of Egypt, out of the house of slavery. You shall have no other gods before Me.	1) Ultimate Authority/Being
2) You shall not make for yourself an idol, or any likeness of what is in heaven above or on earth beneath or in the water under the earth. You shall not worship them or serve them…	2) Image/Representation/ Hierarchy
3) You shall not take the name of the Lord your God in vain, for the Lord will not leave him unpunished who takes His name in vain.	3) Property/Rules/Boundaries

4) Remember the sabbath day, to keep it holy. Six days you shall labor and do all your work, but the seventh day is a sabbath of the Lord your God; *in it* you shall not do any work, you or your son or your daughter, your male servant or your female servant or your cattle or your sojourner who stays with you. For in six days the Lord made the heavens and the earth, the sea and all that is in them, and rested on the seventh day; therefore the Lord blessed the sabbath day and made it holy.	**4)** Sanctions/Consequences/ Judgment
5) Honor your father and your mother, that your days may be prolonged in the land which the Lord your God gives you.	**5)** Time/Continuity/Inheritance

Second Table

Commandment	Covenantal Point
1) You shall not murder.	**1)** Ultimate Authority/Being
2) You shall not commit adultery.	**2)** Image/Representation/ Hierarchy
3) You shall not steal.	**3)** Property/Rules/Boundaries

4) You shall not bear false witness against your neighbor.	**4)** Sanctions/Consequences/Judgment
5) You shall not covet your neighbor's house; you shall not covet your neighbor's wife or his male servant or his female servant or his ox or his donkey or anything that belongs to him.	**5)** Time/Continuity/Inheritance

Ultimate Authority

The opening chapters of this book explain in great detail the relationship between God and logic. God creates logic as He creates the universe and man, and he imputes his order to creation in a way that His image can comprehend, study, learn, and communicate. It should come as no surprise at this point to learn that as the Ultimate Authority and Being, God makes possible and dictates everything about critical thinking. He is the source of all truth, righteousness, and judgment.

The first point of the Second Table may seem a bit trickier at first. How does "murder" relate to Ultimate authority and being, and especially *logic*? It relates in a surprisingly profound way. Man, as God's image, acts as the delegated ultimate authority taking dominion on earth (Gen 1:28; Matt. 28:18–20). As God's image/vicegerent on earth, an attack on man is an attack on God. And as Christ taught us, "murder" extends to much more than the physical act. It includes *any* unjust malicious thought or action toward another (Matt. 5:21–22). Jesus explicitly says that "murder" may even extend to even what we *say* about another person (5:22). Slander is murder; cursing is murder; and certainly we must entertain the thought that deception (and thus fallacy) is murder in the same sense.

Ray Sutton further explains, "To kill man is analogous to killing God. *All rebellion is an attempt to kill God.* Satan tempted man to become 'like' God. Between the lines of Satan's offer was the idea that the true God would be *displaced* (Gen 3:1ff.)."[2] Yet remember that Paul tells us Satan's attack upon God via Eve came as a work of *deception* (2 Cor. 11:3; 1 Tim. 2:14).

Subsequently, Christians must view their reasoning, thinking, and communicating as works of life and death. We have the choice of faithfully confessing the truth or committing murder, even the "murder" of God. That sounds extreme, but it elevates critical thinking to the seriousness it deserves. From this, perhaps we can better understand why Solomon says, *Death and life are in the power of the tongue, and those who love it will eat its fruit* (Prov. 18:21). James as well harshly condemns the tongue (Jam. 3), for *it is set on fire of hell* (3:6).

In short, God is the Ultimate Authority, and His image exercises that authority on earth. Man must witness the truth objectively, else he stands in rebellion to God's ordering of things. Any attempt at bearing false witness or deceiving your neighbor commits a cosmic attack on God's being as well. This is the reason worldview fallacies are *so* rebellious: they begin with the presumption that God does not exist, or define God as something other than He is, and then interpret *all of reality* in light of that faulty assumption. Satan could not have done it better himself.

Images, Representation, and Hierarchy

The second commandment and seventh commandment both deal with the issues of images, representatives, and hierarchy. In the prohibition of idolatry these strike us as common sense—setting up an image as a false representative of God, and thus submitting to a false hierarchy—but how do they relate to adultery?

While this may sound like another strange pairing at first, the Scripture again makes it quite explicit. God represents idolatry as "whoredom" on the part of his people (2 Kings 9:22; 2 Chron. 21:13; Jer. 2:20; 3:1–3; 13:27; Ezek. 16:15–59; Hos. 1:2; Nah. 3:4). He describes foolishness as an *adulteress* (Prov. 5, 7), in opposition to the lady "wisdom" (Prov. 3:15–20; 8–9) who makes an *excellent wife* (Prov. 31:10–31). The pairing works because both involve faithful representation of a covenanted partner. In marriage, each partner submits to the other in a holy, sacred duty (1 Cor. 7:2–4) which binds them to each other exclusively. Anyone who engages in sex outside of their marital vow *replaces* their spouse with a false spouse. They bow before a *false image* of their true spouse.

The early church father Tertullian argued, "The principal crime of the human race, the highest guilt charged upon the world, the whole procuring of the cause of judgment, is *idolatry*."[3] He applies this to separate commandments, including adultery: "Further, you may recognize in the same crime *adultery* and *fornication*; for he who serves false gods is doubtless an *adulterer* of truth, because all falsehood is adultery." You can see the connection: idolatry and adultery both involve to *false representatives* which break a covenant. Further, in order to be, create, or receive a false representative, the offender has to commit a *false witness*, a logical error on a fundamental level. In essence, the idolater says, "This, which *is not* God, *is* God," and the adulterer says, "This, which *is not* my spouse, *is* my spouse."

In relation to these commands, truth, reasoning, and communication also involve representation. Under this point, I have attempted to classify fallacies (at least the ones I have dealt with) that most prominently involve *misrepresentation*. These fundamentally fail in presenting some word, phrase, sentence, or argument as something other than it truly is—as a false "image" of the truth. I suspect a more ambitious writer could even extend this concept to the level of symbols such as those used in advanced logic, but I don't have time or training (or patience) to go that far.

Suffice it to say that God expects us to witness truth, and this means representing truth accurately. To the extent that we slack or slide in this area, we have begun to play the harlot with truth, and worship a false god.

Properties, Boundaries, and Rules

So far the Second Table laws have presented more immediate difficulty to our traditional (torpid, nousomnolent,[4] apathetic) understanding of the commandments, but here the First Table does. We can readily understand "Properties" and "Boundaries" in the sense of "Do not steal," but how does this relate to taking God's name in vain?

Not only does God's name fit with the idea of properties and boundaries, it in fact establishes the category. What's in a name, after all? To name something means to have power over it. We see this throughout Scripture, particularly at the fundamental level of creation. God gave Adam dominion over all the creatures (Gen. 1:28), then He brought the creatures to Adam so he could *name* them (Gen. 2:19–23). When the Israelites suffered captivity (foreign dominion), their new rulers often imposed new names (Gen 41:45; Dan. 1:7). So then, who has ultimate power? Who is the ultimate name-giver? God, of course. God is the only self-named, and thus self-authenticating, Being (Ex. 3:14, John 8:58). To the believer Christ gives a new name which only the individual knows (Rev. 2:17), revealing Christ as his only master and saving him from the tyranny of men.

God stands alone as the ultimate ruler of the universe; He cannot be challenged. As such, His self-given name cannot be challenged. Diminishing or changing God's name in any way denies God's rightful *properties*—all that He is, or as He would put it, all that "I AM." The person engaged in such activity essentially denies who God is, or attempts to use the name of God for his own autonomous purposes. Each case commits a fraud against the divine, similar to taking another person's property, although much worse. Using God's name for human vanity attempts to commit robbery against God Himself.

In the eighth commandment we have equally pressing matters between neighbors. "Do not steal," applies to all areas of life, including the intellect. Today we have a lot of talk about "intellectual property," which applies to things like art, music, authorship of books, etc. In these cases, courts generally uphold the theft of ideas as a crime. In God's courtroom, we must extend this concept to truth itself as well. To distort, withhold, or deny truth in any way essentially robs our neighbor of the truth, to which God entitles all lawfully obedient people (those who wish to destroy life, for example, forfeit their right to the truth—Ex. 1:15–22; Josh. 2:1–7). Fallacy trespasses the boundaries of truth which God has set, and thus "removes" the ancient landmarks (Deut. 19:14; 27:17; Prov. 22:28; 23:10) of the laws of logic.

The thief, we could say, commits a simple fallacy in his actions. He essentially declares: "This is not my property, and (at the same time and in the same relationship) This *is* my property." In other words, the thief refuses to attribute rightful properties to objects, and he refuses to name things according to objective reality as God has revealed it. He refuses to name God's names after him. In the case of lawfully man-named objects, the thief refuses to name lawfully named things according to law. In either case, the thief commits a name-denying, boundary-breaking, rule-breaking error.

This point applies directly to *formal* fallacies—those that pertain to the actual rules and structure of critical thinking. The classical and fundamental laws of logic include the law of identity, the law of non-contradiction, and the law of excluded middle. "Identity," as I have mentioned, finds its ultimate source in the self-identity of God (Ex. 3:14), which He imputes (or "names" via His word) to His creation (compare Heb. 1:3). The law of identity classically says "A is A," or "A thing is the same as itself." This law enforces objective truth: If something is true, then it must be true (not true *sometimes*, or true *if*, but plainly, simply *true*). This is the first "prejudice" of the Biblical thinker: he believes truth exists, and that it does not depend upon what man thinks about it, but it depends upon God.

What we commonly call the law of non-contradiction builds upon identity: it says "Something cannot be A and not-A at the same time and in the same relationship." In other words, "A cannot be both true and false simultaneously." We see such distinction in the Godhead first. God exists as Three Persons—the Father is not the Son or the Spirit, the Son is not the Father or the Spirit, and the Spirit is not the Father or the Son—each retaining their own identity. God imputes His order to creation, where we experience both Unity and Diveristy, and where we must confess that "A is A," *and* that "A is *not* non-A." We cannot rightfully claim that that which has an "identity" of "not-A" is the same as that which has an "identity" of "A." To do so crosses the boundaries of reality, and thus bears false witness.

Finally, the law of excluded middle traditionally claims that something must be *either* true *or* false. Just as something cannot be *both*, it also cannot be *neither*. Something must be either "A" or "not-A." This law reminds us again that reality is objective, but it also reinforces the fact that there is no ultimate neutrality. Either something *is*, or it *is not*; it is either *true* or *false*. No "middle" option exists. God expects us to witness accordingly, "yes" or "no."

You can easily see how the formal laws of logic pertain to the third point: they pertain to "naming" (identity), boundaries (non-contradiction), and rules (excluded middle), all of which are essentially implications of the same rule of identity. While this book does not purse examples of *formal* fallacies (so few actually follow the classical syllogistic forms in real life) the rules remain vitally relevant. Interestingly, some philosophers even argue that *all* fallacies (even informal ones) actually at root commit basic formal fallacies. In other words, all fallacies reduce, ultimately, to infractions of these simple formal laws of logic.[5] While I tend to agree with this in theory, the covenant model helps us understand *how* the rules get broken in various ways within the system of reality God has given us.

In terms of *informal* fallacies—arguments that commit errors despite acceptable form or structure—we must look for errors that misapply names and "property" boundaries. I find these characteristics in the classic "naturalistic" or "Is"-"Ought" fallacy in the area of ethics. The humanistic attempt to derive ethical "rules" from nature itself breaks a very obvious boundary: nature is what it is. If "nature" dictates "good," then murder and rape (occurring every day, all over the world, throughout nature) must be "good." Nature's rules trespass all over the boundaries God has set for proper behavior, and broadening "ethics" according to the standard of nature denies God's control over it.

I also find the same failure in certain category mistakes, especially modern attempts to refute God using empirical means. It should stand as common sense that if the God of the Bible exists, He stands above and beyond human senses, and thus requires a much higher standard of "proof." The use of naturalistic methods to "test" for God at the outset commits blasphemy. It essentially says, "If God exists, He can only be a naturalistic God, and we can only know Him through humanistic science." In other words, He cannot be the Transcendent, Triune God of the Bible, and He cannot be known only through His own revelation to us. All of this is assumed with the category mistake modern atheists commit. This fallacy renames God according to man's standard, and robs God of being the God He Himself says He is.

Sanctions, Consequences, and Judgment

We commonly associate the Sabbath with "rest," but the commandment involves much more than this. In fact, our observance of rest itself grows out of the fact that God proclaimed a positive judgment upon the seventh day: *God blessed the seventh day and sanctified it, because in it He rested from all His work which God had created and made* (Gen. 2:1). The commandment explicitly refers to this event, and not only forbids us to work, but commands us to *remember* God's blessed day and *keep it holy*. In other words, it calls us to perpetuate God's judgment of sacredness and blessing; it calls us to judge God's judgments after Him.

The ninth commandment, which this book places as the central command for the pursuit of truth, plays the exact same role: it calls us to think God's thoughts after Him, to judge God's judgments after Him. God controls all of reality; all of reality is a revelation of His truth. If we deny, distort, or ignore a single revealed fact, or represent facts as other than how God reveals them to us, we bear false witness against our neighbor, and we commit perjury in God's courtroom. In doing so, we call God a liar because we deny His revealed truth. Worse yet, false witness attempts to escape God's judgment of things, and thus attempts to usurp the authority of the Final Judge.

Informal fallacies that relate to the concept of judgment or consequences have to do with whether or not an argument actually *has* consequences for the issue at hand. Does a particular statement actually constitute a critical thought (personal judgment) *about the matter it pretends to address*? The question here is not, "Does the argument represent the issue properly (ambiguity, confusion, bad definitions)?" but, "Is the argument even *relevant*?" Fallacies in his regard tend to skirt the real subject entirely, and thus attempt to pressure false judgments through some means other than faithful reasoning according to truth.

Time, Continuity, and Inheritance

The fifth and tenth commandments both relate to the themes of time, continuity, and inheritance. The command to honor our parents carries the promise, *that your days may be prolonged in the land*. The blessing of *family continuity*, and therefore *continuity of wealth* (land) flows out of proper generational obedience. This command requires that children obey (submit to as true) the commands of their elders, and also that parents not provoke their children to wrath. Failures in either case deny God's respective purpose in regard to time: the young denying the wisdom of the old, the old denying the potential of the young. Instead, God calls us to perpetuate his judgments throughout the generations of history.

While we tend to think of covetousness as a "heart" sin, the law against covetousness aims at much more than spirituality. Like the honoring of parents, it also pertains to inheritance. The commandment forbids coveting specifically your neighbor's *possessions*. The law aims to protect the wealth of the family against all attacks from without the family (other families, persons, institutions, or governments). Since such attacks begin with simple jealousy or covetousness of what someone else has, God aims for the root of the sin.

In regard to truth, this point of the covenant instructs us that God's promises, God's truth, and God's judgments remain the same throughout history. History does not change or determine truth; rather, truth should triumph over time. Fallacies in this regard attempt to impute goodness or condemnation to ideas simply due to time—whether progress versus status quo, ancient versus modern, past performance, or claims of future inevitability. Each case simply ignores that God, not time, imputes truth to creation, and thus what we value about the past, present, or future simply cannot determine the truth of any given idea.

Conclusion

This brief essay has attempted to clarify and elaborate the "five points" mentioned in the Introduction to this book. These points arise from and occur throughout Scripture, and as the pattern of God's covenant with man they help us analyze and systematize our worldview. In this particular study of biblical logic and critical thinking I find that they illuminate the subject tremendously, placing truth itself in God's word alone, and placing man as a witness within God's courtroom. The Supreme Judge of the universe calls us to judge His judgments after Him. As the Judge of all the earth shall do right (Gen 18:25), so let *he that ruleth* do so *with diligence* (Rom. 12:8).

NOTES

1. See Ray Sutton, *That You May Prosper: Dominion by Covenant* (Tyler, TX: Institute for Christian Economics, 1987), 214–280.

2. Ray Sutton, *That You May Prosper: Dominion by Covenant*, 220; emphasis mine.

3. Tertullian, "On Idolatry," *The Ante-Nicene Fathers*, 10 vol., eds. Alexander Roberts and James Donldson, trans. S. Thelwall (Grand Rapids: Eerdmans, 1986), 3:61; emphasis mine.

4. My word, meaning, "sleeping mind."

5. Dale Jacquette, "Deductivism and the Informal Fallacies," *Argumentation* 21 (Spring 1997): 335–347.

CHAPTER 4

THE BIBLE AND CRITICAL THINKING

Many Christians balk at the mention of critical thinking. They associate the phrase with skepticism and "criticism" of the Bible and of religion in general; thus, they want nothing to do with it. "Critical thinking" gets taught at colleges and places where they use reason and logic to lure children away from the faith their parents taught them. While university professors have often stolen away children in the name of "critical thinking," the unbelieving skepticism promoted by these types does not deserve the label: it is not truly "critical" in the least bit, at least not in the *biblical* sense of the term.

That's right, I said the *biblical* sense of the word "critical." I say this because the Bible uses the word "critical" in a very important way. The word "critical" merely comes from the common Greek word *krites*, which means "a judge," and appears in many related forms (*krima, krivo, krisis,* and others). Perhaps the closest sounding equivalent to our English "critical," *kritikos*—meaning "able to judge (or discern)"—appears only once in the New Testament but is attributed to the Word of God: *For the word of God is living and active and sharper than any two-edged sword, and piercing as far as the division of soul and spirit, of both joints and marrow, and able to judge [kritikos] the thoughts and intentions of the heart* (Heb. 4:12). The Bible surely *does* have something to say about "critical" thinking, in fact, the Bible itself sets the ultimate standard for godly critical thinking.

This is the same sense of "criticism" which theologian Herman Bavinck used as I quoted him in an earlier chapter. His comments should now strike us with even greater biblical force:

> If Christianity is in the full sense of the term a religion of redemption and therefore wants to redeem men from the error of his intellect as well as from the iniquity of his heart, if it wants to save man from the death of his soul as well as from that of his body, then it can in the nature of the case not subject itself to the criticism of man, but must subject man to the criticism of itself.[1]

The Bible describes God Himself as the ultimate, fair, righteous judge (Gen 18:25 [*o krivov*]; 1 Pet. 2:23; 2 Tim. 4:8; Heb. 9:27; 12:23), who will critically evaluate and recompense all works (Eccl. 11:9; 12:14; Rom. 2:6; 2 Tim. 4:1; 1 Pet. 1:17), even judging hidden things (1 Cor. 4:4–5; 2 Cor. 4:2), and who will preside at a final judgment (Ps. 1:5; John 5:29; Acts 10:42; 17:31; Rom. 2:16; 3:6; Heb. 10:30; 1 John 4:17).

We can say, even if just for instructional purposes, that the Bible describes God as the ultimate, fair, righteous Critical Thinker. We can maintain this as long as we divest the phrase "critical thinking" of the humanistic, skeptical baggage normally associated with it. If we instead accept God's Word as the *standard* of critical thinking, then we have a proper, powerful, and challenging doctrine of critical thinking. This way we can rescue godly judgment and discernment from the corrupt minds and wills of the humanists.

Jesus Himself, the embodiment and exemplar of faithful human thinking, engaged in faithful critical thinking (judgment) obedient to the will of the Father: *As I hear, I judge [krivo]; and My judgment [krisis] is just, because I do not seek My own will, but the will of Him who sent Me* (John 5:30). We should not *avoid* critical thinking, but rather, as Jesus, engage in *faithful* critical thinking in submission to our Father in heaven. As He is a righteous judge, we also should strive to discern, understand, and make decisions based on righteous critical thinking. In fact, we *must* engage in critical thinking. All decision making involves us in critical thinking; we cannot avoid it. The question is not one of critical thinking versus not critical thinking; the question is one of good critical thinking (wisdom, discernment, judgment) versus poor critical thinking (foolishness, sloth, rebellion).

The obligation to engage in "judgment" may sound foreign to the Christian who has heard all along *judge not, that ye be not judged* (Matt. 7:1). Truly, we should not pass judgment upon other people in the sense that we point out their sins and mistakes while ignoring our own, or hold them to superfluous religious standards that the Bible does not call for (Rom. 2:1; 14:4; Col. 2:16; James 2:4; 4:11; 5:9). Yet this does not mean that we should exercise no judgment at all. Jesus *does* command us to engage in a critical-thinking type of judgment according to righteousness: *Do not judge [krinete] according to appearance, but judge [krisin] with righteous judgment [krinete]* (John 7:24). In other words, work hard to conform your judgments (and life!) to the standard of God's law. This will infuse your thinking with honesty and truth, according to the ninth commandment. Other godly standards such as humility and mercy will dictate that you practice criticism of your own positions first (and thus not so quickly judge others, Matt. 7:1; James 1:19).

We should begin to train our children to think critically *according to biblical standards* at a very young age. Such training in wisdom and judgment should play a core role in education. In fact, Solomon's Proverbs aim at such training:

> *To know wisdom and instruction, To discern the sayings of understanding, To receive instruction in wise behavior, Righteousness, justice and equity; To give prudence to the naive, To the youth knowledge and discretion, A wise man will hear and increase in learning, And a man of understanding will acquire wise counsel.... The fear of the Lord is the beginning of knowledge* (Prov. 1:2–7).

This process of learning and training toward good judgment requires an intimate relationship and strong passion for God's word:

> *My son, if you will receive my words And treasure my commandments within you, Make your ear attentive to wisdom, Incline your heart to understanding; For if you cry for discernment, Lift your voice for understanding; If you seek her as silver And search for her as for hidden treasures; Then you will discern the fear of the Lord And discover the knowledge of God. For the Lord gives wisdom; From His mouth come knowledge and understanding. He stores up sound wisdom for the upright; He is a shield to those who walk in integrity, Guarding the paths of justice, And He preserves the way*

of His godly ones. Then you will discern righteousness and justice And equity and every good course (Prov. 2:1–9).

Parents and other adults who never had such an emphasis in their education (including Sunday School!) should study and exercise their critical thinking skills before God as well. The process begins with a desire to apply God's standards to every area of life. Critical thinking is merely faithful thinking, and we can all use more of it.

Paul shunned worldly wisdom, and in place of it advocated the standard of God's wisdom. He called Christians in light of this standard to *critically examine all things*:

> *Yet we do speak wisdom among those who are mature; a wisdom, however, not of this age, nor of the rulers of this age, who are passing away; but we speak God's wisdom in a mystery, the hidden wisdom, which God predestined before the ages to our glory.... Now we have received, not the spirit of the world, but the Spirit who is from God, that we might know the things freely given to us by God, which things we also speak, not in words taught by human wisdom, but in those taught by the Spirit, combining spiritual thoughts with spiritual words. But a natural man does not accept the things of the Spirit of God; for they are foolishness to him, and he cannot understand them, because they are spiritually appraised. But he who is spiritual appraises [anakrinei: critically examines] all things, yet he himself is appraised [anakrinetai] by no man* (1 Cor. 2:6–7, 12–15).

There that word *krino* (to judge) appears again, only in a purposefully modified form: *ana-krino*, which essentially describes the work of a cross-examiner in a courtroom. Christians must critically examine *all things* by the standard of God's word. We must act as prosecuting attorneys, questioning and trying the testimony of human society and exposing its fallacies. In doing so, we witness and submit to both the sovereignty of God, and the high standard of Christ to which He raises His people: *For who has known the mind of the Lord, that he should instruct Him? But we have the mind of Christ* (1 Cor. 2:16; see Is. 40:13–14).

Christian books on philosophy and logic often refer to the use of the word "reason" in Isaiah 1:18: *"Come now, and let us reason together," Says the Lord, "Though your sins are as scarlet, They will be as white as snow; Though they are red like crimson, They will be like wool."* The Hebrew here, however, merely uses a special version of the standard word for "judge," or "rebuke," and particularly applies to a courtroom setting. The English translation "reason" today carries overtones of individual scholarship or thinking, and these lead us away from Isaiah's context of God's lawsuit against Israel for breaking the laws of His covenant (read Is. 1:1–17, and then read verses 18–20). For this reason, Isaiah evokes a courtroom scene as the Lord essentially challenges Israel, "let us debate our case in court."[2] Perhaps the NRSV (despite its many and great flaws) gets closest: *"Come now, let us argue it out, says the LORD."* God engaged Israel in a debate, through critical thinking that views His word as the standard. Rebellious Israel would have been wise to accept His gracious terms, for they could not have reasoned successfully *against* God's covenant terms. He issued the challenge in order to jerk their thinking to reality, as if He said, "Let us dispute," in order "To know if I do accuse you without cause."[3] The only logical conclusion Israel could have reached required repentance and obedience to His law on their part. Yet God called them *to draw this logical conclusion.*

The Greek Old Testament uses a very strong and pointed word to describe this "reasoning" in Isaiah 1:18: *dielegchthomen*, an enhanced version of the word *elengchi* ("reproof," or "conviction") which, as I will discuss in the next chapter, plays an important role in the concepts of biblical truth and faithful thought. This version means "to refute utterly," or "contradict," as employed by Plato (*Gorgias*, 457e), Aristotle, and others. In the context of Isaiah 1:18 it clearly refers to the work of an expert prosecutor who will utterly refute his opponent's (in this case Israel's) case. The same word only elsewhere appears in the exact same scenario in the Greek Old Testament: *Listen, you mountains, to the indictment of the Lord, And you enduring foundations of the earth, Because the Lord has a case against His people; Even with Israel He will dispute [dielegchthesetai]* (Mic. 6:2). In each case, the Bible places "reasoning" within the scene of God's courtroom, and calls man to witness according to the truth of God and by God's standards. Yet note that it still calls us *to do so.*

So, rather than fear critical thinking, Christians should seek to reclaim, reform, and embrace it. We must exercise *judgment* in conforming our lives to God's word; we *should* seek to expand the area of that influence further into our lives, and thus should embrace the idea of learning to "judge." This follows a scriptural ideal. The apostles, Jesus promised, would sit upon thrones in judgment over Israel (Matt. 19:28; Luke 22:30). Paul argued that *all* Christians will sit in judgment over the *world* and even *angels* (1 Cor. 6:2–3), and should therefore have the critical thinking skills to arbitrate each others' minor disputes (1 Cor. 6:4–6). Moses reminded the Israelites that he taught them God's law, and thus standards for good *judgment*: *I have taught you statutes and judgments just as the Lord my God commanded me, that you should do thus in the land where you are entering to possess it* (Deut. 4:5, 14). We should employ godly logic and reasoning and recapture business, ethics, law, education, and everything else, *destroying speculations and every lofty thing raised up against the knowledge of God, and we are taking every thought captive to the obedience of Christ* (2 Cor. 10:5).

True, sometimes seats of judgment and learning get overtaken by wickedness and unbelief. Sometimes false witnesses make a mockery of judgment (Prov. 19:28, KJV); sometimes wickedness fills the seat of judgment (Eccl. 3:16, KJV), and yet this does not mean reasoning, judgment, or critical thinking are wicked in themselves. A wise man will continue to discern time and judgment (Eccl. 8:5, KJV). Despite the failures (fallacies!) of man's reasoning even in high places, God still expects us to pursue truth through godly critical thinking. In fact, He empowers this pursuit through the work of the Holy Spirit: He convinces the world of sin, righteousness, and *judgment—concerning judgment, because the ruler of this world has been judged* (John 16:8, 11). In this sense, critical thinking moves us to understand that God has judged (condemned) the devil, and Christians must live in light of the judgment that—as Christ said already when He walked the earth—*Now judgment is upon this world; now the ruler of this world will be cast out* (John 12:31).

Returning to my earlier theme, logic simply involves the organized study of discerning and telling the truth. Added to the context of the biblical theme of godly wisdom and judgment, logic becomes much more than simple truth-telling; it becomes clear that logical thinking, to meet a biblical standard, must adopt the larger scope of a consistently biblical worldview. Logic becomes a way of thinking that reflects biblical law, biblical purposes, biblical covenant life, and biblical theology. When the Bible speaks of wisdom and judgment (and thus *krites*) it includes all of these things. Thus, only logic and reasoning that remain faithful to the Bible properly deserve the label "critical thinking," because only reasoning that begins with God constitutes good *judgment*.

NOTES

1. Quoted in Cornelius Van Til, *A Christian Theory of Knowledge*, 40.

2. Paul R. Gilchrist, *"yakah,"* *Theological Wordbook of the Old Testament*, 2 vol, eds. R. Laird Harris, Gleason L. Archer, Jr., and Bruce K. Waltke (Chicago: Moody Press, 1980) 1:377. Westminster Seminary professor William Edgar notes something similar in Isaiah 41:21, and also mentions the Hebrew behind 1:18, though he does not elaborate too much on either case. See his *Reasons of the Heart: Recovering Christian Persuasion* (Phillipsburg, NJ: Presbyterian and Reformed, 2003), 44, 123 ("Chapter 4..." note 1).

3. Geneva Bible note, Is. 1:18. See *1599 Geneva Bible* (White Hall, WV: Tolle Lege Press, 2006), 679.

CHAPTER 5

SOPHISTRY, REFUTATION, AND FALLACY

Just because you can persuade someone does not mean that what you have said is true. People often accept (even embrace!) false ideas based on terrible reasoning. They can do so for many reasons: they may have some inherent bias to *want* something to be true, or they may have made a genuine mistake unwittingly. As a result, they create arguments built on wishes and mistakes rather than solid truth and logic.

Aristotle—the "father" of the study of logic—points out these very facts. He writes,

> That some reasonings are really reasonings, but that others seem to be, but are not really, reasonings, is obvious. For, as this happens in other spheres from a similarity between the true and the false, so it happens in arguments.... [R]easoning and refutation are sometimes real and sometimes not, but appear to be real.... [T]here exist both reasoning and refutation which appear to be genuine but are not really so.[1]

In other words, fallacies happen. Aristotle points out that some people—due to profit, or some other desire—prefer the "apparently real" refutations over truth:

> But since in the eyes of some people it is more profitable to seem to be wise that to be wise without seeming to be so (for the sophistic art consists in apparent and not real wisdom, and the sophist is one who makes money from apparent and not real wisdom), it is clear that for these people it is essential to seem to perform the function of a wise man rather than actually to perform it without seeming so.[2]

Aristotle merely touches the matter here. True, the desire for money, as we all expect, can provide strong motivation to obscure truth with deceptive arguments. But many lusts and desires of fallen human nature can move us, in many ways, to evade the light of truth and cover our cherished ideas. Aristotle also noticed this "double-minded" nature of man. He writes that men "do not wish the same things as they declare that they wish, but they give utterance to the most becoming sentiments, whereas they desire what they think is to their interest."[3]

One of the strongest of these hidden desires derives from fallen human nature itself: how a person relates to God, or how he views religion. This holds true whether he denies God, or improperly represents God's truth. For example, someone living a sexually immoral lifestyle may deny the existence of God merely because they do not like the sexual standards God gives to live by. Such a person may create all kinds of smart-sounding arguments even though they know they can never philosophically prove a negative claim (such as "God does not exist"). Nevertheless, they will embrace the silliest reasoning against God because all the while they have a deeply harbored prejudice against Christian *morality*.

A Christian, however, may read the scenario above and mistakenly adopt it as a refutation against atheism in general. Such a Christian may then tell his random atheist friend, "Atheists deny God's existence because they just want to live deviant, pleasure-driven lifestyles." Such a Christian would likely have committed the Fallacy of Hasty Generalization, which improperly applies attributes of a small sample to an entire group. What may truly apply to one or even many atheists does not necessarily transfer to this particular atheist's case. The Christian would do better to examine his friend's claims about the world, expose the fundamental errors of his worldview, and then show why only the

Christian worldview can account for human experience (including our desires!). Adopting the claim above, however, leaves both the atheist and Christian resting upon fallacies.

In popular media of argument (internet forums, etc.), I have witnessed similar dialogues play out many times over. The most disheartening thing I've seen involves the claim "I've refuted that," or sometimes "You haven't refuted me because you never answered my question." Both of these statements assume that the refutation involved or the question posed actually carries the weight that the proponent thinks it does. More often than not the "refutation" fails badly in some way or other, yet the person behind it thinks that just because they have written five paragraphs in response that they have "refuted" some position. Or they think that because an opponent has ignored a certain question that therefore the particular question has tripped him up. They rarely bother to think that their question misses the point, has inconsistencies, makes no sense, actually received an answer already, or somehow else simply stands irrelevant to the issue at hand. In all of this the out-of-touch opponent really just fails to be self-critical. They fail to engage in genuine *critical thinking*.

A crucial part of godly reasoning involves arriving at a sound conclusion. With a godly world-order in place—a faithful Creator-Judge, an objective creation, critical minds with the capacity for good judgments, and the mandate from God that we exercise godly judgment and avoid false witness—we must learn *discernment*. This means we must learn to tell the difference between deviant reasoning and sound reasoning. In the course of everyday life, and certainly in the course of learning through scholarship, reading—even pulpits and Sunday Schools—the Christian will encounter a barrage of shady claims and arguments. Many such arguments may sound strong, and many may even effectively persuade many people, but the measure of godly logic will always remain the truth, not the effects—God's truth, not the acceptance of men. Discernment, therefore, describes the ability to separate truth from merely persuasive rhetoric, and Christians must train their minds in this art.

SOPHISTRY AND REFUTATION: *IGNORATIO* AND *ELENCHI*

Paul reminded the Corinthians that he purposefully avoided cunning rhetoric in favor of the plain, powerful Gospel:

> *And when I came to you, brethren, I did not come with superiority of speech or of wisdom, proclaiming to you the testimony of God.... And my message and my preaching were not in persuasive words of wisdom, but in demonstration of the Spirit and of power, that your faith should not rest on the wisdom of men, but on the power of God* (1 Cor. 2:1–5).

Historically, however, people give in to the temptation to trick and dupe others by using persuasive words rather than godly wisdom. Aristotle provided the first systematic examination of logic, and he did so primarily because of the prevalence of trained rhetoricians who hired out their persuasive abilities for money. Many became very rich and famous. This group of "sophists" (from the Greek *sophos*, "wise"; of such people see Rom. 1:22) did not care about the truth of any particular issue; they merely cared about winning the argument for their paying clients. Sophists prided themselves on their ability to take either side of any argument and win. As a result, society grew ever more vicious while suppressing and essentially penalizing all concern for truth and righteousness in judgment. The prevalence of sophistry led to the subsidizing of false witness. It paid to lie, and paid better to lie well.

Aristotle, despite his own humanistic flaws, sought to counter "sophistry" by outlining proper ways to reason, and by systematically exposing all the ways in which sophists could create devious persuasions. This latter part of his work bears the title *Sophistical Refutations [Sophistikon Elengchon]*, by which he means "refutations" that do not truly refute anything at all, yet persuade. Such false refutations Aristotle called "paralogical," or "beyond logic," or in other words, not really logical at all. He listed and described thirteen fallacies, all of which later philosophers have included and expanded upon.

Among these thirteen fallacies Aristotle listed one he called *ignoratio elenchi*, or "ignorance of what a refutation is." He explained this fallacy as the neglect to distinguish genuine or false contradictions in an argument, and thus letting some shady definitions slip by. Later, however, he argued that *all* fallacies can fall under the heading of "ignorance of what 'refutation' is."[4] I accept this broader application, for truly all fallacies essentially commit the same error: they fail to compel us necessarily to a true witness (which I explain further below) *because of the the truth of the argument,* and thus fail to deliver a true refutation or reasoning. Aristotle says that "the conclusion ought to follow from the premises laid down, so that we state it of *necessity* and do not merely appear to do so."[5] An argument must compel us *of necessity* to accept it or else we can judge it inconclusive and thus likely fallacious.

In order to avoid such errors, Christians should have a solid view of what *elengchi*—"refutation" or "convincing"—actually is. We can begin with Aristotle himself, and progress into a biblical understanding.

To describe genuine refutations—those that derive from logical conclusions—Aristotle used the Greek word *elenchon*, which plays an important role in later New Testament Greek as well. For Aristotle, the word simply referred to a sound logical refutation of a philosophical argument, the virtue of the refutation resting in the fact that it worked logically from the point of view of huamnistic reason. Later Greeks expanded the concept to include correction in general, but particularly pertaining to basic ways of living as opposed to philosophical arguments.

Biblical writers employ the same term *elegnchon* in order to mean more than general "correction" or "refutation," but particularly to refer to the discipline and education God gives to man in history.[6] This view appears already in the Greek Old Testament (begun about 250 BC). Wisdom cries to man in Proverbs 1:23, *Turn to my reproof [elengchois], Behold, I will pour out my spirit on you; I will make my words known to you.* Here the role of God's Spirit factors in—a crucial feature of New Testament reproof and conviction. God calls his people to accept godly correction: *My son, do not reject the discipline of the Lord, or loathe His reproof* (Prov. 3:11). In fact, correction according to God's standards indicates God's fatherly love for us: *For whom the Lord loves He reproves, even as a father, the son in whom he delights* (Prov. 3:12; see Heb. 12:5–6; Rev. 3:19). A person's acceptance of reproof reveals his character: *Do not reprove a scoffer, lest he hate you, reprove a wise man, and he will love you* (Prov. 9:8; 12:1; 13:18; 15:10, 12; 29:1). The love of logical correction marks godly wisdom; the hatred of it reveals foolishness, and actually self-hatred (Prov. 15:32).

Such a heart for God's corrections will help a person remain patient: listening first, then discerning, then speaking if necessary. The patient, wise listener knows that God's corrections and instruction come in many ways, and from very unlikely, often lowly, sources. God confronted a rebellious Balaam with an angel that only his donkey could see. Balaam beat the God-obeying donkey, and God moved the donkey to "reprove" Balaam. Peter tells us that the donkey gave Balaam a *rebuke [elengxin]* and by that *restrained the madness of a prophet* (2 Pet. 2:16). If God can move a donkey to think critically, He can move you.

God's people ought to engage in critical thinking, and ought to engage each other in reproof, though no doubt in humility and Christian love. Through such confrontation we expose the kinds of errors that clever hearts learn to rationalize and hide: *The first to plead his case seems just, until another comes and examines [elengchetai] him* (Prov. 18:17). And through such examination we actually earn mutual respect and love among the wise: *He who rebukes [elengchon] a man will afterward find more favor than he who flatters with the tongue* (Prov. 28:23).

The New Testament gives the word a very similar thrust, usually referring to correction from sin and including a call to repentance, or change toward right living.[7] This comes out in the very teaching of Jesus, in a passage vital to our biblical doctrine of logic. Jesus teaches that in His absence, the Holy Spirit acts as the power behind correct thinking and living—a power that calls and guides His people in to truth, and condemns those who reject truth. Jesus says of the Holy Spirit,

> *He, when He comes, will convict [elengxei] the world concerning sin, and righteousness, and judgment; concerning sin, because they do not believe in Me; and concerning righteousness, because I go to the Father, and you no longer behold Me; and concerning judgment, because the ruler of this world has been judged. I have many more things to say to you, but you cannot bear them now. But when He, the Spirit of truth, comes, He will guide you into all the truth; for He will not speak on His own initiative, but whatever He hears, He will speak; and He will disclose to you what is to come. He shall glorify Me; for He shall take of Mine, and shall disclose it to you* (John 16:7–14).

The Holy Spirit, testifying of Jesus, refutes our error and convinces us to turn to righteousness. He speaks only the *truth*, and testifies only the truth of *Jesus*. He guides the Christian into truth, refuting error according to the standard of God's law (Jam. 2:9). Jesus personally embodies this law; He is the standard of truth by which God corrects us. As the Truth Himself, no man can offer a refutation of Him: *Which one of you convicts Me of sin?* (John 8:46). The answer to this rhetorical question, of course, is "no one." God's word is complete and final; no man can add to or take away from it without earning refutation from God: *Every word of God is tested.... Do not add to His words lest He reprove [elengxe] you, and you be proved a liar* (Prov. 30:5). Arguments that deny God's word or deviate from His standards of truth, therefore, commit fallacies and deny logic.

A question arises at this point. Can we relate the biblical usage of *elengchos* (reproof) to Aristotle's usage of it (refutation) for the study of logic? I think we can, indeed must. Watching carefully not to assume some fixed meaning of the word from one culture to the other, and making sure not to assume that the New Testament writers had Aristotle's logic in mind when they wrote (certainly they did not!), we can nevertheless see a crucial similarity in the role of *elengchos* as "correcting" a bad notion. To the extent that the usage of the word broadens over time, covering a greater degree of man's intellectual, moral, and eventually spiritual life, we must likewise broaden our view of *logic* as well.

The fact that the New Testament applies the need for "reproof" to a greater degree of human life than did the ancient Greeks simply speaks to the biblical view of human depravity: it extends to the fundamental fiber of man. The issue is not, as it was for the Greeks, a poor argument here or there begging for refutation, but rather a corrupt heart and corrupt mind that need renewing, and therefore require divine correction and guidance. This means, further, that initiative for such renewal comes from God, not man. Man cannot escape his corruption by employing the very corrupt heart and mind that need renewing to begin with. His pathetic attempts to do so advance him no further toward God than the ancient pagans could get. Rather, God, by His power, by His will, and by His standard, calls mankind to repentance from their erring ways, including their fallacious reasonings, and enables them to follow the correct path that He determines. Thus Paul exalts the Scriptures as *inspired by God and profitable for teaching, for reproof [elengmon], for correction, for training in righteousness* (2 Tim. 3:15).

The necessary reliance upon God appears again in Hebrews, in the classic definition of "faith" itself. The author teaches us: *Now faith is the assurance of things hoped for, the conviction [elenchos] of things not seen* (Heb. 11:1). In faith we apprehend conviction of the truth of God—of his very existence as well as his approval and reward (Heb. 11:2, 6). *Without faith*, he tells us, *it is impossible to please him* (11:6). God gives the faith (Eph. 2:8–9), man does not generate it himself, and thus we must credit God with initiating and sustaining all proper reproof, conviction, and assent to truth. Without Him, the means, methods, and goals of critical thinking disappear.

By following God's standards, Christians will not fall prey to erroneous beliefs. They will *not participate in the unfruitful deeds of darkness, but instead even expose [elengchete] them… for all things become visible when they are exposed [elengchomena] by the light* (Eph. 5:11, 13). Paul here simply applies the teaching of Jesus (who is that light—John 1:4–5), that *everyone who does evil hates the light, and does not come to the light, lest his deeds should be exposed [elengchthe]. But he who practices the truth comes to the light, that his deeds may be manifested as having been wrought in God* (John 3:20–21). This teaching about light exposing darkness applies just as much to thinking and reasoning as to other deeds.

What the Greeks developed in the name of human wisdom, the Scriptures reveal as a way of life intimately dependent upon God's standards, the revelation of God in Christ, a relationship with Christ through the Holy Spirit, and a lifetime work of judging and refuting the errors of this world so as to avoid them and walk in righteousness. In short, what so many people throughout history have attempted to develop as a humanistic standard, God reveals as only possible with His total support and provision. Truth belongs to God; the world is His courtroom.

God's word is complete and final; no man can add to or take away from it without earning refutation from God: *Every word of God is tested.… Do not add to His words lest He reprove [elengxe] you, and you be proved a liar* (Prov. 30:5). Arguments that deny God's word or deviate from His standards of truth, therefore, must defy logic and commit fallacies.

LOGICAL FALLACIES

If logic is the systematic study and practice of discerning and telling the truth, then what is a fallacy? The word itself gives us a hint as it shares the same root as the word "false." "Fallacy," "false," and even "fail" all come from the Latin *fallere*, which means "to deceive, trick, dupe, cheat, disappoint."[8] Many variants and uses exist, all with meanings related to failure, deception, or unfaithfulness. Fallacies, according to this understanding, represent the many ways in which people can deceive or create non-truths. In brief, a fallacy is one instance, whether intentional or not, of bearing false witness.

With a biblical view of logic and judgment in place—a view which depends upon a sovereign creator God and his express law for our lives—we can understand logical fallacies as not just instances of tricky expression, but as failures of moral integrity, failures of discerning truth, failures of thinking as clearly or thoroughly as we ought, failures of reasoning according to God's standards, failures to learn from God's reproof, and failures of critical judgment. Fallacies become theological and ethical concerns. For such a reason, St. Augustine could charge the pagan philosophy of the Romans with being "contemptible and *false*" (Latin, *falsio*);[9] pagan worldviews commit basic theological fallacies.

An interesting parallel appears in the Greek language, with the closely related word *sphallo*, which means "to slip, stumble, fall."[10] The few occurrences of this word in biblical literature do not suggest mere accidents of falling, but of falling due to moral error, or due to God's judgment upon His enemies. Moses spoke for God of His enemies, *Vengeance is Mine, and retribution, In due time their foot will slip [sphale]; For the day of their calamity is near, And the impending things are hastening upon them* (Deut. 32:35).[11] Job's friend Bildad rightly knows of the wicked man that *the steps of his strength shall be straitened, and his own counsel shall cast him down [sphalai]* (Job 18:7), even though Bildad improperly implies this for Job. And Solomon, who presents us the virtuous woman "wisdom" against the adulterous whore "foolishness" in Proverbs warns the young man: *Her feet go down to death.... She does not ponder the path of life; Her ways are unstable [sphalerai]* (Prov. 5:5–6). "Unstable" here means "trembling" and "slippery." As a remedy, God's commandments provide us reproof (*elenchos*) and instruction to avoid the evil woman and find the *way of life* (Prov. 6:23–24). In so many ways does God warn us of a link between our moral life and sure footing, an image that presents a useful rule for intellectual endeavors: He that stands with deceptive thinking, falls with it.

Most of the rest of this book deals with logical fallacies. Of course, in studying logical fallacies the Christian (or anyone, really) must have some standard of logic by which to determine the true from the fallacious. Part Two of this book will rely on the understanding of logic discussed in the previous chapters—that logic essentially involves the systematic pursuit of bearing true witness. Thus, the study of fallacies which follows represents the exposure and correction of popular ways to tell lies (whether intentionally or not).

I tend to agree with Gordon Clark where he writes, "Logic books have their flaws. The examples tend to be trivial or artificial. If historical, and not artificial, they tend to be irrelevant."[12] Most books that cover fallacies present mostly manufactured examples, as well as many that create the humor in comic strips, jokes, and Lewis Carroll's works, *Alice's Adventures in Wonderland* and *Through the Looking-Glass*. It seems to me that most philosophers who write on fallacies cannot resist quoting something from the witty but completely silly purposeful nonsense Alice experiences in Wonderland. Gordon Clark tolerates the phenomenon as long as it presents simple examples for beginning students to learn from. I tend to think that the cumulative effect of too many light-hearted examples subliminally weakens the reader's esteem of logic and critical thinking in general. Clark later notes, "[B]e warned that in the affairs of this world, the fallacies are usually complex and not so easily recognized."[13] This book contains dozens of such real-world examples. The reader will find humor here and there as well, but the meat of the lessons involves serious and weighty examples of fallacious thinking.

NOTES

1. "On Sophistical Refutations" (Book 1, Ch. 1), *Aristotle: On Sophistical Refutations; On Coming-to-Be and Passing-Away; On the Cosmos*, ed. and trans. E. S. Forster, The Loeb Classical Library, eds. T. E. Page, et al (London: William Heinemann, and Cambridge, MA: Harvard University Press, 1955), 11, 13.

2. "On Sophistical Refutations" (Book 1, Ch. 1), *Aristotle: On Sophistical Refutations; On Coming-to-Be and Passing-Away; On the Cosmos*, 13, 15.

3. "On Sophistical Refutations" (Book 1, Ch. 12), *Aristotle: On Sophistical Refutations; On Coming-to-Be and Passing-Away; On the Cosmos*, 71.

4. "On Sophistical Refutations" (Book 1, Ch. 6), *Aristotle: On Sophistical Refutations; On Coming-to-Be and Passing-Away; On the Cosmos*, 35.

5. "On Sophistical Refutations" (Book 1, Ch. 6), *Aristotle: On Sophistical Refutations; On Coming-to-Be and Passing-Away; On the Cosmos*, 35; emphasis added.

6. Friedrich Büchsel, "*elencho*," *Theological Dictionary of the New Testament*, 10 vol., eds. Gerhard Kittel and Geoffrey W. Bromiley, trans. G. Bromiley (Grand Rapids: Eerdmans, 1964), 2:473.

7. Friedrich Büchsel, "*elencho*," *Theological Dictionary of the New Testament*, 2:474.

8. Charlton T. Lewis and Charles Short, eds. "fallo," *A Latin Dictionary* (London: Oxford at the Clarendon Press, 1966 [1879]), 721.

9. Aurelius Augustine, *The City of God* (7.5), Nicene and Post-Nicene Fathers, First Series, 14 vol., ed. Phillip Schaff, trans. Marcus Dods (Grand Rapids: Eerdmans, 1983), 2:126.

10. William F. Arndt and F. Wilbur Gingrich, eds. "*sphallo*," *A Greek-English Lexicon*

of the New Testament and Other Early Christian Literature (Chicago: University of Chicago Press, and London: Cambridge University Press, 1957), 803.

11. These Old Testament passages use variants of *sphallo*, of course, in the Septuagint version.

12. Gordon H. Clark, *Logic* (Jefferson, MD: The Trinity Foundation, 1985), 12.

13. Gordon H. Clark, *Logic*, 13.

PART TWO

BIBLICAL LOGIC APPLIED

Fallacies of Worldview

CHAPTER 6

"Leaky Buckets": Fallacies of Worldview

Worldview fallacies occur when people make false assumptions at the level of ultimate issues. In order to account for and justify all of human experience, we must acknowledge a self-authoritative, self-revealing, self-consistent Creator-God who Himself subsumes both unity and diversity within His own self-order. Human experience involves all of these characteristics, and yet no part of human experience itself—no part of creation—can provide final justification for them. Man's attempt to do so all run him into absurdities, contradictions, and chaos. The attempt to erase the Creator from the picture and to account for reality independently through human reason alone always leads to dead ends.

It should stand as common sense that the endeavor of trying to justify human experience *by* human experience will inevitably include circular logic, and thus logical difficulties. Furthermore, the limitations of human experience will naturally stifle the conclusions man can reach about human experience when relying on that standard alone. The fact that human experience, from the Christian point of view, comes only through the filter of *fallen* human nature, intensifies and exaggerates the distortion—both in how man receives his experience, and in how he processes and communicates it.

Thus we enter this study of Worldview Fallacies with double cautions: 1) autonomous human standards for reality will fail logically, and yet 2) fallen man will try every means possible to deny or hide 1).

The Fall of Man and Human Autonomy

Paul teaches us that fallen man has rejected and continually suppresses the knowledge of God and His revelation; yet the same man cannot live without attempting to ground his experience in some ultimate principle. As Augustine famously confessed, "O Lord ... Thou hast formed us for Thyself, and our hearts are restless till they find rest in Thee."[1] Paul explains how the children of fallen Adam wrestle with this restlessness:

> *even though they knew God, they did not honor Him as God or give thanks, but they became futile in their speculations, and their foolish heart was darkened. Professing to be wise, they became fools, and exchanged the glory of the incorruptible God for an image in the form of corruptible man and of birds and four-footed animals and crawling creatures. Therefore God gave them over in the lusts of their hearts to impurity, so that their bodies would be dishonored among them. For they exchanged the truth of God for a lie, and worshiped and served the creature rather than the Creator, who is blessed forever. Amen* (Rom. 1:21–25).

Notice the multiple effects that this rebellion has upon the mind of man:

- *(1) they became futile in their speculations, and their foolish heart was darkened;*

- (2) yet they engaged (perhaps all the harder) in philosophy, and called themselves philosophers (lovers of wisdom), yet to no real intellectual gain (*Professing to be wise, they became fools*);

- (3) they rejected man as the image of God and instead saw him akin to nature only (*exchanged the glory of the incorruptible God for an image in the form of corruptible man and of birds and four-footed animals and crawling creatures*);

(4) they succumbed to self-deception and their foolishness expressed itself in false witness (*they exchanged the truth of God for a lie*);

(5) they still continued in worship, but exchanged worship of the Creator for worship of creation (*worshiped and served the creature rather than the Creator, who is blessed forever*); and thus,

(6) God sends judgment, for now, in the form of their own spiritual corruption, and their futility, foolishness, false piety, false witness, and false worship all become their own condemnation, proving their hearts corrupt (*God gave them over in the lusts of their hearts to impurity, so that their bodies would be dishonored among them*).

In the following section, I will illustrate the intellectual foolishness bred from this rejection of God's revelation, concentrating on the "futility" of such thought. Human autonomy, wishing to justify itself apart from God, grasps and strains at every possible straw of human experience, trying at various times and from multiple angles to create a lasting foundation for existence, knowledge, ethics, meaning, value and progress. With thousands of Adam's rebellious children thinking and writing throughout history, the student will encounter dozens of "isms," ideas, beliefs, or life-stances that have grown out the simple worldview fallacy of human autonomy—all of them equally futile and vulnerable to the same fundamental criticism.

All anti-Christian worldviews have at their core a rejection of the revelation of God, and as such will fail due to the limits of human experience. These limits will appear in the worldview in the form of some logical inconsistency, incoherence, or arbitrary aspects. The following overview covers some of the most common facets in which human autonomy intellectually expresses itself.

Fallacies of Autonomy

Naturalism and Materialism

Beneath every autonomous worldview secretly rests a belief about reality. This belief masquerades as an assumed answer to the question,

"What is real, ultimately"? This assumption can only take two basic forms: supernaturalism or naturalism (excluded middle: S or not-S). All worldviews ultimately fall into one of these two categories, and each category contains many fallacious varieties.

Christian theism can fall under the heading of supernaturalism although it forms a very special case: it constitutes the only viable worldview that involves no indefensible arbitrary assumptions or logical incoherence. In one sense we could categorize all worldviews under the two headings, "Christian theism," and "Human autonomy," but I will stick with what I have set up for now. The rest of the category of supernaturalism includes false religions, cults, New Age beliefs, and the like, all of which believe in an ultimate reality beyond the "nature" perceived by the human senses, but all of which fail in various ways. These particular failures lie beyond the scope of this book, and the reader can find them well documented in various places.[2]

The category of naturalism also contains many permutations which may include even some religions (Confucianism, some forms of Buddhism, Taoism, and some New Age ideas) and broadly describes the belief that nothing exists except "nature." The most popular application of this idea appears among skeptics and "scientific" minded unbelievers. Among these, "nature" can best be defined by what it is *not*, namely, a universe beholden to a personal Creator God who sustains it and "interferes" with "the laws of nature" in answering prayers and performing miracles.

Consequently, this group of naturalists believes in a universe that *never* operates at variance with laws—laws which themselves exist inherently in and because of nature itself. This belief gives rise to a secondary belief called *uniformitarianism*—the idea the universe and everything in it, for all of history, remains uniform in its operation. The universe has always operated, and will always continue to operate, according to predictable and understandable laws.

Many problems arise with such a worldview. Firstly, it is arbitrary, and thus dogmatic. While the universe does display amazing orderliness, all philosophers will agree that the limitations of human knowledge make it impossible to prove a negative claim such as "no Supernatural God exists." So while we can trust the orderliness of the universe to a great degree, engage in science, and generate remarkably precise and accurate predictions, we cannot rightfully abstract that activity and conclude that such orderliness is the primary, let alone the only attribute of reality. To do so would be to operate on an unproven assumption, and thus would reveal more about the naturalist's opinions than about reality.

To maintain his arbitrarily chosen belief about nature, the naturalist "explains away" alternative views from within the confines of, and using the limited tools of, his own worldview. Since he has excluded any miraculous event or supernatural intervention by definition, then no evidence of a miracle could logically change his opinion. Why not? If ever confronted with a miracle—even an extreme miracle, for example, the resurrection of the dead—the naturalist would still attempt to take recourse to a natural explanation. On the one hand he may attempt to offer a "natural" explanation (for example, that the corpse was not really dead to begin with, or that given the right medical circumstances a dead body *can* be brought back to life by CPR and electromagnetic nerve stimulation, etc.). No matter how weak such an explanation may be, it will have the merit (in the mind of the naturalist) of being "natural," and thus for him will provide a more plausible scenario than any supernatural explanation. On the other hand, he may consent that naturalistic science currently has no answer to such a phenomenon, but nevertheless "scientists are working on it" and will ultimately arrive at one. The dogmatism of his position stands out at this point: he would essentially argue, in the face of a miracle, that if *any* explanation is to be given of the event, that explanation *can only be* a natural explanation.

This shows that even the naturalist's own criteria of judgment—that is, natural "evidence"—could never change his fundamental commitments even when it contradicts them. Indeed, since he has already predetermined in his own mind that *nothing* exists except uniform nature, then he will reinterpret any contradictory evidence as somehow not contradictory. This means that "nature" and "evidence" truly do *not* form the basis of the naturalist's worldview (despite how much he boasts of this fact); rather, his *unproven assumptions* form the unchallengeable basis of his worldview.

Jesus speaks of such a problem with unbelievers. In the parable of the rich man and Lazarus (Luke 16:19–31), Jesus teaches about a rich man who ignored God during his life, and after death lay suffering in hell. Shouting to Abraham afar off the man pleaded to have someone sent back to warn his brothers of the torment that waits. The dialogue that follows carries an important lesson about the limitations of miraculous evidence:

> *Abraham said, "They have Moses and the Prophets; let them hear them." But he said, "No, father Abraham, but if someone goes to them from the dead, they will repent!" But he said to him, "If they do not listen to Moses and the Prophets, they will not be persuaded even if someone rises from the dead"* (Luke 16:29–31).

According to Abraham, a man unmoved by the supernatural power of God's word will also remain unmoved by supernatural interventions in nature, even as drastic as a resurrection. Evidence will not move them, for their fundamental commitment is not to nature, but against the Personal Creator God.

From this perspective, the naturalist essentially creates his own intellectual limitations and then arbitrarily (on his own autonomous authority) defines all of reality as falling within those limitations. The old saying applies: "What my net don't catch ain't fish." But this behavior is akin to locking yourself in the closet and then arguing that the rest of the world does not exist because you can't see it. The resulting condition resembles a fish in his bowl pontificating about the non-existence of everything outside.

Examples of this type of rationalizing abound in the literature of secularists and atheists. For example, atheistic philosopher Daniel Dennett has created a metaphor to describe what types of explanations we should accept when talking about the origins of the universe. What kind of explanation do we need to do our intellectual "lifting"? To answer, he contrasts "skyhooks" with "cranes." Quoting the Oxford English Dictionary, Dennett defines a "skyhook" as "An imaginary contrivance for attachment to the sky; an imaginary means of suspension in the sky."[3] Notice the repetition of the word "imaginary" and the inclusion of the word "contrivance." Dennett adds, "Skyhooks would be wonderful things to have.... Sad to say, they are impossible."[4] Rather than refer to the supernatural directly, Dennett uses his metaphor to categorize any explanation of nature that does not creep along step-by-step according to Darwinian theory. In other words, any non-Darwinian, non-naturalistic explanation of the universe is *by definition* (according to Dennett) imaginary, contrived, and impossible. He has defined God away at the start!

Naturalistic explanations, however, he refers to as "cranes." "Skyhooks are miraculous lifters, unsupported and insupportable. Cranes are no less excellent lifters, and they have the decided advantage of being real."[5] Of course, cranes can only lift as high as they can reach, so Dennett (as a faithful Darwinian) stretches the metaphor further. Just as sometimes contractors use smaller cranes to assemble bigger ones, we can understand nature using small steps to achieve greater results.

> Vast distances must have been traversed since the dawn of life with the earliest, self-replicating entities, spreading outward (diversity) and upward (excellence). Darwin has offered us an account of the crudest, most rudimentary, stupidest imaginable lifting process—the wedge of natural selection. By taking tiny—the tiniest possible—steps, this process can gradually, over eons, traverse these huge distances. Or so he claims. At no point would anything miraculous—from on high—be needed. Each step has been accomplished by brute, mechanical, algorithmic climbing, from the base already built by the efforts of earlier climbing.[6]

Ignoring the very fundamental question that arises from this—Where did the first "step" or "the base" come from to begin with?—Dennett's naturalistic assumptions stand out here. He further elaborates:

> a *skyhook* is a "mind-first" force or power or process, an exception to the principle that all design, and apparent design, is ultimately the result of mindless, motiveless mechanicity. A *crane*, in contrast, is a subprocess or special feature of a design process that can be demonstrated to permit the local speeding up of the basic, slow process of natural selection, *and* that can be demonstrated to be itself the predictable (or retrospectively explicable) product of the basic process.[7]

Dennett reinforces my earlier point that naturalism essentially amounts to a negative position, defined not by what it is, but by what it is *not*—it exists merely by denying a Creator "mind" from the universe, not by establishing proof of itself. Notice how this assumption infuses Dennett's explanations: a "mind-first" approach would present an *exception* to the norm, which is *mindless* by definition. The "mindless, motiveless mechanicity" of *natural* selection forms the basis of his worldview. Anything that does not fit this mold he labels as "imaginary."

You can easily see the arbitrariness of this position. Dennett has no *ultimate* justification for choosing a natural versus a supernatural explanation for ultimate reality (not minor changes in nature, but the existence of all of nature and nature's "laws" and constants to begin with). Rather, he chooses his assumption autonomously, based on his own personal experience. With this presupposition of naturalism as the norm in place, he erects the false dichotomy of "skyhooks" versus "cranes" to describe the possible acceptable types of explanations. But his loading of his worldview into the very definitions to start with stacks the deck against anyone countering him. His categories of skyhook and crane do not fairly present the fight between supernaturalism versus naturalism, for they are both naturalistically conceived definitions. To accept his metaphors would be to concede to naturalism up front, and this method simply Begs the Question (more on this fallacy later).

Yet such unfairness characterizes all worldview fallacies, especially that of naturalism. For example, atheist Richard Dawkins takes Dennett's metaphor and runs. Dawkins writes, "[T]he very least that any honest quest for truth must have in setting out to explain such monstrosities of improbability as a rain forest, a coral reef, or a universe is a crane and not a skyhook."[8] This is true, apparently, by definition. He elaborates, exposing his assumption:

> The crane doesn't have to be natural selection. Admittedly, nobody has ever thought of a better one. But there could be others yet to be discovered. Maybe the 'inflation' that physicists postulate as occupying some fraction of the first yoctosecond of the universe's existence will turn out, when it is better understood, to be a cosmological crane to stand alongside Darwin's biological one. Or maybe the elusive crane that cosmologists seek will be a version of Darwin's idea itself: either Smolin's idea or something similar. Or maybe it will be the multiverse plus the anthropic principle espoused by Martin Rees and others. It may even be a superhuman designer—but, if so, it will most certainly *not* be a designer who just popped into existence, or who always existed.

Apparently, Dawkins will accept *any* explanation as possible, as long as that explanation does not involve an Eternal Supernatural Creator. Such a Designer he must rule out immediately by his definition:

> If (which I don't believe for a moment) our universe was designed, and *a fortiori* if the designer reads our thoughts and hands out omniscient advice, forgiveness and redemption, the designer himself must be the end product of some kind of cumulative escalator or crane, perhaps a version of Darwinism or another universe.[9]

"Must be," you see. *Any* designer of this universe *must be* himself the product of a "crane"—a previously existing building block. The *most* god-like being Dawkins can imagine still must bow before the Almighty dictates of nature. Elsewhere Dawkins puts it more bluntly: he speaks of skyhooks as "including all gods."[10] In other words, Dawkins, because of his presupposition of naturalism, refuses to even acknowledge the *possibility* of a supernatural Creator. If *any* kind of a superhuman being exists, that being must be subject to the same natural laws as we. Such beings *must have* evolved (according to Dawkins) by the same evolution humans have, the superhuman beings will simply have progressed further in evolution than we.

As arbitrary (and absurd) as this assumption sounds, Dawkins sticks to it. He reveals further implications of his worldview: aliens. He expounds,

> I do think that there may very well be, somewhere in the universe, evolved beings which are so far advanced compared to us that we would, if we saw them, we might very well be tempted to call them gods; and it is also possible by the same token that if our species goes on evolving either genetically and/or culturally for a sufficient number of millennia, our descendants might be so advanced that we would be tempted to call them gods. However, I don't think I would wish to call them gods, because however advanced they are—however ingenious, however intelligent, however their technology would strike us with awe—they would still be evolved beings. They would be beings that had evolved by a process of slow, gradual, incremental evolution.[11]

In the same lecture Dawkins made it clear that only naturalistic science (and thus never God Himself) can provide reasons. He said, "There may be good reasons for believing in a god, and if there are, I would expect them to come from, possibly, modern physics, from cosmology, from the observations that—as some people claim—the laws and constants of the universe are too finely tuned to be an accident."[12]

Thus, when faced with even pure scientific ignorance on a matter—such as the origins and development of the universe—Dawkins will not remain silent with an "I don't know," but he exercises his *faith* in naturalism. Knowing that physicists have no answer for such a question, he urges, "We should not give up hope of a better crane arising in physics, something as powerful as Darwinism in biology."[13] Of course, for those who think Darwinism provides a *weak* justification for biological origins, then perhaps physics will do good to go a different route. This aside, note Dawkins' persistence in maintaining—without evidence—that the explanations for the physics of the cosmos must be a "crane"—that is, must be natural.

Other naturalists characteristically (almost stereotypically) commit the same error. They assume their position as true by definition rather than proving it. For example, the *Humanist Manifesto II*, published by the American Humanist Association, declares that traditional religion does "a disservice to the human species," because, "Any account of nature should pass the test of scientific evidence."[14] Alright, then, what about "scientific evidence" itself? By what criteria do we account for that? If by scientific evidence, then the circularity of naturalism grows apparent. Of course, the whole standard is arbitrarily imposed anyway. This *Manifesto* continues, "Nature may indeed be broader and deeper than we now know; any new discoveries, however, will but enlarge our knowledge of the natural."[15] At least the document admits its bias up front, and does not attempt to hide it: "As nontheists, we begin with humans not God, nature not deity." They begin by assuming that nothing but nature exists. The conclusion follows logically that *any* new discovery will only reveal more about nature. The assumption itself, however, has absolutely no logical warrant or authority, and therefore presents a fundamental fallacy for those who adopt it.

Like the *Humanist Manifesto II*, atheist Richard Carrier argues "if anything exists in our universe, it is a part of nature, and has a natural cause or origin, and there is no need of any other explanation."[16] It wouldn't bother me nearly as much if he acknowledged the limitations of "nature"; even if he defined "universe" up front as natural and then admitted there may exist something beyond, I would have no problem. But he lets naturalism rule his worldview completely and therefore says that if *anything* exists it has a natural explanation and does not require *any* other explanation. This is a pure assumption.

Carrier quickly denies this charge that his worldview rests on a prior assumption: "This belief is not asserted or assumed as a first principle, but is arrived at from a careful and open-minded investigation of all evidence and reason...."[17] Of course, since his *standards* (evidence and reason) for arriving at this belief themselves lie *within* the worldview of naturalism, and are therefore subject to the limitations of that system, then the conclusion he arrives at should hardly surprise anyone. Again, the fishbowl limits the fish's knowledge as well as the range of assumptions it can make about all other knowledge. The difference comes in the fact that the naturalist self-imposes his own intellectual limitations. Thus, Carrier depends upon his naturalistic standards which he has derived *from* his assumption about naturalism, in order *to define and support* his naturalistic worldview. Reasoning does not get any more circular than this.

Like Dawkins and Dennett, when faced even with what he does *not* know, Carrier imposes his faith in naturalism:

> Likewise, there are certainly other physical "laws" besides those we know—which may even permit things beyond our imagining, things we would otherwise call miraculous, just as a tribal shaman would call a jumbo jet's flight—but these would be no different than the laws we already know: brute properties of the universe that describe how its dimensions and materials manifest and behave. And the cause and origin of all these things we believe to be natural in turn: a simple, non-sentient fact.[18]

Echoing the basic commitment of naturalism, Carrier believes that whatever overarching basis for the universe we may find, that basis will without question be natural and therefore "non-sentient"—that is, not an intelligent Creator or Mind. Like the other examples above, Carrier arrives at this point *because he started at this point*. The assumption of naturalism leads to the standards of naturalism which drives to the "conclusion" of naturalism.

Yet, given the limitations of his position—just as we have seen with Dennett above—he cannot escape the inherent arbitrariness of holding to a "nature only" worldview. These atheists have no justification for rejecting the Creator God by definition, they just do so. They have no authority for such a decision; they rely solely on their own experience and standard. The ultimate authority for such a standard lies in the individual, not any transcendent or objective fact.

This understanding of naturalism therefore exposes the fact that despite the naturalist's claims to objectivity, his worldview (and his behavior) reveals him as logically a subjectivist. Just as his worldview rests on an unproven assumption about the universe as only natural, so do his claims that the universe presents a predictable and uniform order rest on an unprovable assumption. Both are assumptions that *he himself* makes independently and autonomously and thus can represent only his opinion about the universe. Since he cannot prove his worldview without first assuming it, then he cannot communicate it definitively to other people and it cannot stand as authoritative independently of him. This does not mean he cannot persuade others to believe it, for indeed he does; but persuading is not logically proving (as this book will expose over and over), and to the extent that other people join the naturalist in his naturalism they will only be making the same assumptions (and thus the same leaps of logic and faith) that he does. Thus the naturalist will only succeed in creating an army of subjectivists with his skepticism.

So we have seen that naturalism relies on unproven assumptions about nature (not even just nature itself) in order to uphold its worldview. These assumptions render nearly any criticism or contradiction of the position futile since the naturalist will reinterpret even the most outstanding evidence against his view as somehow fitting within his view. The only way to confront the naturalist, then, is to attack the faultiness of the assumption he has made up front—expose the fallacies of the assumption itself. Finally, we recognize that his arbitrary assumptions and his inconsistent treatment of evidence both point to the subjectivism inherent in his worldview: his worldview originates and terminates with his own mind and carries no further authenticity or authority. From here we move from this fallacious authority to see its fallacious effects on all of life.

Subjectivism and Relativism

Once the secularist has presupposed the worldview of naturalism, he has automatically adopted a subjective position. He has unwittingly destroyed the possibility of objective knowledge and communication by creating his worldview on an autonomous assumption. This sounds like an exaggeration. If, however, no overarching authority exists to definitively communicate truth to separate individuals, then each individual stands autonomously in his own experience.

This self-referential standing has as its basis nothing less than the individual, and can use as its tools of proof nothing more than that individual self can produce. Thus, when the naturalist speaks of "reason" and "evidence," we must understand how his worldview logically limits these terms. While he practically operates as if his reasons and the evidence he experiences stand objectively for anyone to experience in the same way, we have already seen that he cannot prove this. He *assumes* an objective natural world, but since this assumption originates from the authority of his own mind (his decision), then his touted objectivity actually rests upon his personal assumption, and thus upon subjectivity. By "reason" and "evidence," then, we can only understand him to mean *his own personal* reason and claims of evidence, and his own personal experiences cannot stand as authoritative for anyone but him (in fact, not even for him). Only if some overarching authority actually upholds the objectivity of the universe could we have any certainty that reason and evidence apply to people in general. In short, those who stand with autonomy also fall with autonomy.

This remains true no matter what theory of knowledge (including learning and communicating) the naturalist chooses to adopt or emphasize at any given moment.[19] If he accepts reason alone as his standard (rationalism), then he still has no guarantee that his thoughts actually correspond to anything outside of him. This causes some problems. First, it denies the autonomous thinker any assurance that his thoughts and reasons—however exact they may be in his mental world of logic and mathematics—actually provide knowledge of the real world of tangible objects. After all, if only abstract truths of reason provide certainty, then how can we trust anything outside of that? As Dr. Frame puts it, "Rationalism seeks the most abstract knowledge possible, but in doing that it finds it can make no specific claims about the world."[20] Honestly, therefore, the rationalist cannot assure himself that anything but his immaterial thoughts actually provide knowledge. Thus, while his theory of rationalism sounds certain and strong, in practice it actually traps him in irrationalism, because he cannot truly know anything besides a small fraction of his own thoughts, if those.

If he cannot assure himself, then he certainly cannot assure anyone else, and therefore the autonomous thinker cannot communicate truth even if he had it. Anything he says can only arrive to another person as sense perceptions (audible voice, observed text, etc.), not deductive reasons. The listener may construct his or her own mental reasons from the perceptions he receives, but then those reasons will not be foundational for that person; these constructed reasons will themselves be derived from something other than pure reason. Each individual can at best manufacture their own pure reasons independent of other people or external stimulation. No one can definitively prove their reasons to another, because communication requires elements of knowledge beyond pure reasoning. It results from this, however, that we can never have a guarantee that the thoughts of any two people actually correspond in any two points. In short, rationalism destroys communication.

Thus in attempting to guarantee knowledge, reason alone fails to assure the thinker of the simplest facts about the world about him. This standard logically traps the reasoner within the solitary confinement of his own mind: he cannot claim to know anything beyond his purest logical and mathematical thoughts, he cannot know any single fact about the world around him or another person, and he cannot communicate the tiny bit that he does know.

Yet, the classical alternative to "reason alone" knowledge fails just as badly. The standard of "evidence" falls under what philosophers have called "empiricism," or knowledge gained solely through the human senses. This is the "seeing is believing" school of knowledge. Such a standard gains wide acceptance today due to the much popularized results of "science." Only that which can humans can detect, observe, measure, and manipulate do empiricists consider knowable, and thus attribute as the foundations of knowledge.

But this standard encounters problems as well. Most importantly, philosophers have long exposed the inconsistency of empiricism because it simply fails its own test. The claim, "Only that is true which can be verified empirically," cannot itself be verified empirically. We have no evidence that proves that only evidence provides truth, or even that it provides any truth. Therefore, to maintain the basic commitment of empiricism requires the autonomous thinker to make a totally unsupported and unsupportable assumption. Thus the adoption of this standard requires the subjective choice of the thinker in which the ultimate authority is the individual.

In addition, "evidence only" thinking ignores many other things: that our senses often deceive us, that science involves a great deal of untestable theory and theory-laden instrumentation in its application, that science includes interpretation, evaluation, and other fallible human input (even downright lying in some cases), that human experience is affected and limited by cultural, personal, and societal expectations and other factors, and that therefore scientists often miss facts that contradict their theories. Likewise, "evidence" can never prove a universal claim (such as "All men are mortal"), justify a universal law (such as "$E=mc^2$"), or provide any knowledge about the future—all because sense experience limits knowledge to the here and now, and cannot pontificate about anything beyond that.[21]

Finally, like "reason alone," "evidence only" also destroys communication. If knowledge is limited to what the senses tell the mind, then no one can ever be sure that what exists in someone else's mind even approximates what occurs in their own. In reality, sensory knowledge amounts to little more than what our minds tell us we have processed. A million deceptions could have crept in between any real world out there, or any other person, and what the brain tells the individual. The only certainty comes in the fact *that* the individual experiences *something*. Once again, this theory of knowledge traps its sensor within his own mind, and denies any certainty or specificity to the alleged facts of his knowledge.

If the autonomous thinker grows clever and attempts—as many have—to combine these two classical theories of knowledge, he must still essentially work with two leaky buckets. No matter how you try to carry the two together—which one you place inside the other—the combination will still not hold water. No arrangement of the two will, and no theory based on the two will. As the former atheist Antony Flew admitted, when arguing the failure of piling up multiple "evidences" as a cumulative proof for God's existence, "If one leaky bucket will not hold water that is no reason to think that ten can."[22] What Flew unwittingly illustrated, however, was not only the failure of "evidence only" thinking to prove the existence of God, but the failure of *any* human-centered theory of knowledge to prove *anything*. Without the existence of a Creator of an objective world, a self-authenticating revealing God, and an ultimate Judge of truth and falsity, we have no guarantee that human reason and experience actually correspond to reality or that the experiences of individual human beings actually occur within an intelligible, social, and mutually accountable environment. Otherwise, the human mind can only arbitrarily assume that objectivity and knowledge exist, thus contradicting the very ideas of objectivity and knowledge.

Thus we see that the first fallout of naturalism is subjectivity, which ultimately manifests itself in society as "relativism." The teaching of relativism says that what is true for one person may not be true for another, and truth in one day and age changes as time progresses. This denial of absolute truths (like, for example, You shall not bear false witness against your neighbor) logically leads to the denial of absolute laws and meaning. The second fallout results: nihilism.

Nihilism and Meaninglessness

If man cannot know anything for certain, it takes only the setting of the sun of personal illusions to darken all hope. Cynicism, apathy and selfishness emerge as the virtues of a generation. If we can know nothing for certain, and all truth grows relative to the individual in any given time and situation, then, "Let us eat, drink, and be merry, for tomorrow we die." Let us get a few kicks before we go.

Why does this make so much sense? Because if we can know nothing with certainty, then even if any moral laws exist, we cannot know them with certainty either. Even if a god exists, if we cannot definitively know him or be certain of his revelation (so the autonomous reasoner must reason) then he becomes meaningless. In fact, if we can know nothing for certain, then everything becomes ultimately meaningless to us. Some philosophers have gone so far as to state that relativism means not only that nothing has meaning, but that nothing *exists*, but this extreme position does little more damage than its sister-philosophy nihilism—the belief that no values, truth, or morals actually exist, but mankind has manufactured all of them. As products of man, they have no genuine authority and carry no obligation for anyone. Therefore, every individual stands free to create his own rules. Every man does that which is right in his own eyes.

The more people give in to this philosophy of personal godhood, the more civilization will devolve into self-aggrandizement, self-promotion, self-gratification. Once they have denied the Personal Creator God, they must logically believe that knowledge and communication are impossible, and therefore all law and responsibility disappear as well. The universe becomes a giant pit of subatomic particles blindly mauling one another for preeminence, the alleged apex of which chaotic brawl we term "consciousness." Then consciousness creates metaphors to understand its journey from nothingness: the universe is a series of small cranes erecting larger cranes which eventually create complex superstructures like sponges and jellyfish, human beings, giraffes, horned frogs, howler monkeys, and vampire fish. Yet despite whatever poetry we create to describe them, these have all arisen from the same chaos: meaninglessness acting upon nothingness producing a cosmic jungle.

What began as a sea of colliding atoms emerges as a struggle for survival between trillions of living things, including (incidentally) about six billion human beings. Logically—aside from all purported atheistic theories of society—life after the philosophy of meaninglessness and nihilism can only become some type of interpersonal struggle.

Evolution and Jihad

Little scholarship has addressed the prevalence of the idea of "struggle" throughout non-Christian worldviews, yet the phenomenon exists. Heraclitus was one of the earliest of philosophers to speak of the idea of struggle as a creative force in metaphysics, and subsequently in history and ethics. He maintained a wide application of this idea, claiming, "War is the father of all things." Darwin was a latecomer who only provided an explanation of struggle palatable to "natural philosophers"— that is, Darwin put the abstract notion of struggle into the scientifically acceptable formula of "natural selection." Nevertheless, natural selection only describes the results of the struggle for existence among the flora and fauna. In the absence of any viable theory of truth, law or accountability, "struggle" (the central mechanism of evolution) must characterize not only the natural development of biology, but *every area of life*.

Interestingly, other non-believing worldviews arrive at a similar view. The atheistic philosophy of Marxism (communism or socialism) focuses on "class-warfare" and "revolution" as the engines of social change. In other words, the non-rich stand in perpetual envy and antagonism to the rich (thus as the incarnation and legitimization of envy). If the non-rich dislike their working conditions, pay, etc., they may rise in violent overthrow of person and property until they achieve what they want. This of course, does not solve the problem ultimately, but only shifts the categories of who is rich and not. Another revolution awaits in the near decades, guaranteed.

Likewise, at the heart of Islam rests the doctrine of *Jihad*. While most people today understand this to mean "holy war," the word more generally means "struggle." It certainly applies to the perpetual holy war between Muslims and "infidels," but it also describes all of life for the Muslim: the individual personal "struggle in the way of Allah," as well as the collective advance of Islam throughout the world. Nevertheless, *jihad* is a "Divine institution of warfare to extend Islam into the Dar alharb (the non-Islamic territories which are described as the 'abode of struggle,' or of disbelief) or to defend Islam from danger."[23] However you define it, "struggle" characterizes every facet of the Islamic worldview.

We could add more, but the point should stand clear: apart from a Christian philosophy of Creation, Providence, law, and personal conversion, renewal, and reformation, human thinking must logically legitimize some form of conflict. More sophisticated autonomous thought will create more complex ideas such as biological evolution through natural selection, or even Marxist economics, but the base idea will remain the same: success depends on the ability to prevail in struggle. In other words, everyman does that which is right in his own eyes, forcefully.

Superman and Other Futurist Fictions

Despite the preceding consequences of the fallacy of naturalism (actually, of all autonomous thinking), those who hold the view still believe in future progress. Despite the chaos, relativism, meaninglessness, lawlessness, and inevitable conflict inherent in their view, they still believe that evolution (as opposed to devolution) occurs and will eventually self-erect a glorious future on top of the rubble of demolished decades. Whatever scenarios arise, the central hope of the autonomous thinker usually appears as the anticipated advent of a highly-evolved man.

The quest for the perfection of man obsesses the pagan mind of almost all worldviews. Mystery religions and Gnosticism, for example, revolve around the idea of gaining secret knowledge and enlightenment, but in each case these are merely means to an end—the end of becoming divine. Their ultimate goal is to compile the knowledge necessary to transcend the material universe into some form or status of divinity. This quest is inherent in the heart of fallen man: *How you have fallen from heaven, O star of the morning, son of the dawn! You have been cut down to the earth, You who have weakened the nations! But you said in your heart, "I will ascend to heaven; I will raise my throne above the stars of God ... I will ascend above the heights of the clouds; I will make myself like the Most High"* (Is. 14:12–14). This belief has manifested in various forms throughout history, and naturalists have no special immunity.

The German philosopher of "nihilism," Friedrich Nietzsche, has famously expounded his philosophy of the "superman." He believed that if man only followed his natural lust for power and denied the oppressive forces of Christian morality, an ensuing social struggle would lead to the triumph of a higher man. The highest aspiration of man, for Nietzsche, is to evolve such a superman—man at his pinnacle, transcending all of his own personal follies and those of all previous races.

Modern thinkers, especially those pursuing the dream of artificial intelligence (including many philosophical "neuroscientists"), have a very similar goal in hoping to fuse the productive capacities of computer chips with the human brain, or to create a computer that subsumes all that human brains can do and much more, thereby creating something of a super-human thinking machine. These thinkers have waged a fierce debate over the belief that they can successfully duplicate the human brain using computers. In short, is the human brain nothing but a powerful computer? (The fallacious assumption of "yes" I deal with later under the fallacy of False Analogy.) They believe so, and fully intend to create artificial intelligence that *surpasses* the human being.

Yet, logically the quest of humanistic thought (in all of its forms) to find the perfect man must always end in despair. The very fact that such "higher man" philosophies and religions exist shows that the humanists themselves know that man in his current condition needs a change. The American journalist H. L. Mencken, himself a fan of Nietzsche, had no illusion in this regard:

> Man, at his best, remains a sort of one-lunged animal, never completely rounded and perfect, as a cockroach, say, is perfect. If he shows one valuable quality, it is al-

most unheard of for him to show any other. Give him a head, and he lacks a heart. Give him a heart of a gallon capacity, and his head holds scarcely a pint. The artist, nine times out of ten, is a dead-beat and given to the debauching of virgins, so-called. The patriot is a bigot, and, more often than not, a bounder and a poltroon. The man of physical bravery is often on a level, intellectually, with a Baptist clergyman. The intellectual giant has bad kidneys and cannot thread a needle. In all my years of search in this world, from the Golden Gate in the West to the Vistula in the East, and from the Orkney Islands in the North to the Spanish Main in the South, I have never met a thoroughly moral man who was honorable.[24]

Little has changed since Mencken wrote this in 1923—save, perhaps, a little more education on the part of Baptist clergymen—because human nature has not changed. We encounter no new material (physical or intellectual) despite Nietzsche's prediction of a higher man. We have faced plenty of war and bloodshed since cultures began more widely to adopt his ideals, but we have experienced no progress in the nature of man.

Nietzsche's attempt at creating a "higher man" provided following generations with plenty of intellectual ammunition with which to assault Christian liberty. Worse yet, under the plan of elevating man to a status where he could truly enjoy life, Nietzsche set in motion the wheels of the war machines of human avarice. He, in a sense, saw this coming. He knew that the overthrow of traditional values, which he saw as lies (funny that someone denies absolutes in morality would worry about lies), would mean the end of human peace. (Again, humanism requires war and struggle to advance.) He writes,

> For when truth enters into a fight with the lies of millennia, we shall have upheavals, a convulsion of earthquakes, a moving of mountains and valleys, the like of which has never been dreamed of. The concept of politics will have merged entirely with a war of spirits; all power structures of the old society will have been exploded—all of them are based on lies: there will be wars the like of which have never yet been seen on earth.[25]

This publication first appeared in 1908; the astute observer will note that history has proven Nietzsche correct in this regard. While some have seen this comment as only metaphorical, Nietzsche elsewhere makes it clear that he means literal war as well:

> We owe it to Napoleon... that we now confront a succession of a few warlike centuries that have no parallel in history; in short, that we have entered *the classical age of war*, of scientific and at the same time popular war on the largest scale.[26]

> I am *glad* about the military development of Europe; also of the internal states of anarchy.... The barbarian in each of us is affirmed; also the wild beast.... [This is an] age of tremendous wars, upheavals, explosions.... where masses of barbarians are crossed with a lack of all restraint for whatever has been.... I am not afraid of predicting a few things and thus, possibly, of conjuring up the cause of wars.[27]

The wars—both literal and intellectual—have indeed been disastrous on many fronts. This inevitably results when man—collective man, governmental man, tyrannous man, machine-gun, tank, helicopter, nuclear missile-armed man, guerilla and terror-wielding man—rejects a higher, divine law, and sets his own law and agenda.[28]

Can we expect anything more than a bleak future under such circumstances, should we consistently follow such a philosophy? And yet, these emerge as the logical conclusions of human thought when suppressing the knowledge of his Creator. When man attempts to determine reality for himself he must ultimately rest on some arbitrary assumption. Whether he settles on naturalism as I have described it does not necessarily matter, for all worldviews that have their origin in autonomous human thinking must stumble at the same logical hurdles, and suffer the same logical deaths. Man-dependent thinking immediately traps the thinker in his subjective experience and destroys knowledge and communication. Relativism in truth results, and leads to nihilism in values, morals, and meaning. In a valueless and meaningless world, the only method of social change and progress becomes struggle. This can take one of many forms—from personal struggle, to class warfare, to holy warfare, to total warfare. Despite such a crude method, humanists entertain beliefs about progress and evolution, always endeavoring to improve mankind. Yet the carnal nature of the worldview fallacy and its attendant doctrine of struggle always exposes the ethical failures of the worldview: it cannot improve man, it can only set him against himself or other men in violent conflict.

And all of this from simply adopting one false assumption about reality. You can see that little logical fallacies, especially Worldview Fallacies, have big consequences. In fact, Worldview Fallacies by their very nature spread into every area of life because they infect the most fundamental beliefs about God, man, law, society and history. A little leaven leavens the whole lump (1 Cor. 5:6; Gal. 5:9). A single false witness, carefully constructed, and then taught and accepted can send an entire generation into an intellectual *jihad* against its Creator.

NOTES

1. Aurelius Augustine, "The Confessions of St. Augustine," 1.1, *The Nicene and Post Nicene Fathers, First Series*, 14 vol., ed. Philip Schaff, trans. J. G. Pilkington (Grand Rapids: Eerdmans, 1983), 1:45.

2. For example, see the works of Robert Morey, Walter Martin, Hank Hanegraaff, Ravi Zacharias, James White, and many others.

3. Daniel C. Dennett, *Darwin's Dangerous Idea: Evolution and the Meanings of Life* (New York: Simon and Schuster, 1995), 74.

4. Daniel C. Dennett, *Darwin's Dangerous Idea*, 74.

5. Daniel C. Dennett, *Darwin's Dangerous Idea*, 75.

6. Daniel C. Dennett, *Darwin's Dangerous Idea*, 75.

7. Daniel C. Dennett, *Darwin's Dangerous Idea*, 76.

8. Richard Dawkins, *The God Delusion* (Boston and New York: Houghton Mifflin Co., 2006), 155.

9. Richard Dawkins, *The God Delusion* (Boston and New York: Houghton Mifflin Co., 2006), 156.

10. Richard Dawkins, *The God Delusion*, 73.

11. Richard Dawkins, Q&A following a book reading at Randolph Macon Woman's University, Lynchburg, VA, October 23, 2006.

12. Richard Dawkins, Q&A following a book reading at Randolph Macon Woman's University, Lynchburg, VA, October 23, 2006.

13. Richard Dawkins, *The God Delusion*, 158.

14. See http://www.americanhumanist.org/who_we_are/about_humanism/Humanist_Manifesto_II (accessed March 24, 2009).

15. See http://www.americanhumanist.org/who_we_are/about_humanism/Humanist_Manifesto_II (accessed March 24, 2009).

16. Richard Carrier, *Sense and Goodness Without God: A Defense of Metaphysical Naturalism* (Bloomington, IN: AuthorHouse, 2005), 67.

17. Richard Carrier, *Sense and Goodness Without God*, 67–68.

18. Richard Carrier, *Sense and Goodness Without God*, 68.

19. The following points I have distilled in general from Cornelius Van Til, Greg Bahnsen and others, but specifically from John Frame's helpful analysis in *The Doctrine of the Knowledge of God* (Phillipsburg, NJ: Presbyterian and Reformed, 1987), 111–122.

20. Frame, *The Doctrine of the Knowledge of God*, 114.

21. Frame, *The Doctrine of the Knowledge of God*, 116–118.

22. Antony Flew, *God and Philosophy* (New York: Harcourt, Brace and World, Inc., 1966), 63.

23. Quoted in David A. Noebel, *Understanding the Times*, 2nd Ed. (Manitou Springs, CO: Summit Press, 2006), 397.

24. "The Good Man," in *A Mencken Chrestomathy*. ed. H. L. Mencken (New York: Vintage Books, 1982 (1949)), 19.

25. Friedrich Nietzsche, *Ecce Homo*, "Why I am a Destiny," 1, tr. Walter Kaufmann. In *On the Genealogy of Morals and Ecce Homo*, ed. Walter Kauffman (New York: Vintage Books, 1989), 327.

26. Friedrich Nietzsche, *The Gay Science: With a Prelude in Rhymes and an Appendix of Songs*, Section 362, trans. Walter Kaufman (New York: Vintage Books, 1974 [1887]), 318.

27. Friedrich Nietzsche, *The Will to Power*, Sec. 127, 130, trans. Walter Kaufman and R. J. Hollingdale (New York: Vintage Books, 1968 [1883–1888]), 78–80.

28. For more on Nietzsche and his idea of a superman in contrast to the true perfect man, Christ, see Joel McDurmon, *Manifested in the Flesh: How the Historical Evidence for Jesus Refutes Modern Mystics and Skeptics* (Powder Springs, GA: American Vision, 2007), 116–120, 128–131.

Fallacies of Representation

CHAPTER 7

"Too Simple": Fallacies of Oversimplification

Many people misrepresent the truth—either the facts themselves or the arguments of other people—by oversimplifying matters. We covet simplicity for its elegance and power, yet it often operates beyond what the facts warrant. The false witness inherent in these fallacies relies on presenting the truth as *less than* it really is—leaving out or diminishing vital aspects. Sometimes, the story as presented is just *too* simple.

Simplicity improves communication and thus persuasion, both of which we desire in news and education. But for the same reasons, simplicity can intensify the influence of false witness. Christians must discern and avoid all forms of oversimplification, including but not limited to the following forms:

False Dilemma

Oversimplification often appears in the form of a False Dilemma. This fallacy occurs when someone attempts to force a choice between two options even though other options may exist. This oversimplifies the truth by pretending that the two options presented are the only options available.

When I was in college I was obliged to take a personality test for one of my classes. I objected that the multiple choices available on many of the questions were not clear or exhaustive enough for me to answer honestly. The teacher asserted that this was a purposeful feature of the test: to force a choice in order to determine allegedly important distinctions. She then tried to illustrate her point of a "forced choice" by holding out a pencil within my close reach, equally between my right hand and left. "Here," she said. I looked at her. She added, "I am forcing you to choose either your left hand or your right."

I smiled at the otherwise smart and gifted instructor, and explained her error. "Those are not the only options. I can choose not to take the pencil from you at all. I can get up and leave, I can sit and stare at you. I can do a hundred things besides take it with either my right or left hand." The problem with such personality tests are often the same: they present simplistic choices of behavior for scenarios in which many other behaviors are possible.

This problem will result in most cases that artificially limit choices, especially those cases that only allow two options. When choices are minimized to two then the potential for fallacy is at its highest. Thus the name "dilemma" which means "two propositions." A false dilemma is a false claim that only two choices exist. The fallacy is also known as *false dichotomy* (meaning "false cutting" or "false division"), as the *either/or* fallacy, or as *bifurcation* (meaning "two prongs" or "two forks").

A man who comes to a fork in the road may seem to face only two options: go left or right. Truthfully, however, he has several other options. He could turn around and go back. He could split the difference and walk down the grassy knoll in the middle. He could leave the paths altogether, and go pick wild berries in the bushes or wildflowers in the fields. He could take a helicopter up and over the area completely. He could sit and meditate for a while on the significance of forked roads and grassy knolls. He could bulldoze the roads and build a house. Rarely does any apparent dilemma turn out to be a genuine dilemma. There are almost always many other options.

This does not mean that all either/or statements are fallacious, nor does it mean that true dilemmas do not exist. A true dilemma actually makes a powerful tool for thinking and debate. If you genuinely can reduce a matter to two contrasting options it can help to clarify or to force a decision or an admission. Nevertheless, you must take care that any either/or decision which you propose actually excludes all other options. Either do your homework well, or run the risk of fallacy.

In the Bible, Jesus faced a False Dilemma when asked about a man's blindness.[1] The disciples fallaciously inquired, *Rabbi, who sinned, this man or his parents, that he should be born blind?* (John 9:2). Jesus disarmed the fallacy easily, pointing out the truth as a third alternative: *It was neither that this man sinned, nor his parents; but it was in order that the works of God might be displayed in him* (9:3). Defeating a False Dilemma can be this easy.

False dilemmas occur very frequently in the public forum, especially in politics where debaters hope to move agendas by applying pressure. Claims such as, "Those who don't support government welfare programs obviously don't care about the poor," are essentially saying "Either you support government welfare or you don't care about the poor," and can be exposed very simply by understanding false dilemmas. A third option is that those opposed to government welfare programs care as much or even more about poverty than their detractors, but they know that private charities minister to the poor more effectively than government programs. Those who continue to employ the false dilemma ignore or suppress this third option, and thus continue to paint their opposition as uncaring and unconcerned about the poor. This is not only fallacious, it is dishonest and slanderous; but its proponents find it convenient for furthering their agenda.

With Us Or Against Us!

Issues of patriotism and war also provide fertile ground for false dichotomies. After the 9/11 attacks, politicians on both sides jumped in. Bush famously said, "Every nation in every region now has a decision to make: either you are with us or you are with the terrorists."[2] In general Bush spoke correctly, but to the extent he applied this fact to physical support of the "War on Terror," he crossed a logical line: countries could well have remained neutral internationally while securing their own borders at home without joining "with the terrorists." Not only Bush, but even former president Bill Clinton proclaimed, "Getting Osama bin Laden is the beginning, not the end, of this process."[3] Really? Could the military not have best planned to apprehend bin Laden through some *process*, or after other necessary steps? Aside from the frank inaccuracy of Clinton's claim (here we sit eight years later with no bin Laden!), his forced choice between "beginning" and "end" creates a False Dichotomy. This poor logic from both Bush and Clinton represents the irresponsibility laden in much of political rhetoric: it aims to frighten people toward a desired course of action while robbing them of time to think through the issue. You may say this rhetoric has "been laden" with "logical terrorism."

"Either you are with us, or you are against us," is a commonly employed pressure tactic based on this fallacy. The phrase is taken from the words of Jesus who surely uses it appropriately: belonging to the Kingdom of God is truly an either/or matter (Matt. 12:30; Luke 11:23). Anyone, however, who tries to apply Christ's words to certain aspects of the civil realm, which realm is itself subject to and judged by the Kingdom of God, had better have clarity of vision and divine wisdom comparable to Christ's own, else they run the risk of misapplying Christ's words to an ungodly cause.

There are those who claim that all who object, for example, to the invasion of Iraq are part of the "blame America first crowd." Essentially they argue, "Either you support the war or you blame America." Put this way, it should be easy for anyone to think of many plausible third options which make it possible, if not compelling, both to oppose the war *and* to support the interests of America. The two ideas hardly exclude each other. Some may even point out that a true patriot should oppose some wars on the very principle of patriotism.

Poor Character and Poor Logic

Examples of False Dilemma appear all over the news media. This form of oversimplification gives journalists and ideologues the chance to polarize an issue and force a choice in favor of their pet position. One headline reads, "Bush's Dilemma: Terrorism or Oil?"[4] which assumes that the two things must mutually exclude each other. Certainly the author could have thought of a better solution. On a more local note, one story reported on a mother, Christina Silvas, who worked as a stripper while sending her daughter to a Christian school. When the school expelled the daughter because Christina broke school rules, she complained, "I want to find a school less concerned with image and more concerned with the welfare of children."[5] Perhaps Christina did not realize that her child's welfare may depend quite a lot on mommy's image, given all that the image of sexual promiscuity can bring with it. For this and other reasons, the complaint creates a False Dilemma.

Rich or Poor? Wallis' False Dilemma

A clear example of a False Dilemma comes from the liberal activist Jim Wallis. He writes,

> **We believe that poverty—caring for the poor and vulnerable—is a religious issue.** Do the candidates' budget and tax policies reward the rich or show compassion for poor families? Do their foreign policies include fair trade and debt cancellation for the poorest countries?[6]

Wallis often uses Biblical language to promote the agenda of political liberals. His book *God's Politics* provides many examples of this type of thinking. The false dilemma in this passage should be obvious to the reader. He presents two scenarios by which to judge whether the political candidates are "caring for the poor" or not: do their budgets and tax policies "reward the rich, *or* show compassion." Wallis therefore implies that tax cuts for wealthier families somehow violate the Christian ideas of "caring" and "compassion." But is this the only way of looking at it? The proper response to Wallis will note the fact that it is possible *both* to "reward" the rich *and* have compassion for the poor. A more helpful way to say this is that the Bible requires us to favor *neither* the rich nor the poor (Lev. 19:15), and to prosecute thieves even if they steal because of their poverty (Prov. 6:30–31).

Biblical fairness means having one law that applies to all people equally, favoring neither the rich nor the poor, and therefore it is improper to set the two against each other in the way that Wallis does. Wallis, for example, might object to a certain tax break for middle and upper-middle class families if the legislation does not also call for similar tax breaks for the lower income brackets (and he has done so), and he will object upon the principle quoted above. But if he does not relate that such tax breaks on "the wealthy" merely reverse the increases levied by previous administrations, and which prior increases were not shared by those in lower brackets, then Wallis stands guilty of suppressing vital information and not putting the argument into its proper historical context. Tax policies that "reward the rich" in Wallis' eyes may actually be a case of Biblical justice in returning the levels of taxation more closely to equal percentages for the rich and the poor (although, the wealthier classes still pay much higher percentages than the lower income classes, and the wealthy still pay by far the largest amount of the tax burden over all).[7]

Thus is it possible to create a false dilemma in principle (by stating a "this or that" scenario in which the two possibilities do not exhaust the possibilities in real life), or by leaving out some of the important facts of the case (sometimes called the fallacy of suppressed evidence).

A Libertarian Slip

Another instance comes from a libertarian writer commenting on a recent FBI scandal. He writes,

> The release of the FBI's "evidence" against Bruce Ivins, the now-deceased Ft. Detrick scientist targeted by the FBI as the alleged culprit in the 2001 anthrax letters case, demonstrates (1) the FBI is covering for the real culprits, or (2) what we are witnessing is a dramatic drop in the intelligence of the average FBI official—maybe it's something in the water.[8]

The columnist who wrote the claim, Justin Raimondo, has presented us with two possible explanations for the alleged weakness of the FBI's evidence in this case. Mr. Raimondo may be right-on with his criticism that the evidence is poor, but his two proposed options for why create a false dilemma. He claims that either the FBI is conspiring to protect the real criminals (true corruption indeed!), or the FBI is totally incompetent. Are these really the only two explanations? Of course not. It could well be, for example, that the FBI is being pressured to solve the case, and they have therefore rushed ahead with what weak evidence they have. This option reflects just as negatively on the Bureau, but it is in fact another option. It may be that the FBI has leads on additional evidence which it has not or cannot yet mention.

Mr. Raimondo has written many smart and probing articles in defense of individual liberty (with which I often agree), and normally writes with a strong bias against intrusive governmental authority (not necessarily a bad thing) and a persistent hatred of war. Despite having put forth many good arguments on many issues, those who hold views so strongly often run the risk of logical fallacy. Mr. Raimondo may turn out to be correct about corruption or incompetence in the FBI, but at this point his proposed either/or scenario does not exhaust the possibilities, and thus commits an informal fallacy.

A Sly Atheist's Dilemma

A final example comes from the atheist Sam Harris, who claims,

> If our worldview were put to a vote, notions of 'intelligent design' would defeat the science of biology by nearly three to one.[9]

I have included this example in order to show you how sneakily a false dichotomy can appear. Sam does not here propose a choice, nor does he use the word "or" which would possibly signal a false choice. Rather he simply assumes a false division by *definition*—in the way he chooses and uses particular words as opposites. Contrasting the ideas of "intelligent design" versus "science of biology" as polar opposites, as irreconcilable enemies, as at war with each other, enables Sam to maintain a false dichotomy between the two. In reality, intelligent design operates as scientifically anything else the "science of biology" can come up with. Sam has merely imposed his atheistic worldview on the situation, calling it "science of biology," and he has deceitfully pretended that "intelligent design" lies outside of this science. Well, it *lies* outside of Sam's atheistic worldview, but to assume up front that it lies outside of "science" simply Begs the Question and here creates a very carefully hidden False Dilemma.

The extreme tenets of the atheistic worldview (or any extreme worldview) can easily lead their proponents to formulate false dilemmas. People with a radical agenda to push often fall into a sharp "us versus them" mentality, and then try to persuade "them" by presenting the agenda as a sharp contrast with "their" beliefs. The overzealous often overstep the bounds of truth and logic and create a fallacious claim. Sam does this in other places in his book. For example, he writes,

> The choice before us is simple: we can either have a twenty-first-century conversation about morality and human well-being—a conversation in which we avail ourselves of all the scientific insights and philosophical arguments that have accumulated in the last two thousand years of

human discourse—or we can confine ourselves to a first-century conversation as it is preserved in the Bible. Why would anyone want to take the latter approach?[10]

Sam makes no attempt at all to conceal this fallacy as he did the last one: he clearly presents it as a choice, and offers two options divided by the word "or." But this example commits the fallacy no less than the last. To begin with, the choice is *not* "simple," and even if it were it would not be simple in the way Sam presents it. More importantly, *no Christian* claims that the Bible explicitly addresses every single moral situation we face today (effectively making the "discussion" of morality to be fully settled by the first century), although it does give us laws and principles which apply to every situation. So Sam's "first-century conversation" option creates a Straw Man.

Further, for Sam to suggest that those of us who do accept the Bible as the source of moral law thereby limit morality to a "first-century conversation" as opposed to a "twenty-first-century conversation" commits two errors. First, just because we accept a first-century document as the source of our moral principles does not mean that we do not avail ourselves of the full history of science, arts, and medicine in order to learn to apply those principles in the most faithful way, and considering the most modern tools and knowledge in doing so. That first-century document in fact *commands* us to do so. Secondly, even those who adhere to allegedly "modern" humanistic standards cannot escape the fact that most of their moral ideas, methods, and conclusions were already arrived at by the ancient Greek philosophers, and thus their's is no more "modern" ultimately than anyone else's "conversation."

In this case, the False Dilemma rests on a Straw Man in the second option. It also dabbles with the Fallacy of Appeal to Progress (discussed later). Sam's accusation about a "first-century conversation" is simply false as no one proposes such a ridiculous standard. Even if they did it would not stand as the only other option to choose from. And, even if it were the only other option, it would not necessarily be bad simply *because* it was conceived in the first century. This is a great example of how radicals many times compound fallacies together in order to prosecute their agenda. The knot of fallacies multiplies the confusion and makes unraveling the illogical ball of yarn all the more difficult.

GENERALIZATION

Generalizations almost always provide fertile soil for fallacies. Any claim that includes the words "all," "any," "every," or similar words (just as the sentence you are now reading) has the potential of committing a fallacy of Generalizing. In most cases groups are composed of objects that share *some* characteristics, but by no means *all* characteristics. For example, we understand that there exist many different types of dogs, but yet we know them all to be dogs. There are vast differences between a Chihuahua and a Saint Bernard, and yet when we see either one of them we immediately recognize it as belonging to the same group: "dog." This is the way classes of things work: some common features vitally link the members together, while each member of the group retains many individual characteristics. This presents possibilities for at least two common errors: 1) a *hasty generalization*, which applies the attributes of a tiny, inadequate, or unrelated sample to a whole category, and 2) a *sweeping generalization*, which applies the general attributes of a group to a single case where they do not necessarily fit.

Hasty Generalization

A *Hasty Generalization* refers to a conclusion drawn about an entire group or class based on information from a single member or too small a sample of members. In such a case the error lies in assuming that the inadequate sample represents every member of a group in one or several characteristics. This assumption ignores vital differences between the sample and the group.

For example, all violinists play violins, but certainly not all of them play violins made by the famous Italian Luthier Stradivari. While his certain instruments are highly famous for their quality and sound they are also very expensive and rare. Few violinists own them and thus, few play them. It would be a hasty generalization to assume all great violinists play a Stradivarius.

A more relevant example to Christians is found in some common objections to the Faith. We often hear things like, "I won't go to church because those Christians are all a bunch of hypocrites." When the person behind such a complaint is asked what led them to such a conclusion they may point to Christian leaders who have been exposed as sinners on TV, or to friends they know who did not live up to their own profession of faith. These experiences can truly sour anyone's taste for Christianity, but they hardly warrant the conclusion that all Christians are just a bunch of hypocrites. The person lodging this complaint is merely painting the whole group of Christians with the image of the minority of bad moral failures who belong to the same group. This is a hasty generalization, and thus is an unacceptable argument.

The complainer may even to add to his evidence: "Actually," he says, "I have dated five girls in the past year, all of whom claimed to be Christians and none of whom lived up to their claims, I have read about three scandalous affairs by pastors and Christian school principals in the last week, and most of the friends I went to college with all claimed to be "born again," and yet partied and got drunk every weekend. Plus, I read that the divorce rate among "born again" Christians is just as high as it is among non-believers."

Such evidence may seem to add weight to his claim, but considering his original claim, that Christians are "all a bunch of hypocrites," he will need a lot more evidence than that which he draws from his own small circle of experience. Despite the fact that such facts and figures (if they actually represent the truth) bring shame upon the faith, there are still literally *hundreds of millions* of faithful believers throughout the world. Not even getting into arguments about Christians struggling against personal besetting sins, the truth is that faithful and dedicated believers are out there *everywhere* for anyone who really wants to find them. Excuses that pin the image of a few known hypocrites onto the whole of the faithful are not cogent arguments, but rather expressions of personal unbelief in action.

Thus people can draw hasty generalizations based on a single bit of evidence or even on a string of evidences compiled together. A common factor that makes either case fallacious: neither considers the ways in which the minority in question *significantly differs* from the group in question. Such claims overlook, ignore, or even suppress evidence in order to maintain an untruth based on a thread of evidence.

An interesting case appears in Paul's letter to Titus, where he states of the inhabitants of the island Crete, *One of themselves, a prophet of their own, said, "Cretans are always liars, evil beasts, lazy gluttons"* (Titus 1:12). This text would provide an example of Hasty Generalization if Paul meant us to take it literally. Would it be proper, based on experience of even many Cretans, to claim that they are *always* liars, evil, and lazy? Is there not a single example of truth, goodness, and productivity among them? Of course Paul does not really mean it this way. In fact, he seems to play a bit with a well-known poetical text in which we find a classic philosophical conundrum—the "liar's paradox." The paradox arises because the poet who wrote it *himself* was a Cretan, so in saying that Cretans always lie he also claimed that he himself always lied. So then, his own statement that Cretans always lie must itself be a lie. But undoing his statement would indicate that Cretans do not always lie, and thus the claim that all Cretans lie would truly be a lie. Well, we can deduce from this that at least *one* Cretan has told at least *one* lie! Perhaps you can see the problems inherent in Hasty Generalizations: it only takes one counter-example to overturn the fallacious claim.

Sweeping Generalization

Somewhat the opposite of the hasty variety, a *Sweeping Generalization* occurs when someone applies a general rule to a specific case in which the rule or characteristic does not necessarily apply. Going back to the earlier example of dogs, someone may think based on their experience of many breeds that all dogs are furry animals. Some have short fur, others long shaggy fur, but they are all furry. Such a person would be startled when introduced to the Mexican hairless dog, or to the Peruvian hairless dog, both of which breeds have no fur. The existence of these hairless varieties exposes the original statement as a fallacious sweeping generalization.

Just as a hasty generalization ignores differences between the individual and the groups, so does a sweeping generalization. The difference between the two is that the first overextends the unique aspects of the individual onto the whole group, while the second ignores the importance of these unique aspects for each individual in the group. The student must pay very close attention to differences between individuals. It may even be true, in some cases, that the individual in question does not even belong to the group or class at all.

Very often generalizations stem from the limitations of one's own experience. Despite human finitude, the urge for students, scholars, debaters (or anyone else in general terms) to pontificate often leads them into the sin of claiming more than they know, or pronouncing judgments that do not apply. When these judgments relate to groups and classes, a fallacious generalization may be in the works.

An illustrative example comes from a recent book titled *The Black Swan*. Common experience in western Europe from ancient times forward included the sight of white Swans. So common was association of "white" with "Swan" that the ancient Roman writer Juvenal wrote of something absurd as being "a rare bird in the lands, and very like a black swan" (this may also account for the saying "he's a strange bird"). Juvenal thought he wrote of an absurdity—something that does not exist—like we would talk about fairies or unicorns today. Proverbs swept western culture: "all swans are white," to refer to any well-accepted truth, and "a black swan," to refer to that which is non-existent. The latter phrase appears in famous works by Sir Walter Raleigh (*A History of the World*, 1614) and as late as Charles Dickens (*A Christmas Carol*, 1843).

The shocks first came in 1697 with the first reported sighting of a Black Swan in Australia, and again in 1726 when two birds were captured as proof of their existence. The news came as a shock because popular sentiment had long been trained by a tradition informed *only by its limited experience of western Europe*. When travel escalated and European explorers began to reach the rest of the globe, many old ideas and beliefs were challenged or shattered. It is currently thought that the population of Black Swans totals something near half a million worldwide. That anything near such a population could survive undetected for so long, and existed in the mind of the entire western world as the symbol of something non-existent for over 1600 years provides a humbling example: if we make generalizations based on our limited experience, we run the risk of transgressing truth and crossing into fallacy. If such generalizations are reinforced by teaching, literature, figures of speech, and other forms of cultural tradition, then the inevitable counterexample will come not as a delightful discovery, but as a culture-shaking revelation. We can minimize such momentous occasions by reducing how often we draw generalizations based on limited experience.

REDUCTIONISM

A third type of oversimplification is *Reductionism*. Reductionism occurs when someone reduces a complex issue to only a single aspect, and judges the whole of the issue as if the single aspect subsumes it. The single aspect presented may only touch one point of the issue at hand, it may create a caricature or "cartoon" version of the true issue, or it may not relate at only but only deceptively seem to apply (see also Red Herring). In any case, the fallacy ignores and/or hides all of the nuances and qualifications which the issue actually warrants, and relies on the reaction produced by the image it has deceptively painted.

This fallacy has been called the "nothing-buttery" fallacy because it essentially represents a thing as "nothing but" one aspect of the thing, or another thing altogether. For example, you have probably heard the claim, "Intelligent Design theory is *nothing but* creationism disguised as science," and likewise that, "Creationism is *nothing but* religion masquerading as science." These claims commit fallacies because they emphasize a tangential aspect of the issue, and downplay the extensive scientific data to which intelligent design theory and creationism point. The claim dishonestly presents something less than even a half-truth as the whole truth for the public. In short, such Reductionism refuses to tell "the truth, the whole truth, and *nothing but* the truth"—the only good form of reductionism. Rather, it contents itself to caricature the truth as *nothing but* whatever it wants the public to perceive. In this effort the phrase "nothing but" often appears, as well as similar words like "merely," "only," or "just."

Examples in Scripture

The Bible relates an example of this fallacy in the story of David and Goliath. In 1 Samuel 17:33 we read, *Then Saul said to David, "You are not able to go against this Philistine to fight with him; for you are but a youth while he has been a warrior from his youth."* In the well-known tale the giant Goliath challenges the Israelite soldiers, all of whom flee in fright. The young shepherd boy David, to everyone's surprise, accepts the challenge. Then David meets his first obstacle: doubt. King Saul, who himself was a mighty warrior and stood a head and shoulders taller than his peers (1 Sam. 9:2), scoffs at David's eagerness to fight the giant: "You are but a youth." The word "but" in the translation here gives away the fallacy, though it would still be fallacious without it. Is David really just a "youth"? Does being a "youth" really mean you cannot accomplish great things?

Elsewhere in Scripture, Paul addresses a similar issue, telling the young pastor Timothy, "Let no one look down on your youthfulness, but rather in speech, conduct, love, faith and purity, show yourself an example of those who believe" (1 Tim. 4:12). Youthfulness brings with it a certain suspicion that the person is unproved and unpracticed. Both Timothy and David had to prove themselves against such opposition. In David's case, he reminded Saul that as a shepherd boy he had already slain a lion and a bear, essentially saying, "Don't be fooled by my looks. I have already proven my faith and bravery." As the story goes, he did so again by killing Goliath. So much for reductionistic thinking.

Evolution and Reductionism

The worldview of evolution forces its proponents into reductionism often. For example, one writer claims, "We humans appear as only slightly remodeled chimpanzee-like apes."[11] Statements like this—that equate to, "Human beings are nothing but highly evolved apes"—echo in classrooms, media, and popular dialogue about the subject everywhere. The claims are not always this clearly and bluntly presented, but many times they are. Sometimes, human beings are represented as nothing but the sum total of material chemicals that make up our physical bodies. The famous atheist Carl Sagan once wrote:

> I am a collection of water, calcium, and organic molecules called Carl Sagan. You are a collection of almost identical molecules with a different collective label. But is that all? Is there nothing in here but molecules? Some people find this idea somehow demeaning to human dignity. For myself, I find it elevating that our universe permits the evolution of molecular machines as intricate and subtle as we.[12]

Sagan displays the same type of fallacy: humans are nothing but water, calcium, and organic molecules that have undergone "evolution." Sagan's statement and the claim about "chimpanzee-like apes" differ only by degree. Both reduce man to something more simplistic than he is, and then claim he has just "evolved" further down a continuum. Each case reduces a human to "nothing but" something simpler: either "molecules" or "apes." Sagan is more honest in his reductionism, taking his definition of "human" closer to his own materialistic beliefs. If the evolutionist's story is correct, then humans are really "nothing but" highly evolved matter. In fact, going back before the alleged "big bang," before matter existed—when "nothing" existed—then humans must be "nothing but" highly evolved "nothing." The truth is that any claim that reduces humans to "nothing but" anything—even if that anything looks or acts as relatively similar as an ape—commits the fallacy of Reductionism. Human beings are nothing but human beings, period. Any other comparison should be highly qualified and nuanced clearly, else it flirts with fallacy.

Another evolutionist goes so far as to say, "In essence, we are nothing but a big fly."[13] This claim was made by a researcher who studies the hearing mechanisms of fruit flies and hopes to apply the results to humans. There is a strong belief among many researchers that many genes found in fruit flies have been retained through millions of years of evolution and continue to appear today in parts of the human genetic code. Thus, solving problems in fruit flies, they presume, may help solve problems with human beings.

Despite the theory of evolution, it may well be true that similar genetic mechanisms appear in many organisms throughout nature. Such a feature may tell us something about a common designer more than a common ancestry of all animals. Nevertheless, to assume, based on the premise that similar genes occur, that humans are "nothing but a big fly," is quite an overstatement—in fact, quite an oversimplification. There is no proof whatsoever that we are even related to flies—this is merely the starting assumption of Darwinism—let alone that we are "nothing but" big flies. The fallacy of reductionism stands out very clearly here.

The same researcher made a similar error later. He said, "Our enjoyment of wonderful symphonies is nothing but the conversion of mechanical energy into electrical signals by the cells in our inner ear."[14] Ironically, he offered this statement as part of the justification for seeing humans as "nothing but a big fly." The problem is that this statement is as fallacious as the one it pretends to support, and it will do no good to pile one Reductionism on top of another.

Is a symphony really "nothing but" the twittering of ear drums converted to neuro-electrical impulses? While the process of enjoying a symphony certainly involves this mechanism, it can hardly be *reduced* to it. There is so much *more* involved! For starters there is the vital element of *information*. No "wonderful symphony" is created without a *composer* who arranges the notes and instruments in such a way as to make it "wonderful" to the ear. Oddly enough, information is the same vital element that the evolutionist leaves out when talking about man. Our DNA involves a magnificent amount of information—highly organized data. Where did this information come from? How did it get organized? Who is the composer of this great symphony called man?

The "big fly" theory of man will have us believe that there is no difference between the information that constitutes a fruit fly, and that which constitutes human genes. It does not, however, take a Ph.D. in biology to figure out the enormous differences between the two. Trying to illustrate his scholarship by pointing to the fallacious symphony idea, this evolutionist makes the fallacy of evolutionism all that more obvious to the discerning thinker. It is now even easier to refute. Almost as easy as killing a fly.

Simplifying versus Oversimplifying

This does not mean, however, that all uses of phrases like "nothing but" automatically qualify as fallacies. We must examine and judge each particular case on its own merits and context. In this process the honest critic will indeed find legitimate instances of "nothing but." For example, the vigorous Austrian economist Ludwig von Mises taught, "Money is *nothing but* a medium of exchange. . . ."[15] Was Mises engaging in reductionism by using the phrase "nothing but"? To argue so would draw one into trifles: money *technically* can also be paper and ink, or metals, etc. These facts, though true, pertain only to insignificant and variable characteristics of money, and thus matter little to the context of Mises' point about the *definition and function* of money. The critic who makes a point of pushing such quibbles will rightfully earn the title "pedant," and will prove that he has nothing substantial to offer to the discussion.

Rather, Mises illustrates a legitimate example of *clarification by simplification*, not a fallacy of *over*simplification which this chapter elaborates. Mises simply confronted the phenomenon of *obscurantism*, in this case in relation to his own academic field of money. Obscurantism (from Latin *obscure*, "to darken") refers to any phenomenon that impedes the spread of knowledge. This can occur due to withholding information from the public, or, in this case, from adding to, dissecting, parsing, qualifying or generally explaining the matter to the point of unnecessary complexity and confusion. When Job ranted at length in complaint against his plight, God confronted him for speaking so much when he actually knew so little: "Who is this that *darkens* counsel by words without knowledge?" (Job 38:2). By talking too much, Job actually *darkened* (obscured) the truth when he thought he was illuminating it. "When there are many words, transgression is unavoidable" (Prov. 10:19), and "a fool's voice *is known* by multitude of words" (Eccl. 5:3, KJV). The same applies to *many arguments*: be wary of over-complexity in discourse or writing. In such cases we should have little fear of reductionism, but rather should *seek to reduce* the issue to its uttermost simplicity.

Mises works to simplify the definition of money, and thus criticizes those who wish to elaborate unnecessarily: "they do not think that due regard has been paid to the significance of money until they have enumerated half a dozen further 'functions.'"[16] He rejects these several "secondary functions" of money as either superfluous or legitimately subsumed under his definition of money as "the common medium of exchange."[17] The student, therefore, should seek to avoid oversimplification, but not fear simplification when the situation demands it. Developing the discernment to reach the proper balance will take practice and self-discipline.

Reductionism and Advertisement

The fallacy of reductionism potently affects modern society because people generally do not take the time and effort to critically think through most issues. We are daily trained by advertisement and fast-paced culture. Subliminal thoughts and desires often override critical thinking skills and drive us into bad decisions. Toothpaste sells because the television ads show people with amazingly perfect teeth, not necessarily because the product actually whitens, straightens, and perfects everyone's teeth in that way (so, such an ad implies "nothing but" white teeth). Pickup trucks are sold by ads that feature tough men driving through mud pits and carrying unbelievable loads: anything to associate manliness and herculean strength with the product ("nothing but" manliness). Fast food is portrayed as fresh and mouthwatering when in reality it often arrives lukewarm and greasy. All of these cases portray complex issues as something less than their true sum total. In advertising, the "single" issues emphasized are often the best aspects, and the worst aspects are left out. People who react to such advertising accept a reductionistic view of reality.

Reducing Grace

Theological debate is filled with reductionisms (which is a painful statement to have to make on behalf of the believing world). For example, those who hold to Reformed theology (Calvinism, or the "doctrines of grace"), and who therefore deny man's "free will" in the choice of salvation, often get portrayed as believing that "people are *just* puppets on a string." In truth, however, Reformed beliefs about man's will, the effects of fallen human nature, God's sovereignty and providence involve much more complex ideas that the caricature of God as a puppeteer and man as a puppet with strings attached to his hands and feet. The debater who attempts this claim refuses to engage the full extent of Reformed theology. This could reveal laziness, prejudice, or a number of other motivations.

Atheism, often relying on the materialistic worldview that claims all of reality is "nothing but physical matter," naturally runs into Reductionistic fallacies. For example, the famous atheist Karl Marx wrote,

> *Religious* suffering is, at one and the same time, the *expression* of real suffering and a *protest* against real suffering. Religion is the sigh of the oppressed creature, the heart of a heartless world, and the soul of soulless conditions. It is the *opium* of the people.[18]

This famous statement represents Marx's critique of religion. He believed that God and the spiritual realm do not exist, and that they can be explained away as the desire of humanity to escape the sufferings of human life. "Opium" is a sedative—a drug used to kill pain and numb the mind. Marx believed that the spiritual world is a self-created illusion used to sedate oneself from reality. In the same work he wrote, "*Man makes religion*, religion does not make man." For Marx, religious beliefs can be reduced to "nothing but" expressions of the desire to alleviate suffering.

Contrary to Marx's view, while religious faith may *include* the desire to relieve suffering, religion can hardly be *reduced* to it. He does not consider or present any other possible aspects of religious faith, nor any other possible view of the facts, but pretends that his narrowly-conceived biased view of religion is enough to explain the whole of religion. Thus he commits the fallacy of reductionism.

It is important to note that Marx does not here use the phrase "nothing but" or anything like it, but rather presents his reductionism in very direct and plain statements. This illustrates how slyly reductionism can appear. Marx is very eloquent and compelling on this point, but is fallacious nonetheless. He does elsewhere employ the "but" approach to his reductionistic view—as he wrote, "The religious world is but the reflex of the real world"[19]—but the key words need not be present for reductionism to flourish. The reader must learn to detect reductionism even when arguments or statements do not include words like "nothing but."

NOTES

1. This example appears also in Norman L. Geisler and Ronald M. Brooks, *Come Let Us Reason: And Introduction to Logical Thinking* (Grand Rapids: Baker Books, 1990), 110–111.

2. Reported in *Newsweek*, October 1, 2001, 17.

3. Reported in *Newsweek*, October 1, 2001, 17.

4. Mark Holloway, "Bush's Dilemma: Terrorism or Oil?" *USA Today*, April 17, 2002, 13A.

5. "Stripper's child returns to Christian school," *USA Today*, May 4, 2002, 3A.

6. Jim Wallis, *God's Politics: Why the Right Gets it Wrong and the Left Doesn't Get It* (San Francisco, CA: HarperSanFrancisco, 2005), xxiii.

7. "The top 1 percent of income earners pay more than one in every three dollars the IRS collects in taxes. From 1986 to 2004, the total share of the income tax burden paid by the top 1 percent of earners grew from 25.8 percent to 36.9 percent, while the total share of the tax burden paid by the bottom half of earners fell from 6.5 percent to only 3.3 percent" ("Did the Bush Tax Cuts Favor the Wealthy?" National Center for Policy Analysis Report, January 21, 2008; available at http://www.ncpa.org/prs/rel/2008/20080121.html, accessed August 27, 2008. Also the report from the House of Representatives Joint Economic Committee, "Top One Percent of Tax Filers Pay Highest Share in Decades," available at http://www.house.gov/jec/news/2008/July/pr110-45.pdf, accessed August 27, 2008.

8. Justine Raimondo, "The Anthrax Follies and the Bizarro Effect," *Antiwar.com*, August 8, 2008; available at http://antiwar.com/justin/?articleid=13270 , accessed August 11, 2008.

9. Sam Harris, *Letter to a Christian Nation* (New York: Alfred A. Knopf, 2006), x.

10. Sam Harris, *Letter to a Christian Nation*, 50.

11. Morris Goodman, quoted in Randolph Schmid, "Team Sees Primate as Chimp Off the Old Block," *The Seattle Times*, May 20, 2003, available at http://community.

seattletimes.nwsource.com/archive/?date=20030520&slug=chimp20, accessed July 30, 2008; also quoted in John G. West, *Darwin Day in America: How Our Politics and Culture Have Been Dehumanized in the Name of Science*)Wilmington, Delaware: ISI Books, 2007), 3.

12. Carl Sagan, *Cosmos* (New York: Random House, 1980), 127; also quoted in A. J. Hoover, *Don't You Believe It!* (Chicago: Moody Press, 1982), 27.

13. Charles Zuker, quoted in "UCSD Study of Uncoordinated Fruit Flies Provides Molecular Clues to Hearing Problems in Humans," (www.biology.ucsd.edu/news/article_032300.html) accessed July 30, 2008; also quoted in John G. West, *Darwin Day in America*, 3.

14. Charles Zuker, quoted in "UCSD Study of Uncoordinated Fruit Flies Provides Molecular Clues to Hearing Problems in Humans," (www.biology.ucsd.edu/news/article_032300.html) accessed July 30, 2008; also quoted in John G. West, *Darwin Day in America*, 4.

15. Ludwig von Mises, *The Theory of Money and Credit*, tr. H. E. Batson (Indianapolis: Liberty Classics, 1980 [1934]), 31, emphasis added.

16. Ludwig von Mises, *The Theory of Money and Credit*, 47.

17. Ludwig von Mises, *The Theory of Money and Credit*, 47.

18. Karl Marx, "Introduction to a Contribution to the Critique of Hegel's Philosophy of Right" (1843); available at www.marxists.org/archive/marx/works/1843/critique-hpr/intro.htm, accessed July 30, 2008.

19. Karl Marx, *Capital*, Vol. 1; available at http://www.marxists.org/archive/marx/works/1867-c1/ch01.htm#219, accessed July 30, 2008.

CHAPTER 8

"NOT CLEAR": FALLACIES OF AMBIGUITY

Whereas Fallacies of Oversimplification reduce or ignore vital information, Fallacies of Ambiguity misrepresent truth by obscuring or clouding it. These fallacies often rest on poor usage of language, both of grammar and vocabulary. Careless (or deceptive) placement and definition of words account for many fallacies in everyday life. The following pages list several types and examples of such falsehoods.

AMPHIBOLY

The fallacy of Amphiboly technically refers to poor sentence structure that causes words or phrases to have more than one clear meaning. Poor word combinations or careless placement of words in a sentence can leave unclear or "double" meanings.

A Little Humor

Examples of this fallacy abound in newspaper headlines and advertisement where every effort is made to minimize wording. Too sparse wording often results in ambiguous meaning. One such example comes from a small town newspaper which advertised free obituaries for locals. The ad concluded, "When you die, ask your funeral director to notify us." The newspaper ad could easily be rectified by rearranging one phrase so it reads thusly: "Ask your funeral director to notify us when you die." It is hard to believe that something so obviously out of order made it into print, but such things are not uncommon.

The Tonight Show host Jay Leno exploits this phenomenon every Monday night in his segment, "Headlines." Not to give the impression that amphiboly is always associated with cemeteries, but here is another example. One caption read, "Lakeview Memorial Estates is a private cemetery. If you'd like information on people buried there, please contact them directly."[1] Of course, by "them" the ad intended the cemetery not the people buried there, though the language suggests the latter.

Another wild headline read, "Man shot with arrow in head feels good after it's removed." What?! What was removed, the arrow or the head? Another read, "Postal chief says faster mail delivery to take at least a year." What will take a year? The mail itself or a new faster system of delivery? It's not clear.

Another example appeared in an Ebay listing, where someone hoped to sell a VHS tape of Dr. Laura Schlessinger lecturing on safe sex. The ad carelessly (or not?) read: "SAFE SEX with Dr. Laura Schlessinger."[2]

Sometimes Amphiboly occurs due to the placement of "ing" words (these words can be noun-like verbs, called gerunds, or verb-like adjectives called participles). I once saw an article caption that mentioned children who were "institutionalized in government holding pens." Were the children all holding pens in their hands, or did the author mean held in "holding pens" as in cages. I'm sure the latter was the metaphor he intended, but the sentence structure could have made it clearer.

Classic Amphibolies include the pharmacy sign, "At our drugstore, we dispense with accuracy!"; the western novel line, "He said, 'Saddle me the ass.' And they saddled him"; and the wartime poster, "Save Soap and Waste Paper."[3]

Amphiboly: The Net Fallacy

The word "amphiboly" literally means "to cast both ways" (Greek *amphi* "both" + *ballein* "throw or cast"). This illustrates the meaning of the fallacy: that in a given arrangement within a sentence, certain words or phrases can be understood in both of two ways. Scripture uses versions of this Greek word to describe the casting out of a net for fishing (Hab. 1:17; Mark 1:16), the net itself (Ps. 141:19; Eccl. 9:12; Hab. 1:15–17; Matt. 4:18), or the fisherman (a "net thrower," Is. 19:8). A theme runs through these passages: that of being caught in a net. No matter which way the hapless fish turns, the net is there. Amphiboly mimics such a net. The fallacy captures its victims (both the proponent and the listener) in a net of confusion.

To escape the confusion the student must unravel the net into a single thread. To do this, rearrange the wording in your sentences to make meanings unmistakably clear. If you are faced with someone else's amphiboly, ask them to clarify their position.

Unraveling Current Events

Examples appear everywhere. One headline reads, "The IDF is drawing up options for a strike on Iranian nuclear facilities that do not include coordination with the United States."[4] The context does not leave us guessing too much, but the sentence itself qualifies due to its poor structure. What, exactly, does "not include coordination with the Unites States"? The sentence does not clarify whether this clause describes Iran's "facilities" or Israel's "options." The context points out the latter: Israel is preparing to strike by itself if need be, without the involvement of the U. S. But as the lead sentence of the article, it should be more clearly written. Perhaps two sentences would be better: "The IDF is drawing up options for a strike on Iranian nuclear facilities. These options do not include coordination with the United States." Or a compound sentence: "The IDF is drawing up options for a strike on Iranian nuclear facilities, and the options do not include coordination with the United States." Or even employ punctuation: "The IDF is drawing up options for a strike on Iranian nuclear facilities—options that do not include coordination with the United States." Sentences like this example illustrate why you should always reread and edit your writing before you publish. A second set of eyes always helps, too. A good editor is priceless.

Wittgenstein's Drunken-Man Fallacy

Amphiboly does not affect only journalists; the most brilliant thinkers among us fall prey as well. The famous philosopher Ludwig Wittgenstein, in the midst of his philosophizing on a no-doubt important point, writes, "For instance, we don't trust the account given of an event by a drunk man."[5] What does he mean? Do we not trust the account of an event because the event itself was carried out by a drunken man? Of course not. It is an account *given* by a drunken man that we would hold suspect. Such amphibolies often occur because of stringing too many prepositional phrases together—so many that they get separated from the word they describe. Wittgenstein could have communicated his point more clearly like this: "For instance, we don't trust a drunken man's account of an event."

This particular mistake may have come from the fact that Wittgenstein spoke German as his native language, English coming secondarily. If so, we quite readily forgive the instance. But that he founded a school of philosophy that prides itself on the detailed grammatical analysis of statements should give us all pause. Seemingly easy-to-avoid errors like amphiboly can happen to the best and brightest of us, even pertaining to our own areas of expertise.

Madden's Big-Ol' Offensive Fallacy

Ambiguity can afflict even professionals in communication. Another example of this came during a Primetime football broadcast, when the commentator proclaimed of one player, "He doesn't like to cut off his right toe [when he's running]." I personally overheard this paraphrased quotation during the telecast of an NFL football game between the San Diego Chargers and the New England Patriots on October 13, 2008. The announcer, the famous John Madden, explained how Chargers running back LaDainian Tomlinson had trouble running in a particular situation. Due to a sprained big toe on his right foot, Tomlinson had difficulty "cutting" to the left because he had to plant his right foot firmly and this intensified his pain. Madden spoke an amphiboly when he said "cut off his right toe." He meant something like "move abruptly left having planted his right toe," but sounded as if he meant "dismember his right toe," an obviously absurd thing for a football player (or most other people) to do. Even professional speakers sometimes misspeak, and then—BOOM!—you have a fallacy.

EQUIVOCATION

Equivocation refers to confusion based on a word that has more than one possible meaning. Whereas amphiboly occurs when the sentence structure allows for two meanings, equivocation may occur amidst good grammar and yet lead to fallacy because the word itself allows for multiple meanings.

For example, one headline read, "West Point cadets train for life in Iraq with weekend in N. J."[6] The humor here lies in the equivocation on the word "life." The article intends it to mean "the way life is in Iraq" or "daily living in Iraq," whereas we could easily take it to mean "a lifetime in Iraq." If a single weekend in New Jersey could prepare you for a lifetime in Iraq, then I'm glad I don't live in New Jersey! All humor aside, let's hope the article's intended meaning turns out to be the case, and the troops return home safely and soon.

From Equivocation to Crucifixion

Jesus encountered a very important equivocation that made the Gospel accounts:

> *Jesus answered them, "Destroy this temple, and in three days I will raise it up." The Jews then said, "It took forty-six years to build this temple, and will You raise it up in three days?" But He was speaking of the temple of His body* (John 2:19–22).

Since Jesus often spoke in parables and often referred to a spiritual understanding of things, his opponents, not unimaginably, did not "get it." In listening only to the literal sense of Jesus words they imagined something completely wrong and often quite unreasonable. In this case the Jews took the word "temple" literally when, as John tells us, Jesus spoke "of the temple of His body." Failing to seek the proper understanding of spiritual language can lead to monumental errors.

It was, after all, the instance involving this very equivocation on the word "temple" which supplied the phony "evidence" used to send Jesus on His way to the cross (Matt. 26:59–62). The "witnesses" who maintained the equivocation are called "false witnesses" by the Bible, underscoring the truth that fallacious thinking is equivalent to perpetuating a lie. Our thinking always bears ethical implications. Even a trivial-sounding fallacy like equivocation can have tragic consequences. No wonder John later ties belief in Christ so closely with truth, and disbelief with lying:

> *Who is the liar but the one who denies that Jesus is the Christ?... The one who believes in the Son of God has the testimony in himself; the one who does not believe God has made Him a liar, because he has not believed in the testimony that God has given concerning His Son* (1 John 5:10).

Equivocation plays many roles in theological discourse. Among various viewpoints the word "God" can have a dozen meanings. Likewise, "Christ," "spirit," "inspired," "holy," "sin," "grace," "works," "justify," "revelation," "ordain," "foreknowledge," "generation," "salvation," and dozens of other terms suffer abuse and infusion with many meanings and shades of interpretation. I remember one woman arguing with me in college, trying to persuade me that the Bible taught New Age-style reincarnation because it says "You must be born again." I laughed: "'Again,' yes, but not 'again, and again, and again.'" Theologians from opposing viewpoints can use the same word while meaning opposite ideas. When this happens across the grid of Christian doctrines a jungle of tangled beliefs and confused arguments grows up. Defining the meanings up front can itself eliminate much theological debate.

This is not to say that equivocation is only a religious folly. Secularists have their ample share of wax words and slippery phrases. Humanist abuses include the words "evolution," "life," "fetus," "nature," "science," and many others.

Equivocation frequently occurs in reply to another claim. If a response adopts a meaning for a given word which the original claim used but intended otherwise, the responder commits an equivocation. Good logic, however, aims to erase the possibility of equivocation by choosing words and expressions in such a way as to minimize possible variations in meaning. Equivocation therefore reminds us of the importance of definitions, as well as our audience's perspective and perception of our words.

Evolving Definitions

One equivocation can invalidate an entire argument, chapter, or book, as occurs in the following example:

> Evolution of the Corvette. Everything evolves in the sense of 'descent with modification,' whether it be government policy, religion, sports cars, or organisms. The revolu-

tionary fiberglass Corvette evolved from more mundane automotive ancestors in 1953 . . . the Corvette evolved through a selection process acting on variations that resulted in a series of transitional forms and an endpoint rather distinct from the starting point. A similar process shapes the evolution of organisms.[7]

The evolutionist author of this passage, Tim Berra, commits an equivocation on the word "evolution" which he, following Darwin, claims to define as "descent with modification." At least he defines it, but then he does not consistently apply his definition. Assuming that the array of different "hominid" fossils is evidence that they are all related in "the drama of human evolution," he compares it to the stages of change in the design of the Corvette over the years. "Human evolution" is similar to the way the "Corvette evolved," he argues. If he sticks with the bare definition of "descent with modification" then there is an element of truth in the argument. But earlier in the same chapter Berra claims to explain the "origins of life and the rise of humans" as part of the overarching "view of evolution from the Big Bang to humans."[8] It is this much broader view of "evolution" which he carries throughout the chapter and into the discussion about hominid fossils and the evolution of the Corvette. He concludes of the fossils that "each new discovery helps fine-tune our increasingly detailed knowledge of human evolution."[9] Not only does his shady use of the word "evolution" Equivocate, but the whole argument also commits the fallacy of False Analogy explained later in this book (see the chapter "Stretching the Facts").

It is impossible to prove that humans have evolved in the way that Corvettes have changed over time. For starters, the car (and everything else in the list of his original quote) had a designer who designed each stage and workers who crafted and assembled each stage. Any "evolution" here is artificially imposed by men using pre-existing information and material. If Berra were consistent he would realize that his analogy implies a designer and creator for humans, too. Furthermore, we have a full knowledge of the idea, origins, design and manufacturing of the Corvette. We have full documented from beginning to end; we have a full view of the historical *connections* between all of the parts of its evidence. We have nothing near such empirical evidence for hominid fossils, let alone their alleged relationship to humans. Berra's theory is, therefore, highly creative speculation. His analogy self-defeatingly rests on a shifty abuse of the word "evolution."

Aborting Logic and Life

Abortion provides another charged issue in which proponents abuse elastic definitions. An example comes from liberal Catholic writer Gary Wills, who writes,

> But is abortion murder? Most people think not. Evangelicals may argue that most people in Germany thought it was all right to kill Jews. But the parallel is not valid. Killing Jews was killing persons. It is not demonstrable that killing fetuses is killing persons.... The question is not whether the fetus is human life but whether it is a human person, and when it becomes one.[10]

Wills here forces a distinction which amounts to an equivocation. A "fetus" he tries to maintain, is "human life" but not necessarily "a human person." At least he admits that he is making such a distinction. Nevertheless, his convenient and unhelpful distinction assumes what he wants to prove (that a fetus is sometimes not a human) and allows him to avoid the heart of the question, "Is abortion murder?" Is there really a distinction between "human life" and "a human person," or is this a sly way for liberals to hedge the debate? Unless opponents agree upon this distinction in advance, the use of the word "fetus" to mean something other than the traditional definition of "unborn child" is dishonest and equivocal. It is therefore fallacious.

Atheist Sam Harris uses a combination of true statistics and Equivocation to create the following shocking claim:

> Of course, the Church's position on abortion takes no more notice of the details of biology than it does of the reality of human suffering. It has been estimated that 50 percent of all human conceptions end in spontaneous abortion, usually without a woman even realizing that she was pregnant. In fact, 20 percent of all recognized pregnancies end in miscarriage. There is an obvious truth here that cries out for acknowledgment: if God ex-

ists, He is the most prolific abortionist of all.[11]

While his statistics are correct, Sam's abuse of the words "abortion" and "abortionist" need some clarification. The term "abortion" as normally understood in relation to the debate of terminating a pregnancy, refers to the *voluntary* decision to artificially terminate a pregnancy. In normal discourse, we purposefully distinguish this idea from that of *involuntary* or *spontaneous* abortion, which most people, wishing to avoid confusion, term "miscarriage." Sam even uses the phrase "spontaneous abortion" when announcing the statistics for miscarriages. He maintains the ambiguous title "abortionist," however, when He hypothesizes the existence of God. Problem is, the title "abortionist" is almost exclusively reserved for *people* who perform *voluntary* abortions, or who support doing so.

If God exists, as Sam hypothesizes, then we have to consider the whole issue from that perspective. Creatures cannot arbitrarily hold an omnipotent Creator, Ruler, and Lawgiver to the same limitations we experience. From a moral perspective, the voluntary abortion of a human in the womb in most cases trespasses God's law against murder. Excepting in situations of just war or capital punishment (where the offenders have rightfully earned the punishment of death) God forbids humans the right to arbitrate death. God Himself, however, *by nature*, is the arbiter of life and death. It is not unjust for him for forbid the unnecessary and artificial termination of a pregnancy, while at the same time inscrutably governing the pregnancies of those who miscarry. This is what God does: He chooses who lives and who dies. This is perhaps what infuriates atheists most about this issue: God is in control and the atheist is not; God is the arbiter of life and death and the atheist is not.

While it may present an uncomfortable question as to why God allows miscarriages (this, in reality, just presents a particular facet of the "problem of evil"), it is inconsistent to apply a label like "abortionist" to God which can only rightfully apply, considering the normal use of language, to humans. That this commits the Fallacy of Equivocation should be clear: God "aborts" in the sense of just and rightful providence, and God has presided over no unnecessary termination. Abortionists abort in the sense of medical expediency, often totally unnecessarily, and thus as transgressors of the law of God and as men wanting to usurp God's role.

As a result, and like many other instances of fallacy, this case of

Equivocation from Sam Harris compounds with another fallacy, namely that of a Category Mistake. We simply cannot take categories such as "abortionist" which apply in one worldview and impose them in another. As an atheist and a naturalist, Sam does not recognize a transcendent realm of the Creator; he understands no Creator-Creation distinction. Thus, he has no problem throwing terminology around in the way he does. But if we even *hypothesize* "If God exists," as Sam hypothesizes, then we must be willing to draw the types of distinctions that such a truth would warrant. Sam fails to do so, and commits two fallacies in the process.

Logos, Logic, and More

Christians commit the same error, as I mentioned earlier in relation to theological terminology. The following example I find in the writings of a great scholar, Gordon Clark:

> The well-known prologue to John's Gospel may be paraphrased, "In the beginning was Logic, and Logic was with God, and Logic was God.... In Logic was life and the life was the light of men."...
>
> But the thought that Logic is God will bring us to the conclusion of the present section.... The law of contradiction is not to be taken as an axiom prior to or independent of God. The law is God thinking....
>
> Not only was Logic the beginning, but Logic was God.... Hence logic is to be considered as the activity of God's willing....
>
> God and logic are one and the same first principle, for John wrote that Logic was God.[12]

While I do find the source of human logic (logic within the created realm) in the character and nature of God (and thus Christ), I cannot follow Clark in his translation of the Greek word *logos* as "logic," for this loads all of the technical meaning of our modern usage of the word *backward* into the biblical text. This is classic *eisegesis* instead of *exegesis*. I can accept Clark's claim that "The law of non-contradiction is not to be taken as an axiom prior to or independent of God," but to equate "Logic" with God crosses both semantic and theological lines. "*Logos*" may include "logic" in some way, but certainly means much more. To argue that they consitute "one and the same first principle" constricts the definition of "*logos*" too much, and greatly risks breaking the second and third commandments. A great gulf exists between Creator and Creation and thus between the "logic" of the Creator's mind and the logic of man's mind. Man thinks as God's image—in a way analogous to God—not as God's exact duplicate, for no such thing exists. *"For My thoughts are not your thoughts, Nor are your ways My ways," declares the Lord. "For as the heavens are higher than the earth, So are My ways higher than your ways And My thoughts than your thoughts"* (Is. 55:8–9).

Clark defends his paraphrase-translation with a double Appeal to Authority. First he appeals to technical expertise, namely that of translating the Greek: "This paraphrase, in fact, this translation, may not only sound strange to devout ears, it may sound obnoxious and offensive. But the shock only measures the devout person's distance from the language and thought of the Greek New Testament."[13] In other words, you must be an expert in New Testament Greek to get a good translation here. And what constitutes a good translation versus a bad one? Well, if you translate it the way Gordon Clark does, of course! He writes, "Any translation of John 1:1 that obscures this emphasis on mind or reason is a bad translation.... In the beginning, then, was Logic."[14] Unfortunately for Clark, maintain an emphasis on the mind and reason does not *necessitate* that we equate God with logic. In addition, the vast majority of Greek scholars would disagree with Clark's narrow translation here, so such an Appeal to Authority actually backfires.

After this appeal to expertise, Clark appeals to the similar situation of St. Augustine. He writes, "Even Augustine, because he insisted that God is truth, has been subjected to the anti-intellectualistic accusation of 'reducing' God to a proposition."[15] While this historical case may parallel Dr. Clark's to some small degree, it certainly does not help prove the truth of his novel translation. The liabilities of Appeal to Authority aside, this particular appeal combines a fallacy of False Parallel as well. Augustine's "truth" is a much broader and more flexible idea than Clark's "logic." Clark's abuse is, therefore, more egregious, and thus the criticism applies more strictly in his case. Nevertheless, whether either Clark or Augustine abused the terms or not, we must decide each case individually. Clark is not justified in appealing to the authority of Augustine's situation, or to any authority for that matter.

In the end, Clark's intentions are clear: he wished to defend the rationality of the Christian worldview both against skeptics who criticize Christianity as irrational, and against liberals and pietists who denigrate rationality altogether in favor of feelings, experiences, and subjectivity. In this effort I heartily stand beside Clark, but I think his good intentions led him to overemphasize reason and logic in this case. The fallacies I find in his defense of his more extreme statements reveal weaknesses that we can otherwise avoid, while maintinaing the integrity of Clark's mission.

Equivocations can have as little insignificance as the guy who complained that the "World Series" in baseball does not really include the "World," but only America;[16] or Equivocations can deal with very serious matters, like the examples above. In all cases, a false witness caused by carelessly using words, or by neglecting to define terms up front, commits a fallacy worthy of attention.

Hypostasization/Reification

Hypostasization, also known as Reification, closely resembles equivocation. This fallacy involves speaking of or treating an abstract idea as a concrete thing. As with many of the fallacies, the root words behind the names prove descriptive. The Greek word *hypostasis* in this context means "real," or "substance." The alternate name "reification" is based on the Latin word *res*, which means "thing," or "object." Thus this fallacy is a "substance" fallacy, or a "think making" fallacy: it wrongly treats abstract ideas or words as if they were real, substantial, concrete things.

We easily understand Hypostasization when discussing "make believe" things: talking about "fairy dust" does not make fairy dust actually exist in the physical world. Take this a step further, however, and apply it to meaningful concepts that happen to reflect abstract ideas, like "nature," "science," "liberty," "equality," "justice," "grace," "faith," and many others. All of these things are not only real and important, but crucial to human life; and yet they are not physical things in the physical world, and that means that we must be very careful about how we employ the words in discourse.

The Fallacy of "Nature" and "Natural"

For example, evolutionists very often talk about "natural selection" as a force behind evolution. But what is "natural selection"? Is it the type of thing that can exert force and mold and shape objects like a craftsman or machinist? No. While, to be fair, many evolutionists use the term carefully, limiting it to something like "a natural process in which those organisms survive which are best fitted to their environment and thus are 'selected' to survive," nevertheless, many other instances occur in which the phrase clearly refers to a power, a force, or a "thing" that is just as much a part of nature as lions, tigers, and bears. This conception commits the fallacy.

Likewise, people treat the "nature" itself as a concrete thing. A typical example states, "Nature produces improvements in a race by eliminating the unfit and preventing them from polluting the gene pool of the fit."[17] This statement attributes to nature the power to "produce," "eliminate," and "prevent" fit versus unfit elements. This essentially attributes personal and animate characteristics to an abstract name "nature" which merely represents an impersonal and inanimate. We give the name "nature" to the created order as a whole; it is not a single concrete thing which has its own intelligent and creative attributes.

Nevertheless, evolutionists speak of "natural selection" as if it had a mind and causal powers of its own. The French atheist and biologist Jacques Monod writes,

> Even today a good many distinguished minds seem unable to accept or even understand that from a source of noise *natural selection* alone and unaided could have drawn all the music of the biosphere. In effect natural selection operates upon the products of chance and can feed nowhere else....[18]

Monod Hypostasizes on two accounts, one with the phrase "natural selection," and again with word "chance." Monod speaks as if "natural selection" has powers of its own so that it could "alone and unaided" create order from chaos. "Natural selection," however, is a name for an alleged occurrence that depends on several aspects of nature corresponding together. It is not a thing that has creative, organizational abilities or powers. Secondly, Monod refers to the "products of chance." "Chance" like "natural selection" is not a thing and thus cannot produce anything. By reifying or concretizing these abstract concepts Monod perpetuates the greatest illusion of Darwinism, which is that the universe and its processes all have created and transformed themselves allegedly by their own powers. There may be processes or phenomena within nature to which we can give names like "natural selection," "chance," or even "evolution," but these are mere names, not things which have powers or capabilities.

The Powers of "Science"

An even worse abuse by scientists occurs widely with the word "science" itself. Artifical intelligence expert M. Mitchell Waldrop offends in this regard:

> Science has given us a universe of enormous extent filled with marvels far beyond anything Aquinas ever knew.[19]

If by "science" we understand "people exploring the universe using the scientific method" then this statement begins to make some sense (begins to), and admittedly those who engage in the fallacy of hypostasization generally intend the word to mean something close to this. But the fallacy allows for people to improperly attribute causes and powers, and this matters greatly for worldview issues. "Science" has no causal powers; it has no ability to make or "give" us anything.

Nevertheless, many writers commit this fallacy with the word "science," especially those who have an anti-Christian agenda and hope to somehow defeat "faith" by contrasting it with "science." These people will attribute all kinds of powers to the abstract idea "science." For example, in the space of one essay, atheist Daniel Dennett imputes to "science" several causal and personal phrases: "science says," "according to science," "Science promises—or threatens—to replace," "science has given," "science gives," "science provides," "thanks to science," "science and technology might subvert," "science has banished," "science has already discovered," and "science must expose dishonesty" among others.[20] That Dennett provided this paper as part of a Presidential Council on Bioethics should concern us all the more.

In a different book Dennett provides a quotation from philosopher Hilary Putnam who engages in the same fallacy: "Science is wonderful at destroying metaphysical answers, but incapable of providing substitute ones. Science takes away foundations without providing a replacement. Whether we want to live there or not, science has put us in a position of having to live without foundations."[21] Not only is this false ("science" cannot destroy metaphysical answers because empircal tests cannot pass judgments upon non-physical phenomena) it fallaciously abuses the word "science" several times.

Faith as a Substance

Some Christians, however, offend in the manner as well. I have in mind here some examples from the popular "Word of Faith" movement:

> Some think that God made the earth out of nothing, but He didn't. He made it out of something. *The substance God used was faith....* (Heb. 11:1). Faith is the substance.[22]

> Faith was the raw material substance that the Spirit of God used to form the universe.[23]

These two quotations each commit the fallacy of hypostasization in a very literal way, and both do so based on a popular "Word of Faith" New Age/Charismatic theology. They both Hypostasize the concept "faith." The literal aspect of this instance has two parts: firstly, the proponents of the movement teach that faith is literally a *substance*; and secondly, they base their belief on a literal reading of the Greek word *hypostasis* in Hebrews 11:1. The passage says, *Now faith is the assurance of things hoped for, the conviction of things not seen.* Older translations (KJV) render the word "assurance" as "substance." Since the Greek word in question is *hypostasis*—the very word from which the name of our "substance making" fallacy comes—we might expect it rightfully to translate as "substance." This usage of the word, however, pertains mostly to the much earlier era of classical Greek philosophy, and it varied and changed greatly over the following centuries. By the time of the New Testament, the usage was quite plastic, and most modern English Bibles translate the word as "assurance."

Even if this were not the case—even if the word were properly translated as "substance"—this would not require that we understand "substance" to be a literal material substance as these teachers insist. The word can be, and often is, used metaphorically. In this sense, faith is *assurance* that what God promises is real, and *conviction* that He will bring it to pass. Faith is the earnest belief that God's promises are *substantial* even if not seen. Faith itself is not a literal substance, but a mental and spiritual state of *"being persuaded"* that what God promises, He will be able to perform (Rom. 4:21).

Even though this "word of faith" theology wins many converts among Christians today, the core of its beliefs depends on a fallacious reading of Scripture. In this case, the Fallacy of Hypostasization—deriving from the Greek word *hypostasis* itself—leads to all kinds of strange ideas about speaking reality into existence with mere words, "faith in faith" itself instead of or in addition to faith in Christ or God, and physically healing or cursing individuals, or creating personal wealth or poverty based merely on your words.[24]

Accent

The Fallacy of Accent occurs when the stress, emphasis, or pronunciation of a word suffers confusion, resulting in emphasis where none was intended, or no emphasis where clarity calls for it. The misplaced or missing emphasis can pertain to whole words, entire phrases, or even merely syllables within words. I also extend this fallacy to translation issues, where misplaced stress within a given language can often lead to mistranslations into a second language.

The description of this fallacy originates from Aristotle's seminal work on logical fallacies. In his original estimation the philosopher concerned himself only with proper accents placed on Greek words in order to secure intended meaning, because some words have shared spellings but different meanings based on how their pronunciation. Later Greek writing developed accent marks (for example, ˆ, ´, `) in order to distinguish syllables requiring emphasis, but this system arose much later than Aristotle's era. Thus, his peers could often misread written words by attributing wrong emphases.

The results of the fallacy can sometimes be minor or even trivial—often amounting to little more than quibbling and pedantry. As a case in point, Aristotle gives the example of certain critics of Homer's *Iliad* (a 500 year-old classic by Aristotle's day). Referring to a stump of wood used to mark a turning point in a race, Homer wrote, "*to men ou kataputhetai ombro*," which means, "that is not rotted by the rains." The accent problem arises with the little word *ou*, which can mean "where," "of," "no," or "not," depending on its use or accented. The traditional reading in this passage has been "not," as in "not rotted." Some critics, however, thought it "unnatural" that a stump of wood should not rot, and thus, as Aristotle tells us, "solve the difficulty by a change of accent."[25] The alternate reading prefers "of," and says of the stump, "part *of it* decays in the rain."[26]

The whole issue is, of course, a large amount of time and energy expended over a completely pointless issue that adds nothing of substance to the epic story. One commentator adds, "This must mark the low water of Homeric criticism."[27] Personally, I suspect that one group of annoying interpreters during Aristotle's time were pushing a presupposition—for example, the belief that no natural things are imperishable—and thus took every possible measure to emphasize their view. In this way, entire worldviews can be wrongfully accentuated to create emphases where none belong. This is how worldviews work: we carry our basic assumptions about reality *into* what we read, and some people purposefully take such behavior to extremes. They will not even let the most minor issue pass without forcing their twist upon it.

This Rock

Other examples can lead to broad theological arguments. One such argument arises over which words to properly emphasize in the following words of Jesus:

> *I also say to you that you are Peter, and upon this rock I will build My church; and the gates of Hades will not overpower it* (Matt. 16:18).

This passage has caused much consternation among Protestants and Evangelicals due to the fact that the Roman Catholic Church bases its doctrine of the Primacy of the Bishop of Rome (the Pope) on it. The Roman church claims that Christ made Peter "prince of all the apostles and visible head of the whole church militant,"[28] and that church pronounces "anathema" upon anyone who denies this. This extreme position is based on the fact that Christ calls Peter a rock (in addition, the name "Peter" comes from the Greek *petros* which literally means "stone," or "rock"), and then proceeds to say that this rock will stand as the foundation for His church. Protestants, understandably, have objected to the extremes to which Rome stretches the application of this text, but in doing so have employed every imaginable strain upon the text so that it may not be understood to say what it plainly says.

Christ very clearly makes a word-play: *you are a rock (Peter, petros), and upon this rock I will build my church.* In order to prevent even the possibility of understanding this as Rome does, Protestants have variously stressed that by "this rock" Christ was stressing something besides the rock he mentioned first, Peter himself. The second mention of "rock"—*this* rock—was really Peter's *faith*, Peter's *confession*, or even Christ Himself instead of Peter. The text, however, gives little if any support to these imposed readings. The Fallacy of Accent enters the picture when we try to remove the natural emphasis of the text away from *Peter* himself as *the rock*.

This in no way means that the Roman church correctly uses this text to perpetuate their dogmas of Peter as "prince of the apostles," or of a succession of Popes ruling the church from Rome. The text itself does not even hint at anything like that.[29] The passage merely states that Peter has a foundational role in the formation of Christ's church, and anyone who has read Peter's sermon in Acts 2, as well as the effects afterward, can surely accept the fact that Christ fulfilled this promise through Peter. The same role as "foundation" later appears in relation to all the other apostles as well (Eph. 2:19–20; Rev. 21:14). We do the faith a disservice when, in order to avoid a poor application of a biblical text, we strain to an opposite extreme.

That Day

Another evangelical example occurs by allowing certain "end-times" assumptions to force unwarranted emphasis onto the text. The following passage from Jesus prophetic "Olivet Discourse" involves the Fallacy of Accent, not due to what Christ was teaching or how He said it, but due to how many prophecy teachers have imposed certain emphases in order to interpret the verse in a particular ways. Pay close attention to the words "this" and "that":

> *Truly I say to you, this generation will not pass away until all these things take place. Heaven and earth will pass away, but My words*

will not pass away. But of that day and hour no one knows, not even the angels of heaven, nor the Son, but the Father alone (Matt. 24:34–36).

The word "this" in the phrase "this generation" receives appropriate stress from those who say "this generation" refers to the generation living at that time. The discourse in Matthew 24 about tribulation and Christ's coming in judgment prophesies of Christ's coming *in judgment* on unbelieving Israel, and all of the prophecy was to take place within the lifetimes of those listening to Jesus at the moment. This is obvious from the references in particular verses which indicate that audience: "*You* will be hearing.... *you* are not frightened" (24:6), "deliver *you* to tribulation ... kill *you* ... *you* will be hated" (24:9), "when *you* see the ABOMINATION OF DESOLATION" (24:15), "*your* flight" (24:20), "if anyone say to *you*" (24:23), "*you too*, when *you* see these things" (24:33), "I say *to you, this generation* shall not pass..." (24:34).

Jesus clearly speaks of a great judgment event that would decimate Israel and send his disciples into flight and persecution. Thus, "this" is rightly emphasized in order to point to the very generation to whom Jesus spoke. The other demonstrative adjective, "that," causes problems for some interpreters. There are some writers who are not comfortable reading *all* of Matthew 24 as fulfilled in the past, and so they must find some dividing point in the text at which they say the prophecy changes from near future fulfillment (A.D. 70) to *far* future fulfillment (yet to be fulfilled). These writers often point to the word "that" in verse 36 as marking the division. "That" as in "*that* day," they argue, points to a different time (here, I suppose, they imagine Jesus waving His hand toward the distance as He talked) in the distant future in contrast to *this generation* which was immediate.

This stress on the word "that," however, is arbitrary and undue. The text itself gives us no reason to change time and audience references at this point. The imposition of an emphasis in order to uphold a certain belief about this passage commits the Fallacy of Accent—undue emphasis that changes the fundamental meaning of the text. "That day," rather, points to the day of His coming in judgment, which formed the subject of the disciples' original question (24:3)—the same subject Jesus remained on throughout the discourse (24:27, 30; compare "it" in verse 33). That many great expositors have held this view of "that" in Matthew 24:36[30] shows once again that even the brightest minds can brush with fallacy.

Eating the Enemy

The Fallacy of Accent rarely occurs in modern speech, though given some wideness in how we understand it, we can discern a few occurrences. A fairly recent example made international news to the embarrassment of many in government and media. The stir revolved around the comment from a French official: "I honestly don't believe that it will give any immunity to Iran ... because you will eat them before."[31]

Since Accent depends so much upon the pronunciation of words, this written example demands some explanation. This particular instance occurred due to an English-as-a-second-language foible. French Foreign Minister Bernard Kouchner, speaking in English, responded in Israel to the possibility of Iran possessing a nuclear weapon and thus posing a threat to Israel. He was recorded as telling the Israelis, "I honestly don't believe that it will give any immunity to Iran ... because you will eat them before."[32] The next day headlines boldly told the Israeli public, "You will eat Iran before it achieves a nuclear bomb."[33]

A BBC news story examined the oddity: "Some Israelis may have choked on their breakfast when a newspaper headline quoted France's foreign minister saying Israel might devour its arch foe, Iran." The Frenchman, however, had not quite meant to say "eat," though his French accent (a literal accent in this case) caused him to pronounce the English word "hit" by dropping the "h" and lengthening the "i" as "ee"; thus his listeners heard him say "eat" instead of "hit." He meant that Israel would engage in a preemptive strike (hit) against Iran if it began developing a nuclear weapon, not that Israel would "eat" the Islamic neighbor. Nevertheless, a hasty reporter, upon hearing, wrote down "eat," and this error made it past the editors and all the way to the headlines.

Such an example of the fallacy of accent reminds us that even the simplest of fallacies can still occur without close attention. The least possible of errors can happen to the best of us when we leave our intellectual guards down.

Assault on Logic and Liberty

Another instance occurred due to a reporter's listening mistake, creating a similar PR mishap. The article read, "We are training debaters who can perform assault ministry, meaning becoming the conscience of the culture."[34] Thanks to Ann Coulter in her book *Godless* for catching this great example.[35] This misquotation of late Liberty University president Jerry Falwell commits a Fallacy of Accent. It is hard to spot, until you realize that an "assault ministry" does not make sense with the context of "becoming the conscience of culture." Rather, Falwell had more characteristically made a biblical reference to "a salt ministry." The mistake probably came honestly, though the reporter did not necessarily speak of Falwell or Liberty University favorably. It is a Fallacy of Accent however you judge it. The original source, *Newsweek*, later posted this correction: "In the Feb. 6 article 'Cut, Thrust and Christ,' NEWSWEEK misquoted Jerry Falwell as using the words 'assault ministry.' In fact, Falwell was referring to 'a salt ministry,' a reference to Matthew 5:13 where Jesus says 'ye are the salt of the earth.' We regret the error."[36]

The article covered the rise of Liberty University's debate club to first place in the country, above Harvard and other elites. The students had mastered the fast-talking, rapid-fire approach to academic debating, where number of arguments per minute often wins. The reporter opened the piece with a gibe against the school's view of prophecy: "When you believe the end of the world is coming, you learn to talk fast." Of course, Falwell himself was a master of rhetorical clarity and erudition, even on the side of talking slowly. The reporter's error simply resulted from poor listening, and perhaps trying too hard to be clever.

Textual Criticism and the Fallacy of Accent

Accent fallacies, however, are not always trivial, but can involve more substantial problems, too. Though the following example may be a bit advanced for some readers, it is worth including. 2 Kings 22 describes part of the rebuilding and reform efforts of King Josiah. Some of his cabinet members discovered the book of the law which the kingdom had previously lost and forgotten. A reading of the law convicted the King of the sins of his nation and he feared the wrath of God. He immediately sent to get a word from a prophet. The interesting part comes in the particular prophet that he chose: 2 Kings 22:14 mentions the woman Huldah the prophetess. Even though Jeremiah and Zephaniah were known to be prophesying at this time, Josiah nevertheless seeks out this seemingly obscure and otherwise unmentioned prophetess to deliver a word. Bible commentators have tried to explain this anomaly by suggesting a temporary absence of those prophets or some problem with the timing of their ministry, but these explanations are purely speculative.

We know nothing of Huldah besides the brief mention of her in this text. Her obscurity, however, grows intriguing due to the long introduction the text gives her: "the wife of Shallum the son of Tikvah, the son of Harhas, *keeper of the wardrobe* (now she lived in Jerusalem in the Second Quarter)." The odd detail that her in-law was a "keeper of the wardrobe" seems trivial to add here where we might expect some important credential instead. Perhaps the in-law was a court member and thus known to Josiah, but it remains unclear whether the wardrobe mentioned is that of the King or the priests, and so this explanation is speculative also.

An interesting possible answer to this question arose from a discussion in a Hebrew Exegesis class.[37] Considering that the ancient manuscripts from which our translated Bibles come were written with *no spaces between the Hebrew letters*, there exists an acute possibility that a version of the fallacy of accent occurred if and when the ancient rabbinic scholars divided words at the wrong place. This is surely a *very rare occurrence*, and we should not manipulate the text as we please, but such mistakes can happen. This represents the fallacy of accent because improper division forces an improper emphasis on a certain letter, resulting in wrong words being translated.

In the case of 2 Kings 22:14 the switch, in very general terms, works like this. The phrase "keeper of the wardrobe" comes from the Hebrew *shomer habegadiym* (written *shmr hbgdym*, as ancient Hebrew used no vowels). A simple shift of the *h* at the beginning of the second word to the end of the first would read *shmrh bgdym*. This resulting phrase makes "keeper" feminine and thus would refer to Huldah, not her in-law. The second word *bgdym* could be a form of *hgdh* which is a word that refers to the tradition of telling the Passover story, and could well be translated as "oral tradition." The phrase could then be translated as "a keeper of oral tradition." This would mean Huldah was a student of the Jews' oral traditions at a time when the written word had been lost. This would make sense of the context and of the reason why Josiah sought her out instead of more prominent prophets. While this possible "fix" to the translation involves some complex issues with the Hebrew grammar, while it seems novel in the sense that none of the commentaries mention the possibility,[38] and while it may seem to some that to even "mess with" the text at all is dangerous, yet this slight shift seems to have positive results for understanding the text. We should at least look at the possibility of the fallacy here.

Concluding Remarks

Unfortunately, like ancient Hebrew, and like Aristotle's system of Greek writing, our system of writing English does not require a written method of emphasis (we *may* use *italics* for emphasis, but the system does not require this and not all writers do so). Thus we today can be liable to the same problems as occurred during Aristotle's time. Fallacious accent can occur when written words lack the proper emphasis they would normally receive when spoken. A classic example is the phrase "I love you." Written plainly it can be interpreted in more than one way, depending on if and where stress is placed. It can mean "*I* love you (the other guy doesn't)." It could mean "(I don't just *like* you) I *love* you." Or it can mean "I love *you* (but I don't love your eight sisters)." Each different meaning derives from emphasizing a different word in the sentence. This is not to say that every sentence *requires* a particular word to be emphasized in order for it to be accurate, but when meaning *depends* on emphasis, be sure to supply it. Making emphases clear in your *writing*, therefore, will help avoid the fallacy.

Likewise, emphases in *speech* must be clear as well. The Fallacy of Accent can, naturally, occur when spoken words are mispronounced or misunderstood to have an emphasis or non-emphasis unintended by the speaker. This is most often true when conversations are beset by adverse conditions such as crowd noise, language barriers, or other impediments to communication. For example, during a conversation at a banquet a man once asked me what I thought of "cremation." I began to explain how I didn't think Scripture mandated any particular type of interment, to which explanation I received confused looks. The inquirer then clarified that he had asked about "freemasonry," not "cremation." Since the two words sounded similar, especially when spoken casually amidst the atmosphere of crowd noise, I misunderstood. The Fallacy of Accent really can be as simple as a misunderstood word or syllable.

NOTES

1. http://www.lofthouse.com/davis/lakevwes.htm (accessed August 14, 2008).

2. Sorry bidders, the auction ended April 19, 2000; Item #307194015.

3. See David Hackett Fischer, *Historians' Fallacies: Toward a Logic of Historical Thought* (New York: Harper Torchbooks, 1970), 267.

4. Yaakov Katz, "IDF preparing options for Iran strike," *The Jerusalem Post*, December 4, 2008; http://www.jpost.com/servlet/Satellite?cid=1227702421218&pagename =JPost%2FJPArticle%2FShowFull (accessed December 5, 2008).

5. Ludwig Wittgenstein, *Lectures and Conversations*, ed. C. Barrett (Berkeley: University of California Press, 1972), pp. 57. CHECK THIS.

6. *Times Herald-Record*, April 3, 2008. Available at http://www.recordonline.com/ apps/pbcs.dll/article?AID=/20080403/NEWS/804030323; accessed August 14, 2008.

7. Tim M. Berra, *Evolution and the Myth of Creationism: A Basic Guide to the Facts in the Evolution Debate* (Stanford, CA: Stanford University Press, 1990), 118–119.

8. Berra, *Evolution and the Myth of Creation*, 70.

9. Berra, *Evolution and the Myth of Creation*, 117. In fairness, the author elsewhere in the book agrees that the definition is often abused (see p. 12), but he does not keep consistent with it himself either.

10. Garry Wills, "Abortion isn't a religious issue," *Los Angeles Times*, November 4, 2007; available at http://www.latimes.com/features/religion/la-op-wills-4nov04,0,2121538.story?track=mostviewed-storylevel; accessed August 14, 2008. See also the critical blog article at http://www.principledpolicy.com/?p=108.

11. Sam Harris, *Letter to a Christian Nation* (New York: Alfred A. Knopf, 2006), 38.

12. Gordon H. Clark, "The Axiom of Revelation (Wheaton Lecture II)," *The Philosophy of Gordon H. Clark: A Festschrift*, ed. Ronald H. Nash (Philadelphia, PA: Presbyterian and Reformed Publishing Co., 1968), 67–68.

13. Gordon H. Clark, "The Axiom of Revelation (Wheaton Lecture II)," *The Philosophy of Gordon H. Clark: A Festschrift*, 67.

14. Gordon H. Clark, "The Axiom of Revelation (Wheaton Lecture II)," *The Philosophy of Gordon H. Clark: A Festschrift*, 67.

15. Gordon H. Clark, "The Axiom of Revelation (Wheaton Lecture II)," *The Philosophy of Gordon H. Clark: A Festschrift*, 67.

16. Al Neuharth, "Real 'World' Series in baseball's future?" *USA Today*, October 26, 2001, 15A.

17. This example is provided by S. Morris Engels, *With Good Reason: A Introduction to Informal Fallacies*, 5th Ed. (New York: St. Martin's Press, 1994), 109.

18. Jacques Monod, quoted in Daniel C. Dennett, *Darwin's Dangerous Idea: Evolution and the Meanings of Life* (New York: Simon and Schuster, 1995), 299.

19. Mitchell Waldrop, "The Age of Intelligent Machines: Can Computers Think?" available at http://www.kurzweilai.net/meme/frame.html?main=/articles/art0103.html, accessed August 15, 2008.

20. Daniel C. Dennett, "How to Protect Human Dignity from Science," *Human Dignity and Bioethics: Essays Commissioned by the President's Council on Bioethics* (Washington D.C.: The President's Council on Bioethics, 2008), available at http://www.bioethics.gov/reports/human_dignity/chapter3.html , accessed August 15, 2008.

21. Quoted in Daniel C. Dennett, *Darwin's Dangerous Idea: Evolution and the Meanings of Life* (New York: Simon and Schuster, 1995), 181.

22. Charles Capps, *Authority in Three Worlds*, (Tulsa, OK: Harrison House, 1982), 24, 25; also quoted in Hank Hanegraaff, *Christianity in Crisis* (Eugene, OR: Harvest House, 1997), 68.

23. Kenneth Copeland, "Authority of the Believer II," (Ft. Worth, TX: Kenneth Copeland Ministries, 1987), audiotape #01–0302, side 1; quoted in Hank Hanegraaff, *Christianity in Crisis*, 69.

24. See Hank Hanegraaff, *Christianity in Crisis*; Curtis I. Crenshaw, *Man as God: The Word of Faith Movement* (Memphis, TN: Footstool Publications, 1994); D. R. McConnell, *A Different Gospel: A Historic and Biblical Analysis of the Modern Faith Movement* (Peabody, MA: Hendrickson, 1988).

25. Aristotle, *On Sophistical Refutations*, Book 1, Chapter 4, tr. W. A. Pickard Cambridge.

26. See Walter Leaf, *The Iliad by Homerus* (London, 1900), notes on Book 23, verse 328.

27. Walter Leaf, *The Iliad by Homerus*, notes on Book 23, verse 328.

28. Chapter 1, "The Dogmatic Constitution on the Church of Christ," *Decrees of the First Vatican Council*, 1870.

29. A great discussion of this text is found in R. T. France, *The Gospel of Matthew*, The New International Commentary on the New Testament, ed. Gordon D. Fee (Grand Rapids, Eerdmans, 2007), 620–623; a view very similar to France's is John Nolland, *The Gospel of Matthew: A Commentary on the Greek Text*, The New International Greek Testament Commentary, eds. I Howard Marshall and Donald A. Hagner (Grand Rapids: Eerdmans, 2005), 667–673; a Roman Catholic view is stated in W. F. Albright and C. S. Mann, *Matthew*, The Anchor Bible, Volume 26, eds. W. F.

Albright and David Noel Freedman (Garden City, NY: Doubleday and Company, Inc., 1971), 195.

30. R. T. France, *The Gospel of Matthew*, The New International Commentary on the New Testament, ed. Gordon D. Fee (Grand Rapids, Eerdmans, 2007), 931–943; Kenneth L. Gentry, Jr., *Perilous Times: A Study in Eschatological Evil* (Texarkana, AR: Covenant Media Press, 1999), 89–93; J. Marcellus Kik, *An Eschatology of Victory* (Presbyterian and Reformed, 1971), 159–161; I agree with the view of Gary DeMar, *Last Days Madness: Obsession of the Modern Church* (Powder Springs, GA: American Vision, 1999), 193–201.

31. Marcel Michelson and Allyn Fisher-Ilan, "Dropped 'h' causes trouble for France's Kouchner," ed. Richard Balmforth, *Reuters*, October 6, 2008; available at http://www.reuters.com/article/oddlyEnoughNews/idUSTRE49579J20081006, accessed October 10, 2008.

32. Marcel Michelson and Allyn Fisher-Ilan, "Dropped 'h' causes trouble for France's Kouchner," ed. Richard Balmforth, *Reuters*, October 6, 2008; available at http://www.reuters.com/article/oddlyEnoughNews/idUSTRE49579J20081006, accessed October 10, 2008.

33. "Israelis Digest Kouchner 'H-Bomb'," *BBC News*, October 8, 2008; available at http://news.bbc.co.uk/2/hi/middle_east/7658728.stm, accessed October 10, 2008.

34. Susannah Meadows, "Cut, Thrust and Christ: Why evangelicals are mastering the art of college debate," *Newsweek*, February 6, 2006; available at http://www.newsweek.com/id/57203?tid=relatedcl, accessed December 29, 2008.

35. Ann Coulter, *Godless: The Church of Liberalism* (New York: Crown Forum, 2006), 15.

36. See Coulter, *Godless: The Church of Liberalism*, 15.

37. This "solution" is based on Thomas F. McDaniel, "Chapter 11, Huldah: The Guardian of Tradition, II Kings 22:14 and II Chr 34:22," *Clarifying Baffling Biblical Passages*, 2007; available at http://tmcdaniel.palmerseminary.edu/ (accessed October 20, 2008). This work was modified, particularly with reference to the word *bgdym* being a form of *ngd* (*hggdh*), and reapplied in class discussion by my Hebrew professor Dr. Rollin J. Blackburn (Reformed Episcopal Seminary).

38. See, for example, T. R. Hobbs, *World Biblical Commentary, Volume 13: 2 Kings*, eds. David A. Hubbard, Glenn W. Barker, John D. W. Watts (Waco, TX: Word Books, 1985), 327; R. D. Patterson and Herman J. Austel, "1, 2 Kings," *The Expositors Bible Commentary: Volume 4 (1 Kings–Job)*, ed. Frank E. Gaebelein (Grand Rapids: Zondervan, 1988), 284.

CHAPTER 9

"Hidden Presumptions": Fallacies of Plain Deceit

Fallacies of Presumption attempt to fool you into accepting a proposition without prior justification. In other words, these fallacies secretly presume certain things as true in order to further their main points. The faithful thinker will discern the hidden presumptions first, analyze them, and then evaluate the overall argument. More times than not, the presumption will prove a swindle. Even if it ultimately reflects the truth, the overall argument remains a fallacy because it relies on another unproven assumption. Until you bring all the hidden parts to light and examine them separately, presenting the claim as true breaks the ninth commandment.

Begging the Question

Many people wrongly use the phrase "begs the question" to point out when any particular argument leaves open or raises other questions. For example, a blogger for the Wall Street Journal reports how perjury (lying in court under oath) occurs more commonly in court rooms than prosecutions for the crime suggest. He adds, *"And this begs the question: 'Why are perjury charges so infrequently brought?'"*[1] It is not entirely unacceptable to use the phrase in this way (as a popular figure of speech), as long as we remember that when speaking of logical fallacies "begging the question" means something different. It does not mean "raises the question," but rather, "assuming the answer which you are supposed to be proving."

The fallacy of "Begging the Question" is also known as "circular reasoning" or a "circular argument." These latter two names more clearly describe what actually occurs in the fallacy. It refers to an argument that assumes in its conclusion what it also states as a premise of the argument. An example would be this popularly quoted "defense" of our faith: "The Bible is inspired by God, and the Bible says that God exists. Therefore, God exists." The fallacy here is that the first premise, "The Bible is inspired by God," itself *assumes* that God exists in order to do the inspiring. The conclusion here just makes a *circle* back around to what was already assumed in that first claim. It "Begs the Question" that it claims to prove.

A more proper formulation of this issue would be like this, "If the Bible is God's Word, then everything the Bible says is infallible and authoritative." We may be tempted as Christians to hesitate at this "If" language, but from the perspective of reason this is acceptable. We simply ask the unbeliever to suppose our beliefs as a hypothesis in order to walk them through the logical benefits of our faith. As Christians we certainly *believe* that God exists, and that the Bible is His infallible word, but these are the precious beliefs of Christianity. Thus, most Protestant creeds and confessions which deal with the issue place the inspiration of Scripture and the existence of the Triune God as *articles of faith*. The Bible itself tells us that we must believe in God's existence and providence before we can approach Him or please Him (Heb. 11:6). In other words, we must presuppose that God exists as the ground of successful human action and reasoning. We must be careful, then, when arguing with nonbelievers, neither to submit God's word to testing (as they would), nor, however, to use our beliefs as tools for bludgeoning the truth upon unreceptive heads. Rather, we can demonstrate *why* our particular beliefs provide a better ground of reality and human prosperity than the competing foundational beliefs of atheism, agnosticism, or whatever else. All worldviews ultimately rely on "circular" reasoning for ultimate questions. The Christians task requires them to expose the vicious circle of unbelieving thought while highlighting the gracious circle of biblical logic.

The fallacy of Begging the Question is anciently known by the Latin name *petitio principii*, which literally means "request of the beginning." In this sense "begging the question" means asking your audience foolishly to accept, without proof, the thing you originally stated. You would be asking the listener to pretend that your beginning claim is true without it being proven true. The foolishness of this rests in the fact that it asks your audience to discount the very thing it wants you to provide: proof.

Stoned Logic

We find a great example of Begging the Question in the following quotation from an article on evolution and fossils: "The rocks do date the fossils, but the fossils date the rocks more accurately."[2] Creation Scientists widely cite this article as an admission of circularity at the heart of evolutionary thinking. Author J. E. O'Rourke argues essentially that geology and evolutionary theory presuppose each other—that one requires the other in order to maintain an air of viability. He writes, "Stratigraphy [classification of rock layers] cannot avoid this kind of reasoning, if it insists on using only temporal concepts, because circularity is inherent in the derivation of time scales."[3] He explains that the circular process "starts from a chronology of index fossils, abstracts time units from it, and imposes them on the rocks."[4] Thus he admits, "Radiometric dating would not have been feasible if the geologic column had not been erected first."[5] Of course, the fact that the "geologic column" consists of the speculations of previous paleontologists about which fossils "belong" in which layer, and which rock layers pre-date others, etc., exposes the whole enterprise as arbitrary and man-made.

In other words, the heart of the process of fossil and rock dating and the reconstructions of history based thereon—upon which so much of evolutionary theory depends—entirely Begs the Question. If the issue begins, "How old is this fossil?" and the answer comes, "As old as this rock layer," then they must have an independent and definitive means of dating the rock layer first. But their standard rolls around upon itself. They answer the logically subsequent inquiry, "Then how old is this rock layer?" by saying, "As old as the fossils found in it." That they get away with such illogic defies all ethical standards. That the theory of evolution rests upon such a logical fallacy at its foundation leaves it one tottering column of stones and bones.

A Stimulus Fallacy

Another example shows up in a recent blog post leftist Christian activist Jim Wallis. He mixes in some Begging the Question with other fallacies. After the passage of the so-called "stimulus" bill of President Obama (February 2009), Wallis assures his readers it was the right thing to do:

> First, economists across the political spectrum agree that the economy desperately needs to be stimulated by federal investment in things that will generate immediate economic activity and jobs. Second, the same analysts also agree that benefits to low-income families will result in immediate economic stimulation as people in distress will spend the money they receive because they have no other choice. In other words, directly helping vulnerable people works because it will quickly help stimulate the economy, and it's right because it will immediately help poor and vulnerable people. How often do we get to do what works and what's right at the same time?[6]

The first two sentences—"economists … agree"—both commit Appeals to Authority (a fallacy I discuss later), and thus cannot logically justify Wallis' assessment that the stimulus plan "works" (especially before the plan even gets tested in practice!). After all, if all the experts jumped off a bridge, would that mean we should, too?

The Question Begging comes when Wallis claims that "helping vulnerable people works … and it's right because it will immediately help poor and vulnerable people." The circularity in argument here is obvious. You simply cannot rightfully argue that "X is right because it is X," unless, of course, there is divine law or an agreed upon consensus among the arguers that X is right to begin with. Of course, then we would not need to argue about it to begin with, would we?

Wallis does continue his post by saying, "At the heart of our religious traditions is the command to help the vulnerable and to have a bias for the poorest among us." It might seem from this that he works from a divine mandate and a consensus that helping the poor is right. But remember his context: his post comments on "federal investment into the economy," not private charity between individuals. The Bible gives no directive for government to take wealth from some people and give it to others, not even the poor; the Bible gives no command for government to have a "bias for the poorest." In fact, Scripture teaches that government must act impartially and explicitly warns against a bias specifically for the poor: *You shall do no injustice in judgment; you shall not be partial to the poor nor defer to the great, but you are to judge your neighbor fairly* (Lev. 19:15); *nor shall you be partial to a poor man in his dispute* (Ex. 23:3; see also Deut. 1:17; Prov. 28:21).

EPITHET AND EUPHEMISM

I find it helpful to understand Epithets and Euphemisms as "name adding" or "word adding" fallacies. They are also, in a way, types of begging the question. Both refer to a descriptive or graphic word which attributes any particular characteristic to the thing or person it is applied. Attributing certain characteristics to a person, place, or thing enters bias into the argument, and thus reinforces the argument with mere language instead of rational proof. Thus the fallacy is a type of question begging because is assumes (using descriptive words) the thing it is supposed to prove.

The word "epithet" comes from the Greek word *epitithemi*, which literally means "to place upon" or "to add to." As a fallacy it generally refers to descriptive words that add a *negative* connotation, although the word "epithet" itself does not require negativity. It can refer to any "label" that slants or biases the terms of a claim. "Euphemism" also comes from a Greek word (*euphemia*) that means "good report" or "good fame," and thus strictly refers to descriptive words that add a *positive* or good spin to an argument.

Both Greek words appear in the original text of the New Testament, and some of their uses there provide helpful images for understanding the fallacy. Epithet (*epitithemi*) is used to describe the Pharisees' legalistic abuses: Jesus said, They tie up heavy burdens and *lay* them on men's shoulders, but they themselves are unwilling to move them with so much as a finger (Matt. 23:4). The abuser of epithets engages in something like the Pharisees' hypocrisy: he wants to have the appearance of winning the debate by loading the language and expecting the other person to carry it, while the fallacious arguer himself gets off easy by not having to prove his point. Any kind of question-begging is thus hypocritical logic, and is, therefore, intellectual sin. This sin grows all the more weighty when we learn that the Bible uses *epitithemi* to describe when the soldiers "put" the crown of thorns on Jesus' head (Matt. 27:29).

Epitithemi describes many other things in the Bible, but just a few more helpful examples are in order. First, it describes how the Roman rulers at Thyatira "struck" Paul and Silas with beatings. The King James reads "*laid* many stripes upon them" (Acts 16:23). This "laying" of stripes—that is, whipping—provides a graphic image of placing a negative judgment upon someone. And this is analogous to what happens in the logical fallacy, only instead of a whip, words are used to inflict a negative judgment. *Epitithemi* also describes the giving of a nickname, especially Christ's naming of Cephas "Peter," and James and John as "Sons of Thunder" (Mark 3:16–17). While Christ's epithets here are not fallacious in any way, the act of nicknaming illustrates in a slightly different way how the fallacy works: it is the labeling or adding a new name in order to affect its perception.

Finally, and perhaps most descriptively, *epitithemi* is used twice in Revelation 22:18 as part of a stern warning: "I testify to everyone who hears the words of the prophecy of this book: if anyone *adds to* them, God will *add to* him the plagues which are written in this book." *Adding* to God's word is a serious sin because it distorts the very message of God Himself—there is no higher form of intellectual dishonesty. This warning from God, however, should serve as a model for all intellectual endeavors. We should strive for perfection in all of our communication, and view all faulty "additions" to reasoning as distortions worthy of contempt. In this case of God's word, God Himself goes beyond mere contempt and promises judgment—in particular the "plagues" written in the book in question, Revelation. Epithet, then, we can understand as the "name adding" or the "word adding" fallacy.

Euphemism (*euphemia*) also has an illuminating Scriptural example. Paul defends his ministry by saying that he and his fellow missionaries were in everything commending ourselves as *servants of God*, in much endurance, in afflictions, in hardships, in distresses, in beatings,... by glory and dishonor, by evil report and *good report* (2 Cor. 6:4–8). The point here is subtle as well: by "good report" Paul is not complaining of flattery or euphemism as a fallacy. He is merely pointing out that through all circumstances he has a singular devotion: to be a faithful servant of Christ. He was distracted from his purpose by neither evil speaking nor good speaking. Faithfulness must be the logician's goal, as it was Paul's, whether encountering evil reports or good reports. Truth must rise above prior value judgments and aim for faithfulness.

Good reports do, however, have an important place in our meditations and general thinking. We do want to present others in as positive a light as possible. For this reason Paul elsewhere teaches directs us thusly: Finally, brethren, whatever is true, whatever is honorable, whatever is right, whatever is pure, whatever is lovely, whatever is of *good repute* [*euphema*], if there is any excellence and if anything worthy of praise, dwell on these things (Phil. 4:8). The fallacy, however, comes when people try to impute goodness (or negativity) with mere words before the claim has been proven.

Two Sides, Two Stories

Examples of epithet and euphemism occur throughout human communication, probably because bias, pride, and prejudice lace every human thought and action. Sometimes it depends on perspective. The "American Civil War" (1861–1865) was called "The War of Rebellion" by Northerners during the war in order to emphasize their viewpoint that the South's Secession was an act of rebellion. The South, however, referred to the war as "The War for Southern Independence." After the South lost and independence was a "lost cause," another common epithet, "The War of Northern Aggression," reaffirmed to many Southerners that the effort to secede was just and only foiled by Northern tyranny. Many other names have been given in order to emphasize differing special interests: The War Between the States (fairly neutral), The Great Rebellion, Mr. Lincoln's War, War to Save the Union, War to Prevent Southern Independence, Slaveholder's War, War for Abolition, Second American Revolution, The Lost Cause, and simply The War. From this one example of the Civil War we can see how people argue not just with structured and reasoned sentences (in fact, rarely so), but with the very words they choose to express their opinions.

The student must learn to decipher and remove such emotional, biased, and question-begging words from the arguments they both make and rebut. Such words add a level of judgment to a premise, whereas judgment (or conclusion) must be reserved until *after* the point has been proven.

"All Men": Totally Depraved Logic

Many Bible students and theologians create Epithets and Euphemisms when they debate passages of Scripture. In an effort to promote a certain interpretation of a passage, they will call their explanation "the plain meaning" of the text, and their opponent's "dubious," "implausible," or some other negative term. The fallacy factors in when such abusers of language provide no good reasons to back their points. This, of course, is one reason they use loaded descriptions to begin with: to hide the fact that they have no good argument.

An example of this appears in Norman Geisler's book *Chosen But Free*, where he attempts to refute the Reformed view of Scripture. For an entire chapter he contrasts his view as "the plain meaning of" a given passage against the "implausible interpretation" of those he wishes to refute. Rarely do his explanations rise above stating what he should prove, or merely labeling his opponents with negative titles. One example actually compounds multiple fallacies in just a couple of paragraphs. In contrasting the "free will" theology view of 1 Timothy 2:3–4 against the Reformed view, Geisler appeals to the "plain meaning," which he assumes comes from merely reading one translation of it: *This is good and acceptable in the sight of God our Savior, who desires all men to be saved and to come to the knowledge of the truth.* Geisler emphasizes the phrase "all men" and argues that the "obvious meaning" here as well as in 2:6 is that "all men" means "the whole human race."[7]

This of course goes to the heart of the "free will" (Arminian) vs. Reformed (Calvinist) debate over salvation: Arminians believe that God wishes to save each and every individual, Calvinists argue that God chooses to save only the elect. Were this passage as "obvious" and "plain" as Geisler suggests, the debate would likely have ended long ago. Geisler *assumes* his view as right, but instead of arguing for it, he uses emotion-laden words to fool the reader—"plain" versus "implausible" and "dubious." This simply commits the fallacies of Epithet and Euphemism.

Geisler compounds this fallacy with others, as I said. To "prove" his point he quotes Charles Spurgeon who agrees with him. Since Spurgeon was a Calvinist, it would seem a damaging admission against Calvinism for him to agree with the Arminian interpretation of 1 Timothy 2. What gets missed is that Spurgeon's opinion, while certainly worth hearing, is pointless in regard to logical proof. To argue so commits a fallacious

Appeal to Authority (which I cover later). Something is not true because some great personality says so. So Geisler has wasted his entire paragraph on a rhetorical stunt instead of logical argument. As long as he continues to assert that his viewpoint triumphs he Begs the Question because he has yet to provide a reasonable argument for it.

What does the verse actually mean if the "obvious" meaning of "all men" is not "whole human race." To begin with we must understand the wide range of possible meanings of the Greek word *pantas* here translated as simply "all." But the widely used word can have several shades and purposes of meaning, including not just "all" as in "every," but "all" as in "all kinds." The word is so flexible that we must look to the context of each passage where it appears to determine exactly what the writer means. The translation "all" needs context to illuminate it.

Another part of the Arminian's problem, therefore, results from isolating the passage from its immediate context, as well as from the larger context of Paul's writing. Notice that 1 Timothy 2 *begins* by prescribing prayer for "all men" (the same phrase), and then specifies *kings and all who are in authority*. Why would Paul's readers need such an exhortation? Because they lived under harsh persecution—a time when Christians would have viewed their rulers as enemies of the faith. Paul exhorts them to pray for even these people, which means that Paul is talking about praying for different *classes* or *types* of people—even ones they may not feel like praying for. Paul says we should do this remembering that God saves all kinds of people—He can even save persecuting enemies (as Paul himself was, and so knew very well!).

Paul elsewhere uses the word in this very way. In Titus 2:11, he writes, *For the grace of God has appeared, bringing salvation to all men.* The word "all" here (*pasin*, directly related to *pantas*) does not mean "each and every single person." Just look at the context. For the ten verses prior Paul is giving specific exhortations to different *classes* of people— old men, older women, young women, husbands, children, young men, masters, *and* servants—all different types of people among whom Paul sought to encourage love and unity, all having received God's grace and salvation equally, and learning from the godly instruction. Likewise, Galatians 3:28 says, *There is neither Jew nor Greek, there is neither slave nor free man, there is neither male nor female; for you are all [pantes] one in Christ Jesus.* Again, "all" here refers to different classes, which the text lists.

Geisler himself admits that Paul sometimes uses the word *panti* (in its various forms) to mean things other than a strict "all" as in "every single." When commenting on Paul's claim that the Gospel has spread "in *all* the world" (Col. 1:6), Geisler calls the phrase an "obvious hyperbole."[8] So why can it be hyperbolic (non-literal) here and yet cannot be in 1 Timothy 2:4? Geisler shows arbitrariness in his interpretation, the reason for which likely involves his prior theological commitments to Arminianism (which forces him to see "all" as literal in 1 Timothy 2), and a futurist "end times" theology (which makes him deny that the gospel covered "all" the world already in Paul's time in fulfillment of Jesus' prophecy (Matt. 24:14; Mark 13:10)). Once again we see how a person's presuppositions form and mold their interpretation of reality and Scripture.

So Geisler and other Arminians simply capitalize off of ignorance when they refer to the simple translation "all" as "the plain reading," while calling a more detailed study of the word and Paul's usage of it "dubious." This tactic deceives and suppresses truth rather than making it "plain."

As fallacious thought would have it, the select quote from Spurgeon itself commits a fallacy here. He argues, "'All men,' say they,—'that is, some men': as if the Holy Ghost could not have said 'some men' if he had meant some men."[9] Geisler adopts this argument: "he could have used the word 'some,' if he had chosen to do so, but he did not."[10] This argument (in stereo) commits two big fallacies: The "Big If" Fallacy (described below), and a Straw Man Fallacy (described later in this book). The Straw Man comes when these men impute to Calvinists a weak argument that Calvinists do not use. None I know argue that "all" means "some." This oversimplifies and thus distorts the position. We use the language and the context to qualify what the word "all" refers to here, not to absurdly change its meaning. As for the second fallacy, apologist James White sniffs it out:

> The argument "he could have used such and such a term" is the weakest that can be offered. Jehovah's witnesses often say "John could have said 'The Word *eternally* existed in the beginning' if that it is what he wanted to communicate." The issue is not what a writer *might* have written, but, what does it mean *in the context as written.*[11]

White is right: it is not about what *might* have been. Spurgeon and Geisler essentially say here, "*If* the Holy Ghost meant 'some,'" then he would have written 'some.'" Of course, now you can clearly see the "Big If" Fallacy: Spurgeon and Geisler cannot predict what the Holy Ghost would have done or done differently in the past. Reading the Big "If" section below will illuminate this more.

All together, Geisler's Epithets and Euphemisms for his interpretations do little more than hide a hand-full of fallacies beneath some name-calling. The Arminian position has no real defense here.

Calvin versus Context

Calvinists, however, are not immune from the fallacy. An unfortunate example of argument by Epithet comes in the writings of John Calvin himself. That such a gifted theologian as Calvin commits this error testifies again to the insidious nature of fallacies—even the best can and do fall prey. When addressing the validity of Old Testament law for civil governments, Calvin does not deeply engage the implications of the question, but skirts them with mere insult:

> For there are some who deny that a commonwealth is duly framed which neglects the political system of Moses, and is ruled by the common laws of nations. Let other men consider how perilous and seditious this notion is; it will be enough for me to have proved it false and foolish.[12]

Instead of providing reasons to back his denial, Calvin merely labels the position "perilous," "seditious," "false," and "foolish." This commits the fallacy of Epithet as clearly as anything. Calvin does go on for a few paragraphs to outline the classic medieval distinction between moral, ceremonial, and judicial divisions of laws in Moses' code, but he provides no argument to show the biblical warrant for this division, nor does he show a biblical basis for deciding his view to be adequate while the revealed Mosaic view to be "false," let alone "foolish." What really drives his persuasion here is the widespread acceptance of his view already, and the Epithets he hurls upon to opposition.

Of course nearly everyone writing during the Reformation employed invective and insult on top of their argumentation, and such practice does not always count as fallacy. God's prophets often spoke in vulgar metaphor and insult against rebellious people. But when the insult itself begins to do the work of persuasion, then we have fallacy. And while Calvin rarely made such a logical slip, on this issue he slid badly.

We could go so far as to argue that the exaggerated severity of Calvin's epithets here really betray the emptiness of his case. Even if Old Testament law did not supply the most biblical and ideal legislation for modern states, could he rightfully argue that such a notion was *seditious* and *foolish*? Are they really *fools* who hold God's prescribed judgments and punishments for theft, etc., in higher esteem than man's?

The historical context in which Calvin wrote makes his appeal to "the common laws of nations" and his rejection of Moses somewhat understandable. The most outspoken proponents of Mosaic law at the time had used the name of Moses as a means to carry out violent social revolution in Münster. Kings everywhere feared that local protestants, wishing to Reform society according to the Bible, would follow the same course and incite violence against the throne. Roman Catholic writers stirred fear amongst these leaders by pointing to Münster's violence and murder as an example of what the Reformers' *Sola Scriptura* (the Bible Alone as our ultimate authority) would inevitably lead to (a Slippery Slope Fallacy!). Into this scene stepped the very young John Calvin.

The furor in Münster began in 1534 and lasted until the middle of 1535. By this time it had gained fame throughout Europe as a symbol of protestant rebellion against the throne. Calvin published the first edition of his *Institutes* in 1536—less than a year later—partly because he wished to distance the true Reformation from the unjust association with the violence done in its name. In his dedicatory epistle to King Francis I, he wrote,

> Lastly, they do not act with sufficient candor when they invidiously recount how many disturbances, tumults, and contentions the preaching of our doctrine has drawn along with it, and what fruits it produces among many. The blame for these evils is unjustly laid upon it, when this ought to have been imputed to Satan's malice.... And frst, indeed, he stirred up men to action that thereby he might violently oppress the dawning truth.

> And when this profited him nothing, he turned to stratagems: he aroused disagreements and dogmatic contentions through his Catabaptists [also called Anabaptists] and other monstrous radicals in order to obscure and at last extinguish the truth.[13]

Calvin thus made it clear that the advancement of God's Word in no way necessitated social disasters like Münster, nor did those violent radicals represent the whole of the Reformation.

In pursuing this defense, however, Calvin unwittingly refuted his own argument against the Mosaic code. Against those who impugned the Reformers' adherence to the Bible by associating it with sedition, Calvin defended,

> Furthermore, how great is the malice that would ascribe to the very Word of God itself the odium either of seditions, which the wicked and rebellious men stir up against it, or of sects, which imposters excite, both of them in opposition to its teaching![14]

I hope you note the irony here when you compare this quotation with the earlier one I cited as a fallacy. Earlier Calvin impugned the argument that Moses applies to modern governments as "seditious." Now he defends adherence to the ultimate authority of the Bible as right and refutes those who ascribe to such preaching "sedition." Why the disparity here? I believe the issue of biblical law at this early stage in Calvin's career to have been a glaring inconsistency—one which his own biblical standard refutes.

Calvin himself provided the refutation in biblical terms. His remarks provide us a way to understand the rightful limits of Epithet and Euphemism as well. As far as God's Word determines "good" and "evil," to that extent we can understand something as "godly," or "foolish," but even then we should take care in our language lest we risk judgment for unjustly slandering a brother (Matt. 5:21–22). Calvin used God's prophet as a frame of reference for the charge of "sedition":

> Yet this is no new example. Elijah was asked if it was not he who was troubling Israel [I Kings 18:17]. To the Jews, Christ was seditious [Luke 23:5; John 19:7 ff.]. What else

are they doing who blame us today for all the disturbances, tumults, and contentions that boil up against us? Elijah taught us what we ought to reply to such charges: it is not we who either spread errors abroad or incite tumults; but it is they who contend against God's power [I Kings 18:18].[15]

Exactly. Epithets and Euphemisms mean nothing if they run counter to God's revealed Will. When they do, we may justly charge them with fallacy. When they do not, we must consider their weight in the light of God's Word. Even then, wisdom and love for our neighbors dictate that we should avoid them when possible.

COMPLEX QUESTION

The fallacy of Complex Question is like begging the question, only in the form of inquiry. This fallacy involves the addition of an unproven claim into the question, and thus essentially assumes the claim to be true before it is proven. Such a fallacious question is invalid because it rests on another proposition which itself needs to be exposed and tested before the initial question can be regarded as acceptable or not.

Classic examples of Complex Questions are: "Does your husband know you're having an affair?"; "Have you stopped beating your wife yet?"; "Why do you believe in higher taxes?" All of these share the common trait of assuming some proposition which itself needs to be questioned first. Thus, a Complex Question is *complex* because it is not just a single question, but usually two. In the examples above the answers to the following questions should *first* be established: "Is the wife having an affair?"; "Does the husband beat his wife (or, Has he ever)?"; "Does the individual believe in higher taxes?" Until these propositions are settled, the original questions stand as *Complex Questions* and thus should be rejected as fallacious.

This fallacy is sometimes called "trick question" since it tries to trick its victim into assuming something without proof. It is also known as a "loaded question" because of the assumption that is "loaded" into the question. The abuser of this fallacy hopes to trick the audience into accepting his assumption, and bear the burden of the illegitimate freight he has laden into the matter.

Every Day Tricks

Sales pitches frequently employ Complex Questions in order to sucker unwitting consumers. During a trip to a furniture store a salesman showed several sofas to my wife and I, none of which impressed us enough to buy. Nevertheless, the man inquired, "So, which one are you interested in?" The truth was that we were interested in none, even though the question assumed that we were. I responded, "I think we'll pass." Salespersons routinely get by with propositions which a good judge would immediately throw out of a courtroom. But, that's why they're salespersons and not judges.

Another piece of marketing from a computer chip company advertises that with their new advanced processor you can "Love your PC again." What is assumed? That you *have fallen out of* love with your computer at some point. Or, more importantly, that even if you are *satisfied* with you computer, you need to buy this new processor to make it more than just satisfactory: you need to *love* your computer the way you did when you first got it and were excited about it. But why spend more money on something you don't need? The ad cleverly appeals to dissatisfaction and lack of excitement, but fallaciously assumes something it has not established as truth.

I used to frequent a Persian deli when I lived near Philadelphia. The owner labeled almost everything on his menu as "the best": "Best Bean Salad," "Best Tabouli," "Chicken Filo, the Best!," "Best Spanakopita," "Best Kabobs"! Many ads claim their products to be "the best," usually with the question, "Why buy anything but the best?" Of course, the ads merely assume without proving that the product in question *is in fact* the best. In the case of my local deli owner, he supplied the proof: he always gave samples of anything his customers wished to try. If his wasn't the best, it was sure close!

I came across a humorous example of Complex Question in the writings of the poet Alexander Pope (1688–1744). Pope once gave a gift to Frederick, Prince of Wales, who resided at Kew, a section of London. The gift was a collar for the prince's dog, engraved with the following witticism:

> I am his highness' dog at Kew;
> Pray tell me, Sir, whose dog are you?[16]

All who stooped to read the pet's tag would receive the jest at their expense!

"What Must We Do?"

Jesus faced a very serious Complex Question recorded in John 6:28–29: *Then said they unto him, What shall we do, that we might work the works of God? Jesus answered and said unto them, This is the work of God, that ye believe on him whom he hath sent.* This inquiry, which Jesus and many of His followers have since faced many times, actually commits the fallacy of Complex Question. Beneath the question of finding God's favor sneaks the assumption that we must *do* some kind of *work*. Jesus, in this particular situation, corrects the error directly, by teaching the people that God's favor is expressed in *believing on Him*, and that this is not a human work, but *the work of God*. The author of this Gospel carried this teaching faithfully into his epistle: *This is His commandment, that we believe in the name of His Son Jesus Christ, and love one another, just as He commanded us* (1 John 3:23).

Jesus faced a very similar query from the rich young ruler, who asked, *Teacher, what good thing shall I do, that I may obtain eternal life?* (Matt. 19:16). In this case, Jesus used a more indirect method of correction. He directed the ruler to examine the law, which the ruler foolishly thought he had kept perfectly from his youth up. Jesus knew better. He challenged the ruler to examine the extent of the law more closely: *go and sell your possessions and give to the poor, and you will have treasure in heaven; and come, follow Me* (Matt. 19:21). This tried the ruler's view of the law on several accounts. First, it exposed his true god, his wealth—a violation of the first commandment, and perhaps the second. Secondly, his failure to let go of his possessions exposed his covetousness—a violation of the tenth commandment. His claim to have kept "all these things" turns out to be almost laughable when the depths of the heart are considered. The fact, however, that none of us can stand as blameless when the law is expounded in all its fullness means that none of us can be saved by our works. Jesus was showing the ruler, step-by-step, that his question was ill conceived. There *is no "good thing"* you can do to inherit eternal life. It is beyond our works. The way to eternal life is through faith.

Oftentimes, when people ask, "What must I do to be saved?" and then begin to quibble about the commandments, they are really asking, "What is the least I can get by with having to do, and still be saved?" The answer, "You cannot do anything to get saved," usually presents a shock. Faith is a very hard doctrine to arrive at for many people, for most have to be broken by the law in order to arrive there. "Broken," unfortunately, is not what most people have in mind for their religious pilgrimage? It is the natural fallen human tendency to "do" something, to see salvation as something you earn instead of a gift. So the complex question always comes, "What must I *do* to get saved?" As Peter answered this on the day of Pentecost, *Repent, and each of you be baptized in the name of Jesus Christ for the forgiveness of your sins* (Acts 2:38). The repentance of the heart—not a work, but new faith—must precede the joining into the covenant. Anyone genuinely interested in eternal life will have to forget about "doing" first and start believing first. The only godly works we will ever do will flow *from* that faith. God's work of faith must be there first.

Lawyer's Tricks

Politicians and lawyers often attempt to push their agendas by entrapping their victims in Complex Questions. The following example involves both a politician and lawyer in one person:

> Towards the end of a town meeting discussing the topic "Race in America", when a participant argued that the issue was not affirmative action but "racial preferences", the moderator, President Bill Clinton, responded by asking the participant, "Do you favor the United States Army abolishing the affirmative-action program that produced Colin Powell? Yes or no?"[17]

Clinton posed a classic trick question that assumed that affirmative action had actually produced Colin Powell. The participant could easily have refuted the fallacious claim by pointing out this unproven assumption. Truth be told, affirmative action probably had nothing to do with Powell's military and later political success. Colin Powell's unique gifts, performance, and a host of other factors all in God's providence "produced Colin Powell." In light of this and the many attending downfalls of affirmative action, the participant could strongly respond "Yes, I wish to abolish affirmative action."

Cops and Consequences

Like many of the other fallacies, Complex Questions have effects even more serious that the political obscurantism Clinton exemplified. One of the most troubling abuses of this fallacy occurs in police (and perhaps military, etc.) interrogation techniques. In one case, interrogators pressured a young man by using loaded questions such as "Where did you hide the murder weapon, in the field or in the chimney?"[18] While a judge would not allow such a question in a courtroom (assuming that the young man had not assented to *having* the murder weapon, let alone *hiding* it to begin with), the interrogation room still allows such trickery under the excuse of possibly getting *some*, *any*, information. In this particular case, the young man suffered from a mental handicap, and the police intimidated and deceived him into giving a false confession. He said he *had* hidden the weapon in the chimney. A police search found nothing, and later an already-incarcerated criminal confessed to the murder, and the young man bravely admitted that police has manipulated him into lying.[19]

The philosopher who studied this case concludes:

> This case indicates how the fallacy of many questions works in a context of dialogue. Instead of allowing a respondent to answer a connected sequence of questions in proper order, so that the respondent can reveal his real commitments, the use of complex questioning technique limits the respondent's options so that he is forced [in many cases] to accept propositions that he is not really committed to, and would disavow, if given a reasonable chance to do so.[20]

Coupled with the environment of intimidation that interrogation by authorities naturally creates, Complex Questions can lead to rank injustice in the legal system. God calls us to a higher standard of justice, and therefore He calls us to a higher standard of truth.

Draining Logic

The fallacy of Complex Question can show up in very subtle ways, sometimes by a mere suggestive action. For example, an old anecdote tells how mental asylums would employ the "bathtub test" to determine sanity. The "doctors" would fill a bathtub, offer the patient a spoon, a teacup, and a bucket, and then direct them to empty the tub. The question implied was, "Would you use the spoon, teacup, or bucket?" The temptation to answer "bucket," because it is the biggest tool offered, overlooks the obvious solution, "None of the three; I'd pull the plug, thank you." The doctors were presenting a trick question which assumed that the only three ways to empty the tub were the three that they *mentioned*. A sane critical thinker will look beyond the question *as it is presented* and point out the fallacy. The tub will drain itself, because fallacious thinking won't hold water.

The fallacy of Complex Question is much like False Dilemma (see the Chapter "Too Simple"). False Dilemma present two options as *the only options* from which to choose. The fallacy lies in the fact that other possibilities lie hidden or unmentioned, and thus the proposition as presented is oversimplified, or "too simple." Complex Question does a very similar thing, only it more often *adds* an untrue assumption into the question, and thus carries "hidden presumptions." A False Dilemma hopes that its victim will not look for the further possibilities it has hidden; whereas a Complex Question hopes its victim will unwittingly accept the false assumption it has added to the issue.

DOUBLE STANDARD

Double Standard, often called "special pleading," is as self-explanatory as it sounds: it refers to a claim that allows itself a special standard of judgment—a standard which it denies to other similar cases or claims. This fallacious standard is "double" because it creates two standards—one for the argument itself, and another for every other case. It is "special pleading" because it asks for itself to be treated as special while it does not allow other cases—even very similar cases—to benefit from the same special considerations.

As fallen and fallible humans we can succumb to the fallacy of double standard in at least two significant ways: either by prejudicing the criteria by which we judge other arguments, or by misrepresenting arguments so they either pass or fail (according to our desires) fair criteria. The first case involves simply judging other arguments more harshly than we do our own. By allowing ourselves a "free pass" on certain criteria that we impose on others, we commit the fallacy. The second scenario is more sinister, because it pretends to work according to a fair standard. The problem is that under this guise of fairness it slips a double standard in the presentation of the two sides. Perhaps it presents an opposing view weaker than it truly is (see also the fallacy of Straw Man, described later), or exaggerates the favored position just enough to gain influence. Both ways result in deception, and the discerning student will point out the "treat me special" fallacy.

Spin as Special Pleading

This special twist on double standards flourishes during election times. Political ads often attack an opposing candidate by presenting only part of the truth about his position, emphasizing an aspect of his campaign that sounds negative, while ignoring issues that could explain or mitigate this negativity. Likewise, these "attack ads" often suppress very similar issues that could prove problematic to the platform of those who run the ads.

For example, during the 2008 presidential election, Barak Obama ran an ad that claimed, "John McCain admits, if the election's about the economy, he's going to lose." During this spoken line a quotation appeared on-screen next to a photo of McCain. It read "If we keep talking about the economy we're going to lose." The ad then criticized McCain for attacking Obama's character and running negative "attack" ads. The problem is that McCain never said what the ad attributed to him. Rather, a "top McCain strategist" was quoted by a liberal newspaper as saying "If we keep talking about the economic crisis, we're going to lose."[21] The news story, however, did not offer any context beyond what they quoted, and it is not uncommon for media outlets with an agenda to "soundbite" their political opponents. The quotation may have contained some truth, but to attribute it to McCain was inaccurate. So the irony unfolds that the Obama ad was itself being less than honest, and engaging in the very type of attack ads that it denounced. Examples like this abound on all sides throughout the political world.

Discerning Double Standards

Be sure to note that not all alleged "double standards" qualify as a fallacy. There are legitimate reasons, sometimes, for drawing distinctions between certain cases that at first glance look similar. For example, atheists often accuse Christians of "special pleading" when it comes to the authority of the Bible. Why do we condemn other religions' holy books—like the Koran—by employing every possible means of criticism, and yet not apply as strict a standard to our own Bible? Atheists would argue that the Bible itself fails the same tests Christians apply to the Koran, and yet Christians do not reject the Bible.

This scenario is facile and contrived. It is facile because it ignores that many theologians and historians *have* applied the same tests to the Bible by which we reject the Koran, and the Bible indeed stands unsurpassed in coherence and historical accuracy. Likewise the claim glosses the fact that theologians and historians have subjected the Bible to extensive research and skepticism many times over, and the readily available knowledge of such research the skeptics pass over with little or no mention. In the light of these facts, the criticism is contrived, because atheists have to make a large stretch and ignore several facts in order to draw the comparison. We can legitimately maintain a distinction in the quality of the Bible versus other holy books, and thus our choice of Christianity does not rest on a double standard. Rather, by refusing to admit the vast amount of research that confirms both a scholarly acceptance of the Bible and a rejection of other "holy books," skeptics and atheists set up their own double standard and thus fall prey to their own criticism.

Perhaps no fallacy more than Double Standard exhibits the nature of the fallen heart. In the introduction I quoted C. S. Lewis regarding the "Great Sin" of pride, and reviewed several passages of Scripture in relation to the effects of hidden sinful forces in our hearts. The fallacy of double standard very often stems from too high esteem of ourselves, our causes, our argumentation, or an unfair prejudice against competing views or ideas. Fears of "losing face," being proven wrong, losing credibility, feeling exposed, bested, beaten, shamed, etc., can all pressure us into applying unfair standards of judgment. Learning to discipline these fears requires intellectual and spiritual courage, but as we discussed in the introduction, we have nothing to lose and everything to gain by doing so.

Sam's Double Standard

Great examples of double standard abound in the recent works by militant atheists. Some of them seem to always allow themselves great leniency in regard to atheist atrocities in history while exaggerating and excoriating every possible bad thing any Christian has done. Here's a clear example from Sam Harris:

> You probably think the Inquisition was a perversion of the 'true' spirit of Christianity. Perhaps it was. The problem, however, is that the teachings of the Bible are so muddled and self-contradictory that it was possible for Christians to happily burn heretics alive for five long centuries.... Martin Luther and John Calvin advocated the wholesale murder of heretics, apostates, Jews, and witches.... Christians have abused, oppressed, enslaved, insulted, tormented, tortured, and killed people in the name of God for centuries, on the basis of a theologically defensible reading of the Bible....

Yet he later writes,

> Christians like yourself invariably declare that monsters like Adolf Hitler, Joseph Stalin, Mao Zedong, Pol Pot, and Kim II Sung spring from the womb of atheism. While it is true that such men are sometimes enemies of organized religion, they are never especially rational.... The problem with such tyrants is not that they reject the dogma of religion, but that they embrace other life-destroying myths.[22]

Notice the double standard that strains Harris' portrayals: he harshly blames the Christian religion for any historical evils that professing Christians perpetrated. Yet at the same time he makes every effort to downplay and absolve atheism for the far greater mass atrocities that professing atheists have carried out. Many of Sam's followers have adopted his arguments and thus perpetuate this very fallacy, so we do well here to expose it. These defenders of atheism basically argue that Christians carried out their evils in the name of their beliefs about God, but the atheist leaders' mass homicides had little or nothing to do with their atheism. Sam argues that the Christian crimes derived directly from Christian teachings whereas atheist crimes stem from sources other than atheism itself. Thus, he blames Christianity, but atheism gets a free pass.

In this scenario Sam uses highly selective evidence and biased interpretation of the sources. He does not apply the same standard of criticism to both sides. He has presented the ways in which the Bible can be used to justify evil, and he has presented a way in which atheism can be excused for its evil, *but he has stopped there*. If he employed a consistent standard of judgment, he would also present the many ways in which the Bible and Christian history decry and denounce the evil that some Christians have perpetrated in God's name, as well as the many ways in which atheism conversely has justified mass murder and violent political revolution. Adding these vital pieces of information drastically tilts the balance of evidence in favor of the Christian religion.[23] Sam may purposefully leave out a thorough examination of the evidence since it would damage his case, or he may simply not have studied the issue thoroughly at all.

Accuracy would demand for Sam not only to make the criticism more equal but to completely turn it around. He should argue that when Christians commit crimes, they do so in direct opposition to the most clear parts of Scripture—*you shall not murder ... you shall not steal* (Ex. 20:13, 15). Even if a Christian leader tries to expunge himself saying, "God told me to," that leader will have spoken in direct contradiction to the commandments and Scriptural precedent. Atheists have no such standard to hold them accountable. Neither humanistic philosophy—which has justified every ethical position imaginable—nor history provides a clear standard or precedent by which to judge. So we should say that Christians who have committed crimes stand *condemned by their own standards* despite their profession of faith; atheists, on the other hand, who commit atrocities in history, do not necessarily break any rules by their own standards.

That Sam can present his case in a persuasive (to some) way attests to the power of special pleading: a double standard can go a long way in making an untruth appear compelling to the public. This is why Proverbs warns us not to accept a single argument without cross-examination and fact-checking: *The first to plead his case seems right, until another comes and examines him* (Prov. 18:17).

Feminism Out Of Fashion

Humanists of all sorts have employed Double Standards in order to persuade (I should say "dupe") the public. Feminists have offended in this regard perhaps even worse that atheists, though some of their own scholars have begun some in-house criticism. For example, one feminist article says,

> In the 1970s and 1980s social convention began to change with regard to the role of women, possibly due to the rise in women's participation in the work force. Advertising changed and began portraying women as confident individuals who could effectively balance their personal and private endeavors.... Many products that were traditionally marketed to men, or the household as a whole, are now marketed to women.... However, despite the movement toward affirming women as self-confident and successful, there is also another trend that appears to discredit their accomplishments and demean them as sexual objects. Marketers present the idea that women must be physically perfect in order to be truly accomplished. This quest for the perfect body has made it now socially acceptable to openly discuss one's latest cosmetic surgery....
>
> Critics of advertising ... believe that the use of perfectly airbrushed models and those with extremely thin bodies suggests to women that they should be just as attractive as the models. This quest for perfect beauty has contributed to the explosive growth of the plastic surgery industry in the United States.... [It] feeds into the problem of distorted body image and low self-esteem of many young women.[24]

This example shows a Double Standard within one of the main currents of feminist thought. The argument runs that the social standards of beauty are set by men and channeled through powerful advertising. These "patriarchal" standards oppress women in that they set an impossibly high standard of beauty and then impel women to buy clothing and products in order to attain the image they have been taught to reach for.

This vicious cycle turns women into mere objects of sexual desire based on male-generated images and targeted marketing. Coincidentally, one particular wave of feminism has urged women to buck this trend by dressing in certain ways to oppose it. Women who choose traditional attire face insult as the feminists outcast them as "collaborators in their own oppression."

In this approach lies an inherent Double Standard. Feminism has centrally argued against the oppression of women. This would imply that women should be left free to determine their choice of dress for themselves. But feminism rarely speaks out for this type of individual freedom. Rather, feminists marginalize, ignore, or even persecute those women whose practice of personal choice in the areas of beauty or fashion conflict with the mainstream feminist critiques. Thus, in order to maintain their anti-fashion and anti-beauty crusade, many feminists must maintain a Double Standard in which they claim to support the liberation of women, but simultaneously try to press their own standards on those they claim to liberate.

This phenomenon is a fallacy of reasoning at a very fundamental level. The feminists who wage this anti-beauty critique engage in Double Standard because they hold a very high standard of "oppression" for the "patriarchal" society they attack, and yet do not hold their own ideas to anywhere near the same level of criticism. These feminist proponents decry the oppression of women by societal standards of appearance, and then turn around and create their own standard of appearance to which they feel justified in forcing women to conform. Yet they cannot see, or will not admit, that in the name of fighting the oppressors, they themselves have become the oppressors.

Some feminists have seen this contradiction and have begun to fight it from within their own ranks. Linda Scott, professor of gender and women's studies at the University of Illinois at Urbana-Champaign, wrote book titled *Fresh Lipstick: Redressing Fashion and Feminism*. Scott relates,

> Feminist writers have consistently argued that a woman's attempt to cultivate her appearance makes her a dupe of fashion, the plaything of men, and thus a collaborator in her own oppression.... Though this wisdom has seldom been open to question as a matter of principle, it has always produced discord at the level of practice.[25]

Scott argues that beauty and adornment serve more than mere sexual attraction. To those who contrast "beauty" with a "natural" appearance, she would argue that there exist few things more natural in practice than improving or adorning one's appearance.

This inner contradiction within feminism effectively exposes the true nature of much of feminist though. It in reality cares little for individual female freedom of choice, and thrives on perpetuating a mentality of oppression and victimization. Perhaps no one has exposed feminism's Double Standard more clearly than conservative pro-lifer Phyllis Schlafly. In an article about female vice presidential candidate Sarah Palin in 2008, Schlafly calls out the feminists for the inequality in their disrespect. Schlafly writes,

> Feminist anger against Sarah has exposed the fact that feminism is not about women's success and achievement. If it were, feminists would have been bragging for years about self-made women who are truly remarkable achievers, such as Secretary of State Condoleeza Rice, or former Hewlett-Packard CEO Carly Fiorina, or Sen. Elizabeth Dole, or even Margaret Thatcher. Feminists never boast about these women because feminism's basic doctrine is victimology. Feminism preaches that women can never succeed because they are the sorry victims of an oppressive patriarchy.[26]

Schlafly goes on to point out even more blatant Double Standard at work in the feminist culprits:

> After 40 years of telling wives and mothers to get out of the home (which Betty Friedan called "a comfortable concentration camp"), put their children in day care (tax-funded, of course) and join the workforce, these same feminists now tell Sarah to stay home with her children.[27]

Even the fallacious article that began this example itself admits that personal choice, not "oppression," in reality determines the ultimate outcome: "The average consumer has a plethora of choices available to him or her in an infinite marketplace.... Ultimately it is the consumer who chooses to listen to or ignore the message that is presented."[28] Yet these feminists and those that think like them refuse to let freedom reign either according the tried conventions of Christianity or according as a majority of women themselves may choose.

Due to the conflicts among its proponents, as well as the double standard often applied, we do not have to stretch to say that what is called "feminism" has very little at its core but rebellion. In fact, the attempts to define exactly what "feminism" is have fomented so many conflicts and arguments within the movement itself that the Stanford Encyclopedia of Philosophy concludes, "Is there any point, then, to asking what feminism is? Given the controversies over the term and the politics of circumscribing the boundaries of a social movement, it is sometimes tempting to think that the best we can do is to articulate a set of disjuncts that capture a range of feminist beliefs."[29] This does not stop the entry, or the movement, from continuing, but in doing so they only prove Schlafly's "victimology" thesis correct. One prominent feminist admits, "Feminism is grounded on the belief that women are oppressed or disadvantaged by comparison with men, and that their oppression is in some way illegitimate or unjustified."[30] Such an assumption up front lends its believers to formulate Double Standard arguments by nature.

The "Big If"

The "Big If" fallacy goes by several names: "Hypothesis Contrary to Fact," "Speculative Fallacy," or "Fallacy of Fictional Questions." All highlight the same fallacious feature: the pontification of *what would be now* based on what *might have been*. In other words, this fallacy refers to a statement of how things would be different presently *if* some given event would have happened, happened differently, or not happened (based on the particular case) in the past. Since, however, the hypothetical "if" event, as proposed, has not really occured, any verification of what "would be" proves impossible. In short, non-testable and non-provable speculations can never provide even reasonable certainty. This fact is basic to the scientific method of *testing* hypotheses, not assuming their validity up front.

The judgment of this fallacy rests on the fact that we *cannot* test speculations about the past. We cannot go back in time—into the *exact* historical scene with *all* of its interconnected variables—and replay things over again. Therefore, you cannot derive accurate predictions from alternative theories of the past. It is not only unlikely, *it is impossible*.

In fact, few if any hypothetical "might have been" scenarios give accurate insight into how present conditions *could* change at all. History involves too many interwoven complex factors. To postulate that alteration of one (or even a few) of these countless factors would directly result in some particular change in the present presumes an oversimplification of reality. Things just aren't that simple. Even if history were so simple, the vast realm of infinite possibilities presents plenty of problems to any single hypothesized scenario.

We can make one exception to this rule for the Person who has perfect omniscience. This Person can indeed determine an accurate and precise outcome despite the multifarious complexity of history. Of course, this Person is not only omniscient and omnipresent, but also *omnipotent* and *sovereign:* He not only knows history, but decrees it according to His will. Thus, when Christ announces alternative outcomes of history (what *would be, if* something had happened) He does not engaging in fallacy, but an expression of His divinity (see Matt. 11:20–24).

We can also avoid this fallacy simply by changing the mood of our language. Instead of speaking of a hypothetical event leading to a definite change, leave the postulated change in the speculative as well. It is not fallacious, in other words, to speak of what *may be* today (instead of what *would* be) based on a hypothetical past. As long as we limit our discussion to the realm of *possibility* we do not err. When we claim or even imply certainty or even great likelihood, we cross the line into fallacy. You cannot prove such a thing.

Our Fate in 1588?

Sometimes, however, writers mix such careful language with equally careless reasoning. For example, some of the most popular historians in recent times, Will and Ariel Durant, engaged in fallacious claims concerning the defeat of the Spanish Armada in 1588. This vaunted event turns out to have had less definitive effect on history than once told, as I describe under the "After This" Fallacy. Perhaps the perceived grandiosity of the battle drives the Durants' to speculate vast historical changes had the Spanish won instead of the British. They write,

> Had the Armada been more wisely built and led, Catholicism might have recovered England, the Guises may have

prevailed in France, Holland might have succumbed; the great burst of pride and energy that raised up Shakespeare and Bacon as the symbols and fruit of a triumphant England might never have been; and the Elizabethan ecstacy would have had to meet the Spanish Inquisition.[31]

Note firstly that this argument does not claim these results based on the results of the battle, but only on the construction and leadership of the Armada, though it implies the result. That issue aside, the Durants carefully use the word "might" throughout the argument except in the last phrase: Protestant England under Elizabeth "would have" had to meet the Spanish Inquisition. Had Spain gained control of England such a meeting would likely have been almost inevitable. But this assumes, for one, that had Spain won the naval battle then they would have inevitably moved on to conquer the English throne. Such an envent may have enjoyed great likelihood, but we have no way to tell for sure.

On top of this failure, the poorly worded beginning to this argument makes it less than compelling. Even if the Spaniards had "built and led" the Armada "more wisely" it would not guarantee a victory in any particular battle. Many more factors figure into a naval battle than these two. In fact, historians love to tell one particular part of the story: soon after the Armada departed from Lisbon on its way to England, a storm arose that blasted the fleet off course and damaged the ships. It forced the Armada to harbor, repair, and set off again days later. Who knows what affect those few additional days of English preparation had in the outcome? And this, not based on the factors men control, but upon those of nature and nature's God. In all historical matters, forces exist beyond human control, beyond human knowledge, and much of them probably beyond human comprehension. To say we can determine outcomes based on changes of just one or a few historical factors equates to claiming that footprints on the wet beach permanently change the shape of the ocean.

Iffy Details, Gore-y Logic

One example from not-so-current current events arose out of the controversial presidential campaign between George W. Bush and Al Gore. The controversy arose out of ballot counting in South Florida: the counts tallied so closely that Gore challenged for a recount. Due to poor handling by voters, officials could not count many ballots in the highly liberal area. Liberal commentators spoke out angrily that Bush "stole" (an undue Fallacy of Epithet) the election. Newspapers joined the fallacy-factory of liberal chorus, one headline reading, "If the Vote were Flawless…" The article claimed, "If no one had ever heard of hanging chads, if the butterfly ballot had never flown, if no voter had bungled in the booth, who would have won Florida and the presidency of the United States."[32] Any definite answer to this question would cross the fallacy line. Perhaps recognizing this, the paper hedged its language, yet could not resist conducting an "analysis" that "suggests": "Florida would likely have gone to Al Gore—by a slim 23,000 votes—rather than George W. Bush… by the wispy margin of 537." Of course, "The Gore campaign called it 'compelling evidence.'" Bush's people, not much more logically, called it "statistical voodoo" (thus bordering on Epithet). A Bush spokesman argued, "If you want to divine voters' intent when there isn't even a mark on the ballot, you'd do better to hire a palm reader than a statistical analyst." In the world of common sense, people call speculative fallacies "grasping at straws." Yet partisan activists apparently do not mind trying to override logic with wishful thinking.

Newton versus Darwin

The recent wave of atheism and its attendant emphasis on "science" and evolution have given rise to at least one (probably more) "Big If" Fallacy. Since no "true" scientist today rejects Darwin's theory (so they argue), then the great scientists from centuries past (whom none will deny as "true" scientists) who believed strongly in creation would certainly have accepted Darwin had they lived to hear him. An example of such argument looks like this: "Newton didn't know about evolution, so he couldn't have rejected it.… *If* Newton were alive today you can be sure he would accept evolution.…"[33]

This example of the speculative or "Big If" fallacy comes from Larry Moran, Professor of Biochemistry at the University of Toronto. Similar arguments from atheists have claimed the same scenario for past scientists such as Newton, Pascal, and Mendel. These atheists and Darwin promoters claim that any "real" scientist who lived before Darwin would have agreed with Darwin on human evolution *if* they would only have lived to read what Darwin wrote. The fallacy here is obvious because it follows a very standard pattern of stating a hypothetical event (*If* Newton were alive today…) and claiming that a *certain* change would concur (…we can be *sure* he would accept evolution). Hiding behind this overtly fallacious statement is another fallacious implication: *If* Newton would have known of evolution, he would have agreed with it.

Even if Prof. Moran's statement avoided fallacy, it would still face strong counterarguments. For example, Isaac Newton aside, some bright and successful scientists living today still reject Darwin's theory, even though they have read Darwin. Despite not only Darwin, but an onslaught of teaching about evolution in every phase of education, many bright scientists reject it. Thus to postulate that Newton or any other pre-Darwin scientist would assuredly accept evolution is to deny the living examples of the contrary.

On top of this, the claim that Newton did not know about evolution is an inaccurate statement. Newton, granted, lived before Darwin's formulation of evolution by natural selection, but evolutionary thought in general has existed since ancient Greece, and Newton was keenly aware of the naturalism of Lucretius and the evolutionary ideas of Empedocles among others. Despite knowing these philosophers well—whose philosophies formed the foundations of Darwin's own—Newton rejected them.

At least one Intelligent Design (ID) proponent has faced this fallacious claim with proper critical thinking. William Dembski, Research Professor of Philosophy at Southwester Seminary and author of the blog *Uncommon Descent* relates his experience: "I remember speaking at the University of Toronto in 2002 when a biologist challenged me about how holding to ID renders one a nonscientist. I asked him if that disqualified Isaac Newton from being a scientist. His instant response was, 'but he didn't know about evolution.'"[34] The biologist, therefore, implied that if a brilliant scientist merely *knows about* evolution he will accept it as true. Against this "Big If," Dembski's logic is correct: merely understanding a theory does not necessitate that one believe that theory. Not all theories are true, sometimes even popular theories are untrue, and sometimes even very persuasive and compelling theories prove untrue. Even if unbelieving scientists such as Prof. Moran believe that "the evidence for evolution is overwhelming," this does not require other people to agree with them. Particularly, to assume that men of great genius, such as Newton, would interpret that "evidence" in the same way he does is the very image of unscientific bigotry and dogmatism.

The fallacious nature of the "if Newton were alive today" argument leaves our evolutionist with nothing but insults and *Ad Hominem* against his opponent. In the same blog post from which this example comes Moran blurts that when Dembski spoke in 2002, "if you rejected evolution you were an idiot.... In the 21st century, anyone who rejects these fundamental concepts in science doesn't deserve to be called a scientist." Of course, since he has failed to prove his original point without fallacy, these emotional tirades carry absolutely no force except to illustrate the logical emptiness of his position.

Such speculative fallacies commonly arise out of the unbelieving worldview, perhaps because its proponents must try hard to suppress the knowledge of God which manifests itself everywhere (Rom. 1:18–20). This act of suppressing the obvious requires a full time effort, yet the nonbeliever has only inadequate tools to perform it. Part of this task of suppression includes suppressing the obvious truths of the past—truths which cannot be hidden or denied, and thus can only be reinterpreted. Thus, when it comes to understanding history, such critics must create hypothetical schemes to deceive themselves and others.

Paine's Bold Speculation

One such desperate attempt comes from the well-known colonial-era critic, Thomas Paine. He claimed,

> Had it been the object or the intention of Jesus Christ to establish a new religion, he would undoubtedly written the system himself, or *procured it to be written* in his lifetime. But there is no publication extant authenticated with his name. All the books called the New Testament were written after his death.[35]

In his work of skepticism, "The Age of Reason," Paine elucidates the position of many atheists and skeptics concerning the New Testament. While the authorship and authenticity of the New Testament books certainly provide matter for scholarly study, Paine's formulation of the argument is dogmatic and question-begging. We could have as easily classified this example under Begging the Question, but since he makes his claim as a hypothetical scenario—"had it been"—it qualifies as the Fallacy of the "Big If." In truth, Paine has no more knowledge about what Christ would have done, how He would have done it, or when He would have done it than anyone else does. To pretend so places man's powers of divination and prediction in judgment over the mind of God. Not only is his statement fallacious in the special sense, it is also generally confused. Who has ever claimed that Jesus intended to "establish a new religion"?

NOTES

1. Ashby Jones, comment on "The Elusive Perjury Charge (Yeah, Yeah, That's the Ticket!)" The Wall Street Journal Blog, comment posted on September 13, 2007. http://blogs.wsj.com/law/2007/09/13/the-elusive-perjury-charge-yeah-yeah-thats-the-ticket/ (accessed August 27, 2008).

2. J. E. O'Rourke, "Pragmatism versus Materialism in Stratigraphy," *American Journal of Science* 276 (January 1976):53. Cited in Henry M. Morris, ed., *That Their Words May Be Used Against Them: Quotes from Evolutionists Useful for Christians* (Green Forest, AR: Master Books, 1997), 245.

3. J. E. O'Rourke, "Pragmatism versus Materialism in Stratigraphy," 53.

4. J. E. O'Rourke, "Pragmatism versus Materialism in Stratigraphy," 51.

5. J. E. O'Rourke, "Pragmatism versus Materialism in Stratigraphy," 54.

6. Jim Wallis, comment on "The Best Thing for the Economy, the Right Thing for the Poor," God's Politics Blog, February 12, 2009; http://blog.sojo.net/2009/02/12/the-best-thing-for-the-economy-and-the-right-thing-for-the-poor/ (accessed February 12, 2009).

7. See his discussion, *Chosen But Free: A Balanced View of Divine Election* (Minneapolis, MN: Bethany House, 1999), 201–203.

8. Norman L. Geisler, "Colossians," *The Bible Knowledge Commentary: An Exposition of the Scriptures by Dallas Seminary Faculty*, ed. John F. Walvoord, Roy B. Zuck (Wheaton, IL: Victor Books, 1983), 670.

9. Quoted in Geisler, *Chosen But Free*, 201.

10. Geisler, *Chosen But Free*, 202.

11. James R. White, *The Potter's Freedom: A Defense of the Reformation and a Rebuttal of Norman Geisler's Chosen But Free* (Amityville, NY: Calvary Press Publishing, 2000), 144.

12. John Calvin, *Institutes of the Christian Religion*, trans. Ford Lewis Battles (Grand Rapids: Eerdmans, 1975 [Original 1536]), 215. The wording remains verbatim in the two volume edition of Calvin's later version of the *Institutes* (4.20.14) 2:1502.

13. John Calvin, *Institutes of the Christian Religion*, 1536 Ed., 11–12.

14. John Calvin, *Institutes of the Christian Religion*, 1536 Ed., 12.

15. John Calvin, *Institutes of the Christian Religion*, 1536 Ed., 12.

16. Alexander Pope, "Epigram Engraved on the Collar of a Dog Which I Gave to His Royal Highness," *The Complete Poetical Works of Alexander Pope: Cambridge Edition* (Boston and New York: Houghton Mifflin Co., 1903), 131.

17. Douglas Walton, "The Fallacy of Many Questions: On the Notions of Complexity, Loadedness and Unfair Entrapment in Interrogative Theory," *Argumentation* 13 (1999): 381. The article cites Clinton in *Newsweek*, December 5, 1997, 35.

18. Noted in Douglas Walton, "The Fallacy of Many Questions: On the Notions of Complexity, Loadedness and Unfair Entrapment in Interrogative Theory," *Argumentation* 13 (1999): 382.

19. This case comes from Douglas Walton, "The Fallacy of Many Questions: On the Notions of Complexity, Loadedness and Unfair Entrapment in Interrogative Theory," *Argumentation* 13 (1999): 382.

20. Douglas Walton, "The Fallacy of Many Questions: On the Notions of Complexity, Loadedness and Unfair Entrapment in Interrogative Theory," *Argumentation* 13 (1999): 382.

21. Thomas M. DeFrank, "Insults fly as Barack Obama & John McCain prepare for second debate," *Daily News*, October 5, 2008; available at http://www.nydailynews.com/news/politics/2008/10/05/2008-10-05_insults_fly_as_barack_obama__john_mccain.html, accessed November 4, 2008.

22. Sam Harris, *Letter to a Christian Nation* (New York: Alfred A. Knopf, 2006), 11, 12, 23, 39–40, 41.

23. See my *Return of the Village Atheist* (Powder Springs, GA: American Vision, 2007), 6–13, for more on Sam's double standard.

24. M. L. Walden and Peg Thoms, eds., *Battleground Business* (Greenwood Publishing Group, 2007), 321, 324–325.

25. Quoted in Craig Chamberlain, "Feminism has suffered because of its views on beauty and fashion, author says," *New Bureau, University of Illinois at Urbana-Champaign*, available at http://news.illinois.edu/news/04/1214fashion.html, accessed November 3, 2008.

26. Phyllis Schlafly, "Feminists against Palin — shame on you," *The San Francisco Chronicle*, September 21, 2008; available at http://www.sfgate.com/cgi-bin/article.cgi?f=/c/a/2008/09/20/IN5U13026F.DTL, accessed November 3, 2008.

27. Phyllis Schlafly, "Feminists against Palin — shame on you."

28. M. L. Walden and Peg Thoms, eds., *Battleground Business*, 326.

29. "Topics in Feminism," *Stanford Encyclopedia of Philosophy*, available at http://www.science.uva.nl/~seop/entries/feminism-topics/#Gen, accessed November 3, 2008.

30. Susan James, quoted in "Topics in Feminism," *Stanford Encyclopedia of Philosophy*, available at http://www.science.uva.nl/~seop/entries/feminism-topics/#Gen, ac-

cessed November 3, 2008. The article cited is Susan James, "Feminism in Philosophy of Mind: The Question of Personal Identity, " *The Cambridge Companion to Feminism in Philosophy*, eds. Miranda Fricker and Jennifer Hornsby (Oxford: Oxford University Press, 2000).

31. Will and Ariel Durant, *The Age of Reason Begins: A history of European Civilization in the Period of Shakespeare, Bacon, Montaigne, Rembrandt, Galileo, and Descrates: 1558–1648*, The Story of Civilization: Part VII (New York: Simon and Schuster, 1961), 37–38.

32. Anabelle de Gale, Lila Arzua, and Curtis Morgan, "If the Vote were Flawless…," *Miami Herald*, December 2, 2000. Viewed via print-out from an email. Link provided no longer works.

33. Larry Moran, comment on "Does Disbelieving Evolution Reflect a Lack of Understanding of It?" *Sandwalk* blog, posted January 12, 2007; available at http://sandwalk.blogspot.com/2007/01/does-disbelieving-evolution-reflect.html, accessed November 10, 2008.

34. William Dembski, "Does understanding coerce belief?" *Uncommon Descent* blog, posted January 12, 2007; available at http://www.uncommondescent.com/evolution/does-understanding-coerce-belief/, accessed November 10, 2008.

35. Thomas Paine, "The Age of Reason," *Selections from the Writings of Thomas Paine* (New York: Carlton House, no date), 206.

CHAPTER 10

"Stretching the Facts": Fallacies of Distortion

Misrepresentation also commonly occurs in the form of distorting the facts. Such fallacies involve attempts to make improper comparisons, misapply characteristics based on groupings or classifications, present vague effigies or parodies of existing truth, or deny important distinctions based on degrees or increments of measurement. In each case, people present a deceptively jaded version of the facts as the true objective facts. In short, these fallacies simply stretch the facts. The Christian must discern the actual facts, and then contrast the fallacious version against the truth.

False Analogy

Broadly speaking, an analogy instructively compares two things based on similarities between them. Broadly speaking, then, a *False* Analogy occurs when someone tries to sustain an argument using a faulty or weak comparison. One scholar helpfully defines analogy as *"the relation of likeness between two things;* a relation which obtains only when the two things are neither totally alike nor totally unalike, but share one or more attributes or have similar attributes."[1] A *false* analogy, then, will claim that one thing is like another, or that one thing parallels another, when in reality the similarity or correlation between the two does not hold.

The fallacy generally occurs when an argument leverages a relationship established on *one* similarity and overextends that relationship to another feature that is in fact dissimilar. In other words a false analogy often involves this form: A and B share feature X; A also has feature Y, therefore B also has feature Y. But this assumption stretches the facts beyond what they warrant. X only represents *one* similarity between A and B; other features such as Y do not follow automatically. We must judge each alleged similarity on the merits of its own case.

The word "analogy" comes from the Greek *analogia*, which means "according to a ratio," or more simply, "in proportion." The Greek mathematician Euclid originally used the word to refer to mathematical ratios that have exact common multiples.[2] The idea, however, soon received broader application than mathematics. By New Testament times the usage had broadened to mean "according to," "right relationship to," or in its verb form to "consider" in the sense of "reason" or "compare." The word appears in Romans 12:6 where Paul says, "Having gifts that differ according to the grace given to us, let us use them: if prophecy, *in proportion to* our faith" (ESV). Having said earlier in verse 3 that each believer should walk humbly, thinking with "sober judgment, each according to the *measure* of faith God has *assigned*." Both terms "measure" and "assigned" (or "divided") recall a mathematical-type relationship, and thus we may likewise understand Paul's use of *analogia* in verse 6. Paul teaches here that believers must exhibit both personal discipline and participation in ministry *in proper proportion* to the faith and gifts God has given each of them. Our lifestyle must create a recognizable analogy to the faith we profess.

Also, the author of Hebrews employs the term *analogia* in its verb form. The entire following passage helps us in that it both employs the *word* and provides a biblical *example* of an analogy (of which there are many):

> *fixing our eyes on Jesus, the author and perfecter of faith, who for the joy set before Him endured the cross, despising the shame, and has sat down at the right hand of the throne of God. For* consider *Him who has endured such hostility by sinners against Himself, so that you will not grow weary and lose heart. You have not yet resisted to the point of shedding blood in your striving against sin* (Heb. 12:2–4).

The word subtly translated "consider" here probably deserves a more refined distinction: "examine," "inspect," "think over again," "investigate," "calculate," "reason critically," "compare." After using such a specialized word (used only twice in the New Testament) to invoke a thoughtful meditation, the author invites us to the very *comparison* he intends. Consider the determination and faith of Christ, who withstood sin even to the point of the Cross and bloodshed, all because He knew the triumph that lay beyond. *Compare this* to your own Christian walk, in which, for whatever trials you may face, you have not had to shed your blood in order to avoid or overcome sin. For whatever problems we may complain of, a quick comparison to our Lord will reveal that we have it quite easy (because of Him, by the way).

The analogy here proves to be valid in respect to the fact that both Christ and Christians have a "race" to run: a race that involves obstacles, trials, setbacks, and yet a joyful triumphant prize to be had in the end. The analogy, however, is purposefully *false* in respect to the severity of the trial of Christ versus that of the trials of the epistle's readers. The author intends for his readers to see this disconnect, for the lesson is, "You don't have so much to complain about. Christ took on the burdens of sin and God's wrath which were *impossible* for us. Therefore, the lighter 'discipline of the Lord' (Heb. 12:5) that you now endure is 'for your good' and will yield 'the peaceful fruit of righteousness' (Heb. 12:10–11)." So here we have a good example of the use of analogy, as well as an acceptable *rhetorical* use of a false analogy to provide a clear contrast. These could simply fall under the categories of comparing and contrasting. But only with such skillful use would a false analogy provide a helpful tool.

The Bible is full of examples of analogies. All of Christ's parables are in fact analogies. In fact, nearly *any* comparison can qualify as an analogy, and this includes figures of speech such as metaphors and similes. Poetic imagery also qualifies, and the better the correspondence between the image and the theme of the poetry, the more power the poetry wields.

Analogies can be strong or weak. Strong analogies occur when the things compared have many points of similarity, or when the points of similarity are particularly relevant to the argument. Weak analogies result when someone strains to make a comparison where few similarities exist. A *False Analogy* can result due to an analogy's weakness, or by involving superficial or irrelevant similarities.

One memorable (and harmless) analogy comes from the movie *Forrest Gump*, with the memorable line, "Life is like a box of chocolates: you never know what you're going to get." This comparison, which did not mean to prove a philosophical claim, but rather instill folk wisdom using its subtle charm, holds as far as Forest's mama intended: just as you cannot predict what any given chocolate will have inside, you cannot predict what will come next in life. It would be faulty, however, if someone stretched the analogy to prove things that are not similar at all. For example, the claim that since your life is like a box of chocolates, and a box of chocolates costs about ten bucks, therefore your life is worth about ten bucks, would create an absurd False Analogy.

It would be great if all false analogies were as trivial as the one I just concocted, but unfortunately this is not the case. In fact, since nearly every poetic image and figure of speech constitutes an analogy, they show up in many arguments from the trivial to the very weighty. They require constant attention, and the student will be on constant lookout for claims such as the following classic false analogy from David Hume's essay "On Suicide": "It would be no crime in me to divert the Nile or Danube from its course, were I able to effect such purposes. Where then is the crime of turning a few ounces of blood from their natural channel?"[3] Diverting your flow of blood really *is* analogous to rechanneling a river *in the very limited sense* of both being flows of liquid that get redirected from their existing course. But it is a *false* analogy for Hume to compare the *criminal import* of the two: bloodletting a jugular has quite a different effect on one's immediate health than digging a ditch.

Consider also a classic example from Francis Bacon (no insignificant logician himself):

> No body can be healthful without exercise. Neither natural body nor politic; and, certainly, to a kingdom, or estate, a just and honorable war is the true exercise. A civil war, indeed, is like the heat of a fever; but a foreign war is like the heat of exercise, and serveth to keep the body in health; for in a slothful peace, both courages will effeminate and manners corrupt.[4]

Bacon's insistence that just as an individual body needs physical exercise, so does a "body" politic leaves much to be desired from such a giant of education and logic. Not only does the analogy not hold at the point of physical exercise (compare the effect of push-ups and sit-ups with that of cascading mortar rounds and bombs), but the example also partakes of other fallacies: that of Equivocation (on the word "body"), and perhaps of Composition (in that the whole of a nation is said to bear the same characteristics as the individuals that make it up).

Artificial Intelligence: Computers in Man's Image

One of the most powerful False Analogies in modern times results from the advancement of artificial intelligence (AI). Based on a resemblance in function between a computer and a human brain, many unbelieving scholars, writers, and entrepreneurs have created a strained analogy and loaded all their hopes and efforts into AI as the avenue to human advancement (evolution). One atheist in particular writes,

> Computers obviously do not think quite like humans, and I do not claim that the computer of today [1988] is necessarily a valid model of the human brain. But computers process data and make decisions based on that data, which is all that the human brain does under the label of thinking. A prime area of study today is artificial intelligence (AI), and its practitioners harbor few doubts that someday computers will be made to do all the operations normally associated with human intelligence, and many more. If the intelligence that results is not strictly human, that is not to say that it will necessarily be inferior. Perhaps artificial intelligence will be superior, with characteristics and capabilities the human mind cannot even imagine....
>
> Future computers will not only be superior to people in every task, mental or physical, but will also be immortal....
>
> If a computer is 'just a machine,' so is the human brain....[5]

This case involves atheist author Victor J. Stenger discussing the future possibilities of artificial intelligence (AI), and in the process, creating a False Analogy. Stenger works from one point of similarity—that both computers and brains process data and make decisions based on that processed data—but takes too much liberty in allowing other points to necessarily follow. For example, he claims that if we can call a computer "just a machine," then we must also say so for the brain. Besides dabbling in Reductionism, the point does not follow at all. By the same logic we could argue, "If a computer plugs into a wall socket, so does the human brain. If a computer wears out in five years, so does a human brain." We can legitimately classify a computer as a machine. We cannot, however, place the human brain under the same category. Yes, computers do some things that brains do, and brains do some things that computers do, but one given similarity does not necessarily imply any others. To claim otherwise commits the fallacy of False Analogy.

While disavowing that the computers of his day can reasonably compare to a human brain, Stenger holds that in the future, technology will catch up with nature. This certainly holds true to a degree. Chips work much faster and more powerfully today than when Stenger wrote twenty years ago. "Moore's Law"—formulated in 1965—so far has accurately predicted the exponential increase in computing power for microchips. Based on this regular progress, many futurists project that by 2035 (give or take), computer chips will reach the processing capacity of the human brain. Then, it will proceed beyond that power at exponential speeds.

One theory argues that once these superfast machines are programmed to design other superfast machines, they will soon leverage their superior "brain power" on their own to create even more superior machines. In theory, we will have robots creating robots. One of the early writers on the future of AI concluded that "the intelligence of man would be left far behind.... Thus the first ultraintelligent machine is the *last* invention that man need ever make...." For those of you who, like me, have visions of *Terminator* from this theory, the professor candidly adds, "provided that the machine is docile enough to tell us how to keep it under control."[6] Many other authors and scientists joined in this naïve vision, including such famous names as Isaac Asimov, Carl Sagan, Ray Kurtzweil and novelist Verner Vinge.

Perhaps the most famous contribution to this field came from Alan Turing, who is considered the father of modern computer science. Turing proposed that if a computer program, under certain conditions, can imitate human intelligence closely enough to fool a human judge, then we should accept the idea that machines "think" in the same way we do. This creates quite a debate among philosophers and scientists, and has created a massive wave of scholarship within the relatively new discipline of neuroscience. Computer scientists, physicists, psychologists, philosophers, and neuroscientists constantly buzz about the future of AI.

All these debates and theories aside, however, the question will always remain whether something successfully imitating human intelligence indeed *equals* human intelligence. Even in such a wild future as these scholars, including Stenger, imagine—even if AI far surpasses the abilities of the human brain in many ways—Stenger's analogy will still face the risk of being False. The human brain may yet have capacities and means that the binary computations of a computer chip can never approximate, despite outward appearances in function, performance, or subjective evaluations by humans.

I mentioned the fallacy of Reductionism in regard to Stenger's claim. Fueling his bad analogy, the Naturalistic Fallacy at the base of his worldview basically reduces all of reality to physical reality. In order to remain consistent, Stenger must argue that "processing data" in the same way that a computer does "is *all* that the human brain does under the label of thinking." But is this really true? Can we really reduce human "thinking" to a purely physical process? Christian scholar Stanley L. Jaki, in his book *Brain, Mind and Computers*,[7] argues against such "radical reduction of thought processes to physical ones."[8] He cites, among countless others, the classic philosophers including Pascal. Pascal created one of the earliest adding machines—a proto-computer—and had clear thoughts about the possibility of AI. Of his machine he said, "A calculating machine achieves results that come nearer to thought than anything done by an animal. But it does nothing that enables us to say it has will, as we say animals have."[9] Jaki essentially concludes that despite faster and more complex computers, equating mechanical computation with human thought ignores too much evidence to the contrary—that "the machine analogy of mind is patently insufficient to account for" human intuition, comprehension, meaning, and judgment, among other things.[10]

Forcing the naturalistic worldview and reducing all thought into its artificial mold produces all kinds of fallacies; Stenger's False Analogy of AI is just one expression of them. The computer-brain idea is definitely artificial, but definitely not the best of intelligence.

Friedan's Famous Feminist False Analogy

Earlier in this book I exposed a Double Standard within feminism. Since it relies on such a fallacious method, it should not surprise us to find the most famous and outspoken of its voices relying of misrepresentations like False Analogy. Perhaps the worst and most destructively influential of these follows:

> In a sense that is not as far-fetched as it sounds, the women who 'adjust' as housewives, who grow up wanting to be 'just a housewife,' are in *as much danger* as the millions who walked to their own death in the concentration camps.... In fact, there is an uncanny, uncomfortable insight into why a woman can so easily lose her sense of self as a housewife in certain psychological observations made of the behavior of prisoners in Naxi [Nazi] concentration camps. In these settings, purposefully contrived for the dehumanization of man, the prisoners literally [an abuse of the word "literally"] became "walking corpses." Those who "adjusted" to the conditions of the camps surrendered their human identity and went almost indifferently to their deaths. Strangely enough, the conditions which destroyed the human identity of so many prisoners were not the torture and the brutality, but conditions similar to those which destroy the identity of the American housewife....
>
> [I]s her house in reality a comfortable concentration camp? Have not women who live in the image of the feminine mystique trapped themselves in the narrow walls of their homes? They have learned to "adjust" to their biological roles.[11]

This comes from one of the most famous of American feminists, Betty Friedan. In her 1963 book *The Feminine Mystique* she argued that social norms had trapped the women of her generation into the lonely and unfulfilling role of housewife, and had brainwashed them into accepting that fate as the only available life for a woman, despite its droning, repetitive, menial nature. In order to enforce her faulty view Friedan drew on many undesirable images and events, creating this nasty false analogy in the process. Her comparison between the housewife's home and a Nazi concentration camp was rhetorical genius. To those women who indeed felt burdened by their home-life, the "concentration camp" metaphor gave the excuse they needed to rebel against tradition. Of course, this is the nature of fallacies: they can strongly persuade those who have the slightest motivation not to think critically and thoroughly.

For those who do think critically, Friedan's metaphor is an eye-rolling False Analogy. The most glaring difference that the comparison ignores is that victims of the Nazi camps were *forced at gunpoint*. Not only was force involved, but relentless force *throughout* the German nation. For Friedan's analogy even to stand a chance of holding she would need to prove that social norms created an equally strong *and* prevalent dominance over the human will as did the police power of the Nazi SS. Likewise, the warning that housewives were in "as much danger" as concentration camp victims who walked to their death is a great example of melodrama and an awful example of logic, integrity, and responsibility as a social leader.

Critics of Friedan have since shown her claims to fail on more than one ground.[12] Friedan's assessment inaccurately regarded both the societal portrayal of women at the time, and the social roles available to women. One scholar writes that the hundreds of popular magazine articles of the era she studied

> did not simply glorify domesticity or demand that women return to or stay at home. All of the magazines sampled advocated both the domestic and the nondomestic, sometimes in one sentence. In this literature, domestic ideals coexisted in ongoing tension with an ethos of individual achievement that celebrated nondomestic activity, individual striving, public service, and public success.[13]

Another adds that Friedan's work does not represent the awakening of a simple housewife as she claims, but rather the calculated work of a radical leftist activist—a role Friedan played for nearly twenty years prior.[14]

This last fact helps us understand the *making* of logical fallacies. As I have stressed, fallacies have as their effect and often as their *goal* the deceiving of the public. Radicalism's greatest weapons are human vice and human ignorance. If you can stoke someone's envy and then exaggerate their situation, you can easily motivate them to action. Friedan's "comfortable concentration camp" is just the type of False Analogy that provides the needed exaggeration. This case, unfortunately, has had tremendous impact in American culture.

Even if Friedan's analogy held true in its most basic comparison—that both housewives and concentration camp victims can lose their "sense of self"—this would by no means indicate that 1) the parallel occurred due to the "same conditions," or 2) that we could consider housewives as prisoners, in danger, walking to their death, or in any other way similar to concentration camp victims. In fact, to use the two categories of "housewife" and "victim" (of any sort, Nazi camp or otherwise) in the same comparison not only abuses analogy but also falls into the fallacies of Ad Hominem, Epithet, and classic guilt-by-association.

To give you an example of how fallacious this abuse is, we could just as easily create an analogy of feminist activists as Nazi SS officers marching in goose-step, saluting their leaders, hailing the great cause of the National Organization for Women, desiring their Third Wave (Reich?) to manifest in political power. A couple academic-sounding references and some well-chosen rhetoric could make the analogy just as salable as Friedan's, if the audience were there for it.

More Feminist Fallacy

Another feminist attacked the Southern Baptist Convention's 1998 resolution to adhere to the biblical teaching of male headship. She protested: "Wifely submission?... Why not slaves? Why don't they hold slaves, too?"[15] Her argument rests on a False Anology:

> As with slavery, however, wifely submission was an ancient cultural norm. Rome was a rigidly structured patriarchal society. Roman wives had few rights; children and slaves, none....
>
> When Paul urged wives to submit, he was trying to control a chaotic situation. Because it threatened the family, the new church might be persecuted. Therefore, Paul urged wifely submission as a way to prove Christians' fidelity to Roman society and mitigate the charge of treason to the empire.[16]

In other words, she argues that since slavery only grew out of ancient culture, and Christians only endured it until they could escape it in a socially acceptable way, so too does male headship of the family only pertain to ancient societies. Paul only allowed wifely submission as a way of not angering Caesar. So her analogy rests between slavery and wifely submission.

This explanation only touches half of the truth, and confuses that half. If Paul really feared angering the Roman Empire, he might have dropped his perpetual claim that "Jesus is *Lord*"—a title of political power notably applied to Caesar and printed on public buildings and currency.[17] By saying "Jesus is Lord," Paul essentially proclaimed "Caesar is not." You cannot get more subversive than that. So his urging of wifely submission requires a different explanation. We find this explanation in the created order and man's fall (Gen. 2–3; 1 Tim. 2:11–15), and subsequently in the true analogy of the marriage between Christ and His church (in which the church submits to her Lord; see Ephesians 5:22–33). Making an analogy between slavery and marriage as both culturally-bound institutions ignores the fact that God ordained the marriage order as part of the order of creation. Slavery crept in long afterward as a result of human depravity. The feminist's analogy between the two simply will not hold.

Fallacy Foils Feuerbach, Marx, and More

Very closely akin to feminism, and actually at the root of it, lies Marxism. Being a materialist and atheist (just as with the AI example above) forces Marx to distort the truth about the religious positions he hates. The following somewhat advanced example illustrates one of Marx's distortions:

> Feuerbach starts out from the fact of religious self-alienation, the duplication of the world into a religious, imaginary world and a real one. His work consists in the dissolution of the religious world into its secular basis.... [T]he chief thing remains to be done.... The [secular basis] must itself, therefore, first be understood in its contradiction and then, by the removal of the contradiction, revolutionized in practice. Thus, for instance, once the

earthly family is discovered to be the secret of the holy family, the former must then itself be criticized in theory and revolutionized in practice.[18]

Marx here recognizes that certain earthly realities—such as the structure of the family—have traditionally been organized according to (we could say "analogous to") religious ideals. By "holy family" here Marx refers to the traditional image of Joseph, Mary, and Jesus. That this paints an ideal of the traditional family unit in Western culture needs little explanation. Marx, being an atheist, believed that the religious story is false, but worse than this he condemned it as a tool of oppression. He believed that the church fabricated the image of the "holy family" as an abstraction of the earthly family, and then used that image to force society into a predictable, maintainable norm. Not content to simply deny the "holy family" as real, Marx believed that a change in societal norms—that is, abolishing the family unit in practice—must correspond.

This all creates a complex example of a false analogy intertwined with Marx's materialistic, atheistic worldview. In general Marx believed that all non-material ideals are illusory, imaginary, and not real. He further believed that changing conditions in the real world would eliminate the need for such "illusions" as religion. Thus, for Marx, the analogy which holds between the "holy family" and the natural family necessitates that the abolition of the natural will lead to the end of the religious ideal as well. This is an example of a false analogy in that one set of similarities between the two—"holy" and natural families—is assumed to necessitate further relationships between the two. Just because "earthly family" corresponds to "holy family," does not necessitate that "abolished earthly family" leads to "abolished holy family." Nor does tearing apart earthly families even abolish the *need* or importance of the ideal family. Also, this whole argument is bound up with Marx's worldview of materialism, and thus it not only constitutes a False Analogy, it partakes of a Worldview Fallacy, and also a bit of Reductionism.

In addition to the fallacious logically in Marx's view, history itself refutes him many times over. The harder the Bolshevik State, for example, tried to create programs and systems to change social structures and thus eradicate religious faith, the more strongly many of the Russian religious population adhered to their beliefs. Even officially atheistic leaders in the government still baptized their children, got married in the Church, gave Christian names, and participated in the loftiest rituals of the Church.[19] Marx himself believed strongly in the abolition of the traditional family unit, the removal of children from parental influence and authority (by replacing home education with socialized public education), and destroying the traditional marital boundaries for sexual activity.[20] Even if, however, Marxist societies successfully forced these practices on the people, it would not logically prove the religious ideal false nor necessitate its abolition. Thus Marx's revolution fails both logically and practically.

Sadly, there are some today who continue openly to promote Marx's view. At a meeting of atheists in 2007, Hollywood screenwriter and author Matthew Chapman echoed Marx almost verbatim:

> The church takes care of people ... and how does atheism compete with that? I don't think it can. I don't believe atheism actually can ever succeed in isolation; only as a result of a much larger political change.... It's quite clear that the better a country takes care of its citizens, the less religion there is.... I don't think atheism can succeed in a country as primitive as this one [the U.S.] now is; a country where politicians deride their own profession, sneering at the political process as if it was the problem not the solution, who deride the idea that government should help, protect, and raise up its weaker citizens; where the current government has turned over the delivery of basic needs to religion and made them a matter of charity.... [W]ithout gigantic social change, the church will have to remain the only place where ordinary people can go to find community, and equality.... If atheism—if reason—is to flourish, it will only do so when people feel protected by a rational system in which they have involvement, and which is run on principles of compassion, not profit.[21]

In other words, eliminate the physical roles of the church in society, and religious faith will disappear. This is Marx's fallacy redux. Chapman was not coy about it, either. He literally cursed the idea that we shoudl frown upon "big-government," and retorted, "I am *for* big-government," and to even my surprise—and having studied them for a while now, I usually am not surprised by the antics of the atheist crowd—the audience heartily applauded. There is, indeed, much education in logic needed out there.

Analogies are powerful teaching aids in that they provide striking images by which to understand more subtle or complicated ideas. One of the reasons Jesus taught so powerfully and effectively pertains to His use of *parables*—pictorial stories which drive home spiritual truths. On the flip side, the fallacious use of analogy can have just as much power, only with an adverse effect. The fallacy of *False Analogy* can severely impair understanding and create strong delusions for its victims.

COMPOSITION AND DIVISION

These related fallacies are very similar to the fallacies of Generalization, discussed in the chapter "Too Simple," and also similar to False Analogy, discussed above. Both fallacies—Composition and Division—concern the relationship of members of a group to the group as a whole.

The *Fallacy of Composition* refers to applying the characteristics of the members as individuals to the group as a whole. For example, a single stick may be easy to break. But to infer, based on this, that a bundle of sticks is also easy to break, is to commit the fallacy of composition. Even if you can break individually every stick in a bundle, you still may not—probably cannot—break the bundle as a whole together.[22] Imputing the weakness of one stick to the group as a bunch commits the fallacy.

The *Fallacy of Division* commits the opposite error. This refers to applying the characteristics of the group as a whole to each individual member of the group. For an example of this, take the converse of the bundle of sticks. Because the bundle as a whole is tough to break does not necessitate that any individual stick in the bundle is tough to break by itself.

Awareness of this fallacy guards against the neglect of ancient wisdom, in fact, revealed wisdom. Both Scripture and ancient traditions remind us that when similar things come together as a group, they acquire properties and characteristics inaccessible by the individuals alone. The Preacher in Ecclesiastes writes,

> *Two are better than one because they have a good return for their labor. For if either of them falls, the one will lift up his companion.*

> *But woe to the one who falls when there is not another to lift him up. Furthermore, if two lie down together they keep warm, but how can one be warm alone? And if one can overpower him who is alone, two can resist him. A cord of three strands is not quickly torn apart* (Eccl. 4:9–12).

This, of course, is not to say that individuals have no value, but only to point out that groups acquire qualitative differences from the individuals that compose them. The same is true in reverse: individuals may each have qualitative differences that do not transfer to the group.

Solidarity and the Church

One of the glories of the Church as the Body of Christ is that *both* the individual members *and* the body as a whole possess indispensible, irreplaceable attributes which the other does not, and thus both need each other. Paul teaches both aspects in 1 Corinthians 12. The long passage is worth quoting:

> *For even as the body is one and yet has many members, and all the members of the body, though they are many, are one body, so also is Christ. . . . For the body is not one member, but many. If the foot says, "Because I am not a hand, I am not a part of the body," it is not for this reason any the less a part of the body. And if the ear says, "Because I am not an eye, I am not a part of the body," it is not for this reason any the less a part of the body. If the whole body were an eye, where would the hearing be? If the whole were hearing, where would the sense of smell be? But now God has placed the members, each one of them, in the body, just as He desired. If they were all one member, where would the body be? But now there are many members, but one body. And the eye cannot say to the hand, "I have no need of you"; or again the head to the feet, "I have no need of you." On the contrary, it is much truer that the members of the body which seem to be weaker are necessary; and those members of the body which we deem less honorable, on these we bestow more abundant honor, and our less presentable members become much more presentable, whereas our more presentable members have no need of it. But God has so composed the body, giving more abundant honor to that member which lacked, so that there may be no division in the body, but that the members may*

have the same care for one another. And if one member suffers, all the members suffer with it; if one member is honored, all the members rejoice with it. Now you are Christ's body, and individually members of it (1 Cor. 12:12–27).

Amidst Paul's elaboration of the fact that the Church is indispensable both as individuals and as a whole, he works in some practical applications of this doctrine. As individuals we have differing gifts; we must use our own gifts as well as respect the various gifts of others whether small or great. Likewise, we must respect the collective nature of the body, and when one mourns or rejoices, we all do together. As a Church, a divine fellowship, we must maintain both individual responsibility and mutual solidarity.

Perhaps nowhere in modern history has the theme of Solidarity (of members uniting as one group and gaining strength thereby) applied more prominently to the Church than in Poland under Communistic rule in 1980. A strongly Roman Catholic country by tradition, Poland suffered food and supply shortages in the waning decade of the atheistic, communistic dictatorship. In 1978, during this time of state atheism and suppression of religion, the Roman Catholic Church elected Karol Wojtyla, Bishop of Krakow, as the first ever Polish Pope. Renamed John Paul II, the new Pope quickly traveled to speak in Poland in 1979 where millions received him with cheer. In defiance of the official atheism and oppressive conditions, he preached for freedom of religion, human rights, and an end to violence. He inspired the nation—as well as much of Eastern Europe and the rest of the world—to believe that something bigger than communism stood on their side. They only needed the bravery to stand together in faith.

Within a year, after the communistic government vaulted meat prices during an already acute shortage, self-organized strikes broke out all over Poland. The price hikes came on July 1. Meanwhile, the government continued plundering supplies to send to Moscow for the 1980 Olympics, scheduled to begin on July 19. In an ironic twist, a rail worker in the city of Lublin was poking around some freight cars that sat waiting for shipment to Moscow. Spying the cars full of paint cans, the worker curiously popped one open. To his surprise he found it packed with allegedly scarce choice meats.[23] More cans revealed more scarce goods. The news spread. The workers immediately made the connection. The government had secretly hoarded loads of food to make the failing Soviet Union appear prosperous as nations and media flooded in from around the world for the Olympics.

People were furious. Strikes spread like wildfire. The rail workers welded the train's wheels to the rails and distributed the meat and food to the people.[24] A month later, support grew so strong throughout the people that they created a non-governmental trade-union named "Solidarity" and forced the government to begin to back down.

The communist State immediately reacted, however, enforcing martial law and outlawing the Solidarity union. But the attempt to destroy the union failed, only driving the united movement underground. In 1983, another visit from the Pope provided a stage for massive regathering and rallying of Solidarity with hopes and expressions of eventual victory.[25] His message to the Poles remained constant from 1979 until the communist State ultimately fell: "Fear not."[26] Pope John Paul II's efforts at toppling communism reached far beyond his 1979 visit to Poland. He had lived through dictatorship himself, worked with underground churches throughout the Eastern Bloc in direct defiance of Communist rule. His leadership among the Poles is now widely accepted as a key factor leading to the end of Soviet rule.[27]

The lesson of Solidarity teaches us that when individuals unite as one body around a legitimate purpose, they gain a strength that can overcome the greatest of enemies. Had the Poles remained as disassociated individuals, they would likely never have had the strength to oppose the enemy. To believe they would have had, as individuals, the strength to end the reign of communism would be a delusion of grandeur. To claim so would, in fact, commit the fallacy of Division—wrongly attributing the strength of the group to the individuals.

Families as Democracies?

Examples of these Fallacies do not appear publically as frequently as others, but they do occur. A questioner challenged conservative columnist John Rosemond on the question of authoritative parenting. The question reads,

> You yourself have repeatedly said that parents should raise
> their children such that they are familiar and equipped to

deal with the real world. If the real world is democratic, then shouldn't American families be democracies?[28]

The question commits the Fallacy of Division, assuming that since the nation is governed as a democracy (by the way, it is not: it is a representative republic), then the institutions (in this case family) that make up that nation should function democratically as well. Rosemond has no trouble countering the fallacy: "The idea that the USA would be a 'better' democracy if its families were little democracies is baseless." Not only baseless, I must add, but logically unsound. Rosemond approaches the same criticism when he responds that "although the political process in the Unites States is reasonably democratic, our society is definitely not. Rather it is composed of institutions that are structured hierarchically.... Within them, persons of greater authority are found instructing, directing and dictating to persons of lesser authority." He points out that this holds true even within the "democratic" government itself: you cannot ignore laws you do not like in the name of "democracy," you must abide by the authoritarian principles of law. Nevertheless, from a logical point of view, we must reject the viewpoint that the democracy of the larger group (nation) must also apply to each member of that group (families). This view commits the fallacy, and thus does not reflect the truth.

Practical Notes

Many find it easy to confuse these two fallacies, Composition and Division. Here are some suggestions you may find helpful to keep them separate in your mind. To compose a group assuming the characteristics of its members is to commit the Fallacy of Composition. Conversely, to assume that the characteristics of a group divide out to each member is to commit the Fallacy of Division. So, to move from individuals to a group is to *compose*, thus *Composition*. To move from the group to individuals is to divide, thus *Division*. Composing begins with individuals; dividing begins with groups. I believe this provides a helpful way of remembering. If, however, you still find the two confusing, it will be enough to remember them together: that you cannot assume *either* that attributes transfer from individuals to a group or from a group to its members.

There are many expressions of these fallacies in human behavior. The evils of racism, sexism, and other related prejudices express these two fallacies in social ways. The beliefs that "all blacks are X, therefore this black man must be X" or that "a black family I knew was X, therefore the black race is X," and all similar claims fall into the categories of Composition or Division. Of course, few racists actually state their belief so clearly and categorically as this, but this is a valid logical representation of what occurs in practice. Stereotypes in general commit this fallacy (as well as False Analogy), because they create an abstract image that allegedly represents a group of people; the stereotype then allows others to classify individuals as members of that group, and then uncritically to apply aspects of that imaginary group to each alleged member of that group. This stretches the facts in the worst way: it not only deceives people, but misrepresents them, marginalizes and oppresses them. When fallacious argumentation masks racism and other unfounded prejudices, then the moral and ethical implications of logic become obvious.

STRAW MAN

Straw Man does not describe a unique classification of fallacy, but rather a fallacious practice of creating, in any way, a false caricature of another position. Thus, the Straw Man argument generally occurs in response to an already existing claim or position, although it can simply misrepresent an already existing fact. It is the fallacy of representation *par excellence*. It thrives by presenting an opponent's position as something resembling it, yet distorted, extreme, exaggerated, absurd, emaciated, and with its strongest aspects removed or rendered offensive in some way. The resulting claim, as presented, is thus very easy to counter and defeat. It is like setting up a straw man and knocking him down instead of taking on a real fighter. Thus the name, *Straw Man*.

A Paine-ful Fallacy

As an example, consider this tirade against the Bible written by Thomas Paine:

> Whenever we read the obscene stories, the voluptuous debaucheries, the cruel and torturous executions, and unrelenting vindictiveness, with which more than half the Bible is filled, it would be more consistent that we

called it the word of a demon, than the Word of God. It is a history of wickedness, that has served to corrupt and brutalize mankind; and, for my own part, I severely detest it, as I detest everything that is cruel.[29]

Aside from its overflow of other fallacies such as Epithet (which I have covered) and Abusive Ad hominem (which I shall cover in a later chapter), Paine's statement stands as one big Straw Man. While the Bible does contain some stories that can make us feel uncomfortable—the idea of divine retribution and blood sacrifice are not for the weak hearted—you can hardly represent the Bible, or even just the Old Testament, as "unrelenting vindictiveness" or "a history of wickedness," with any degree of accuracy or respectability. God certainly does vindicate His justice, yet He can hardly be called "vindictive," let alone "unrelenting." Since in most cases the justice of God falls upon those who have blatantly rejected the heart of the Old Testament law—"You shall not take vengeance, nor bear any grudge against the sons of your people, but you shall love your neighbor as yourself; I am the Lord" (Lev. 19:18)—we can quite easy to accept the occasions of God's wrath as just and good. The Bible is not a "history of wickedness," but rather a history of God dealing—in grace and mercy as well as judgment—with a world full of *wicked people*. If Paine truly detested "everything that is cruel," then he might have at least paid lip service to even the harshest of God's works as efforts at setting things right in a cruel world. Did Paine truly believe in the title of his work, "The Age of Reason," he might also have tried to employ reason and logic to tame the "unrelenting vindictiveness" of his own tongue. Modern day proponents of atheism and critics of religion have made little progress in this area either.

The Straw Man is perhaps the most common of all fallacious encounters. It takes a particular type of mental lapse to commit most types of fallacies. They represent distinct failures of mind, will, or heart. Straw Men however, represent the general tendency of fallen man to avoid representing our opponents in their full vigor. Instead of facing up to the full truth, a Straw Man evades it by creating a caricature of it. Instead of looking truth in the face, it diverts attention to a false representation of truth, yet in the name of intellectual pursuit. Thus Straw Man is an evasion tactic and a diversion tactic. It ultimately expresses fear that our opponent's position may have some merit, and thus betrays an intellectual cowardice to face that position squarely. It also fears that an audience may be persuaded by strength of the opponent's real position, and thus fails to trust in God's truth, the power of His Spirit to convert, His providence to bring such conversions to pass, and finally His command to bear accurate witness even if no conversions follow.

This is the strength of the Straw Man—it relies on psychology and propaganda rather than truth. The psychological aspect pertains both to the one making the argument and to those listening. Many arguers value winning the argument more highly than arriving at truth or learning. But advancing against tough arguments requires much learning, lots of practice, lots of humility and patience. Those who merely desire to win usually have few if any of these character qualities. Even those who do possess such character may nevertheless succumb to the temptation to slander their opponents for public gain. As a result, many arguers tend to cut corners by misrepresenting their opponents' viewpoints. By presenting the opposing argument as lifeless, weak, and lightweight, the debater can easily dispense of it. If the audience before which he presents harbors some inclination or predisposition to want to hear his particular conclusion—even though he arrive at that conclusion in a fallacious manner—then the Straw Man, sadly, will likely succeed. Willing ignorance compounds itself with self-deception, but both will only succeed for a while. Both will incur the judgment of God.

Dawkins Taking Paine's

Very similar to Thomas Paine's outburst above concerning the Bible, the following now-infamous line from the atheist Richard Dawkins uses the whole hay stack to construct a Goliath of a Straw Man:

> The God of the Old Testament is arguably the most unpleasant character in all of fiction: jealous and proud of it; a petty, unjust, unforgiving control-freak; a vindictive, bloodthirsty ethnic cleanser; a misogynistic, homophobic, racist, infanticidal, genocidal, filicidal, pestilential, megalomaniacal, sadomasochistic, capriciously malevolent bully.[30]

Like Paine's fallacy-laden scarecrow, Dawkins' comment stands bristling with Abusive Ad Hominem and name-calling Epithet, all of which work together to represent the God of the Old Testament as something decidedly more extreme, distorted, and maligned than the Old Testament reveals. In some cases, and like most Straw Men, Dawkins' description holds enough similarity to make a connection with reality (in every lie there remains some element of truth, else it would be completely unbelievable). For example, God is in fact omnipotent and provident, meaning that He is all-powerful and controls history according to His will. He is, in fact, *in control*. But does this mean Dawkins correctly labels God a "control-freak"? Of course not. "Control-freak" is an extreme caricature which only appropriately applies to some *humans* who *wish* to interfere and control everyone else's business *when they should not do so*. The God of the Bible *by the nature of His existence and character* is *in fact* in control *and should be*. Control is not an anxiety or a lust that God has, it pertains to Him naturally due to the fact that He is God. Again, this is perhaps what makes atheists most angry: God is in control and they are not.

In some cases, Dawkins' rhetoric swerves from distortion into the just plain false. Is God "unforgiving"? Granted, God did exercise his wrath on many occasions, but He also gave second and third chances to many of the frankly undeserving. "Forgiving" is a bedrock of God's character (Ex. 34:6–9). Forgiveness undergirded the sacrificial system of the Old Testament (Lev. 4) and the New (Heb. 9:12–15, 28). The theme flows through all of God's redemptive history (2 Chron. 7:14; Is. 1:16–18; Jer. 31:31–34). Dawkins presents the exact opposite of the case. To make such a drastic misrepresentation is to declare oneself uninterested in truth.

Dawkins even realizes a weakness in the description he gives of God, and he states, "It is unfair to attack such an easy target."[31] But he apparently believes that his hyperbolic ridicule of Yaweh presents an accurate picture, and thus cannot see that the weakness he senses in his definition belies a Straw Man of cosmic proportions. He quickly and candidly offers to tackle the God question more fairly, saying, "I am not attacking the particular qualities of Yaweh, or Jesus, or Allah,... Instead I shall define the God Hypothesis more defensibly," and then gives a broader, more general definition of "God." We must abandon any hopes, however, that Dawkins would abide by this professed integrity but a few pages later as he returns to his Straw Man and decries the monotheistic religion of the Jews as "originally a tribal cult of a single, fiercely unpleasant God, morbidly obsessed with sexual restrictions, with the smell of charred flesh, with his own superiority over rival gods and with the exclusiveness of his chosen desert tribe."[32]

Some day, Dawkins will find his misrepresentation corrected as he views the Supreme Judge Himself face-to-face. The chaff (and the Straw) will be separated from the wheat.

Sam Harris: End of Faith, Beginning of Fallacy

Another atheist, Sam Harris, has erected a Straw Man, not only to attack God Himself, but to unduly criticize religious people. He writes,

> What can be said of the nuclear brinkmanship between India and Pakistan if their divergent religious beliefs are to be "respected"? There is nothing for religious pluralists to criticize but each country's poor diplomacy—while, in truth, the entire conflict is born of an irrational embrace of myth. Over one million people died in the orgy of religious killing that attended the partitioning of India and Pakistan. The two countries have since fought three official wars, suffered a continuous bloodletting at their shared border, and are now poised to exterminate one another with nuclear weapons simply because they disagree about "facts" that are every bit as fanciful as the names of Santa's reindeer.[33]

This is just one more example from that prolific compiler of fallacies, Sam Harris. His 2004 runaway best-seller *The End of Faith* leveled the charge that religious faith is completely unnecessary for, and quite dangerous to, human existence. Sam's overarching thesis includes the idea that religious faith in general (meaning that of all religions) is the very key element of religion that allows and leads its adherents to commit all kinds of atrocities. In order to maintain his thesis, however, he must often distort the facts in many cases. In this effort, Sam rarely misses any opportunity to smear, blur, suppress, exaggerate, or otherwise misrepresent the role of religious faith in *causing* radical behavior.

I have chosen this example in order to illustrate just *how true* a series of facts can be while the conclusion drawn from them remains exaggerated and fallacious. Sam correctly mentions the level of brutality throughout the series of Indo-Pakistani Wars beginning in 1947. But with the mere addition of the words "constant bloodletting" he creates a Straw Man which implies that the wars have raged without end for sixty years now. In truth, the mass of atrocities pertain to the few outbreaks of war, though continual tensions and sporadic terrorism have marked the border.

Even more egregiously, Sam makes the claim—partaking as well of the Fallacy of Reductionism—that, "in truth, the entire conflict is born of an irrational embrace of myth." Here we have another example of the great degree of truth Sam presents: the "myths" of Islamic and Hindu/Secular faiths do lie at the very heart of this conflict. The nation of Pakistan was *created* because its people were Muslims and wanted to divide from non-Islamic Indian rule. Yet it is hardly true to say that the entire conflict is born only because of embracing irrational religious tenets. Yes, the Pakistanis are Muslim and the Indians are mostly Hindu, but there are many more reasons that fuel age-long wars.

Land, race, resources, pride, injustice, retribution, and revenge can all motivate hatred irrespective of one's religion (or non-religion). It is in fact worth noting that one of the primary Indian leaders during the early part of this blood-bathed epoch, Jawaharlal Nehru, drew his political and philosophical inspiration from the decidedly atheist philosopher Bertrand Russell, and his revolutionary inspiration from the communism of the atheists Stalin and Mao.[34] Nehru's daughter and successor even more firmly entrenched herself as a leftist, anti-Hindu, and favored an alliance with the atheistic Soviet Union.[35] That Sam presents the cause of these wars as solely an expression of religious faiths distorts reality and of human nature beyond farce. It is an example of atheistic fundamentalism creating fallacies in order to perpetuate itself.

Sam realizes the extremity of his statements (and he makes many such statements throughout his writing), and he is at least consistent in upholding his extremeness. After relating a graphic description of war atrocities from one reporter, Sam holds the line, "The cause of this behavior was not economic, it was not racial, and it was not political.... The only difference between these groups consists in what they believe about God."[36] While it is true that Pakistan was created and now exists as independent because of its Islamic faith, it is by no means the case that the *only difference* between them is their beliefs about God. To maintain this while purposefully denying the many economic, political, and racial aspects of the countries is to behave as badly, logically, as the radicals who perpetuate the wars. It is to suppress information in order to further a personal ideology. This is Sam's intellectual *jihad*.

This example interests me because, as a Christian, I have no real incentive to take the side of either a Muslim or Hindu simply because they are Muslim or Hindu. From my perspective, both sides need conversion. I agree with Sam that we must accept and criticize the full extent to which religion has played a fundamental and central role in starting and perpetuating these atrocities. Anyone who denies the religious aspect must be asleep intellectually and morally, or perhaps has their research funded by the government. Yet, we cannot follow Sam's Reductionism and blame only religion, nor accept the religious aspect of the case as "further evidence" that we should abhor religious faith *in general*. To go to this extreme is no better than the extremists Sam wants to criticize. The Straw Man here comes at two points: first, in that Sam misrepresents the conflict as solely religious and nothing else. Secondly, Sam claims that "religious pluralists" criticize nothing but the two countries' lack of diplomacy. Most scholars of the conflict do, in fact, recognize the religious aspects of the conflict. What really bothers Sam, however, is that they look at other reasons also, and do not follow his fallacious method of blaming *everything* on religion. Sam has misrepresented both the conflict itself, and the scholars who study it.

I must also add that the extremist anti-faith view itself creates problems, and itself cannot eradicate the premeditated violence and prejudice as Sam seems to suggest. Because he maintains his thesis in such a way, he sees *all* religious faith as potentially dangerous. Worse yet, he sees "belief" in itself as an inevitable wellspring of action, and thus *some beliefs* as so deadly we should seek them out and forcibly remove them. He shockingly claims, "Some propositions are so dangerous that it may even be ethical to kill people for believing them.... If they cannot be captured, and they often cannot, otherwise tolerant people may be justified in killing them in self-defense."[37] More shockingly, Sam retained thousands of followers after writing this. Apparently "religious faith" is not the only wellspring of bloodthirstiness, if indeed it primarily is at all.

A Millennial Straw Man

But atheists are not the only ones liable to creating Straw Men—by no means. Famous Christians in modern times have done so as well. The well-known prophecy writer Hal Lindsey set up the following Straw Man:

> There used to be a group called "postmillennialists." They believed that Christians would root out the evil in the world, abolish godless rulers, and convert the world through ever-increasing evangelism until they brought about the Kingdom of God on earth through their own efforts.[38]

Based on popular appearances and not informed opinions, many Christians at the time (1970) accepted Lindsey's suggestion that postmillennialists belonged to a past era. The claim did hold some truth, as postmillennialists had largely died out after the two World Wars. But they did, however, still exist. For example, both Loraine Boettner's *The Millennium* (1957) and J. Marcelus Kik's *An Eschatology f Victory* (part of which appeared as early as 1948) were both available expressions of postmillennialism from well-known, Bible-believing scholars.

In addition to this, Lindsey also perpetuated a popular caricature of postmillennialism that had grown to be perceived as a liberal humanist belief. Thus he added the pernicious phrase "through their own efforts." While some—perhaps many—liberal "Social Gospel" Christians believed this way, it hardly characterizes the position historically, and certainly does not form a necessary tenet of postmillennialism. As orthodox holders of the doctrine would argue, God triumphs in history by the power of His Holy Spirit—not human efforts. Orthodox postmillennialists no more believe in bringing about the Kingdom by their own works than they believe in salvation by their own works.

Using such Straw Man fallacies to deny rival positions, Lindsey succeeded in perpetuating a popular myth that historical decline somehow disproved the optimistic view of postmillennialism. It was a widely held belief at the time, as Merrill Unger attests, "This theory, largely disproved by the progress of history, is practically a dead issue."[39] That Lindsey's and others' criticism rested merely on the temporary shift of history should signal the fallacy to any Christian, because the primary interpreter of the Bible must be the Bible, not current events. This error led one writer to complain of interpreters like Lindsey as "newspaper exegetes."[40] Nevertheless, even before the time Lindsey wrote, a growing number of Christians have seen the biblical merits of the optimistic view of postmillennialism and have made the switch. That they were never neither extinct nor all liberals exposes Lindsey's comment as a Straw Man (and, in fact, a very Hasty Generalization).

A Gay Straw Man

Speaking of liberal Christians, they have a favorite Straw Man tactic of their own. They will often quote Scripture in support of leftist political positions but leave out important aspects, verses, etc., which contradict the interpretation they want you to accept. This type of Straw Man some writers call the Fallacy of Suppressed Information, though I think Straw Man covers it well enough. An example of this appears in an article by former president Jimmy Carter addressing homosexuality. He writes,

> The apostle Paul makes it plain that homosexual tendencies, along with other temptations, should have been resisted: "Be not deceived; neither fornicators, nor idolaters, nor adulterers, nor effeminate, nor abusers of themselves with mankind, nor thieves, nor covetous, nor drunkards, nor revilers, nor extortioners, shall inherit the kingdom of God." (1 Corinthians 6: 9,10). *Then he immediately goes on to say that all these acts had been forgiven.*[41]

With this mention of forgiveness Mr. Carter apparently assumes he deflates the conservative Christian's case. In actuality, however, he misrepresents Paul's point. If you know your Bible, you will already have spotted the crucial aspects that Carter suppresses. Paul wrote to a specific audience *of Christians*. Of course, these Christians had received forgiveness for these sins, even egregious sins like homosexuality. But they had also stopped living according to those sins, and certainly would not have approved when their culture or government exalted or specially treated such behavior (which did prevail around them). Most importantly, Paul did not preach a blanket forgiveness of these sins, but rather only to those Christians who had repented, submitted to baptism, and committed to follow Christ. In fact, for those who had once repented, yet slipped back into sexual immorality, Paul dealt harshly, even by banning them from the church until they repented (1 Cor. 5:1–5). Paul even scolds the rest of the church for not having condemned the sin themselves already (5:2).

I think Carter knows this about the Bible, but perhaps dislikes the wide support that the issue of homosexuality, when emphasized, helps conservatives draw from religious voters. As a liberal, Carter must combat this issue. In doing so he has to suppress some information. Along with this, he erects an even more obvious Straw Man: "We must make it clear that a platform of 'I hate gay men and women' is not a way to become president of the United States of America." What politician from any side has made "I hate gays" their platform? None. This is Carter's caricature of conservatives who oppose homosexuality. But opposing homosexuality is not the same as hating homosexuals, as Paul shows and conservative politicians show as well. It would be nice if liberals like Carter would represent conservatives in at least as good a light as they do homosexuals.

Dealing With Straw Men

If an opponent distorts argument or statement of your own into a Straw Man, then you must counter this by pointing out the error: "Your refutation misses the mark, for what you have pretended to refute is not *actually* my position. You have created a caricature of my argument and knocked it down, and thus you have not yet even addressed my actual statement." Keep him honest. Then proceed to give your position in all of its strength. The clear contrast between your actual position and the Straw Man should create a point of embarrassment for your fallacious critic. If the audience is on board with your opponent, then they are complicit in his fallacy, and your reply will chastise them as well. You may enlighten a few, especially any genuine seekers of truth.

The biggest reason, however, for being aware of the human propensity for Straw Men is to avoid creating them yourself. It is easy to set up tin cans and shoot them down. But if your enemy is an army tank—not a tin can—then it will do you little good to pretend he is a tin can. Likewise, it will profit you little to use weapons designed for knocking down tin cans. You need bigger weapons, more skill, and a stronger counter-argument. Face up to the real argument in all of its glory, in all of its greatest strength. Present your opponent's position in the best possible light. Maybe even go so far as to strengthen it where it could use strengthening. Then proceed to intellectually confront, surround, deleverage, dismantle, destroy. It would be better to face your opponent in his strength and achieve a stalemate, than it would be to defeat an intellectual effigy. If you defeat a Straw Man you can at best gain an empty and groundless fame. At worst you could be exposed as dishonest and lose all credibility. If, however, you meet your opponent squarely, you can at worst lose the argument but learn to revise your own position; you may learn to strengthen your position in an extended intellectual exchange. At best, you will defeat your enemy at the apex of his strength, thus completely obliterating his position and leaving him with nowhere to stand intellectually.

Some tips to avoid presenting a Straw Man are as follows. First, you must understand your opponent's position. You cannot properly reply to something you do not know; you cannot thoroughly respond to something you do not thoroughly understand; you cannot accurately counter something you do not accurately comprehend. Take the time and patience needed to learn what someone says before you play critic and try to shoot them down. You may, in fact, learn that you have much in agreement with them.

Secondly, you must make a commitment to honesty. The Ten Commandments have something to say about false witness, as I have discussed. They have nothing to say about us knowing everything and coming out on top of every intellectual exchange. It is more important to abide by the moral precepts of God's law than it is to win the argument. A commitment to truth will lead us to many intellectual triumphs, but it will require many learned lessons along the way as well. God requires that his children remain faithful but teachable. This requires a mind open to testing new ideas in the light of God's word, and it absolutely demands a heart supple enough to admit being wrong. It is the mark of a fool *to despise* learning, and *not to learn* from instruction (Prov. 1:7; 9:7–10). Anyone creating a Straw Man displays an interest in dishonest evasion rather than honest truth. A commitment to honesty will help overcome the temptation to intellectual cowardice.

Thirdly, once you have thoroughly understood your opponent's position, and you have resolved to be as painfully honest about presenting it as it requires, proceed to give your opponent's argument the clearest, most positive, most vigorous presentation it has ever received. In this way, your opponent will have no grounds to object. And, if you succeed in countering his position, he will have no excuse for retaining it.

FALLACY OF THE BEARD

The "Incremental" or "Continuum" Fallacy popularly receives the name "Fallacy of the Beard." This name comes from the difficulty of answering the question, "When is a beard a beard?" Does the first sign of stubble count as a beard? If not, why not? It is the *same hair*, after all, when it is a wee bit of whisker as when it's a full Grizzly Adams. Nevertheless, we find a distinct difference between a five-o'-clock shadow and a belly-length beard. A line must be drawn somewhere between the extremes. Defining exactly where to draw that line may prove difficult, but that does not warrant denying or fudging the clear difference between the extremes, or even increments towards those extremes. Thus the fallacy: denying the difference between degrees due to the difficulty in defining where the increments start and stop. We may well find difficulty distinguishing many of the shades of gray between black and white, but this hardship does not allow us to deny the distinction between black and white, or even between the shades of gray for that matter.

An interesting myth that illustrates this fallacy comes from the mischievous Norse god Loki. Loki made a bet with some dwarves with the stakes being the loser's head. Loki lost, but when the dwarves came to collect their gruesome prize, Loki protested that while they had a right to take his head, they had no such right to touch any part of his neck. So the intellectual trap was sprung. Unable to determine specifically where to draw the line between what was head and what was neck, the dwarves had to give up taking their prize. But they did not submit to the fallacy completely. Since they had a full and rightful claim to Loki's head, they sewed his mouth shut. Besides providing an illustration of the fallacy, this should serve as a warning to all would-be philosophers who hedge their bets on fallacies.

More realistic examples of this fallacy may include arguments about moral actions, the point at which life begins, determining when an addiction begins, and many similar problems. For example, an alcoholic might argue that his body can tolerate one drink. Once consumed, he might protest that since he can tolerate one, he can handle one more. This may become a refrain, but soon it will grow obvious that "one more" has led to one too many. The small increments add up, and the drug has cumulative effects in the body. There is a vast difference between one drink and ten: one makes a drink, the other a drunk. Addictions thrive on the idea of "just a little bit," or "just one more, then I'll quit." This pertains not only to alcohol and cigarettes, but to any drugs, eating, pornography, shopping, credit cards, and bad habits in general. The phrase, "Just once more won't hurt," capitulates to the Fallacy of the Beard.

Tax Shavings

Political speech can be filled with Continuum Fallacies, often leading to abuses of words like "rich," "poor," "middle class," and many others. By way of example, the U. S. Census Bureau defines the poverty level (2007) of a couple with one child as having income of $14,291 per year or less.[42] But politicians rarely refer to official definitions when they base their stump speeches on casually thrown out terms such as "rich" versus "poor." Especially in times of economic downturn, most people can identify with "poor" when trying to maintain their lifestyle. Pundits and actvists easily persuade millions by demonizing things like "tax cuts for the rich." After all, who would consider it fair to decrease the taxes of "rich" people while not doing so for "poor" people who can barely get by? Further, politicians and bureaucrats can easily manipulate tax brackets in order to extract more taxes from those deemed "rich" or "able to pay." They do so by simply pushing the dividing lines a little further: either by increasing taxes a few percentage points here or there on certain groups, or by sliding the line a little further between "rich" and "middle class," etc. "Just a little more won't hurt," reveals the politician's (and many voters') addiction to tax revenues.

What often happens in political discourse is that "rich" is quietly defined as something like "making more than $250,000 per year" and "poor" is left undefined, and not much is said of the vast group of people who fall in between. Since so few people fall into this "rich" category, not many object to taxing the "rich" more and more. The problem, however, is that the top 5% of earners in the U. S. (averaging $153,542 per year) already pay a whopping 61% of the tax burden.[43] The top 1% ($388,806/year) pay almost 40% of the taxes. In contrast, the bottom *50%* (a full *half* of U. S. income earners!) pay an insignificant 2.99% of the tax burden. This group includes those making $31,987 per year and less. In other words, even those *making more than twice the official poverty level* pay hardly any taxes in this country. In fact, almost 33% of all tax returns end up paying no tax at all.[44]

The facts, therefore, create a vastly different picture of U. S. tax policy. The "poor" already pay little to no taxes, so talking about "tax relief for the poor" misapplies the word "poor" for political gain. The truly "rich" already pay an overwhelmingly unfair proportion of the taxes—far more than most other groups combined. Tax cuts for the "rich" in this case are hardly "unjust" as many politicians would have us believe. "Just" and "fair" would be for *all groups* to pay an equal percentage, and thus tax cuts for the "rich" would likely be the fairest thing to do at this point.

The "One God Further" Fallacy

Incremental Fallacies do not appear too commonly, but they do pop up from time to time, often in obscure ways. Atheist Richard Dawkins provides us an example. He writes,

> I have found it an amusing strategy, when asked whether I am an atheist, to point out that the questioner is also an atheist when considering Zeus, Apollo, Amon Ra, Mithras, Baal, Thor, Wotan, the Golden Calf and the Flying Spaghetti Monster. I just go one god further.[45]

Consider Dawkins' fallacy with an analogy: You may safely pace off ninety-nine steps towards a cliff, but if the next step goes over the edge you might want quickly to reconsider your convictions about "one step further." By Dawkins' illogic as displayed in this example, every step is like the other, there is no difference. But this is obviously ludicrous. Ignoring any difference in denying God Almighty of the Bible and denying Zeus and the Flying Spaghetti Monster commits, among other fallacies, the Fallacy of the Beard. It also commits a Category Mistake and perhaps a False Analogy. But even if not—even if we had no evidence that the God of the Bible did not warrant a different category that these others—the fact that one can easily deny all the other gods alone does not justify denying one God further. Each *increment*—in this case each god—must stand or fall on his own merits.

In most public discourse, logic and definitions rarely enter the discussion. Impressions, appearances, emotions, and fear generally override factual analysis. But in order to faithfully follow God's commandments we must commit to bearing accurate witness—to analyze the facts, discern the truth, and tell the truth. Part of doing this includes questioning the use of words that fall on a continuum of definition, or that can have many increments or degrees of value. There may not be an "official" definition for the topic under discussion, but whether there is or not, you must have clear agreement on such terms for your discussion to have much meaning. Either abusing or allowing others to abuse words in this way commits the Continuum Fallacy, or the Fallacy of the Beard, and a sharp student will give such hairy definitions a good close shave.

NOTES

1. Richard A. Muller, "analogia," in *Dictionary of Latin and Greek Theological Terms: Drawn Principally from Protestant Scholastic Theology* (Grand Rapids, MI: Baker Books, 1958), 32.

2. Euclid, *Elements of Geomtetry*, Book 5, Definition 3, 6, ed. and trans. Richard Fitzpatrick, 2008; available online at http://farside.ph.utexas.edu/euclid/Elements.pdf; accessed November 11, 2008.

3. Quoted in S. Morris Engel, *With Good Reason: An Introduction to Informal Fallacies*, Fifth Ed. (New York: St. Martin's Press, 1994), 162.

4. "Of the True Greatness of Kingdoms and Estates," *Selected Writings of Francis Bacon*, ed. Hugh G. Dick (New York: The Modern Library, 1955) 83; quoted also in S. Morris Engel, *With Good Reason: An Introduction to Informal Fallacies*, 162–163.

5. Victor J. Stenger, *Not By Design*, quoted in David A. Noebel, *Understanding the Times: The Story of the Biblical Christian, Marxist/Leninist, and Secular Humanist Worldviews* (Manitou Springs, CO: Summit Press, 1991), 128.

6. I. J. Good, "Speculations Concerning the First Ultraintelligent Machine," *Advances in Computers* (1965) 6:33; See http://en.wikipedia.org/wiki/I._J._Good, accessed December 30, 2008.

7. Stanley L. Jaki, *Brain, Mind and Computers* (New York: Herder and Herder, 1969).

8. Jaki, *Brain, Mind and Computers*, 17.

9. Quoted in Jaki, *Brain, Mind and Computers*, 23.

10. Jaki, *Brain, Mind and Computers*, 250–251.

11. Betty Friedan, *The Feminine Mystique* (New York: Dell Publishing, 1963), 294, 296.

12. See the summarized criticism on http://en.wikipedia.org/wiki/The_Feminine_Mystique; accessed November 13, 2008. Ihave picked up the following two footnotes from here.

13. Joanne Meyerowitz, "Beyond the Feminine Mystique: A Reassessment of Postwar Mass Culture, 1946–1958," *Journal of American History* 79 (March 1993): 1458.

14. Daniel Horowitz, "Rethinking Betty Friedan and the Feminine Mystique: Labor Union Radicalism and Feminism in Cold War America." *American Quarterly*, 48:1 (March 1996), 1–42.

15. Diana Butler Bass, "Southern Baptists take Scripture out of context," *The Atlanta Journal-Constitution*, June 14, 1998, D7.

16. Diana Butler Bass, "Southern Baptists take Scripture out of context," *The Atlanta Journal-Constitution*, June 14, 1998, D7.

17. See Joel McDurmon, *Manifested in the Flesh: How the Historical Evidence for Jesus Refutes Modern Mystics and Skeptics* (Powder Springs, GA: American Vision, 2007), 76–77; and N. T. Wright, *What Saint Paul Really Said: Was Paul of Tarsus the Real Founder of Christianity* (Grand Rapids: Eerdmans, and Cincinnati, OH: Forward Movement Publications, 1997), 55–57.

18. Karl Marx, "Theses on Feuerbach," *Basic Writings on Politics and Philosophy: Karl Marx and Friedrich Engels*, ed. Lewis F. Feuer (Garden City, NY: Anchor Books, 1959), 244.

19. See N. S. Timasheff, *Religion in Soviet Russia: 1917–1942* (New York: Sheed and Ward, 1942), 58–94; René Fueloep-Miller, *The Mind and Face of Bolshevism: An Examination of Cultural Life in Soviet Russia* (New York: Harper Torchbooks, 1965), 185–222; and James D. Bales, *Communism: Its Faith and Fallacies, an Exposition and Criticism* (Grand Rapids, MI: Baker Books, 1962), 176–178.

20. See "Manifesto of the Communist Party," *Basic Writings on Politics and Philosophy: Karl Marx and Friedrich Engels*, 24–26.

21. Matthew Chapman, plenary session at "Crystal Clear Atheism," Atheist Alliance International Convention, Crystal City, VA, September 29, 2007.

22. This helpful example, and its following coverse, is provided by S. Morris Engel, *With Good Reason: An Introduction to Informal Fallcies*, 5th Ed. (New York: St. Martin's Press, 1994), 114.

23. Imanuel Geiss, *Zukunft als Geschichte: Historisch-politische Analysen und Prognosen zum Untergang des Sowjetkommunismus, 1980-1991* (Stuttgart: Franz Steiner Verlag, 1998), 101.

24. Marek Jan Chodakiewicz, "Miracle of Solidarity Ended Communism: Polish Patriots Changed History 25 Years Ago," *Human Events*, September 26, 2005; available at http://www.freerepublic.com/focus/f-news/1492257/posts, accessed December 1, 2008.

25. Andrew Nagorski, "After Pope John Paul II: Look to Home," *The New Republic*, April 18, 2005; available at http://info-poland.buffalo.edu/classroom/JPII/nag.html, accessed December 1, 2008.

26. Marek Jan Chodakiewicz, "Miracle of Solidarity Ended Communism: Polish Patriots Changed History 25 Years Ago."

27. Marek Jan Chodakiewicz, "Miracle of Solidarity Ended Communism: Polish Patriots Changed History 25 Years Ago."

28. Quoted in John Rosemond, "Should families be democracies? No way," *The Atlanta Journal-Constitution*, January 13, 2002, M6.

29. Thomas Pain, "The Age of Reason," *Selections from the Writings of Thomas Paine*

(New York: Carlton House, no date), 200–201.

30. Richard Dawkins, *The God Delusion* (New York: Houghton Mifflin, 2006), 31.

31. Richard Dawkins, *The God Delusion*, 31.

32. Richard Dawkins, *The God Delusion*, 37.

33. Sam Harris, *The End of Faith: Religion, Terror, and the Future of Reason* (New York: W. W. Norton and Co., 2005), 26–27.

34. Paul Johnson, *Modern Times: The World from the Twenties to the Nineties* (New York: HarperPerennial, 1991), 472–472.

35. Paul Johnson, *Modern Times: The World from the Twenties to the Nineties*, 568.

36. Sam Harris, *The End of Faith: Religion, Terror, and the Future of Reason*, 27.

37. Sam Harris, *The End of Faith: Religion, Terror, and the Future of Reason*, 52–53.

38. Hal Lindsey, *The Late Great Planet Earth* (Grand Rapids: Zondervan, 1970), 176.

39. Quoted in R. J. Rushdoony, "Introduction," to J. Marcelus Kik, *The Eschatology of Victory* (Presbyterian and Reformed Publishing Co., 1971), vii.

40. R. J. Rushdoony, "Introduction," to J. Marcelus Kik, *The Eschatology of Victory*, viii.

41. Jimmy Carter, "Judge Not," *The Atlanta Journal/The Atlanta Constitution*, February 27, 1996, A17; emphasis added.

42. The figure changes based on the number of children and people living together in a household.

43. National Tax Payers Union, "Who Pays Taxes? See Who Pays What,"; available at http://www.ntu.org/main/page.php?PageID=6, accessed December 5, 2008.

44. National Tax Payers Union, "Who Doesn't Pay Taxes?"; available at http://www.ntu.org/main/page.php?PageID=155, accessed December 5, 2008.

45. Richard Dawkins, *The God Delusion*, 53.

Fallacies of Property

CHAPTER 11

"Breaking Boundaries": Fallacies of Property

By fallacies of "Property" I do not mean property in the sense of land and real estate, though that may make a helpful metaphor. "Property" here refers to the rightful attributes of any object or idea, and as well to the rightful boundaries of a given fact, theory, or truth. In other words, informal Fallacies of Property break necessary *rules*—rules for defining truth itself, and *rules for deriving rules* themselves as well.

Every worldview assumes *some* standards for these rules. As I mentioned under Worldview Fallacies, a naturalistic standard destroys communication and ethics. This chapter deals with two Fallacies of Property that flow out of the naturalistic worldview due to its breaking of God's boundaries for truth. These fallacies appear frequently in the arguments of recent atheists and skeptics. The first of the two, the "Is"-"Ought" Fallacy, attempts to ground ethics and morals in naturalism. Very serious problems result, and yet naturalists still work very hard, and claim to succeed, in accounting for moral directives on a naturalistic basis. I will show you how their assays remain fallacious. The second fallacy, Category Mistakes, pertains to definitions and classification when naturalists attempt to talk about God. The errors here have serious consequences as well although most of the instances of this fallacy stand out so obviously as to appear almost comical. In each case, exposing the root assumption of naturalism will help you unravel the fallacy, overcome the seductions of naturalism, and respond to the critic.

The "Is"-"Ought" Fallacy

The "Is"-"Ought" fallacy involves the attempt to derive moral directions from descriptions of nature. Why does this commit a fallacy? Because it ignores the fundamental characteristic that distinguishes what morals, ethics, and values are: they prescribe how society *ought* to be, as *opposed* to how it naturally and currently *is*. The fallacy lies in assuming that allegedly impersonal nature can direct personal and social standards of living. You cannot derive an "ought" from an "is."

Ex-Huming Hume

Philosophers generally credit this insight to the Scottish thinker David Hume (1711–1776), who attempted to provide a Newtonian-scientific account of human morality. He writes,

> In every system of morality which I have hitherto met with, I have always remarked that the author proceeds for some time in the ordinary ways of reasoning, and establishes the being of a god, or makes observations concerning human affairs; when of a sudden I am surprised to find that instead of the usual copulations of propositions *is* and *is not*, I meet with no proposition that is not connected with an *ought* or an *ought not*. This change is imperceptible, but is, however, of the last consequence. For as this *ought* or *ought not* expresses some new relation or affirmation, it is necessary that it should be observed and explained; and at the same time that a reason should be given for what seems altogether inconceivable, how this new relation [ought] can be a deduction from others [is], which are entirely different from it.[1]

Hume, however, did not add this note as a critique of naturalistic accounts of morality, for he himself attempted to construct such a system. Instead, he wrote against arbitrary or non-existent justifications for assumed morals. He concluded this section of his work persuaded "that this small attention would subvert all the vulgar systems of morality and let us see that the distinction of vice and virtue is not founded merely on the relations of objects, nor is perceived by reason."[2]

Nevertheless, Hume also realized that nature in general could not provide a foundation for morals, nor could it define the boundaries of good and evil. No matter how you understand the word "nature," it cannot provide a foundation for "ought" statements.

> [N]othing can be more unphilosophical than those systems which assert that virtue is the same with what is natural, and vice with what is unnatural. For in the first sense of the word "nature," as opposed to miracles, both vice and virtue are equally natural; and in the second sense, as opposed to what is unusual, perhaps virtue will be found to be the most unnatural. At least it must be owned that heroic virtue, being as unusual, is as little natural as the most brutal barbarity. As to the third sense of the word [as opposed to artificial], it is certain that both vice and virtue are equally artificial and out of nature.... It is impossible, therefore, that the character of natural and unnatural can ever, in any sense, mark the boundaries of vice and virtue.[3]

So how does Hume transcend nature as a foundation of morality? I do not think he ever did. Despite treating the topic at length he concluded on a very vague note, that human morals arise from within us, find expression in our feelings and reactions to pleasure and pain, and receive stimulation and development through sympathy with other people and characters.[4] Yet what are pleasure and pain but *natural* reactions? What is sympathy with other people but a natural relation of objects? Unless by "character" he means the divinely revealed perfect person of Jesus Christ (highly unlikely), I find Hume's attempt to escape his own "is-ought" trap extraordinarily feeble. Could he not see the fact that what he argues applies just as strongly to his own conclusion as it does to "nature" in general? His conclusion, therefore, commits the fallacy of Special Pleading (a fallacy I deal with later).

Perhaps you can see how the worldview fallacy of naturalism falls prey to the "Is"-"Ought" Fallacy as well. Or, you could equally say that the "Is"-"Ought" Fallacy repeats the errors of naturalism: assuming that all things, including morality, have a natural explanation. We can shrug of Hume's weak attempt at explaining morality, and yet thank him heartily for showing how it is "unphilosophical" and "impossible" to find a basis for morals in mere descriptions of the natural.

A Moore Better Fallacy

Another philosopher, G. E. Moore, expanded on what Hume began. He argued Hume's thesis more consistently and said that ethical decisions cannot rest upon pleasure and pain, for these reactions arise from nature as well. Moore calls this the "naturalistic fallacy," and explains that if a man merely defines the word "good" according to any natural standard he commits the fallacy: "[I]f he confuses 'good,' which is not in the same sense a natural object, with any natural object whatever, then there is reason for calling that a naturalistic fallacy."[5] While Moore recognized that "How 'good' is to be defined, is the most fundamental question in all of Ethics,"[6] he strictly refused to allow any naturalistic definition of the term. This rejection comes forcefully:

> My objections to Naturalism are then, in the first place, that it offers no reason at all, far less any valid reason, for any ethical principle whatsoever; and in this it already fails to satisfy the requirements of Ethics, as a scientific study. But in the second place I contend that, though it gives a reason for no ethical principle, it is a *cause* of the acceptance of false principles—it deludes the mind into accepting ethical principles, which are false; and in this it is contrary to every aim of Ethics.[7]

Whatever Moore may have personally postulated for ethics beyond this point bears little consequence for what he here provides: the total destruction of the naturalistic view of ethics. Naturalism not only cannot generate foundations for ethics, or even ethical statements, it actually creates a delusion for those who try.

By applying Hume's idea consistently, Moore moved later philosophers to look somewhere besides nature when seeking a basis of our moral consciousness. This effort can lead logically to only two answers: (1) morality has a supernatural origin, or (2) there is no such thing as morality. I have already described how naturalism devolves into relativism, nihilism, and meaninglessness—a position that denies that values and ethics have any meaning. I mentioned Nietzsche in regard to a bold denial of all values. A more recent but no less consistent atheist, A. J. Ayer, has confirmed the same logical conclusion that Nietzsche popularized. Beginning with naturalism and following a rigorous standard of "evidence only" thinking, Ayer inevitably concludes of ethics:

> We find that ethical philosophy consists simply in saying that ethical concepts are pseudo-concepts and therefore unanalysable.... There cannot be such a thing as ethical science, if by ethical science one means the elaboration of a true "system" of morals. For we have seen that, as ethical judgements are mere expressions of feeling, there can be no way of determining the validity of any ethical system, and, indeed, no sense in asking whether any such system is true.[8]

There you have it: instead of seeking for the metaphysical and religious foundations of ethics, just deny that ethics exist at all. Argue that ethics reduce to mere subjective feelings and that to even study ethics is to pursue a non-subject. With this decided, Ayer determines that the only study left for ethics involves the study of individuals' feelings and reactions, and this study "is a task for the psychologist."[9] Philosophy, according to this view, should forever abandon values, morals, and ethics.

This conclusion I take as an admission and confirmation that naturalism precludes morality; it destroys the possibility of developing, recognizing, and communicating ethical values. You cannot derive an "ought" from an "is," and since we can observe only the "is," it makes no sense to even mention the "ought." Consistent and honest naturalists like Ayer admit this logical outcome.

Recent Atheist Ignorance: Sade Calls Out Sam

More recent popular atheists, however, tend to ignore the logical conclusions of their position, and thus run into the "Is"-"Ought" Fallacy in the very attempt to refute it. For example, Sam Harris ventures a naturalistic basis of morality and asserts,

> We can easily think of objective sources of moral order that do not require the existence of a lawgiving God. For there to be objective moral truths worth knowing, there need only be better and worse ways to seek happiness in this world.... Everything about human experience suggests that love is more conducive to happiness than hate is.[10]

Sam's view fails by the same criticism I have offered above and in the preceding chapter. "Happiness" is hardly an objective principle. In fact, it may represent the *most* subjective aspect of human experience: individual approval or taste. How can you measure "happiness" in order to provide scientific assessments that apply equally to everyone? Impossible. What makes one person "happy" saddens, annoys, infuriates another. Even if one experience makes two individuals happy, we have no way of guaranteeing that they experience anything like an equal amount of happiness. We have no way of guaranteeing even that one person's *claim* to be happy indicates that he actually is happy. This puts the lie to any claim about "objective" happiness. No such thing exists if we have no overarching Guarantor and Judge of human experiences.

We can further illustrate the subjectivity of this position in that Sam's claim that "love is more conducive to happiness than hate is," Begs the Question. What, after all, *is* "love"? Sam provides no definition; any definition he could provide from within his naturalistic worldview must rest on subjective human evaluations of human experience, and therefore must simply circle around on itself. What makes us happy? Love? Well then, what is love? That which makes us happy? And what makes us unhappy? Hate? And what is hate? The natural man simply labels as "bad" or "hate" anything that impedes his happiness, and thus "hate" is that which makes us unhappy. Again, these things could vary from person to person. Ultimately, in the Sam's naturalistic world, every personal determines his own values arbitrarily, thus reasoning in a fallacious circle.

The biggest argument against the standards of "nature" or "happiness" comes once again from the consistent atheists of years past. The clearest refutation of natural morality appears in the person of the Marquis de Sade (1740–1814). Sade held high contempt for religion and morality, and he constructed his own philosophy of life from only nature. To his fellow Frenchmen he wrote, "what should we, who have no religion, do with law?"[11] Denying God, Sade proclaimed that the "foremost law of your new government" should be only "Nature, dictating vices and virtues to us."[12]

The results—which he followed with logical rigor and then lived according to—turned out horridly. R. J. Rushdoony is one of the few historians who have had the stomach to read Sade's extensive writings. He summarizes:

> The morality of love for one's neighbor was for Sade, absurd. Sade opposed capital punishment, and laws against murder. The only proper morality for a republican government was its self-perpetuation. One can add that it was to exist to prevent the existence of Christianity and its laws: republican manners required immorality to demonstrate equality. All women should be the property of all men: there should be *no exclusiveness* in any sphere of life. He held that he had the right of possession over any woman, and "I have incontestable rights to the enjoyment of her; I have the right to force from her this enjoyment, if she refuse me it for whatever cause may be." This should be true of females from their early years. Sade favored incest: he wanted it made into law, and also sodomy. Savages are closest to Nature and the most ferocious, as all should be, Sade believed. Child-killing to avoid "over-population" he also favored.[13]

Sade himself ridiculed Sam's standard of "happiness" by his rigorously applied lust. He wrote,

> True wisdom, my dear Juliette, does not consist in repressing our vices, because these vices constitute almost the only *happiness* in our life to wish to repress them would be to become our own executioners. But it consists in abandoning ourselves to them with such secrecy, and such extensiveness that we may never be caught out. Do not be afraid that this may diminish their delight: mystery adds to the pleasure. Moreover, such behavior ensures impunity, and is not impunity the most delicious nourishment of debauchery?[14]

Nietzsche consciously (and happily?) drew the implications as well: "'*There is nothing else on earth but immoral intentions and action*,' if we view things from the traditional and Christian perspectives, but, in reality, 'there is no such [thing] as a moral or an immoral action.'"[15]

The modern atheists realize that this fallacy traps them in an unpopular spot. Most of them do not want to take the unpopular route of Nietzsche, Sade, and others who deny any objective morality, or even that we can talk about morality, at all. To do so risks losing respectability with the billions of normal people who believe that such things as good and evil exist and that we "ought" to live accordingly. So some of the modern atheists (naturalists) actually deny the validity of the fallacy itself and argue that we actually *can* derive moral values from natural states. Of course, in order to remain consistent with their worldview *and* yet appear to retain a belief in popular morals, they *must* claim this. Rushdoony described such intellectual cowardice: "Many academicians are simply housebroken versions of Nietzsche."[16]

For example, Daniel Dennett has attempted forcefully to refute the "naturalistic fallacy," or what I have referred to as the "Is"-"Ought" Fallacy. Confronted with the fallacy he retorts defensively, "Well, so what?" He continues,

> If "ought" cannot be derived from "is," just what *can* "ought" be derived from? Is ethics an *entirely* "autonomous" field of inquiry? Does it float, untethered to facts from any other discipline or tradition? Do our moral explanations arise from some inexplicable ethics module implanted in our brains (or "hearts," to speak with tradition)? That would be a dubious skyhook [remember Dennett's arbitrarily defined "skyhooks"?] on which to hang our deepest convictions about what is right and wrong....
>
> From what can "ought" be derived? The most compelling answer is this: ethics must be *somehow* based on an appreciation of human nature—on a sense of what a human being is or might be, and on what a human being might want to have or want to be.[17]

Dennett's conclusion—"must be *somehow*"—is a naturalist's trick of desperation. He tries very hard, covers every philosopher, names names classical and contemporary, all in order to obscure the fact that he willingly, consciously ignores the supernatural answer to the question. Ethical values come from above nature and call nature (including man) to the image it ought to conform to. Yes, this involves human nature, but only in calling that fallen nature to become something higher, not as a prescriptive of the ideal it ought to conform to. Dennett's seemingly significant objection actually only carries weight if you *assume naturalism to begin with*. In short, he Begs the Question.

But this question-begging creates a problem. Only if the world needs no improvement to begin with can a description of how things naturally occur translate to a moral directive. Another way of looking at this is to say that if anything "ought" to be other than it "is," then describing how it is—despite studying it in the greatest detail—can only inform us of one way it ought *not* to be. The "ought" describes how nature needs to be changed; the "is" can only describe that which needs the changing. The "ought" must come from some other source than the fallen world around us.

This type of thinking led the Dutch theologian and polymath Abraham Kuyper to teach a distinction between two schools of thought:

> Must religion be *normal* or abnormal, i.e., *soteriological* [teaching salvation]? The distinction which I have in mind here is concerned with the question, whether in matter of religion we must reckon *de facto* with man in his present condition as *normal*, or as having fallen into sin, and having therefore become *abnormal*. In the latter case religion must necessarily assume a soteriological character. Now the prevailing idea, at present, favors the view that religion has to start from man as being *normal*.... [I]mperfect religious development continues to be the rule. But precisely in this slow and gradual progress from the lowest forms to the highest ideals, the development demanded by the normal view of religion contends that it has found confirmation.[18]

Delivering these lectures in 1898, Dr. Kuyper engaged the doctrines of man built on Darwinism and well anticipated the "crane" theories of men like Dennett. Kuyper continues:

Now, this whole theory is opposed by that other and entirely different theory, which,... maintains that the first man was created in perfect relations to God, *i.e.*, as imbued by a pure and genuine religion, and consequently explains the many low, imperfect and absurd forms of religion found in Paganism, not as the result of his creation but as the outcome of his Fall.[19]

These two views logically engender two opposite views of ethics which consequently imply vastly divergent ways of living. Rushdoony explains,

> If the God of Scripture is the Supreme Being, then His law-revelation and His incarnation in Christ define the truth. However, if Nature is ultimate, then the truth is whatever occurs in Nature, and the lie is whatever opposes Nature, i.e., Biblical law and morality. The truth meant for Sade and his successors murder, rape, incest, sodomy, etc. *Nothing in Nature requires the punishment of any such acts.*[20]

Sam Harris must openly admit this fact, and gives a similar confession as Sade: "There is, after all, nothing more natural than rape."[21] He quickly adds that no one would argue that rape is good simply "*because it may have had evolutionary advantages for our ancestors*,"[22] but he cannot provide an *ultimate* refutation of rape as natural and thus "conducive to happiness" in principle. Besides, the claim that "no one would argue that rape is good" ignores the facts: Sade and his followers obviously *did* exalt the act of rape as "good," perhaps even the highest good. They did so *because* they had no refutation of the act arising from nature, and unlike Sam, they did not pretend that they had one.

So, those Christian critics of atheism and naturalism who claim that "Without God, all things are permissible," have a very strong philosophical case despite the atheists' persuasive efforts. Without an overarching Judge and Lawgiver, every man can justify whatever he wants; he need only to convince others or take his depraved deeds underground to get away with them. As Dennett concluded above, ethics in a naturalistic world reduce to "what a human being might want to have or want to be." Thus, naturalism pits every man's *wants* against the others. The supreme court of the universe is not God's but man's will. Dennett unwittingly agrees with Sade's dictum, "what should we, who have no religion, do with law?," and with Nietzsche's "Will to Power" as guides for living.

The atheist A. J. Ayer himself also helps us refute the inconsistent atheists. "In short," he concludes, "we find that argument is possible on moral questions *only if some system of values is presupposed.*"[23] Of course, Ayer argues that any such presupposed system will ultimately arise from human feelings and thus have no logical validity. His conclusion, however, betrays the assumed nature of the ethical standards modern atheists assert. The air of authority with which they make their claims should strike us as all the more laughable in light of such an analysis.

I should note that sometimes nature and our moral ideas appear to overlap, leading naturalists like Dennett to confuse the order of the "ought" and the "is." The naturalist will observe, for example, bravery in action, and then come away from that observation thinking he has witnessed a virtue in a natural phenomenon; he thus feels he stands prepared to give a pure description of what "is" as a prescription for how others ought to behave. This, of course, simply conflates the matter, for how did the naturalist judge the particular action as "brave" and thus desirable to begin with. While we may rightly judge that we genuinely ought to value behavior that conforms to his natural description of bravery, nevertheless we do not ultimately derive this moral imperative *from* the description, but rather recognize the behavior as bravery based on our understanding of certain values that already exist. Our naturalist has not given us a "ought" from an "is," but rather a description of an already existing "ought" in action. The brave man is not a natural rule-maker, but a nice role model.

Category Mistakes

Category Mistakes refer to the improper attribution of some property to an object or concept to which such a property simply cannot belong, or it can refer to improperly assigning something to a group to which it does not belong. A "category" refers to a class or group of things or properties. A "Category Mistake," therefore, describes a logical mistake in classification or application of properties.

For example, the phrase "yellow banana" makes sense, because the property "yellow" does in fact apply to such an object as "banana." Likewise, to speak of "banana" as "fruit" makes sense because bananas belong to the class of things known as fruits. The phrase "infinite banana," however, commits a Category Mistake because the property "infinite" cannot logically apply to a finite object such as a banana. Likewise, to speak of "banana" as a type of "radial tire" also commits the fallacy because bananas do not belong to the same class of things as tires.

We could create many such examples. Perhaps the most outstanding example committed today occurs in the debate with modern atheists who make all kinds of attacks on the idea of God from within the limited standpoint of a naturalistic worldview. Naturalists particularly commit this fallacy as their assumption that all things must have a natural cause makes them susceptible to ignoring or dogmatically denying other possibilities.

A good example of this occurs in atheist Richard Dawkins' *The God Delusion*. Among the many amateur philosophical stunts in this atheistic tantrum appears his use of a quip made by 1920s atheist Bertrand Russell, known as the "parable of the celestial tea pot."[24] This story intends to prove that even though the existence of God cannot be *disproved*, it is still far from *likely*. Dawkins' warms to this idea as he admits that while one cannot completely disprove the existence of God, we still have no good reason to take Him seriously, any more than we have reason to believe in a "flying spaghetti monster" or an "invisible, intangible, inaudible unicorn."[25] He relies on Russell to demonstrate this. I will show you why Russell's tea pot, like Flew's buckets, holds no water.

The story as Russell told it, and as Dawkins affirms it, goes like this:

> If I were to suggest that between the Earth and Mars there is a china teapot revolving about the sun in an elliptical orbit, nobody would be able to disprove my assertion provided I were careful to add that the teapot is too small to be revealed even by our most powerful telescopes. But if I were to go on to say that, since my assertion cannot be disproved, it is an intolerable presumption on the part of human reason to doubt it, I should rightly be thought to be talking nonsense. If, however, the existence of such a teapot were affirmed in ancient books, taught as the sacred truth every Sunday, and instilled into the minds of children at school, hesitation to believe in its existence would become a mark of eccentricity and entitle the doubter to

the attentions of the psychiatrist in an enlightened age or of the Inquisitor in an earlier time.[26]

We find one of the silliest fallacies circulating among the atheists—in fact, one of their staple arguments these days—in this attempt to shift the "burden of proof" in the debate over God's existence. It has grown increasingly popular—and from what we have seen above, you can understand why—for the atheists from the start to assume their naturalistic worldview as *normal*, and refuse any theistic claim as a deviation from nature that must be "proven" (of course, what constitutes "proof" will factor heavily, as I will show below). "Atheism" they would claim, is not a worldview in itself, but merely the common-sense denial of the alleged "additional" and "extraordinary" belief in a god, over and above the natural world that we experience.

The Nature of the Matter

Russell's intellectual ingenuity almost certainly derived from the stalwart educational foundations he laid for himself during his university years. Part of an elite secret intellectual society at Cambridge—the "Apostles"—Russell would meet for late night discussions with the most brilliant minds of the era. Among intellectual giants the likes of John Maynard Keynes, Ludwig Wittgenstein, and Alfred North Whitehead, Russell expanded his mind debating such head-scratchers as, "Does Youth Approve of Age?," "Ought the Father to Grow a Beard?," and "Is this an Awkward Age?"[27] An historian of the era candidly recounts, "It was that early Edwardian failing of the Apostles trying to be clever for the sake of being clever and often when there was nothing to be clever about."[28]

But there was a real philosophical shortcoming among Russell's group. G. E. Moore, the same philosopher who helped describe the "Is"-"Ought" Fallacy above, delivered a paper to the peers boasting their ultimate belief in nature alone: "In the beginning was matter, and matter begat the devil, and the devil begat God."[29] Here we find the underlying force of Russell's skepticism: the classic belief in "materialism," that nothing exists except matter. Since God by definition is immaterial, then according to materialism He can't exist. Very simple, isn't it? Just define your universe so that it can hold no God, and *voila*, we have no evidence for God.

With this as his background, Moore went on to argue that "then there was the death, first of God, then of the devil, and matter was left as it was in the beginning."[30] Even if Moore spoke tongue-in-cheek, it shows the utter circularity of the materialistic worldview. If in the beginning you only have matter, then that is all you will ever have.

Perhaps this view fits many atheists' wishes, but it says very little about the naturalist's (and thus also the materialist's) philosophical rigor. With the phrase, "In the beginning" taken from the Bible, Moore reveals to us that the materialistic worldview, which is almost universally assumed by atheists today, depends no less on faith than the opening sentence of Holy Writ. And while the atheists assume their alleged "scientific" worldview as normal and thus superior to the Christian's, they cannot even consistently answer the most fundamental questions that arise for their own system: where do laws come from? Is there ultimate justice? Why even care about justice? Why is murder, theft, rape, etc., *wrong*? What exactly is *reason*? Is it material? It should not surprise us that the historian to wrote this account of Moore and Russell, *et al*, concluded, "They thought they were the equal of the German philosophers, yet none of them were in the same class."[31]

Once you expose the ultimate assumption of materialism, the claim that atheism relies on no worldview becomes laughable. It only removes the philosophical argument one step. The theist may simply reply, "Ok, supposing I grant your definition of atheism, please tell me *why you adhere to this definition*." If pushed to reveal the standard by which he judges that atheism is the norm, the atheist will ultimately have to reveal his materialism, or some other form of naturalism, at its root. If he does not, then he proves he either has little philosophical training, or does not care to reason honestly. Of course he will try desperately hard not to admit his materialism, for it signals the philosophical dead-end describe already. You will more likely hear diversions like that of Dawkins himself: "I shall suggest that the existence of God is a scientific hypothesis *like any other.*"[32]

Here the Category Mistake begins to grow obvious. "Like any other"? What does that mean? Press him further, and get him to answer this question. If he thinks honestly and consistently with his materialism, he will admit that he will only accept as "proof" finite, measurable, material evidences, and, of course, anything only finite and material automatically disqualifies God for consideration.

This is the evasive failure of the materialistic worldview to grapple honestly with the existence of God—and yet, this naturalism forms the standard by which modern atheists try to set themselves up as the supreme court which ultimately decides the matter. Once they assume materialism at the outset, there remains little sense in debating about "evidence." In order to accept only material evidence as grounds for argument, the theist would automatically surrender at the outset. Instead, he should point out the underlying assumption, and then combat the worldview resting on that assumption, not just the mere word-cloak of the name "atheism," at least not until he fully understands that atheism and divests its meaning of all pretenses.

The Creator-Creation Distinction

Once we distinguish between the different Categories involved here—one which includes created things, another which allows a Creator—then we can see that Russell's tea pot argument holds no water at all. It misses the point as widely as it is silly.

Russell's argument meant to address an issue called the "burden of proof." But if the terms of proof include only materialistic or naturalistic categories, then you could only ever prove the existence of a material God, and thus no God at all. As I have written elsewhere, this kind of limitation imposed by unbelief proves nothing except that if you set your bar low enough, you can achieve any philosophical goal.[33] This procedure simply will not do. It may free us from the fierce cosmic tyranny of orbital teapots, but it says absolutely nothing about the Triune God of Christianity, who belongs in an entirely different class of things than "all material objects." Once introduced, the distinction between Creator and Creation in Christian theology exposes the Category Mistake inherent in Russell's story.

This refutation applies equally to a related argument that the modern atheists like to use. They claim that no one believes in the gods of ancient mythology; all (or most) people are, therefore, "atheists" with regard to these gods. The atheists, including Dawkins, boast that they just "go one god further."[34] This rhetorical saccharin vaporizes in the steam of real philosophy, and it sweetens nothing. It simply places the Christian God in the same category as "Zeus, Apollo, Amon Ra, Mithras, Baal, Thor, Wotan, the Golden Calf and the Flying Spaghetti Monster,"[35] and thus once again commits a Category Mistake. Instead, the object in question requires proof commensurate with the *nature of the thing in question*. Thus atheists cannot rightly deny the existence of the God of Christianity by drawing gratuitous parallels to material objects like dizzy tea pots or frightening pastafarian creatures. Likewise, while we do not have space here to line them all up, the Christian God also qualitatively and categorically differs from all of the pagan gods one can list. One may rightly believe as "atheists" with regard to ninety-nine mythological gods, and yet remain completely unjustified in simply going "one step further," because that step crosses into a different category than all the others. If you are ninety-nine and a half paces from the edge of a cliff, and stride off those first ninety-nine with confidence, would you, therefore, based on mere prior experience, simply take that next step? Or would you take a long hard look at the abyss before you, and consider how different one "leap" of faith can vitally differ from another?

It will take more than an attempt to straw-man the definition of God into something farcical and only material, and then pretend to have ousted God from the universe. We can call this the "straw-god" fallacy (a special version of the Straw Man Fallacy described later). The real philosophical challenge remains to disprove an all-powerful God Who created the material universe, upholds it, and thus transcends the material universe. Such a God defies all attempts at measurement by finite standards,[36] or calls to any finite bar of judgment. For Him to stoop to meet such a standard would require Him automatically *to deny both His Sovereignty and His own existence*. The very act of submitting Himself for verification elevates something besides Him to the status of ultimate Judge and standard. Whether this standard be the will of man, Nature, a tea pot, or anything else merely natural, such a standard denies the God of the Bible *by definition*, and thus fallaciously, not by logical analysis.

So, the Christian need not fear the audacity, shock, or silliness of tea pot arguments. Rather, reject any such argument that refuses to tackle the existence of the kind of God who *created* tea, and the rest of the world for that matter. Expose the Category Mistake and establish fair terms for debate from the start. Once atheists become honest about this issue, they must re-establish the "burden of proof" more squarely, and the debate over God will move from the atheist's comfortable tea-room of materialism, to the *transcendental question* that it is.

Worldviews and Probability

Dawkins, however, following Russell, argues that since God is allegedly just like this teapot, then even though he cannot *disprove* God's existence, it is still much less likely than it is probable. Dawkins says, "[A]vailable evidence and reason may yield a probability far from 50 per cent."[37] We have already seen the fallacy behind Russell's teapot, which Dawkins starts with here, so how does the critique of that teapot apply to Dawkins' conclusion about probability?

Dawkins' naturalistic assumptions limit and rule his view of probability, just as they determine his fallacious definition and classification of God. It only stands to reason that if you presume only a natural world at the outset, then the most probable occurrence in that world can only be a natural occurrence. But that Begs the very Question under debate, does it not? Dawkins, like the other naturalists, merely defines God out of his mental world with mere words. It may make for a nice little chat over tea with an old chap, but not very careful thinking at all.

Probability, however, will tally quite differently in a materialist universe than in a Biblical universe. If we hold the atheist to a tougher logical standard, and do not allow him to impose his naturalistic beliefs on the question of God, then he will have to take seriously the possibility of something other than a natural explanation as the most probable one. As Jesus said, "With God, all things are possible" (Matt. 19:26; Luke 18:27). Obviously, if we assume from the outset that no God exists, then an explanation that involves God will not only be unlikely, but absurd and impossible. But if we prevent the atheist's arbitrary assumptions from ruling the argument, then the *most* probable answer will involve a supernatural God, and we will have to find a different way of approaching the question than through that very limited range of evidence that we can see, touch, smell, etc.

If the Christian makes the mistake of shifting into the arena of *naturalistic probability*, then he has already subjected the God of the Bible to a category which denies the very possibility of His existence. Probability, as the naturalist calculates it, deals only with empirical, sensory, phenomena. God by definition does not fit into this mold, so talking about Him in such a way which limits Him in those terms, denies Him at the outset. No wonder Russell, Dawkins, and other atheists love to talk about God in such a way. *Probability*, in this sense, is the devil's ill-fated prayer, and Dawkins—the self-dubbed "Devil's Chaplain"—kneels at its mention, chants it in rhythm, and crosses himself with its capital "P."

Conclusion

The popularity of the tea-pot argument illustrates how skepticism needs little intellectual rigor to satisfy its customers. A little creative ridicule, a little mythological image keeps them happy. At the intellectual root, however, these customers cannot stand God, and so they try to suppress the knowledge of Him at every turn, even by defining Him away with mere words. They try to reduce Him to something as superfluous as a celestial tea pot. Minimize Him, scrutinize Him, box Him in, trivialize Him—do whatever they can to suppress the knowledge of Him. They want to put Him in a bottle, like "I dream of genie." Problem is, the God described in the Bible and throughout Christian tradition will not fit in. The attributes ascribed to the Triune God of Scripture require the would-be critic to deal with God as God—Creator, Redeemer, King—and as nothing else, certainly not as any aspect of creation. They cannot liken Him to some orbital fantasy, then critique that fantasy, and then pretend they have said anything at all meaningful about the God of Scripture.

NOTES

1. David Hume, "Treatise of Human Nature" (Book III, Part 1, Section 1), *Approaches to Ethics: Representative Selections from Classical Times to the Present*, 2nd Ed., eds. W. T. Jones, et al. (New York: McGraw-Hill Book Company, 1969), 263.

2. David Hume, "Treatise of Human Nature" (Book III, Part 1, Section 1), *Approaches to Ethics*, 263–264.

3. David Hume, "Treatise of Human Nature" (Book III, Part 1, Section 2), *Approaches to Ethics*, 266.

4. See David Hume, "Treatise of Human Nature" (Book III, Part 3). *Approaches to Ethics*, 266–275, includes only the first of six sections to Part 3.

5. G. E. Moore, "Principia Ethica," (Sec. 12), *Approaches to Ethics*, 486.

6. G. E. Moore, "Principia Ethica," (Sec. 5), *Approaches to Ethics*, 481.

7. G. E. Moore, "Principia Ethica," (Sec. 14), *Approaches to Ethics*, 490.

8. Alfred Jules Ayer, *Language, Truth and Logic*, 2nd Ed. (New York: Dover Publications, Inc., 1952 [1946]), 112.

9. Alfred Jules Ayer, *Language, Truth and Logic*, 112.

10. Sam Harris, *Letter to a Christian Nation* (New York: Alfred A. Knopf, 2006), 23.

11. Quoted in Rousas J. Rushdoony, *To Be As God: A Study of Modern Thought Since the Marquis de Sade* (Vallecito, CA: Ross House Books, 2003), 13.

12. Quoted in R. J. Rushdoony, *To Be As God*, 13.

13. R. J. Rushdoony, *To Be As God*, 13–14.

14. Quoted in R. J. Rushdoony, *To Be As God*, 14–15.

15. Quoted in R. J. Rushdoony, *To Be As God*, 177.

16. R. J. Rushdoony, *To Be As God*, 177.

17. Daniel C. Dennett, *Darwin's Dangerous Idea: Evolution and the Meanings of Life* (New York: Simon and Schuster, 1995), 467, 468.

18. Abraham Kuyper, *Lectures on Calvinism* (Grand Rapids: Eerdmans, [1898] 1961), 54.

19. Abraham Kuyper, *Lectures on Calvinism*, 54.

20. R. J. Rushdoony, *To Be As God*, 122; emphasis added.

21. Sam Harris, *Letter to a Christian Nation* (New York: Alfred A. Knopf, 2006), 90.

22. Sam Harris, *Letter to a Christian Nation* (New York: Alfred A. Knopf, 2006), 90–91.

23. Alfred Jules Ayer, *Language, Truth and Logic*, 111.

24. Richard Dawkins, *The God Delusion* (Boston and New York: Houghton Mifflin Co., 2006) 51.

25. Dawkins, *The God Delusion*, 53.

26. Quoted in Dawkins, *The God Delusion*, 52.

27. Richard Deacon, *The Cambridge Apostles: A History of Cambridge University's Élite Intellectual Secret Society* (New York: Farrar, Straus & Giroux, 1985), 71.

28. Richard Deacon, *The Cambridge Apostles*, 70.

29. Quoted in Richard Deacon, *The Cambridge Apostles*, 69.

30. Richard Deacon, *The Cambridge Apostles*, 70.

31. Richard Deacon, *The Cambridge Apostles*, 70.

32. Dawkins, *The God Delusion*, 50; emphasis added.

33. Joel McDurmon, *Manifested in the Flesh* (Powder Springs, GA: American Vision, 2007) 115.

34. Dawkins, *The God Delusion*, 53.

35. Dawkins, *The God Delusion*, 53.

36. I realize that Christian theology must make some qualification of this statement due to Christ, the Incarnation of God.

37. Dawkins, *The God Delusion*, 50.

Fallacies of Relevance

CHAPTER 12

"Doesn't Matter": Fallacies of Dogmatism

By "dogmatism" I mean illegitimate and incorrigible authorities. Fallacies based on false authorities essentially boil down to attempts to justify truth by man's influence or decree alone. These classify as fallacies of relevance because man's influence by definition cannot *guarantee* objective truth, and thus appeals to the authority of man does not count as a relative standard by which to judge. This claim requires some subtle qualifications as I will show, but in general, truth does not depend on the person telling it, unless that Person is God. The Christian will wisely discern between claims that rest on genuine authority (and thus have genuine relevance), and those that try to persuade based on the false authority of man. We stand in God's courtroom. He is the Creator and Judge. When it comes to God-revealed truth (in Scripture *or* nature), man's authority just simply "doesn't matter."

Appeals to Authority (One, Many, or Elite):

A fallacious Appeal to Authority attempts to persuade by leveraging expertise, tradition, boasted credentials, fame, social status, celebrity, etc., when these characteristics do not necessarily pertain to the issue at hand. Even when cited authorities have legitimate expertise in the topic, their *expertise itself* does not guarantee the truth of the argument under discussion, nor does it even prove the cogency or soundness of the argument. Even the most learned individual can make mistakes, and even the most practiced expert can formulate poor arguments. So, whenever you encounter a declaration that amounts to, "Expert X accepts Position A as true, and Expert X is an expert, therefore, Position A must be true," you have just witnessed an Appeal to Authority, and you have no necessary obligation to accept Position A as true simply because Expert X does.

This fallacy leverages the fact that society pays particular respect to certain people, acts, etc. Such people may in fact have genuine authority in many ways. Pastors, professors, judges, etc., all wear robes of authority, and rightfully so. Likewise, policemen, referees, teachers, babysitters, governors, presidents, and legislators all possess differing degrees of authority that we must obey. But this natural or institutional authority does not in itself guarantee the truth of what such people say. We do obey them out of expedience, duty, or good manners, and also because, in many cases, we may incur some punishment if we do not obey. But we cannot use their authority as a test for truth.

The fallacy assumes a link between authority and truth that does not of necessity exist. In the movie *Tombstone*, Wyatt Earp and the other deputies impose gun control laws inside town. As members of the outlaw gang "Cowboys" turn in their guns, one of them sneers at Earp, "Wearing that badge don't make you right." As odd as it may sound to say, the bad guy was correct, logically anyway. The deputy had authority, and he could lawfully impose his authority with force, but his "badge" of authority did not prove his opinions, or certain laws he imposed, necessarily "right." The truth of the proposition, "The best policy is to outlaw the possession of firearms within the city limits," may be debated on many grounds, and reasons given for both sides. But to argue merely that "The marshal says 'no guns,' so that's the best policy," would be logically fallacious. It may sound persuasive, and legal, but it is fallacious.

The abuse of this fallacy also, however, does not mean that the argument in question is necessarily *wrong*. Rather, the fallacy simply errs in offering as proof that which does not count as proof, namely, authority of some sort. The argument remains, therefore, *un*proven because of the fallacy, not *dis*proven. The proposition could turn out true for many other reasons, despite the fallacious Appeal to Authority. The appeal itself simply has no connection, and thus no bearing on the argument, expert or no expert, true or false, valid or invalid, pro or con. For this reason, the fallacious Appeal to Authority classifies as a "Doesn't Matter" fallacy.

The fallacy does, however, also contain a strong emotional and psychological element. A traditional Latin name for this fallacy is *Argumentum Ad Verecundiam*, which means "Argument to modesty" or more accurately "Argument to shame." In other words, it describes an appeal to your personal sense of shame in not agreeing with purported experts or traditions. Who could be so immodest, after all? Would you dare set your limited knowledge, your lack of credentials, your lack of standing, your unpublished, untested opinions up against the 40 years of study of the Nobel Prize-winning Professor Garret P. Servis, Ph.D., D.Litt., Ed.D., J.D., Dr.rer.nat., Th.D., D.D., F.R.S., F.R.S.L.? Would you dare? Perhaps even from this rather farcical example you can understand why Appeals to Authority can have great effect. People generally revere authority, and calling authority to your side in a debate adds a persuasive thrust to your case.

By putting its victim under such pressure, the fallacy also creates a diversion. Like many "doesn't matter" types of fallacies it secretly slides a "Red Herring" across the path. Once the authority is called for support, the person placed in the position of arguing against it now has the apparent burden of answering *why* he or she would dare stand against such revered or accepted "truth." "You disagree with the experts, huh? What makes *you* so special?" So the issue shifts from the original position—whatever that may be—to an interaction and comparison with the cited authority. This holds true, of course, only for those who allow themselves to fall victim to the fallacy. If you point out immediately that appealing to even the greatest authority doesn't prove the case, then you can avoid the added burden and stay focused on the original issue.

The example above pokes fun at academic authority, or the authority of much learning and expertise. This is only one manifestation of the Appeal to Authority. It can come as a reference to an otherwise authoritative figure: "Thomas Jefferson wrote…" Or one expert: "Prof. Herringbone, the world's foremost scholar on the subject, said…" Or an appeal to a scientist: "Einstein himself thought…" A particularly common and clever example is the following combination of Hypostasization and Appeal to Authority: "Science tells us…" (No it doesn't. "Science" can't talk).

The fallacy can also come as an appeal to a *group* of experts: "The Textbook Review Committee recommends…"; "Nine out of ten doctors agree..." But we must hold *group* authority, though it may sound even more persuasive than an individual, to the same *logical* standards. A group of experts can no more guarantee proof *by means of its authority* than can an individual. In fact, in many cases, the nature of group-politics should give us a warning: a *group* of people publishing a decisive opinion often indicates some kind of agenda at work. An Appeal to Authority of a group may represent an even greater level of bias or human error than that of an individual. For this reason, the Bible explicitly warns Christians against group-appeal and peer-pressure: "You shall not follow the crowd toward evil, nor sway a controversy by leaning after the crowd" (Ex. 23:2).[1] This biblical advice applies also to the Fallacy of Peer-Pressure or "Mob-Appeal," which I cover later.

Appeal to Authority can also appear as some expression of *elitism*. This latter variety of the fallacy harnesses "star power" or implicates its victim as either "in" or "out" of an exclusive group. It shows up commonly with Hollywood celebrities backing a cause or product, and also in advertisement: "Actors Michael J. Fox and Christopher Reeve speak out in favor of embryonic stem-cell research"; "U2's Bono calls upon Congress to direct billions of dollars for third-world relief." Such headlines imply that because such famous people support these causes, then these causes must be worthwhile, and therefore you should support them, too. Of course, little mention gets made of *why* such celebrities get involved; the celebrities rarely give logical arguments or any reasons at all, let alone the arguments against the position. Elitism compounds the fallacy by not even selecting genuine authorities for the subject, but rather popular figures who can somehow sway public emotions or sentiments (see also Appeal to Pity). The use of elitism often proves powerful in swaying public opinion, but it remains fallacious nonetheless. Even if Bono had overwhelming expertise in international economic policy, this in itself would not mean that his policy was just, righteous, good, or even helpful in the long run.

Authority and Apologetics

Authority in general can be a tricky subject, mainly because there does exist such a thing as *legitimate authority* that can act as final arbiter of intellectual disputes. In fact, every worldview *must have an ultimate authority*. In the world of evangelical Christianity, the Word of God, the Bible, stands as the unchallengeable ultimate authority. What Scripture says we accept as infallible, inerrant, and authoritative. An appeal to the authority of the Bible, therefore, is not automatically a *fallacious* Appeal to Authority. Of course, this only holds for a *proper* interpretation of the Bible. There are many, many appeals to the Bible which wrest the context or otherwise mishandle the revelation so that such an appeal *is* in fact fallacious. In short, not everyone who appeals to the Bible as an infallibly authoritative proof escapes the fallacy.

Non-Christian worldviews may laugh at our idea that the Bible is an ultimate authority, but they have their ultimate authorities as well. Secularists, for example, may argue that such an appeal to the Bible is a case of Special Pleading—holding the Bible to a different standard than we treat every other matter by. But when pressed to justify their ultimate concerns, they will speak of "evidence" or "reason." A problem arises with how they define "evidence." If it means "what we can scientifically see, touch, measure, repeat, etc.," then *legitimate authority* has been reduced to what can be known *only from the physical world*. Such a definition automatically denies the existence of non-physical things, such as a supernatural God; but it also ignores the nature of other absolutes such as law, reason and logic as sources of ultimate authority, for none of these things have *physical* attributes that count as "evidence." See the problem? The secularist standard Begs the Question concerning God, and relies on an *ultimate authority* which fails its own test of authoritativeness.

As a result of thinking in terms of their respective ultimate authorities, Christians and non-Christians alike often engage in fallacious Appeals to Authority. Christians often leverage the fact that many famous scientists have believed in God and practiced the Christian faith in earnest. This is a perfectly acceptable reply to those who claim that science and Christian thought are incompatible, or to those who argue that anyone who thinks scientifically must reject the truth of Scripture, or even the more popular version that says, "Any thinking person will not accept the supernatural tales of the Bible." It fails, however, as an argument for the *truth* of Christianity or the even the existence of God. Such great men as Kepler, Newton, Pascal, and Mendel all stand as testimony that Christianity and science are compatible, but their weight of authority cannot prove anything by itself.

The opposite appeal occurs in more modern times. Atheists and secularists argue that the vast majority of "intellectuals" and scientists are atheists or agnostics, thereby appealing to the "authority" of I.Q., academic position, and the societal favor of science and technology in order to disgrace those who disagree. But this simply commits a fallacious Appeal to Authority. Atheists employ such a fallacy, not to answer a legitimate inquiry, but to shame Christians as unintelligent, dim-witted, and uneducated. Shame is the key factor. In fact, recent atheist Sam Harris openly called upon the use of "embarrassment" as a tool to fight religious faith: "I think we should not underestimate the power of embarrassment."[2] In these comments, Sam openly confesses to the use of the fallacy of an Appeal to Authority (or more clearly in this case, Argument to Shame) in order to further his agenda:

> So public embarrassment is one principle. Once you lift the taboo around criticizing faith and demand that people start talking sense, then the capacity for making religious certitude look stupid will be exploited, and we'll start laughing at people who believe the things that the Tom DeLays, the Pat Robertsons of the world believe. We'll laugh at them in a way that will be synonymous with excluding them from our halls of power.

Of course, laughter is the ultimate diversion tactic from actual argument. It is the ultimate Appeal to Authority, in which a certain position is assumed to be so authoritative that to argue against it makes one an object of ridicule. The problem arises when the subject in dispute—religion in this case—becomes the assumed basis for ridicule. This again Begs the Question, and leverages emotion and shame in order to persuade (really, to bully) instead of using reasons and argument. If one can incite laughter against a position before proving it wrong, they have committed the fallacy. They may prove victorious in public, but they will have done so at the cost of intellectual integrity. Sam even admits this when he mentions "excluding them from the halls of power," which exposes the agenda of those who rely on fallacious Appeals to Authority: they are not interested in truth, but *power*.

Variations of False Authority

In addition to the forms stated above, Appeals to Authority can infect arguments in many subtle ways: through excessive use of "big words," technical jargon or tedious phrases, frequent appeals to references (where we should expect rational explanation and elucidation), excessive footnoting or end-noting to give the appearance of academic weight, excessive length of prose (especially hard-to-read, turgid writing), or frequent references to statistics, mathematical formulations, or scientific language.[3] Each of these employs some form of pseudo-authority in order to intimidate its audience into accepting a proposition without proving it.

Additionally, you will rarely see this fallacy appear with a definitive claim that "therefore X is true." It generally employs implication rather than a deductive logical statement. For example, you will see something like "This is proposition X. It has already received support from leading politicians, financiers, and celebrities." Such claims will usually not go so far as to add, "Therefore, proposition X is true." In public situations, this addition is not necessary, though it is usually implied. The abusers of the Appeal to Authority let the "star power" do the talking, or persuading.

The following example is filled with such "star power":

> Silicon Valley tycoons, Nobel laureates and Hollywood celebrities are backing a measure on California's Nov. 2 ballot to devote $3 billion to human embryonic stem cell experiments.... Some 22 Nobel laureates and many other scientists support Proposition 71.... Among those bankrolling the measure is Bill Gates ... Google investor John Doerr and eBay founder Pierre Omidyar.... Several prominent Republicans have also endorsed the research, most notably former first lady Nancy Reagan. Also, millionaire developer Thomas Coleman.... The measure has also been endorsed by actors Michael J. Fox, who has Parkinson's, and Christopher Reeve, who was paralyzed in a riding accident.[4]

This great example of Appeals to Authority fires several big guns at once. It appeals to the Status of both individuals and groups. It combines Appeals to tycoons, politicians, Nobel laureates, scientists, a former First Lady, and Hollywood all at the same time. It even throws in another fallacy, Appeals to Pity, with references to actors who suffer from conditions—Parkinson's and spinal injury—for which embryonic stem cell research claims to promise hope.

The Reformation and Authority

Of course, this fallacy does not only occur in modern times or use only "stars." The 16th-Century Reformers battled Appeals to Authority at a time when that authority had a much more powerful and imposing face—the Roman Catholic Church. Against the Reformers, the Roman Church Appealed directly to her own alleged Authority. One of her Bishops, Jacopo Sadoleto, wrote to the council of Calvin's own town Geneva:

> [C]ertain crafty men, enemies of Christian unity and peace, had ... cast among you, and in your city, the wicked seeds of discord, had turned the faithful people of Christ aside from the way of their fathers and ancestors, and from the perpetual sentiments of the catholic Church, and filled all places with strife and sedition (such is always the appropriate course of those who seek new power and new honors for themselves, by assailing the authority of the Church)....
>
> For we do not arrogate to ourselves anything beyond the opinion and authority of the Church; we do not persuade ourselves that we are wise above what we ought to be; we do not show our pride in contemning the decrees of the Church ... but (I speak of true and honest Christians) we proceed in humility and in obedience, and the things delivered to us, and fixed by the authority of our ancestors (men of greatest wisdom and holiness), we receive with all faith, as truly dictated and enjoined by the Holy Spirit."[5]

Sadoleto employed these words (and many others) to urge the Genevan city council to return to the Roman Catholic Church instead of following the Reformers, specifically John Calvin. Despite its humble tone, Sadoleto's 1539 letter rests upon the weight of the Church's (and his personal) authority, and that to disagree with this authority constitutes sedition and discord. He twice mentions his position as Bishop and once his elevation to Cardinal—and this just in his opening paragraphs. He then proceeds continually to ring the note of "the authority of the Church" throughout the rest of the letter.

In his elucidations Sadoleto creates many variations of the fallacy, all of which support the main idea that the Church of Rome stands as the one true Church. He appeals both to the institution's bare authority as well as the authority of its antiquity ("fathers and ancestors"), and this latter feature crosses into Chronological Snobbery also (a fallacy I cover later). But the ultimate fallacy comes when he claims that these ancient ideas, "fixed by the authority of our ancestors," actually represent the infallible dictates of the Holy Spirit Himself! Such is the Roman Catholic view of authority—what their Church teaches is God's word, and what God's word teaches only their Church properly interprets.

Calvin saw through the Cardinal's fallacious construct, and in his reply to Sadoleto he quickly made his case plain: "Athough your letter has many windings, its whole purport substantially is to recover the Genevese to the power of the Roman Pontiff, or to what you call the faith and obedience of the Church."[6] In dismantling the fallacious Appeal to Authority, Calvin exposes Sadoleto's ascription of the Holy Spirit's authority to the Roman position, and corrects it with the only legitimate authority between them: "[T]he Spirit goes before the Church, to enlighten her in understanding the Word, while the Word itself is like the Lydian stone, by which she tests all doctrines...."[7]

Calvin then illustrates how Sadoleto, for all of his appeals to the authority of the Church, really ignores the true meaning of the word "church," and forces it to mean "Roman Catholic Church." Calvin writes:

> Now, if you can bear to receive a truer definition of the Church than your own, say, in future, that it is the society of all the saints, a society which, spread over the whole world, and existing in all ages, yet bound together by the one doctrine and the one Spirit of Christ, cultivates and observes unity of faith and brotherly concord. With this Church we deny that we have any disagreement. Nay, rather, as we revere her as our mother, so we desire to remain in her bosom.[8]

Thus, Calvin essentially argues, the Roman Church had assumed the authority of the Holy Spirit to itself, and had arbitrarily assumed itself to be the one true Church exclusively led by the Holy Spirit. Calvin goes on to show how these ideas diverge from Scripture *and*, actually, from ancient tradition as well. Sadoleto's claims based on authority fail, therefore, as fallacious Appeals to Authority, and as inaccurate ones at that.

Yet the Roman Church has never budged on its view of its own authority. Immediately in an effort to answer the Reformation as a whole, the Roman Church convened the Council of Trent (1545–1563). The document continually refers to the authority of "the Church," and assumes the authority of the Holy Spirit for its own proclamations. For example:

> Whereas the Catholic Church, instructed by the Holy Ghost, has, from the sacred writings and the ancient tradition of the Fathers, taught, in sacred councils, and very recently in this oecumenical Synod, that there is a Purgatory, and that the souls there detained are helped by the suffrages of the faithful, but principally by the acceptable sacrifice of the altar; the holy Synod enjoins on bishops that they diligently endeavour that the sound doctrine concerning Purgatory, transmitted by the holy Fathers and sacred councils, be believed, maintained, taught, and every where proclaimed by the faithful of Christ.[9]

In order to avoid such fallacy, the followers of Calvin and other Reformers placed safeguards in their Confessions against the authority of the Church. For example, the Westminster Confession of Faith (1646) reminds us that "the purest Churches under heaven are subject both to mixture and error,"[10] and that "All synods or councils, since the Apostles' times, whether general or particular, may err; and many have erred."[11] The Confession denies that the Pope has authority over the church, and asserts, "There is no other head of the Church but the Lord Jesus Christ."[12] With authority purely vested in Christ and not man, the Church can avoid fallacious Appeals to Authority. Knowing your Creeds and Confessions doesn't hurt, either.

A Quantum Vacuum of False Authorities

Those who have no creeds and confessions have just as great a likelihood of grasping at false authorities. In secular thought, "scientists" and "experts" fill the fallacious role once taken up by Popes and allegedly infallible councils, as the following example illustrates:

> Furthermore, modern physics and cosmology make even the chaos deity, and indeed any creator, unlikely....
>
> Several detailed theoretical papers have been published by reputable scientists in reputable journals that provide various scenarios by which our universe could have arisen spontaneously from nothing but the quantum characteristics of a vacuum, in a way consistent with all existing knowledge.[13]

With this claim, atheistic scientist Victor J. Stenger creates an Appeal to Authority so grand it almost qualifies as comedy. His argument for why the existence of a creator is unlikely includes Appeals to the following Authorities: "modern science and cosmology" (a Hypostasized authority), "*several* papers" (not just papers, but *detailed* and *theoretical* papers), "reputable scientists," "reputable journals," and "consistent with all existing knowledge" (the authority of unanimity and experience). Notice that not only does he employ several types of authority, but nearly every instance itself Appeals to multiple authorities.

Let us see just how badly this example commits the fallacy. Stripping away the Appeals leaves Stenger with the following bald statement: "papers have been published that provide various scenarios by which our universe could have arisen spontaneously from nothing but the quantum characteristics of a vacuum." This version takes nothing away from his argument itself, but only removes the greater air of plausibility that the pressure of scientific Authority brings to bear on it, especially in the modern climate. The Authority adds nothing to the logical merits of his argument or to the papers that it mentions, but it does make the statement sound more persuasive. This bald form, therefore, reveals how weak the argument actually sounds.

Furthermore, the fact that these "papers" describe only what "could have" occurred to make a creator "unlikely" also reveals the weakness of the modern scientific attack on God: it can really never *prove anything* about the supernatural. It can only pronounce "maybe" or "could have" about natural things. What's more, Stenger's critique cannot even entertain certainty about these limited claims. It may well turn out that these papers all fall flat when evaluated further. In such a case we should find it prudent to wait in calling these scientists and journals "reputable."

In any case, the final statement really makes me chuckle: "in a way consistent with all knowledge." This phrase acts as an intimidating Authority—who can argue with that which is "consistent with all existing knowledge" after all? More fallaciously, it also presents an impossibility: *no one* can have *all* existing knowledge, and thus no one can rightly claim that any given theory is "consistent with *all* existing knowledge." Not even a large group of experts pooling their data can attain to such a comprehensive level of knowledge. One could only substantiate a claim about *all* knowledge if they possessed *omniscience*. At best, Stenger could argue that no one has yet refuted these papers publically, but this would only leave him with the possibility that they remain true. To argue any logical proof from such a position would commit an Appeal to Ignorance, which I cover below. Nevertheless, in the face of impossibility and ignorance, atheists such as Stenger can only Appeal to Authority to make their hypothetical dreams sounds persuasive.

False Authority, Idolatry, and Violence

An earlier generation of atheists operated upon just as vacuous Appeals to Authority, only instead of merely academic nonsense like Stenger's, they resorted to hero worship and even violence. The infamous Communist leaders provide such Appeals as these:

> Marx and Lenin—these are our two supreme guides in the sphere of social research. For the younger generation the way to Marx is through Lenin.... Leninism is the highest embodiment and condensation of Marxism for direct revolutionary action in the epoch of the imperialist death agony of bourgeois society. The Lenin Institute at Moscow must be made a higher academy of revolutionary strategy. Our Communist Party is permeated by the mighty spirit of Lenin. His revolutionary genius is with us. Our revolutionary lungs breathe the atmosphere of that better and higher doctrine which the preceding development of human thought has created. Thus it is that we are so profoundly convinced that tomorrow is ours.[14]

This appeal to the authority of Marx and Lenin represents the classic mentality of Communist leaders during the first half of the twentieth century. The language of this example, from Leon Trotsky, verges on worship—something ironically quite common within the allegedly non-religious movement which ultimately embalmed their great leader Vladimir Lenin in a glass case and has preserved it to this day via chemical baths and preservative injections. Despite its rigid atheism, the movement could not suppress the human impulse to worship, so it created a classic idol.

Trotsky here does not so much commit the Appeal to Authority in its explicit form, but he presents his authorities as unchallengeable authorities, and he bases his argument that "tomorrow is ours" purely on the fact that he and his audience follow these authorities. Thus he essentially argues, "We follow Marx and Lenin. Marx and Lenin said we shall triumph if we follow them. Therefore, tomorrow is ours."

This version of the fallacy also adopts Special Pleading because it assumes its authorities as an ultimate standard not to be challenged. This type of thinking permeated (and still does) communist movements. They consistently assumed Marxism as the standard by which they criticized everything else, and yet never allowed Marxism itself to suffer criticism. Thus, Chinese leader Mao Tse-Tung could say things like, "According to the Marxist theory of the state, the army is the chief component of state power. Whoever wants to seize and retain state power must have a strong army.... Yes, we are advocates of the omnipotence of revolutionary war; that is good, not bad, it is Marxist."[15] The subtle argument, "This is Marxist, so it has to be good," commits an Appeal to Authority, Special Pleading, and Begs the Question.

Statements like this fill Mao's writings, which you can view on nearly every page of his "Little Red Book": "The seizure of power by armed force, the settlement of the issue by war, is the central task and the highest form of revolution. This Marxist-Leninist principle of revolution holds good universally...."[16] "We are Marxists, and Marxism teaches...";[17] "Marxist philosophy holds...";[18] "Concrete analysis of concrete conditions, Lenin said, is 'the most essential thing in Marxism, the living soul of Marxism.'"[19] This last quotation commits a double-fallacy: "Lenin said that Marx said." Again, these do not appeal directly so as to say "Marx said, therefore it is true," but they assume the authority of the men up front, and then appeal to them. This version commits the fallacy every bit as much as the standard form, and essentially forms the basis of a worldview fallacy.

As dictatorial authority is, so it does: Mao's government forced every citizen to own a copy of his Book. Such is the manifestation of the Appeal to Authority: the grasp of political power and coercion. "Believe me because Marx said so," has as its root, "Believe me because *I* said so." In the political sphere it gets worse: it devolves into an Appeal to Force. In Mao's China, anecdotes relate that failure to produce your copy of the book on demand could result in beating or imprisonment. When logic and ethics fail in the political sphere, jail, or the gun decides the matter. I will cover Appeal to Force more fully in the next chapter.

APPEAL TO IGNORANCE

The fallacy of Appeal to Ignorance attempts to establish a proposition based on lack of knowledge. The argument takes forms like: "X is true because no one has disproven it," or "No evidence has been found for X, therefore X is false." It promotes the fallacious idea that *un*proven means *dis*proven, or that not-refuted means irrefutable. We simply cannot justify claims about what we know based on what we do not know. The person who does so essentially presents their own individual word as ultimate authority.

The fallacy commits the basic error of assuming that an absence of evidence equals evidence of absence, or that absence of proof means proof of absence. But this assumption fails examination. Primarily, we must account for the limitations of human knowledge. You cannot legitimately move from the fact of "no evidence *found*" to say "no evidence *exists*." Even if every living person in history searched the world over for the duration of their lives over multiple generations and still found no "evidence," this would not prove that no evidence exists, for the simple fact that the universe is infinitely larger (and infinitely smaller) than even the sum total of all human experience. To make a definitive claim that no evidence exists, you must be able to search every corner of the universe simultaneously at every moment. It is impossible, therefore, to prove such a negative claim unless you possess omniscience and omnipresence.

I remember my wife once telling me she had seen a black squirrel. I naively told her that she must have mistaken a grey squirrel in dim light, or something, because, as I fallaciously claimed, "Black squirrels don't exist." "Yes they do! I saw it," she retorted. I reasoned, "I've never seen one. I've never even heard of such a thing!" Knowing that I grew up in the country, have taken interest in nature for a long time and generally know what I talk about, she decided to not to press (a fallacy of authority, as well!). Not more than a few weeks passed before we were out driving one day and, to my disbelieving eyes, there scurried a coal-black squirrel across a split-rail fence and stopped right on the corner by the road. It sat there, tail twitching and all, as if to say, "Look at me!" My wife shouted with delight, and I immediately (as duty demanded) confessed that I was wrong. I stopped the car and we just stared at the bushy black subject crunching away at a nut.

In hindsight, I must say that my logic was a bit cracked as well. Resting on my own ill-founded, limited knowledge of squirrel species, and limited personal experience, I proclaimed that such could not exist, because "I've never heard of such a thing!" What a paltry reason for anything! An argument from ignorance, to be sure—and one that no one could make unless he had observed every squirrel in existence, and checked every corner of the cosmos for the existence of any and all squirrels to be checked, and all at the same time so that none even momentarily escaped his examination. (Also, as a side lesson, it is better to trust your wife than to pretend you know everything.)

So, short of assuming to ourselves the attributes of God, we must avoid such arguments that Appeal to Ignorance. "Ignorance" describes a lack of knowledge; "ignorant" describes the person who rests in it. This is not mere name-calling, but an applicable description of those who choose ignorance as a supportive tool.

Both Christians and non-Christians can fall prey to Appeals to Ignorance. Christians may be tempted to argue something like, "God cannot be disproven, therefore He exists." While it is true that you cannot "disprove" God, by the same method you also cannot disprove the existence of the tooth fairy or leprechauns. Shall we therefore believe in these also? You can see the fallacy of using non-evidence as proof. We must use some other criteria to justify the existence of God.

Likewise, for the unbeliever, non-evidence does not amount to non-existence. Even *if* "no evidence" has been given for God (as an atheist would say), this would not allow the conclusion that God does not exist. Besides, plenty of "evidence" has been given, and upon any given piece of evidence a worldview battle takes place. What the atheist really means to say is that no evidence has been given that he accepts. Of course, his non-acceptance of certain evidence as requiring a theological explanation derives from his own worldview and definition of "evidence" which automatically excludes the supernatural to begin with (as discussed above in relation to Appeal to Authority). As well, we must consider the fact that God (the God of Scripture) and creation belong to different intellectual categories, and thus require different *types* of evidence and inference as proof. I discuss this further under the fallacy of Category Mistakes. Here it suffices to point out that attempts by either Christians or non-Christians to prove their respective cases by hiding behind the unknown or the unknowable will qualify as fallacious Appeals to Ignorance.[20]

This fallacy simply attempts to shift the burden of proof, which by rule always rests on the person making the proposition. If you make a statement or claim, the burden rests on you to provide reasons to support that claim. It will not do to ignore this duty and then retire to the defense that your proposition has yet to be refuted. Perhaps this is true, but you have not *proven* it either, so why should someone else consider it? Returning to the preceding debate between the atheist and Christian, each side represents different claims—the one confidently states that God does not exist, the other that God does exist—and thus each has a unique burden of proof. This is why either side can engage in the same fallacy: both can make their respective claims without proving them. Rather than rely on ignorance, as discussed above, the atheist's burden of proof consists of offering positive evidence that God does not exist. The fallacious Appeal to Ignorance that says, "I have not seen any evidence," simply ignores the obligation to give evidence for its own claim and rests arrogantly (and foolishly) in its own tower of ignorance.

Dewey's Dogma

The following claim, widely attributed to the "father of American public schooling" John Dewey, abuses an Appeal to Ignorance in the most profound way:

> [F]aith in the prayer-hearing God is an unproved and outmoded faith. There is no God and there is no soul. Hence there are no needs for the props of traditional religion. With dogma and creed excluded, then immutable

truth is also dead and buried. There is no room for fixed, natural law—or moral absolutes.[21]

At the outset of the quotation the author allows that God is *un*proven, and therefore (humoring this claim for the moment) he should recognize that it is not *dis*proven. This statement admits only *ignorance* of the fact, meaning that no evidence has proven the existence of God false. But then the author moves directly from this admission of not-knowing to a decisive statement of non-existence: "There *is no* God...." The argument does not warrant this jump. Moving from a statement of ignorance to a conclusion of non-existence overtly commits the fallacy of Appeal to Ignorance.

This example provides another example in an odd way. I said that this quotation is widely *attributed* to Dewey. Indeed, a broad and deep search of the internet as well as canvassing several books turns up several references to Dewey's authorship of this fallacious statement. Yet, I have not found a single source to pinpoint exactly where or when Dewey actually wrote it. Christian scholar David A. Noebel (a class-act of a scholar) carefully references Ronald H. Nash, who indeed says that Dewey "once wrote" the statement. But Nash himself reveals that his source—a book by secularist Susan D. Rose—provides no source for the questionable quotation. So, how do we know Dewey truly authored this fallacious statement? We don't at this point. This, of course, does not prove that Dewey didn't write it, but to say that he did without having proof, as Nash does, is to implicitly Appeal to the Authority of the previous author, as well as to make a positive statement in the face of Ignorance.

The quotation sounds very much like something Dewey would say, and resonates with his well-published beliefs. We have no reason to believe that Dewey did *not* write it; but we also have no evidence that he did.

Dewey wrote extensively on nearly every subject in the social sciences, including logic, and yet (if indeed it was Dewey who wrote this) he fails the test of logical coherence here.

Dewey's Disciples

Other modern humanists and secularists fail in the same regard, and on the same subject. Consider the following:

> We find insufficient evidence for belief in the existence of a supernatural; it is either meaningless or irrelevant to the question of survival and fulfillment of the human race....
>
> But we can discover no divine purpose or providence for the human species. While there is much that we do not know, humans are responsible for what we are or will become. No deity will save us; we must save ourselves....
>
> There is no credible evidence that life survives the death of the body. We continue to exist in our progeny and in the way that our lives have influenced others in our culture.[22]

This series of three Appeals to Ignorance comes from the *Humanist Manifesto II* (1973), signed and endorsed by a couple hundred scholars, professors, authors, and dignitaries from around the world. With the aim of advancing humanism throughout the world, this document consistently denigrates traditional religious ideas and calls to replace them with humanist ideas. In the endeavor, however, they commit several fallacies.

Each of the three examples above commits an Appeal to Ignorance in an obvious way. Each one makes a statement of ignorance about their respective subjects, and yet proceeds to draw a definite conclusion based on their non-evidence. "We find insufficient evidence for the existence of the supernatural; therefore it is meaningless or irrelevant." No. A consistent thinker would conclude, "Therefore, we cannot further comment on it." "We discover no purpose or providence; therefore no deity will save us." No, "Therefore, we cannot conclude one way or the other on providence." It is not God's fault if these people did not "discover" Him, especially when fallen minds actively "suppress" the knowledge of Him (Rom. 1:18) and thinks in hostility toward Him (Rom. 8:8). Not finding Him doesn't mean He's not there. In fact, His Providence may *determine* that they not find Him. Likewise the fallacious comment, "There is no credible evidence of the afterlife; therefore only our memory lives on, and that in *this* life," commits the same error. An honest and logical thinker who found "no credible evidence" for the afterlife would conclude, "Therefore, the matter is undecided; it may or may not exist."

The entire *Manifesto* oozes the Worldview Fallacy of Naturalism, which leads it into its many errors. It states, "As nontheists, we begin with humans not God, nature not deity. Nature may indeed be broader and deeper than we may know; any new discoveries, however, will but enlarge our knowledge of the natural." Again, it makes an Appeal to Ignorance, but refuses to allow even the possibility of a supernatural explanation. "Whatever answers may come must be *natural* answers." They cannot prove this any more than they can their previous fallacious statements. It is *blind faith in naturalism* at work. It should not surprise us to find this humanist document candidly call itself "an expression of a living and a growing faith." Humanists should take note: their beliefs do not represent pure reason and science, but a competing *faith*—faith in man as opposed to God. Stripping humanist fallacies away helps expose this faith, and understanding this at the outset will help you strip away its fallacies.

Atheist: "The Universe Does Not Recall"

Nevertheless, humanists and atheists continue creating the same fallacious arguments. Atheist physicist Victor J. Stenger claims,

> No laws of physics were violated when the universe came into existence....
>
> The universe at its beginning was in a state of total disorder and zero information. Order and information evolved later. Thus the universe retains no memory of a creator—or of that creator's intentions.[23]

In this example, Stenger weasels in an Appeal to Ignorance with help from a Worldview Fallacy, again that of Naturalism. He does not commit the fallacy of Appeal to Ignorance overtly—so that it would be obvious—but sets the trap of naturalism and by that presupposition argues that the universe contains "no memory" of Creative purpose. So he does fundamentally Appeal to Ignorance in order to deny the role of a Creator, essentially arguing, "We have no evidence of a Creator, therefore the universe evolved by itself."

In order to maintain this fallacy, he argues that the universe could, in fact, have arisen from *nothing* without violating any laws of physics. One wonders, of course, where the laws of physics came from. Likewise, Stenger does not realize that his claim that information later evolved from zero information only permutes the same old argument about "something coming from nothing" which he claims to refute. If *zero* information existed, then how in the world did *some* information come about later? Was it due to the laws of physics acting on chaos? This will not do for an answer, for in such a case we must realize that the order *inherent* in the laws of physics, as well as those laws themselves, must be considered "information."

With this string of arguments Stenger has only succeeded in imposing his belief in naturalism onto the story of Creation. By assuming up front that "no laws of physics were violated," he absolutely *must* conclude that "the universe retains no memory of a creator." Simply define the Creator out of the picture initially, and *viola!*, no Creator shows up in the "evidence." Of course this ultimately Begs the Question, commits a Worldview Fallacy, and, in this case, includes a subtle Argument from Ignorance. In the same article, Stenger employs a fallacious Appeal to Authority as well, which I discuss above.

Appeal to Silence

The fallacy of Argument from *Silence* forms a subset of Appeals to Ignorance. This version of the fallacy attempts to base an argument on what someone did *not* say. In particular it states, "Person A did not mention X, therefore Person A did not know about, or believe X." This represents a version of the "absence of evidence" idea, and often appears in historical arguments. The existence of "silence" does not prove ignorance on the part of Person A who remains silent, nor does it prove that Person A rejected the proposition on which he is claimed to have been silent. Silence in such cases only proves silence, and nothing beyond that. What Person A knows or believes we may or may not determine by other means, but not by anything he did not say. How many times, after all, have you known the answer to a question, and yet not said anything? Did your silence therefore prove that you did not know the answer? Thus the fallacy described here.

Appeal to Silence frequently populate the arguments of the "Jesus-mythicists" who claim that Jesus never existed as an historical person. Of course, I have already mentioned the futility of trying to prove *any* universal negative—that any given thing does not or never existed. Frequent abuses by these mythicists deal with alleged "contradictions" between the Gospels, and also with the Apostle Paul. For example, the once popular mythicist book, *The Jesus Mysteries*, tries to fault the doctrine of the virgin birth of Jesus by claiming a "startling contradiction" between the genealogies in Matthew and Luke, and then going on to use Mark as further "evidence." They write, "Mark, on the other hand, doesn't mention Bethlehem, the virgin birth, or Jesus' family descent from David at all. Why does he leave out these extremely pertinent facts? Something fishy is going on here?"[24] Their reasoning itself sounds fishy. Rather than actually draw some definitive conclusion, they just state "something fishy is going on," which implies that Mark did not know or believe in the virgin birth. Such carefully ambiguous language shows that they realize their logic and evidence are both very thin here.

To even conclude "something fishy" from Mark's *silence* on the matter of Jesus' birth commits the fallacy of Appeal to Silence. Not only do multiple possibilities exist that may explain the apparent discrepancies between Matthew's and Luke's genealogies, etc.,[25] the fact that Mark remains silent here can indicate many things as well. For starters, the fact that Mark begins his Gospel with Jesus as an adult—leaving out *everything* about his birth, infancy, and childhood—shows that the author focused on the ministry and work of Jesus. This shortest and most condensed of the Gospels portrays Jesus as a man of action—decisive, active, and heroic in a fast-paced narrative. These characteristics of Mark's account make it clear that his purpose and audience did not require much preceding the acts of Jesus. Yet on top of this, Mark still introduces Jesus as "the Son of God" (Mark 1:1), which hardly contradicts with the idea of a virgin birth. Freke and Gandy's reliance upon an Appeal to Silence, and thus an Argument from Ignorance, plagues their entire effort to deny that Jesus Christ never existed as an historical person.

Another example from a similar mythicist appears in Brian Flemming's film *The God Who Wasn't There*. Among many similar claims, Flemming fallaciously argues that Paul did not believe Jesus ever walked the earth. Flemming states,

> And here is the interesting thing, if Jesus was a human who had recently lived, nobody told Paul. Paul had never heard of Mary, Joseph, Bethlehem, Herod, John the Baptist, he had never heard about any of these miracles. He never quotes anything that Jesus was supposed to have said. He never mentions Jesus having a ministry of any kind at all. He doesn't know about any entrance into

> Jerusalem. He never mentions Pontius Pilot or a Jewish mob or any trials at all. Paul doesn't know any of what we would call the story of Jesus, except for these last three events, and even these, Paul never places on Earth. Just like the other savior Gods of the time, Paul's Christ Jesus died, rose, and ascended all in a mythical realm. Paul doesn't believe that Jesus was ever a human being. He is not even aware of the idea....

I cannot think of a more boldly fallacious Appeal to Silence. And yet other mythicist works brandish the same erroneous argument: "It is a completely remarkable fact, however, that Paul says nothing at all about the historical Jesus!"[26]

To anyone who has actually read the Bible, these claims prove nothing but the ignorance of those who make them. For starters, most of the statements in these arguments have no basis in fact at all. Paul did speak of Jesus as an historical person (Rom. 1:3; 9:5; 2 Cor. 5:16; Gal. 3:16–19; 4:4; Eph. 2:15–16; Col. 1:21–22), he did mention Pilate (1 Tim. 6:13), and he did often explicitly quote or reference Jesus' words (Acts 20:35; Rom. 12:14; 13:9; 1 Cor. 4:12–14; 7:10; 9:14; 11:23–25; 13:2; Gal. 5:14; 1 Thess. 5:2). So these guys cannot even write good fallacies. But even if Paul did offer only silence on all these aspects of Christ's historical life and ministry, the apostle's silence would not prove that "Paul doesn't believe that Jesus was ever a human being. He is not even aware of the idea." Paul could (and did) have many reasons, stemming from the audience, nature, and purposes of his writings, for not including narrative accounts of Christ's life in the way the Gospels do.[27]

Flemming's claim so classically commits the fallacy of Appeal to Silence that I cannot think of a better example. That so many people base their atheistic beliefs on such arguments as these, claiming that "Jesus never existed," attests to the foolishness of atheism (Ps. 14:1). As an anonymous Dutchess proclaimed of the atheistic philosophers of the eighteenth century, so must I conclude about the "Jesus-mythicists": "They do not believe in Christianity, but they believe every possible absurdity."[28]

Concluding Remarks

Ignorance is no basis for knowledge. It is, in fact, the antithesis of knowledge. Wisdom includes the ability to know *that* you don't know, and to avoid basing a conclusion on what you don't know. One who trusts in ignorance displays intellectual laziness, not doing the hard work to provide the necessary information. The fallacy also may reveal intellectual cowardice—the fear or personal disgust of facing reality for what it may genuinely hold. Like a child who covers his eyes and says, "I can't see you, so you're not here," the abuser of this fallacy blinds himself, hoping to avoid reality. Like an ostrich with its head buried in the sand,[29] so the Appeal to Ignorance hides in fear from what might be. The act of running from the truth exhibits the psychology of a sinner: "The wicked flee when no one is pursuing, But the righteous are bold as a lion" (Prov. 28:1). Christians need the boldness to accept truth and represent it faithfully (Ex. 20:16).

NOTES

1. This is my translation, which I think is more faithful to the Hebrew. For comparison, the Geneva Bible translates it, "Thou shalt not follow a multitude to do evil, neither agree in a controversy to decline after many and overthrow the truth." The New King James says, "You shall not follow a crowd to do evil; nor shall you testify in a dispute so as to turn aside after many to pervert justice" (Ex. 23:2).

2. Sam Harris, "Sam Harris: The Truthdig Interview," interview by Blair Golson, April 3, 2006; available at http://www.truthdig.com/report/page5/20060403_sam_harris_interview/, accessed December 16, 2008.

3. David Hackett Fischer elaborates on many of these in *Historians' Fallacies: Toward a Logic of Historical Thought* (San Francisco: Harper TorchBooks, 1970), 283–290.

4. "Gates, others lead California effort for stem cell research," USAToday.com, August 26, 2008; available at http://www.usatoday.com/news/health/2004-08-26-stem-cell_x.htm, accessed December 19, 2008.

5. Jacopo Sadoleto, "Sadoleto's Letter to the Genevans," *A Reformation Debate: Sadoleto's Letter to the Genevans and Calvin's Reply*, ed. John C. Olin (Grand Rapids: Baker Book House, 1976), 30–31, 37.

6. John Calvin, "Calvin's Reply to Sadoleto," *A Reformation Debate: Sadoleto's Letter to the Genevans and Calvin's Reply*, 53.

7. John Calvin, "Calvin's Reply to Sadoleto," *A Reformation Debate: Sadoleto's Letter to the Genevans and Calvin's Reply*, 61.

8. John Calvin, "Calvin's Reply to Sadoleto," *A Reformation Debate: Sadoleto's Letter to the Genevans and Calvin's Reply*, 61–62.

9. "Decree Concerning Purgatory," *The Council of Trent, The Twenty-Fifth Session*, December 4, 1563.

10. *Westminster Confession of Faith*, Chapter 25, Section 5.

11. *Westminster Confession of Faith*, Chapter 31, Section 3.

12. *Westminster Confession of Faith*, Chapter 25, Section 6.

13. Victor J. Stenger, "Where Can God Act? A Look at Quantum Theology," *Free Inquiry* 28, no. 5 (Aug-Sep 2008): 36.

14. Leon Trotsky, "The Tasks of Communist Education," *The Communist Review*, December 1922, Vol. 4, No. 7; available at http://www.marxists.org/history/international/comintern/sections/britain/periodicals/communist_review/1923/7/com_ed.htm, accessed December 29, 2008.

15. Mao Tse-Tung, *Quotations from Chairman Mao Tse-Tung* (bi-lingual edition, no publishing info, no date), 123.

16. Mao Tse-Tung, *Quotations from Chairman Mao Tse-Tung*, 121.

17. Mao Tse-Tung, *Quotations from Chairman Mao Tse-Tung*, 395.

18. Mao Tse-Tung, *Quotations from Chairman Mao Tse-Tung*, 401.

19. Mao Tse-Tung, *Quotations from Chairman Mao Tse-Tung*, 403.

20. Norm L. Geisler and Ronald M. Brooks use this example in *Come Let Us Reason: An Introduction to Logical Thinking* (Grand Rapids: Baker Books, 1990), 95–96.

21. Attributed to John Dewey in Ronald H. Nash, *The Closing of the American Heart: What's Really Wrong With America's Schools* (Probe Books, 1990), 91; Nash is referenced by David A. Noebel, *Understanding the Times: The Story of the Biblical Christian, Marxist/Leninist, and Secular Humanist Worldviews* (Manitou Springs, CO: Summit Press, 1991), 55–56. Nash himself references Susan D. Rose, *Keeping Them Out of the Hands of Satan: Evangelical Schooling in America* (New York: Routledge, 1988), 39, whom he says provides no source for the original quote attributed to Dewey.

22. *Humanist Manifesto II*; available at http://www.americanhumanist.org/about/manifesto2.php, accessed December 30, 2008; also quoted in David A. Neobel, *Understanding the Times*, 55.

23. Victor J. Stenger, "Where Can God Act? A Look at Quantum Theology," *Free Inquiry* 28, no. 5 (Aug-Sep 2008): 36.

24. Timothy Freke and Peter Gandy, *The Jesus Mysteries: Was the "Original Jesus a Pagan God?* (New York: Three Rivers Press, 1999), 141.

25. See, for just one discussion of the many possibilities, Darrel L. Bock, *Luke: Volume 1: 1:1–9:50* (Grand Rapids: Baker Books, 1994), 903–909, 918–923.

26. Freke and Gandy, *The Jesus Mysteries*, 151.

27. For more on these ideas of Paul, see Joel McDurmon, *Manifested in the Flesh: How*

the Historical Evidence of Jesus Refutes Modern Mystics and Skeptics (Powder Springs, GA: American Vision, 2007), 57–85.

28. Quoted by John Adams, *Discourses on Davila* (Boston: Russell and Cutler, 1805 [1790]), 93.

29. This common belief is actually mythical. Ostriches do not bury their heads in the sand. But as a useful image it remains irresistible.

CHAPTER 13

"No Sweat": Fallacies of Emotion

Relevance requires that persuasion rely necessarily on truth, not the person telling it, *nor* the person hearing it. Unfortunately, many fallacies rely on tactics aimed at manipulating the emotional or mental state of their audience. Fear, intimidation, sense of belonging, guilt, and pity all provide powerful tools for the would-be deceiver. The Christian will discern truth from emotional manipulation and will criticize such methods. The faithful thinker will overcome Fallacies of Emotion with "no sweat."

Appeal to Fear/Force

An Appeal to Fear or Force essentially ignores logical connections and pressures its opponent with some kind of threat. It overrides truth with consequences. It kills philosophy with power. The fallacious argument could threaten bodily harm, blackmail, loss of position or money, demotion, or any other violation of person, conscience, or property.

The classical Latin name comes to us as *Argumentum Ad Baculum*, which means "Argument to the Stick." "Stick" merely stands as a symbol for any type of intimidating weapon. In other words, such an argument appeals to the fear of harm as a means of persuasion. Some scholars have called it "Appeal to Intimidation."

The fallacy could possibly appear in a very open and bold manner, but more often comes in a subtle or veiled form. Not many people lower themselves enough to say, "Agree with this or I'll beat you with a stick" (although instances this blunt could occur). Rather, you will more likely encounter something like these: "My idea is the right one, and before you argue with it, remember that I sign your paycheck"; "It's morally right to bring our troops home now, before they come home in body bags"; or, "Despite the accuracy of this paper, I cannot give it passing grade until you revise it according to my comments." The latter example occurs frequently on college campuses, especially when a student's conclusion clashes with a professor's agenda. Most people who would abuse a position of power in order to force assent will probably need to disguise or hide their pitifully fallacious behavior in some way. Such behavior is both unethical and morally reprehensible; whoever adopts it must not get caught, must feel assurance that some institution will protect them (such as a university, court system, medical system, the "scientific community," teacher's union, etc.), and they must also have some means of deluding themselves that something or other justifies their overt fallacy. In so many ways can politics or power successfully defy logic and reason!

A recent political example comes along with the Senate discussion about accepting the replacement for Barak Obama. The Congressman involved crudely argued,

> Let me just remind you that there presently is no African-American in the U.S. Senate.... I will ask you to not hang and lynch the appointee as you try to castigate the appointer. I don't think that anyone—any U.S. senator who's sitting in the Senate right now—wants to go on record to deny one African-American for being seated in the U.S. Senate....
>
> The recent history of our nation has shown us that sometimes there can be individuals and there can be situations where...you have officials standing in the doorway of school children. You know I'm talking about Orval Faubus back in 1957 in Little Rock, Arkansas; I'm talking about George Wallace, Bull Conner...and I'm sure that the U.S. Senate don't want to see themselves placed in the same position.[1]

These incendiary comments from African-American Congressman Bobby Rush (Democrat-Illinois) came after the Senate refused to seat Roland Burris. Appointed by Illinois governor Rod Blagojevich in the wake of his scandalous attempt to sell the seat vacated by Obama, Burris faced massive opposition. Rush, who himself originally opposed the action, performed an about-face on the issue based on race: Burris would be the only African-American in the 100-member Senate.

Unfortunately, Rush employed a fallacious Appeal to Fear—and a very disgraceful one at that—in order to push his point. Referring to the era of segregation and recalling the names of famous racists from that time, he tried to insinuate that by blocking Burris from the seat the other Senators would be acting like old-time segregationists. The insinuation threatened that if Burris didn't get the seat, then Rush would lead the charge labeling the Senators as "racists" who wanted to "lynch" the African-American.

Of course, the issue of race falls beside the point of the baggage clinging to Burris due to the widely publicized Blagojevich scandal. Race was hardly the point. Even President-elect (at the time) Obama argued against seating *anyone* appointed by Gov. Blagojevich. Even if race played some role, the analogy of lynching would hardly seem accurate or appropriate. So, in summary here, we find Representative Rush committing a Red Herring, and a False Analogy, on top of the Appeal to Fear at the heart of his argument.

Legitimate Fear

Is fear ever a legitimate motivator? Fear of harm can never logically prove the truth of any proposition. A statement is true or not irrespective of how we feel about it, and irrespective of whether or not we fear to accept it or to dismiss it. No amount of punishment for dissent can transform a false claim into a true one. Fear of a conclusion may *coincide* with the truth of an argument, but it cannot prove it true. Nevertheless, this does not mean that fear never plays a legitimate role in our intellectual lives.

In order to understand this role, we must make some important distinctions. First, we must distinguish between different types of "fear." Since we use the word in different ways, we need to impose some consistency on our thought in relation to our usage. The Bible teaches, *The fear of the Lord is the beginning of knowledge* (Prov. 1:7), and *to man He said, "Behold, the fear of the Lord, that is wisdom; And to depart from evil is understanding"* (Job 28:28). "Fear" in the sense that we should "fear the Lord" does not mean "groveling, knee-shaking, terror," though God can invoke this response in many ways. Rather, the fear of the Lord means "reverence, awe, and respect." It means a regard for the holiness of God, and the sacredness of God's law.

Everyone lives with this type of fear for *somebody*. Everyone concedes ultimate respect and reverence to some person or principle in their life. If not God, it will be self, some other person, a group of people, or an ideal person. Even the person who adamantly objects, "I fear nothing at all," ultimately fears something, most likely the possibility of missing something pleasurable or important in this short life. Even the atheist who denies God and believes that the only goal to life is to get a few kicks before she dies—if she truly believes this—lives with the ultimate fear that she will not get those kicks before her candle is snuffed. No one can escape ultimate authority, or the fear of not satisfying that ultimate respect in their life.

Many humanists complain that by fearing God believers give up critical thinking completely and live in blind submission. This argument ignores that by removing our ultimate Respect from anything in this world, we simply refuse to submit to the ultimate authority of man. Believers guard themselves from the greatest possible source of error—the whims and dictates of man. Jesus taught us, *Do not fear those who kill the body but are unable to kill the soul; but rather fear Him who is able to destroy both soul and body in hell* (Matt. 10:19). Likewise, Paul taught that, for the purpose of overcoming the trickery, craftiness, and deceit of man, God provides for believers to have sound discipleship and training: *As a result, we are no longer to be children, tossed here and there by waves and carried about by every wind of doctrine, by the trickery of men, by craftiness in deceitful scheming* (Eph. 4:14). Simply put, then, Christians follow Peter's example and say, *"We must obey God rather than men"* (Acts 5:29).

Secondly, we must also distinguish exactly what position an Appeal to Force actually intends to enforce. Every threat implies some rational proposition, but usually in an obscure manner. Some logicians distinguish between bare threats and threats that intend to back an argument. For example, one philosopher argues that if a thief holds you at gunpoint and says, "Your money or you life,"[2] he has confronted you with a threat, but not an argument, and therefore not this particular fallacy. But this scenario really only hides the fallacious argument in the form of a demand. An armed robber, once we critically analyze his position, actually advances a fallacious argument something like this: "Whatever money people give me belogns to me; You will give me yours or I will kill you and take it anyway; therefore your money belongs to me." Such criminal behavior involves many fallacies and contradictions; for example, the fact that the money is not the thief's property and yet he implicitly declares that it is. Now, if you are ever robbed at gunpoint (God forbid it should ever happen), it will probably not be the best time to engage in a lesson on logical reasoning. Of course, this is exactly the advantage of the armed robber: he wants to override both law and logic by inducing fear and panic. Nevertheless, a logical proposition does lie beneath the threat of force, it just happens to be another fallacious proposition. The thief knows this, and therefore knows he must rely on force to advance it.

This does not mean, however, that every appeal to force covers a logical fallacy. It simply reveals that force provides the last resort to overcome resistance (whether good or bad). Depending on the worldview and the situation, force may represent either an attempt to enforce poor logic, or an effort to protect good logic. Resistance to theft, for example, comes from moral integrity: honest people work hard for their money and resist giving it up for no good reason. The thief instills enough fear for the honest victim to override their sense of wrong and of loss. Yet we recognize *legitimate* fear from the opposite perspective, since we can also understand "resistance" as rebellion against the proper moral order (everything from disbelief to theft, rape, or murder). We would applaud if police tackled the thief, hauled him in, and a judge sentenced him to pay restitution to his victims. It takes lots of force and fear to move a criminal to do so, but as this fear comes as a legitimate punishment for a criminal offense, we do not cry "fallacy!" Rather, we recognize that every moral order must ultimately rest on force as a means of punishing those who defy the laws of that order. Reason and logic come into play in determining how we should take the laws God has given us and apply them to specific situations, and in determining what punishments to apply where, but not in determining the moral order itself.

Likewise parents use legitimate Appeals to Fear when disciplining children. For those who refuse to learn through instruction, the Bible directs the use of the rod: *He who withholds his rod hates his son, But he who loves him disciplines him diligently* (Prov. 13:24). Such describes how to deal with what Scripture often calls "foolishness"—which amounts to hard-headedness and hard-heartedness. The fool refuses to make himself humble and teachable, and refuses to learn through teaching: *He who corrects a scoffer gets dishonor for himself, And he who reproves a wicked man gets insults for himself. Do not reprove a scoffer, or he will hate you, Reprove a wise man and he will love you. Give instruction to a wise man and he will be still wiser, Teach a righteous man and he will increase his learning* (Prov. 9:7–9). Thus, the child who prepares his or her spirit and heart to receive instruction engages in a spiritual and moral exercise—education is not merely an intellectual pursuit, as I have stressed. But scripture teaches that this exercise is tough, and requires discipline: since *Foolishness is bound up in the heart of a child; The rod of discipline will remove it far from him* (Prov. 22:15). Here we see the legitimate Appeal to Fear: wielding power in order to train and to enforce a godly moral order.

The threat of corporal punishment takes well-known forms during childhood (from wooden spoons to paddles!), but in truth continues in different forms throughout life. Historian David Hackett Fischer cites as examples of the fallacy the outbreaks of student riots during the late 1960s, when radical students "disrupted classes, damaged buildings, destroyed books, and injured people, and committed many outrages when professors made statements with which they disagreed."[3] The cure for such violence, he argues, is for the legal rule of force to regain order: "Knock-down arguments, alas, must be overcome not with a syllogism but a stick. Liberty *and* order are the prerequisites for reason."[4] In other words, you can't reason with a scoffer. That most of these students were adolescents called, in Fischer's analysis, for stronger parenting: "Let us have the courage, patience, and wisdom to *enforce* restraint (without repression) upon our erring children."[5]

As well for adulthood: we do not respect a foolish adult who revolts at learning and yet argues hard-headedly: *On the lips of the discerning, wisdom is found, But a rod is for the back of him who lacks understanding* (Prov. 10:13); *A fool's lips bring strife, And his mouth calls for blows* (Prov. 18:6). This, of course, does not legitimize interpersonal violence and fighting to solve disputes. Rather, it indicates that many must "learn the hard way," even to the point of facing criminal litigation and punishment. It also describes the sad fact that at some point, some "fools" will receive a fist for their antagonism, but the Scripture does not legitimize this as legal behavior between private individuals.

Aside from these unfortunate cases, even average adults need spiritual "discipline." Scripture explains that this comes in the form of some undesirable stress, and yet also as an expression of God the Father disciplining us His children:

> *and you have forgotten the exhortation which is addressed to you as sons, "My son, do not regard lightly the discipline of the Lord, Nor faint when you are reproved by Him; For those whom the Lord loves He disciplines, And He scourges every son whom He receives." It is for discipline that you endure; God deals with you as with sons; for what son is there whom his father does not discipline?* (Heb. 12:5–7).

Thus, when Paul pleads with the Corinthian church to grow humble and receive instruction, he speaks to them as children facing the option to learn or to earn chastening. In doing so, he literally appeals to the stick: *I do not write these things to shame you, but to admonish you as my beloved children.... What do you desire? Shall I come to you with a rod, or with love and a spirit of gentleness?* (1 Cor. 4:21). Paul simply threatens legitimate disciplinary force in order to enforce the behavior called for by the very covenant the church has voluntarily entered into.

In light of the idea of legitimate force, we can see that some writers have mistakenly pointed to Revelation 22:18 as an example of this fallacy: *If any man shall add unto these things, God shall add unto him the plagues that are written in this book; and if anyone takes away from the words of the book of this prophecy, God will take away his part from the tree of life and from the holy city, which are written in this book.*[6] Unfortunately for these writers, John does not appeal to force in the illegitimate sense of trying to prove the statement he made. Rather, the outcome of God's judgment in history will provide the final evidence that His word is, in fact, the truth. Therefore, this passage does not commit a fallacy. Instead, John merely repeats the sanctions (rewards or punishments) involved in God's covenantal relationship with man.

The Bible contains many such references to salvation, wealth, damnation and other historical judgments based on obedience or disobedience. That some writers and scholars tend to reference the same single passage suggests that they may have merely copied from each other, rather than engaged Biblical thought for themselves.

Some critics have pointed to threats of damnation in general as examples of the fallacy of Appeal to Force, but rarely does a clear example actually appear in real life. One website, for example, summarizes Pascal's Wager thusly: "You should believe God exists because, if you don't, when you die you will be judged and God will send you to Hell for all of eternity. You don't want to be tortured in Hell, do you? If not, it is a safer bet to believe in God than to not believe."[7] They then complain that "A god is not made any more likely to exist simply because someone says that if we don't believe in it, then we will be harmed in the end." But notice that the original argument (hypothetical as it is) does not claim to prove *that* God exists; it simply announces the moral obligation why you *should* believe that He exists, and that it is a *safer* bet to believe so. Few Christians if any will argue, "God exists *because* you will go to hell if you don't believe." From the proper perspective, the skeptic must allow that *if* the Bible is true, then both God and hell exist, and the consequent appeal to force represents a legitimate threat. It will not do simply to brush aside the claim as a fallacy, unless it is actually stated in a fallacious form. The atheist may rightly argue that the original argument "Begs the Question," but this charge requires a different discussion than Appeal to Force, and we can go to the worldview fallacy if we need to.

Once we recognize the inescapability of an ultimate fear, we will realize that arguments over Appeal to Force and God's existence actually involve deeper worldview issues than just language and logic. A biblical worldview involves knowledge of our Creator, Redeemer, and Sustainer. He reigns all-powerfully, all-knowingly, and everlastingly. Nothing escapes Him. He sits atop all authority, power, and wisdom. God by His very nature cannot err, fall, change, or suffer defeat. Humans obey or disobey Him, and face the rewards or punishments He has determined. He reigns whether we agree or disagree, whether we fear Him or not. The decision whether or not to relate to Him, therefore, is less an intellectual determination than a moral and ethical decision. The biblical threats against disbelief do not intend to try to prove God's existence, but rather rest upon His existence as the Almighty Judge—the beginning and end of all human life and behavior.

Fallacious Appeals to Fear

The Bible contains many instances of people fallaciously Appealing to Fear or Force in order to persuade. For example, when Pilate could not get an answer out of Jesus, he tried to pressure Him with fear: *You do not speak to me? Do You not know that I have authority to release You, and I have authority to crucify You?* (John 19:10). Jesus stood firm in the face of fear: *You would have no authority over Me, unless it had been given you from above* (John 19:11). Jesus certainly understood the Old Testament that He Himself fulfilled: *You shall not fear man, for the judgment is God's* (Deut. 1:17); *The fear of man brings a snare, But he who trusts in the Lord will be exalted. Many seek the ruler's favor, But justice for man comes from the Lord* (Prov. 29:25–26).

Appeals to Force occur frequently whenever institutionalized power or ego feels it has something to protect (which is usually), despite the fact that Appeals to Fear or Force embody perhaps the crudest of all logical fallacies. While many skeptics and atheists constantly refer to the "the Inquisition" and the events surrounding Galileo as examples of religion resorting to force in order to quell opposition, the truth falls far from the extreme stories they tell. More importantly, the most frightening examples occur in modern times, and usually come from secular institutions. Fischer notes as obvious modern examples the suppression and atrocities that enforce censorship of media and scholarship in totalitarian nations.[8] Imperial Japan, Soviet Russian, Nazi Germany and others all held their writers and students in check with threats of demotion, imprisonment, or execution should they express opposition.

The Appeal to Fear, however, did not afflict only these "bad" nations. The total blackout of atrocities under Communist regimes crept throughout the media and universities in the west, simply because the leftist participants believed in their wealth redistribution scheme. Thousands of leftist voices in America hailed the great wonder of Soviet Russia while refusing to report that millions were starved or shot to death in labor camps.

The Velikovsky Affair

Meanwhile, examples abound in American academia. In 1950, psychologist and interdisciplinary scholar Immanuel Velikovsky published a book making admittedly radical claims about astronomy, geology, mythology, and much more. The book, *Worlds in Collision*, disturbed some professors and university men so strongly that they launched an all out attack on Velikovsky and his work. Rather than refute his arguments, however, they resorted to abusive *Ad Hominem* and strong-arm techniques.[9] One edgy professor, Harlow Shapely, threatened Velikovsky's publisher, Macmillan, with a textbook boycott should it continue with publication. The Appeal to Force, however, backfired badly. Though Macmillan itself did melt under the pressure, Doubleday picked up the publishing and (likely due to the raging stir of controversy) the book became a bestseller. Nevertheless, the attacks on Velikovsky continued to grow, headed by even the American Association for the Advancement of Science and the science popularizer Carl Sagan.

The episode so perturbed the conservative sociologist Robert Nisbet that he decried the persecution of Velikovsky as a new Inquisition. While liberals love to twist the Galileo story to make liberal scholars look like heroes versus an oppressive Church (hardly the whole story), Nisbet exposed their vast hypocrisy:

> Anyone who believes that inquisitions went out with the triumph of secularism over religion has not paid attention to the records of foundations, federal research agencies, professional societies, and academic institutes and departments.... It was twentieth century science, not theology, that sought to prevent by every possible means the publication in the 1950s of Velikovsky's *Worlds in Collision*. The Church did not go that far with Galileo.[10]

Liberals vs. Liberals: Jews, Power, and Sociobiology

In March 2006, when two Harvard professors released an academic paper for review entitled "The Israel Lobby and U. S. Foreign Policy," a melee erupted involving professors, politicians, and donors threatening to withdraw money due to the claim that Jews have oppressive influence in American politics and education (you almost get the feeling that the reaction proved the thesis right!). The response was one big Appeal to Fear, and it worked. According to one investigation, the vast majority of faculty at Harvard simply remained silent, refusing even to comment on the paper at all.[11] Some even cited the likely consequences for doing so as reason for their silence.

Jewishness seems to play a role in more than one of the modern episodes. California State University at Long Beach professor Kevin MacDonald has spent years writing in the field of evolutionary psychology. MacDonald accepts Darwinian evolution, which makes him typical as far as university professors go; but he extends Darwin's thought more consistently and argues that genetic differences among humans logically extend to mental, psychological, and social differences between races as well. He has particularly spent his career writing about the Jewish race and its social power as a racial unit. Despite any academic defensibility of his work (let alone professions of "academic freedom"), fellow academicians and many activist groups have blasted him with every possible verbal abuse as well as attempts to get the University publically to disavow his work. Attacks on him come relentlessly and harshly, trying to pressure him out of his position.[12] "Agree with us, or we'll get you fired!"

In a very similar situation, though three decades earlier, socio-biologist Edward O. Wilson published a similar Darwinian thesis. Again, despite his academic credentials and academic tone of his work, fellow academics Stephen Jay Gould and Richard Lewontin, along with activists, created a propaganda campaign designed to discredit and silence Wilson. During a speech delivered in Washington, D.C., a radical activist group stormed the podium and stole the microphone. They shouted while waving Nazi symbols in mockery of Wilson's ideas. Finally, a woman snuck up behind Wilson and dumped a pitcher of ice water on his head, while the rest chanted, "You're all wet!"[13] A massive, organized Appeal to Fear if one ever existed.

In both of the cases of MacDonald and Wilson, liberalism exploits liberalism. I cannot subscribe to the views of either of these scholars. I think, in fact, that the criticisms comparing their brands of Darwinism to Nazism and racism probably have much truth, but I also think their Darwinism is more consistently thought out that those that criticize them. I find it ironic that liberals idolize Darwinism, and protect it institutionally with force, unless, of course, that Darwinism begins to cross other liberal taboos, such as the sacred topic of race and certainly that of the Jewish race—we must never speak of these topics in a critical manner, ever! In fact, thirteen European countries currently have laws banning anyone from publically revising or denying the extent of the Holocaust.[14] Universities bend just as squeamishly. Despite my strong disagreements with Wilson and MacDonald, I find the strong-arming and Appeals to Force of modern academia and governments on these issues even more sickening. This is the institutionalizing and militarizing of intellectual cowardice—unrespectable and a failure of logic and reason.

Liberals vs. Christians: The Anti-Intelligence Attack

One thing, however, can unite all Darwinists: the successes of creation science and intelligent design theory. The recent documentary *Expelled: No Intelligence Allowed* highlighted several instances where universities or museums have shunned, impeded, fired, or otherwise discriminated against scholars and teachers for their intellectual positions. Even if such cases did involve "religious" beliefs in the science world, the tactics employed against these scholars cry out "logical fallacy": "Either tow the party line, or you'll get fired or shunned, and your career ruined." One reporter relates an incident of shunning at the Smithsonian Museum of Natural History: the victim's supervisor related of the institution, "There are Christians here, but they keep their heads down."[15]

Many examples exist of Darwinists attacking and persecuting Christians or even just non-Darwinists.[16] *Expelled* merely popularized the tip of a massive iceberg. Already in his 1984 book *The Criterion*, scientist Dr. Jerry Bergman chronicled and described around a hundred cases of discrimination.[17] According to Bergman, one department supervisor exclaimed, "You creationists are Stone Age Neanderthals, and if I had my way I would fire every one of you."[18] Likewise Bergman relates how one hypocritical department head censored an article by tearing it out from the peer-reviewed journal *Systematic Zoology*—not because it was religious, but because it merely critiqued natural selection. He weakly defended his actions by waffling, "Well of course I don't believe in censorship in any form, but I just couldn't bear the idea of my students reading that article."[19] In other words, "I claim not to believe in censorship but I do believe in censorship, and I practice it." More recently Bergman has continued his laudable efforts at exposing such Darwinist bigotry, documenting many more cases (some of which involve pending court cases for discrimination) in detail in his book *Slaughter of the Dissidents*.[20]

Fear the Truth: Its Force Shall Prevail

Appeals to Force remain alive and well in American education, as well as in politics and society. In fact, one might say they describe the norm. The homosexual lobby, racial pressure groups, special interest groups, planned parenthood and other pro-choice groups, all attempt to use political power to further their agendas, and often target individuals (with whom they disagree) for smear campaigns that aim to frighten anyone else from opposing them.

But with God as the righteous Judge of history, these fallacious fear-mongerers must ultimately fail. Such attempts at control of education and knowledge, not ironically, often have adverse effects. The persecutions vaulted Velikovsky's career, and helped solidify Wilson international recognition. MacDonald would probably have languished in academic obscurity had it not been for the vicious attempts on his career by pressure groups. Fischer concludes about past efforts:

> German historiography has perhaps suffered more severely in this respect than that of any other nation. Sixty years ago [1910], its historians set standards for the world. Thirty years ago, its great centers of learning were purged of every vestige of open anti-Fascism. Today in historical scholarship, Germany is a stagnant backwater.... [T]he decline of German universities since 1932 testifies to the dangerous power of an argument *ad baculum*, not merely over the specific victim, but over everybody in the vicinity.[21]

Perhaps heralding such an ominous warning itself verges on an Appeal to Fear—"A thriving culture requires the absence of Appeals to Fear; Avoid them or face societal decay"—but can you think of a more legitimate Appeal to Fear outside of hell itself?

APPEAL TO PEER PRESSURE

An Appeal to Peer Pressure uses the emotional and psychological feeling of inclusion in or exclusion from a group as a means of pressuring its victim to adopt a position. Crude examples say, "Everyone else is doing it. You won't be cool if you don't," or "If you wish to join the club, you will agree with its perspectives." We can also call this fallacy the "Appeal to the Mob" where the title fits, or accept the traditional name of *Argumentum Ad Populum*, "Argument to the People." The fallacy threatens an individual with exclusion or ostracizing based on the desires of the majority, the possible anger or fury of the majority, the traditions, beliefs, ideology, or any other attribute of a group of people. "It is the kind of argument that plays to the galleries, not to the facts."[22]

Peer Pressure overlaps a bit with Appeal to Authority since a group of "peers" can establish behaviors and "traditions" which comprise a type of social authority. To dissent from the group, in these scenarios, implies social hubris and immodesty—the very ingredients that create the pressures behind an Appeal to Authority. Appeals to Peer Pressure also interrelate with Appeals to Fear because the group engages the dissenter with fear of not belonging, shunning, or disenfranchisement for his individualistic actions.

The pointlessness, logically, of Appealing to a Mob as a means of rational proof stands out almost as clearly as that of Appealing to Force. Even if everyone in the world accepted a proposition as true, their consent would not prove it true (thus pure Democracy is not necessarily a good idea!). Very popular ideas have often turned out badly false. We need only to remember the wild popularity of Adolph Hitler in the 1930s. Hailed as a political messiah, Hitler became the mass murderer history remembers him as. Yet he rode into power on a radical wave of popularity. Likewise, the pressures we endure when wanting to fit into even a small group cannot justify accepting a position as true. Many Christians in all sorts of situations will keep their faith quiet, or even act contrary to it, in order to maintain a job, position, or place in a certain group. Yet caving to such pressure does not prove the truth of any particular proposition, either. The Appeal to Peer Pressure has very powerful benefits socially for those dishonest enough to employ it, but it fails any test of logical consistency.

In considering Appeals to Peer Pressure, keep in mind that the "group" involved can appear in many forms. It may be large or small, organized or chaotic, personal or not, friendly or not. For example, a teacher seeking tenure at a university will face the peer pressure of a small organized group of other university faculty. However, these faculty members may know the applicant as a friend, and thus aim to help her, or they may see her as a threat to their own published work or agenda, and thus treat her as a potential enemy. In a different scenario, a political candidate faces the whole conglomerate of the general public as the "group" he must please. Few of them know him personally, and they have little organization amidst their great masses. In times of crisis when the masses grow desperate for jobs, money, safety, etc., politicians can easily lose control to mob-like actions. When running for office, opponents realize how fear moves the masses, and they often attempt to present their opponent as a fearful prospect before the public. Both cases exemplify the fallacy. In as many forms as the "group" may appear, so may the fallacy.

Peer-pressure fallacies appear commonly in marketing. One spammer boasted, "1,000,000 People Can't Be Wrong: More than 1,000,000 people decided our 85% off Target, Wal-Mart, Sam's and Office Depot prices was right for them." The ad concluded, "IT'S RIGHT FOR YOU TOO!" This last claim commits a Fallacy of the Beard on top of the Peer Pressure. Also notice the emotional pressure added by the ALL CAPS!—another feature to get you excited enough to STOP THINKING AND ACT! But the heart of this spam rests on the "1,000,000 people" claim: peer pressure at its best. Can you argue with "a million people"? Well, actually, yes. Consider that 1.22 Billion people worldwide smoke cigarettes daily, millions use illegal drugs resulting in thousands of deaths and over a million emergency room trips, tens of millions of people bought adjustable-rate mortgages with millions later forced into foreclosure, and millions upon millions each day contract a computer virus by clicking through spam emails. So I would say the "1,000,000 people" argument does not guarantee what's "RIGHT FOR YOU TOO." It may, in fact, have something terribly wrong waiting ahead for you.

Populism at Its Height

In regarding this fallacy, philosopher and logician E. Morris Engel reminds us of perhaps the most powerful display of oratory in American history, William Jennings Bryan's "Cross of Gold" Speech, delivered at the 1896 Democratic National Convention.[23] Despite focusing on a narrow subject—the use of silver to back currency, as opposed to only gold—Bryan hailed his mission as "the cause of humanity," and included several other Appeals to the Masses. He concluded,

> Our ancestors, when but 3 million, had the courage to declare their political independence of every other nation upon earth. Shall we, their descendants, when we have grown to 70 million, declare that we are less independent than our forefathers? No, my friends, it will never be the judgment of this people.... If they dare to come out in the open field and defend the gold standard as a good thing, we shall fight them to the uttermost, having behind us the producing masses of the nation and the world. Having behind us the commercial interests and the laboring interests and all the toiling masses, we shall answer their demands for a gold standard by saying to them, you shall not press down upon the brow of labor this crown of thorns. You shall not crucify mankind upon a cross of gold.[24]

Bryan's overt Appeal to the Masses actually abuses the fallacy several times, referencing the increased numbers of people in the country (thus implying their greater collective might), referring to the courage of the elite group of founding fathers, and calling upon the "producing masses," the "toiling masses," and "labor" as a collective group (outright Marxist language, actually). All of these have the effect of Appealing to the emotions and desires of the particular group, and urging them to act as a group to achieve the agenda. All of this pushes aside reasoning and logical connections, and ignores any possible logical conclusions to the contrary, but rather assumes Bryan's socialist platform as true and acceptable for society.

While Appeals to the Populace carry much weight, those who live by them can die by them—especially in politics, where an Appeal to the Mob suffers defeat by a Bigger Appeal to a Bigger Mob. In Bryan's case, his speech proved wildly popular to 1896 Democrats who immediately nominated him as their candidate; but he lost the general election by a wide margin to William McKinley. He subsequently lost twice more: again to McKinley in 1900, and finally to William Howard Taft in 1908. Bryan's career ended in disgrace as the agnostic lawyer Clarence Darrow publically mocked him in the witness box at the 1925 Scopes "monkey" trial. Bryan died a few days after the trial at age 65.

A Skeptic and a Saint Agree

The satirist and cynic Ambrose Bierce stumbled upon the roots of this fallacy in his *The Devil's Dictionary*. Defining the word "multitude," he wrote:

> A crowd; the source of political wisdom and virtue. In a republic, the object of the statesman's adoration.... If any men of equal wisdom are wiser than any one of them, it must be that they acquire the excess of wisdom by the mere act of getting together. Whence comes it? Obviously from nowhere—as well say that a range of mountains is higher than the single mountains composing it. A multitude is as wise as its wisest member if it obey him; if not, it is no wiser than its most foolish.

Bierce, who held no love for religion, ambled upon the depravity of man in its collective effects. Human wisdom does not increase because several people, or millions, agree. In fact, human vices and avarice tend to amplify when compounded as mob lust. The greatness of "democracy" is a myth, and the old saying *vox populi, vox dei* (the voice of the people is the voice of God) makes a political idol out of fallacious reasoning. Oddly enough, the first person to record this Latin proverb was the British cleric and scholar Alcuin of York (AD 735–804), who also subsequently refuted it. He wrote to Charlemagne, "Nor are those to be listened to who are accustomed to say, 'The voice of the people is the voice of God.' For the clamor of the crowd is very close to madness."[25]

Bierce's skepticism and Alcuin's wisdom combine to remind us that "wisdom" is a gift from God which requires God's nurture to grow. Wisdom does not arise from mere societal consent or "groupthink," which could sooner plunge society into rebellion than enlighten us. We need wisdom from outside the darkened mind of the human race in order to enlighten the human race. This comes from the wisest member of the human race, Jesus Christ. If "a multitude is as wise as its wisest member if it obey him," then let us not give into Peer Pressure, but follow Christ.

The Bible on Peer Pressure

Not many people realize, unless they have read the Bible carefully, that under the principle of not bearing false witness God's law *forbids* His people to give into Peer Pressure. *You shall not follow the crowd toward evil, nor sway a controversy by leaning after the crowd* (Ex. 23:2).[26] Commenting on this passage, the learned Baptist John Gill explained that "it is not the number of witnesses, but the nature, the evidence, and circumstances of their testimony, that are to be regarded."[27] Exactly. Peer Pressure—though a powerful force—has no bearing on determining truth. Truth stands or falls on its own merits, not on popularity. As Norm Geisler puts it, "When did reality become a democracy?"[28] This is the biblical view.

The Bible contains many examples of man's failure to withstand Peer Pressure, and the evils that can result. When Moses remained on Mt. Sinai for forty days and nights, the people grew restless waiting for him. They rashly denied Moses and demanded of Aaron to *make us a god who will go before us* (Ex. 32:1–2). Aaron thus faced the pressure of a restless mob, despite the fact that they wished to blatantly break the First and Second Commandments that they had heard God Himself speak just a few days earlier. Aaron gave in and created the golden calf. As a result, God sent Moses down to execute the offenders, and a plague fell upon those who did not receive the death penalty (Ex. 32:25–35).

Likewise, Saul, the first king of Israel, ended his career in ruin due to his inability to withstand the people. Despite God's blessing in securing the defeat of the Amalekites, Saul *with the people* refused to destroy the entire enemy, but rather saved King Agag as well as the best of the cattle (1 Sam. 15:9). This act played toward popularity (like a president's "approval ratings" today) instead of God's explicit command. When Samuel confronted Saul for his rebellion the king confessed, *I have indeed transgressed the command of the Lord and your words, because I feared the people and listened to their voice* (1 Sam. 15:24); and yet he still desired to retain the favor of the people. He pleaded with Samuel, *I have sinned; but please honor me now before the elders of my people and before Israel, and go back with me, that I may worship the Lord your God* (1 Sam. 15:30). Saul ended his life defeated on the battlefield: wounded by arrows, he committed suicide on his own sword before the enemy could finish him (1 Sam. 31:4–6). The Philistines defeated Israel and took over their cities and towns (1 Sam. 31).

Other biblical instances of Appeals to the Mob occur in Peter's denial of Jesus, certainly in fear that the people might have treated Jesus' disciples as badly as they had Jesus (Matt. 26:69–75). Also, certain unbelieving Jews tried to inflame the entire city of Thessalonica with hatred against Paul and the Christians there. The assailants, *taking along some wicked men from the market place, formed a mob and set the city in an uproar; and attacking the house of Jason, they were seeking to bring them out to the people* (Acts 17:5). Classic Mob action. As well, when Felix, the Roman governor at Caesarea, interrogated Paul, the governor wished to maintain good political favor with the local Jews. Despite Paul's accusers' inability to prove their charges, *wishing to do the Jews a favor, Felix left Paul imprisoned* (Acts 24:27). When Festus succeeded Felix, he feared the people as well (Acts 28:9).

Perhaps the worst biblical case of an Appeal to the Mob comes from Pontius Pilate. Fearing that the bloodthirsty mob would turn to riot on his watch, Pilate released the murderer Barabbas instead of the innocent Jesus. Scripture clearly states that he did so out of fear of the people: *Wishing to satisfy the crowd, Pilate released Barabbas for them, and after having Jesus scourged, he handed Him over to be crucified* (Mark 15:15); *When Pilate saw that he was accomplishing nothing, but rather that a riot was starting, he took water and washed his hands in front of the crowd, saying, "I am innocent of this Man's blood; see to that yourselves"* (Matt. 27:24).

We find an even more insidious and wicked aspect of this story in the Pharisees' explicit use of Mob Appeal to create the pressure on Pilate. They purposefully incited the mob: *But the chief priests and the elders persuaded the crowds to ask for Barabbas and to put Jesus to death* (Matt. 27:20; Mark 15:11). And the crowd, acting in defiance of the Exodus 23:2 law against following a crowd to do evil, willingly obeyed the Pharisees: *But they were insistent, with loud voices asking that He be crucified. And their voices began to prevail. And Pilate pronounced sentence that their demand be granted* (Luke 23:23–24). This sad episode illustrates the power of fallacious reasoning: an Appeal to Peer Pressure effected our Lord's torture and death.

Fallacies are sins, and as *the wages of sin is death* (Rom. 6:23), so can wicked judgment have deadly consequences. So often does a mob wield such power, and so often do those with wicked motives attempt to create mob opinion behind their agenda. Yet for those who reject Jesus, the Truth, they will stand with that final multitude that shall not prevail, where only Truth shall prevail, where Christ's judgment shall move the multitude instead of the crowd bending justice (John 5:26–29; 2 Cor. 5:10; Rev. 20:11–15). God shall not be swayed by the mob. His people should not be, either.

Academic Peer Pressure

In the previous section on Appeal to Fear/Force, I mentioned the many cases of discrimination against non-Darwinists by Darwinists. These cases, as they often occur among academic faculty, pertain to Appeal to Peer Pressure as well. Consider the Peer Pressure created by a group of faculty implicitly threatening to end your academic career—which you have trained for all your life—simply because you disagree with them on the issue of origins. Once they peg you with the label "creationist," they can force you to the fringes of academia, if you can remain at all. One professor of biology at Wheaton College, who is not even a classic "creation scientist," reveals the effects of the vast pressure: "I hate to hear the name *creationist*, because I am a creationist—but I don't want to be treated by my colleagues as a cultic person."[29]

As well, the instance of the two Harvard professors and the paper "The Israel Lobby and U. S. Foreign Policy," bears repeating. The vast majority of faculty at Harvard simply remained silent, refusing even to comment on the paper at all.[30] The reason for the self-imposed silence? It was fear; yet it was a fear imposed by academic Peer Pressure. One reporter noted, "Call it the academic Cold War: distrustful factions rendered timid by the prospect of mutually assured career destruction.... [P]rofessors fear taking a stand on either side."[31] Professors feared saying anything for or against the paper, afraid that another colleague would use that controversial statement against them somehow. So they collectively engaged in silence—the exact opposite of what academic life stands for, particularly regarding controversial issues.

POISONING THE WELL

One especially insidious means of tarnishing a debate with emotional bias occurs when someone attempts to discredit information by maligning the source of the information. Some people often adopt the old saying, "Consider the source," in order to end an argument before they properly evaluate it.[32] The fallacy of Poisoning the Well lies in the fact that even a disreputable person can sometimes offer a formidable argument; even a liar sometimes hits on the truth, even sometimes when he intends to lie! The truth of an argument does not necessarily depend on the reputation or character of the source making it. While corrupt character may imply a greater likelihood of mischief, no strictly logical connection exists between reputation and truth.

Literally poisoning a well was an act of warfare used in ancient and medieval times to plague and kill unsuspecting villages. Even today, poisoning a water supply remains a feared tactic of terrorism. If you poison a well—the source of water—then anyone who draws water from it will get infected. If someone knows you have poisoned their well, they will refuse to accept water from it. Likewise, if someone successfully discredits their intellectual opponent, then an audience will instinctively reject that opponent's arguments as well. Both activities are nearly as criminal as the other—the one defrauds property, the other the reputation. The particularly evil aspect of Poisoning the Well lurks in the fact that by wrongly discrediting someone, the perpetrator discredits not only their immediate argument, but pretty much everything they say in response afterwards.

Newman's Defense

The name "Poisoning the Well" in reference to logic comes originally from the writings of John Henry Cardinal Newman. In the "Preface" to his famous work *Apologia Pro Vita Sua* ("A Defense of One's Life"), Newman responded to the fallacious attack by novelist Charles Kingsley. Kingsley had written, "I am henceforth in doubt and fear, as much as any honest man can be, *concerning every word* Dr. Newman may write. *How can I tell that I shall not be the dupe of some cunning equivocation...?*"[33] Kingsley here attempted to smear Newman's character, and thus render as suspect *every word* which Newman would thereafter write. Such thinking crosses far beyond the line of fallacy, and approaches slander. It well warranted Newman's rebuttal:

> [W]hat I insist upon here is this unmanly attempt of his, in his concluding pages, to cut the ground from under my feet;—to poison by anticipation the public mind against me, John Henry Newman, and to infuse into the imaginations of my readers, suspicion and mistrust of ev-

> erything that I may say in reply to him. This I call *poisoning the wells*.
>
> "I am henceforth in *doubt and fear*," he says, "as much as any *honest* man can be, *concerning every word* Dr. Newman may write. *How can I tell that I shall not be the dupe of some cunning equivocation?*"...
>
> Well, I can only say, that, if his taunt is to take effect, I am but wasting my time in saying a word in answer to his calumnies; and this is precisely what he knows and intends to be its fruit.[34]

Newman countered Kingsley's accusation by pointing out the fallacy at the root of it: by Kingsley essentially arguing, "This man is a liar, and you can't trust anything he says," the attacker poisons the public mind against anything Newman could say. No matter how truly Newman may argue in return, Kingsley could twist and interpret everything he says as the desperate attempts of a liar—the court of public opinion having already decided against him, Newman could not prevail. The fallacy lies in attacking the person and in sewing prejudices rather than addressing the arguments. Newman noted this much as well: "Controversies should be decided by the reason; is it legitimate warfare to appeal to the misgivings of the public mind and to its dislikings? Any how, if my accuser is able thus to practise upon my readers, the more I succeed, the less will be my success."

Newman elaborates on how the tactic follows upon the first poisoning of the public mind:

> If I am natural, he will tell them, "Ars est celare artem [It is cunning to conceal cunning];" if I am convincing, he will suggest that I am an able logician; if I show warmth, I am acting the indignant innocent; if I am calm, I am thereby detected as a smooth hypocrite; if I clear up difficulties, I am too plausible and perfect to be true. The more triumphant are my statements, the more certain will be my defeat.[35]

In the movie, *The Emperor's New Clothes* (2002), actor Ian Holm plays Napoleon in a fictional and somewhat humorous rewriting of the emperor's later years. After he escapes from exile on the island of St. Helena, Napoleon's plans to reinstate his rule get foiled when a look-alike imposter who took his place on St. Helena refuses to reveal his true identity and thus spark a panic. Then the real Napoleon arrives at his contact officer's home and finds him in a coffin ready for burial. As he recalculates, the old emperor befriends the locals and captures the love of his former soldier's widow—all good, except, the aging ruler still desires to regain power. Yet whenever he attempts to reveal his identity, everyone refuses to believe him. Even his new love thinks he suffers from delusions of grandeur, and so does the local psychiatrist—a rival love interest. Once tricked into entering an asylum, Napoleon faces dozens of deluded residents all wearing "Napoleon hats" and claiming to be the emperor! The realization sets in, and the old man flees back to a quiet life with his lover and new family.

Sorry for the spoiler, but the scene of a real Napoleon having to distinguish himself from insane pretenders against public consent illustrates how this fallacy works. As Newman explained to his readers: "There is a story of a sane person being by mistake shut up in the wards of a Lunatic Asylum, and that, when he pleaded his cause to some strangers visiting the establishment, the only remark he elicited in answer was, 'How naturally he talks! you would think he was in his senses.'"[36] Once the public "knew"—via his institutionalization—that he was insane, nothing he could say could change their mind. Likewise, once a debater fools an audience into thinking that his opponent is a bad source for truth, then whatever that opponent says gets interpreted automatically as untrustworthy. It is victory by automatic dismissal.

In response to this fallacy you must do two things. First, you must point out the obvious fact: "Even if I am the vilest person on earth, yea even the devil himself, my arguments may yet stand all the tests of truth. Since you have not even ventured to refute my argument, but instead have attacked my reputation, my argument stands undefeated." With this you can disarm the poison—"I may well be vile, but..."—and at the same time expose the fallacy—"The argument remains untouched." With this follows the realization that the opponent has engaged in fallacious—in fact, quite dishonest—argumentation, and opens him to the charge of corruption himself. Also, his neglect of the actual argument exposes him to a variety of insinuations as to why he chose character assassination instead of honest debate. Intellectual cowardice comes to mind: "Is he afraid to address the real thing?"

Secondly, you can now easily turn the tables on the accuser. Newman above uses the Latin phrase *Ars est celare artem,* which means "It is cunning to conceal cunning," or more generally, "It takes skill to hide skill." This reply encapsulates the fallacy of Poisoning the Well: once the poison has been injected, no however powerfully the victim rebuts, the abuser can respond, "This poisonous lie is but more poison springing from the well of a liar! He is using lies to cover his lies!" But this claim on the part of the accuser is *itself a deceitful tactic,* and thus he is the one engaging in covering his cunning with more cunning. The one objective fact that the victim has on his side—that he actually argues earnestly— will aid him in countering the accuser's deceitful attack: "You have not proven a single one of my arguments wrong! Until you do, the only deceit concealed here lies in *you* labeling *me* deceitful. You are guilty of deceiving the audience, and of hiding that cunning with more deceits, not me!"

The Value of Character

The assassination of character or smearing of someone's reputation closely associates with this fallacy. Not all instances of Poisoning the Well involve an untrue attack on an individual's character, but many do. Scripture addresses this particular sin explicitly. Leviticus 19:16 states, *You shall not go about as a slanderer among your people.* Surely falling under the more general command against bearing false witness (and the command again theft, actually!), this command against slander—defrauding your neighbor's reputation—reveals another facet of God's standard for truth. In protecting our neighbor's name we bear witness to the image of God in that neighbor as well as ourselves: we must refuse to take God's name in vain, and likewise refuse the name of God's image—our neighbor—to suffer any discredit either.

Commenting on the idea, John Calvin argues that God's standard of truth requires that our tongues serve "both the good repute and advantage of our neighbors."[37] Scripture teaches this, "For if a good name is more precious than all riches [Prov. 22:1], we harm our neighbor more by despoiling him of the integrity of his name than by taking away his possessions."[38] We often fail in this regard, and we "delight in a certain poisoned sweetness experienced in ferreting out and in disclosing the evils of others." Yet, "That God is concerned about it should be enough to prompt us to keep safe our neighbor's good name." The child of God should avoid all "hateful accusation arising from evil intent and wanton desire to defame."[39] In other words, we should not only avoid Poisoning the Well in our claims (despite any "sweetness" involved in doing so), but we should actively attempt to protect the reputation of those we interact with.

Many Types of Poisoning

Remember that in addition to a direct personal attack, Poisoning the Well can appear in the form of tainting *any* source related to an argument. Well-poisoners may attack not only people, but nations, races, eras, universities, schools of thought, ideologies, disciplines, classes, occupations, and more. An argument, for example, that says, "Don't believe anything coming from the Marxist camp. Marxism begins with atheism!" commits the fallacy quite overtly, only the victim is not a single opponent but a whole ideology. Note: this is not to endorse Marxism or anything it teaches, but rather to point out one logically fallacious way of criticizing it. You do not need to Poison the Well in order to successfully refute their claims by other methods.

Besides, as Fred Schwarz titled a book long ago, *You Can Trust the Communists (...to do exactly as they say!)*. The point being, Marx and his followers often wrote explicitly enough to condemn themselves with their own words. The earnest student will find ample material to refute within the corpus of Marxist writings, including their atheistic formulations, but pointing to any aspect of Marxism with which to condemn all of Marxist thought risks Poisoning the Well, which the earnest student must avoid out of duty.

Interestingly enough, Schwarz noticed this risk, and therefore made the correct argument that the evil that resides in Communist thought stems from their own explicit arguments. He wrote that "they believe what they say they believe ... and their moral code is the one they have announced without shame.... In the battle against Communism, there is no substitute for specific knowledge."[40] Schwarz had the proper attitude: specific knowledge trumps prejudice, therefore go to the actual claims and arguments and set them before the public in all their glory.

We have no need to Poison the Wells when our opponents poison themselves! Lenin wrote:

> All worship of a divinity is necrophily [love of dead bodies].... [A]ny religious idea, any idea of any god at all,

any flirtation even with a god, is the most inexpressible foulness ... it is the most dangerous foulness, the most shameful "infection". A million *physical* sins, dirty tricks, acts of violence and infections are much more easily discovered by the crowd, and therefore are much less dangerous, than the *subtle*, spiritual idea of god...."[41]

Likewise, Marx wrote, "Communism begins at the outset with Atheism."[42] No need to argue about the intolerance of the Communists; they make it clear for us. Of course, we must still contend with the possibility that, even though they denounce religion and promote atheism, parts of their thought may contain some truths. Nevertheless, they have settled the question of whether or not they will tolerate religion ultimately. They clearly reveal that their hostility, and this means that they probably do not have your best interests at heart. Consider that worldviews affect every area of life and action, this revelation of the heart of Communism warrants suspicion for the whole movement.

Jesus and Poisoned Wells

The Pharisees engaged in Poisoning the Well when they accused Jesus of casting out demons by the power of the prince of the demons. After Jesus cast out a demon, the Pharisees conspired to argue, *This man casts out demons only by Beelzebul the ruler of the demons* (Matt. 12:24). By this they attempted to attribute Jesus' power to a demonic source, so that the people would view anything He said or did as an act of the Devil. But we know that Jesus lived a sinless life and had a good reputation among the people, so it did little good for the Pharisees to malign Him: He easily deflected their fallacy by pointing to His unparalleled good works: *the tree is known by its fruit* (Matt. 12:33). Likewise, He pointed out how the Pharisees' claim contradicted common sense, and thus proved futile. How could the Devil's kingdom advance if he was casting out his own demons? *Any kingdom divided against itself is laid waste; and any city or house divided against itself will not stand* (Matt. 12:25). The well, in this case, turns out not poisoned, but the Well of Life (compare John 4:14; 7:37–40).

Jesus also pointed out that words have ethical consequences, thus rebuking the Pharisees' fallacious argument:

For the mouth speaks out of that which fills the heart. The good man brings out of his good treasure what is good; and the evil man brings out of his evil treasure what is evil. But I tell you that every careless word that people speak, they shall give an accounting for it in the day of judgment. For by your words you will be justified, and by your words you will be condemned (Matt. 12:34–37).

Jesus also had special insight into the Pharisees' agenda, and Scripture shares this with us. Before Jesus cast out the demon, he had healed a man's lame hand on the Sabbath, and *the Pharisees went out and conspired against Him, as to how they might destroy Him. But Jesus, aware of this, withdrew from there* (Matt. 12:14–15). Later, after Jesus cast out the demon, the Pharisees tried to Poison the Well, but Jesus knew their thoughts (Matt. 12:25), and He ably refuted them in public.

Earlier in the Gospels, Jesus had to refute rumors that had poisoned public opinion against God's work. He preached, *For John came neither eating nor drinking, and they say, "He has a demon!" The Son of Man came eating and drinking, and they say, "Behold, a gluttonous man and a drunkard, a friend of tax collectors and sinners!"* (Matt. 11:18–19). That public opinion had dismissed both servants of God—John the Baptist and Jesus—shows how easily those who wish to Poison the Well can twist the truth to their purpose. No matter that each appeared differently—John as an ascetic, fasting and living in simplicity, and Jesus identifying with the common man—those who desire to criticize will find some reason to do so. Jesus' closing comment, *Yet wisdom is vindicated by her deeds*, takes on important meaning here: just as those bent on criticizing will find a reason, those who seek wisdom will prevail in that pursuit. Both will receive judgment accordingly.

Paul and Poisoned Wells

Paul also faced this fallacy (probably often!). When he drew the attention of the philosophers in Athens, some of them treated him with contempt. *And also some of the Epicurean and Stoic philosophers were conversing with him. Some were saying, "What would this idle babbler wish to say?" Others, "He seems to be a proclaimer of strange deities"* (Acts 17:18). The statement about "strange deities" seems fair enough—to them Paul's message in fact set forth a God they had never heard of—but the name-calling of "idle babbler" clearly crosses the line into Poisoning the Well. The

Greek word is actually *spermologos*, which more literally means "seed-picker," or "one who picks up scraps of information."[43] Like a bird that scavenges scraps of bread from the sidewalk, so this little man Paul spouts bits of wisdom probably stolen from other philosophers. In a culture that crawled with sophists—philosophers who made a living by using rhetoric to win audiences—such upstart "seed picking" philosophers likely presented a common sight. Nevertheless, to label Paul thus before hearing his arguments simply Poisoned the Well. Fortunately for Paul, the power of God's word in his preaching actually won some of them over (Acts 17:32–34).

Likewise, as Paul stayed in Ephesus after he preached there, one of the local silversmiths, who made idols for worship in the temple of Diana, rounded up all of his guild members and persuaded them that if Paul's teaching prevailed, their entire craft would collapse as demand for idols fell. This purely economic incentive intended to Poison the Well against Paul's messages. No matter how he argued for it, the conclusion remained the same for the craftsmen: they would lose business! The fallacy here lies in preferring money gained by idolatry rather than reforming their work around godly conversion. The efforts of the tradesmen set the city in an uproar, which built up until a local official persuaded them to settle the matter lawfully (Acts 19:21–41). The whole problem arose from a Poisoned Well, and Appeal to Fear (loss of money), and an Appeal to the Mob. So much for the tradition of philosophy and reason in Greek culture!

Reductio Ad Hitlerum

One particularly relevant modern abuse of this fallacy bears the special title *Reductio Ad Hitlerum* (Reduction to Hitler), and seeks to Poison the Well by aligning an opponent with Hitler, Nazism, the Holocaust, anti-Semitism, etc. It essentially argues that "Hitler did X, therefore X is bad." But, as the philosopher who coined the phrase explained, "A view is not refuted by the fact that it happens to have been shared by Hitler."[44] Political writer and scholar Thomas Fleming explained the fallacy,

> If Hitler liked neoclassical art, that means that classicism in every form is Nazi; if Hitler wanted to strengthen the German family, that makes the traditional family (and its defenders) Nazi; if Hitler spoke of the "nation" or the

"folk," then any invocation of nationality, ethnicity, or even folkishness is Nazi....[45]

He explained how the fallacy plays out in cultural debate, and suggests a dark motive behind the abuse:

> The propagators of the new religion of the holocaust are not actually interested in the sufferings of the Jews but in the destruction of every good thing that can be tarred with the Nazi brush: Lutheran and Catholic Christianity, patriotism and the affection for one's own people and traditions, conventional morality, traditional art and literature.

This Poisons the Well in a very purposeful way—for the advancement of a political agenda. But this special abuse not only commits the fallacy, it gives us an opportunity in which to clearly exhibit why Poisoning the Well constitutes a fallacy. Just consider the question, "If Hitler said, 'Two plus two equals four,' would you deny the truth of that statement because Hitler said it?" Once again: truth stands or falls on its own merits, not on the merits of those who proclaim it.

Abuses similar to the *Ad Hitlerum* version appear often when liberals attack conservatives. Because many terrorist groups or human rights violators cloak their crimes in the name of God or religion, many leftists, liberals, and atheists try to smear all religious conservatives with the image of terrorism, or the like. The recent outbursts of atheism from Sam Harris and Christopher Hitchens exemplify this extravagance, echoing the classic tactics of the liberal agenda. A headline from over fifteen years ago reads, "Family Values and K.K.K." The guilt-by-association, well-poisoning tactic pours from the leftist article:

> I entered a time warp recently while listening to a tape recording of a political rally in May 1963.
>
> The 29-year-old celebrations of "family values" playing in my earphones were strangely similar to the sentiments expressed at the Republican National Convention two weeks ago.
>
> There were tributes to God... wives... civic pieties and denunciations of Communists, journalists and Democrats.

> The 1963 spectacle was a Ku Klux Klan rally in Birmingham, Ala.
>
> Family values was the centerpiece of the old Klan ideology.... They insisted that their anti-black terrorist mandate came from G-O-D....
>
> The Republican Party of 1992 won't need so grotesque a hypocrisy to show how corrupt the ideology of "family values" can be.[46]

According to this reasoning, behind all rhetoric of "family values" we should suspect K.K.K.-style racism, terrorism, and the like—a Fallacy of Sweeping Generalization if ever one existed. Aside from this, the Poisoning of the Well stands out: we should reject "family values" because *some* people who have promoted "family values" have also promoted racism and terrorism. Again, we have Hitler pronouncing "2+2=4." The writer of this column, to remain consistent with her illogic, would have to deny *any* truth—even the most fundamental truth—if uttered by a maniac. For her, the source dictates the truth of the position. So, what if God Himself dictated the truth of family values? What will the leftist say when called to account for that one?

In the area of theology, our dispensational brethren often abuse the poisonous association of "Hitler," "holocaust," and "anti-Semitism" in order to halt criticism of their position. Their particular abuse essentially commits the same error as an *Ad Hitlerum*, but commits it more broadly. By defining "Jews" as physical-national Israel, and making that narrow group the central object of God's special favor, they can then draw from the power of the modern label "anti-Semitic" in order stifle anyone who wishes to challenge their arguments. Once such an emotionally charged label enters the dialogue, the whole rational side of the debate suffers and usually dies out. But this tactic merely avoids the real debate, and Poisons the Well with a powerful epithet.

We find examples of this throughout dispensationalism, but also in recent classical premillennial authors. For example, premillennialist Barry Horner declares his "disturbance" that many Reformed Christians believe "that the Jew today, on account of stubborn unbelief, is covenantally and eternally *persona non grata* in the sight of God."[47] Despite the fact that this description is a Straw Man (no Reformed believer I know of has completely written off Jews to this extreme), Horner then lets the fallacy fly: "Perhaps most disturbing of all in this regard has been an evident form of theological anti-Judaism among a considerable number of those holding Reformed convictions."[48] He later implies that he has chosen the label "anti-Judaism" instead of "anti-Semitism" in order to avoid the racial aspect of the latter term, but he does not explicitly state this. Whichever thrust he intends, the effect remains the same: he Poisons the Well of his opponents so that however they may respond, they will be viewed as attacking "Jews." Even the fact that past Christians have mistreated ethnic Jews in various situations does not warrant such a deceitful and damaging tactic in Horner's (or anyone else's) scholarship.

"Religion Masquerading as Science"

In a very similar manner many evolutionists try to immunize their Darwinism by labeling any criticism from Christians as "creationism" or "religion masquerading as science." Eugenie Scott, an outspoken defender of Darwinism and opponent of intelligent design frequently resorts to Poisoning the Well, titling her articles against intelligent design, "Creationism Evolves,"[49] and "The Latest Face of Creationism in the Classroom."[50] In her book, *Evolution Vs. Creationism: An Introduction*, she quotes a speech prepared for Congress against the language of the No Child Left Behind Act of 2001. The Hon. Rush D. Holt railed,

> The implication in this language that there are other scientific alternatives to evolution represents a veiled attempt to introduce creationism—and, thus, religion—into our schools. Why else would the language be included at all? In fact, this objectionable language was written by proponents of an idea known as "intelligent design." This concept, which could also be called "stealth creationism", suggests that the only plausible explanation for complex life forms is design by an intelligent agent. This concept is religion masquerading as science.[51]

Evolutionists have gotten plenty of mileage out of this phrase, "religion masquerading as science." The phase, however, commits a classic Fallacy of Poisoning the Well. This means, of course, that the continued success of activists and some legistators in this regard depends in large part upon a lie. But then, evolution as a theory of human origins itself rests on a mammoth Worldview Fallacy, and if they swallow that, they'll likely swallow anything.

APPEAL TO PITY

An Appeal to Pity defies logic as it attempts to persuade using feelings of guilt or mercy. It argues, "Accept Position X, because it benefits the poor, needy, blind, lame, destitute, little children, orphans, widows, elderly, etc." It escapes the nets of logic by tugging on heart strings.

This fallacy includes one particularly evil aspect in that it urges a Christian duty in order to dodge another Christian duty. It exalts mercy and pity towards the unfortunate—in essence, making an appeal to "love your neighbor"—at the expense of Truth. But "you shall not bear false witness" also falls under the rubric of "love your neighbor," and thus we must have wisdom to discern truth in cases that involve human suffering. In this way, Appeals to Pity not only defy the Ninth Commandment, but set God's word against itself, and thus bring confusion into Christian life.

The truth is, God's word requires us to show mercy, and anyone who loves God and their neighbor will *want* to show mercy. This does not mean that such cases of mercy can necessarily serve as proof for any given proposition; the mandate for mercy derives from *its own* proposition as given by God. In fact, given that humans bear God's image, and thus that God designed us to identify with each other in our sufferings, to Appeal to that God-given faculty in order to suppress or evade truth abuses and mocks God's created order. Such a fallacy on the one hand *acknowledges* our duty to love one another, because it acknowledges that we are designed specifically for doing so; but on the other hand it *denies* our obligation to love one another through bearing faithful witness.

Scripture provides a good example of how these two mandates apply when they appear to conflict. Proverbs 6:30–31 explains that we must uphold justice even when a thief steals due to poverty: *Men do not despise a thief if he steals to satisfy himself when he is hungry; But when he is found, he must repay sevenfold; He must give all the substance of his house.* Notice the acknowledgment of both issues: the fact of men's feelings of pity, and yet also of the duty to obey God's law. In such a case, the law requires that we punish civil disobedience *even though we feel pity* for the thief. Likewise, in argument we must follow a logical conclusion even if we do not feel comfortable doing so. We must not allow pity, mercy, feelings of guilt, or any other feeling, to move us to pervert the truth—even if that feeling naturally fits the situation.

Christian Pity and Pitiful Logic

One glaring example (among many) of an Appeal to Pity fills the pages of Ron Sider's best-seller *Rich Christians in an Age of Hunger*. The title itself suggests the fallacy. The text spills it:

> Hunger and starvation stalk the land. Famine is alive and well on planet earth. Millions of people die of starvation each year.... One billion people have stunted bodies or damaged brains because of inadequate food....
>
> American Christians have failed to declare God's perspective on the plight of our billion hungry neighbors....
>
> What can be done? U.S. citizens must demand a drastic reorientation of U.S. foreign policy. We must demand a foreign policy that unequivocally sides with the poor....
>
> What are the fundamental biblical principles we need to keep in mind as we think of structural change in society? The most basic theological presupposition, of course, is that the sovereign Lord of the universe is always at work liberating the poor and oppressed and destroying the rich and mighty because of their injustice....[52]

Sider's well-intended proposition has some flaws (both logical and biblical). First, he has exaggerated his "most basic theological presupposition." God does not unequivocally side with the poor and against the rich in the way that Sider's language here implies. Wealth and might do not necessarily imply injustice, and poverty does not secure God's favor. In fact, poverty often results from God's judgment (Deut. 28:15–68), though it does not automatically indicate punishment. Rather, God's law requires us to avoid favoring either the rich *or* the poor in our judgments (Ex. 23:3; Lev. 19:15). Sider himself notes these laws, and yet fails to apply them consistently.[53]

Secondly, even if Sider's presuppositions held true, they would still not justify his proposed solutions to the hunger problem. Even if God set our priority as Christians to side with the poor above all else (now

I'm exaggerating, on purpose), this would not necessarily demand that we do so through foreign policy or foreign aid, or any other government programs. Yet Sider calls for many of these in his book, and though he softens much of his language in later editions, he finds even more areas in which he thinks government should impose economic regulations and taxes—measures that many Christians would indentify as running counter to Biblical principles. Instead, while biblical religion mandates that we in fact address poverty, we must debate and determine biblical solutions and methods to the problems separately. To rush into what Sider says we should "demand" due to our natural pity for a "billion hungry neighbors" engages in logical fallacy (times a billion) on his part, and risks ignoring genuinely biblical solutions on ours.[54]

Worse yet, Sider finished off the Appeals to Pity in his first edition with an Appeal to Fear: "The present division of the world's resources dare not continue. And it will not. Either courageous pioneers will persuade reluctant nations to share the good earth's bounty or we will enter an era of catastrophic conflict."[55] In the intro to that work Sider suggested the possibility of poverty-stricken nations (he mentioned India) resorting to nuclear strikes if the U.S. did not send the aid they needed.[56] Such fear mongering displays the crudest of logical fallacies. Compounding that with Appeals to Pity, as well as Euphemism ("courageous pioneers" for those who follow his advice) exhibits the poorest possible reasoning, especially for a Christian.

Marriage in the Pitts

Another example comes from a local newspaper columnist who tackles the radical topic of gay marriage. Leonard Pitts, guest columnist in *The Atlanta Journal-Constitution*, promotes a typical liberal non-argument that derives all of its persuasive strength from the pity generated by an anecdote. He begins by describing a typical family, only constructing the story so that reader plays the assumed husband's role, vacationing with his wife and kids on a cruise ship. Suddenly mommy falls ill and the scene transfers to a hospital room. Anxiously awaiting news of his wife's condition, he paces the halls periodically getting stalled by doctors. Finally, he reaches her bedside only to watch a priest administer last rights as she dies. Then come two shocking twists: this story really happened on Feb. 18–19, 2007, in Miami, *and* the anxious husband was not a husband, but a lesbian lover.

Notice how merely by the way the writer constructs the argument—placing the sympathetic reader in the midst of it with certain traditional assumptions in place—he succeeds in building the emotional power he needs to pull off the intellectual scam. Then, once the reader's emotion naturally engages the "couple," the writer completes the heist, switching the gender of the "husband," and thus stealing the legitimate pathos for an illegitimate cause.

This bait-and-switch merely begins the author's Appeal to Pity. He writes,

> Politicians and alleged religious leaders have routinely invited us to hate gay people and call it morality. They have taught us to frame gay lives in cloudy abstracts of tradition and values. But this isn't abstract, is it?[57]

Then he pours it on:

> No, it's Janice and Lisa, meeting in college and falling in love, 20 years ago. It is a "holy union" service in a local church,... "We were dirt poor ... but we pulled it off."
>
> It is taking in foster kids no one else wants, drug babies, HIV babies, babies with fetal alcohol syndrome. It is adopting four of them and Lisa deciding she wants to be a stay-at-home mom and Janice saying OK, and wondering how the six of them will manage on a social worker's salary.
>
> It is Janice, diagnosed with multiple sclerosis, and Lisa, bashful Lisa, becoming the family extrovert, cheering the kids at "toddler tumbling time," shepherding them to swimming lessons and story time at the library.
>
> It is Lisa, who loved pecan sandies, the movie "Beaches," and Mitch Album's book "Tuesdays with Morrie," stricken by an aneurysm. It is Lisa, for eight hours, dying alone. It would be good if someone remembered her next time we are invited to hate an abstract. And remember Janice, who could not ache more deeply even if her name was Joe.[58]

Where in any of this did Mr. Pitts approach a substantial argument? Well, in fairness we should note that he consciously used the Appeal to Pity in order to make us aware of the fact that not legalizing gay marriage *does* in fact have real life consequences. This he promotes against "politicians and alleged religious leaders" who have "routinely invited us to hate gay people" and "frame gay lives in cloudy abstracts of tradition and values." Of course, what politician has actually invited you to "hate gay people"? The reader can easily see that the heart of this argument is a Straw Man, weakly mocking as "hate" the conservative and majority platform that opposes gay marriage. In Mr. Pitts' world, opposition gets labeled "hate," and "values"—at least values he doesn't agree with!—are "cloudy" and "abstract." With such a weak caricature of the real conservative position, the Straw Man stands out. Likewise, with such loaded words such as "hate," etc., the fallacy of Epithet applies as well. Additionally, Pitts Begs the Question. Instead of presenting an argument to prove that traditional marriage values are wrong, he *assumes this*, and then tells his story based on that assumption.

But is it true, for example, that opposing gay marriage invites us to hate an "abstraction"? Do conservative and religious believers who promote same-sex marriage ignore such real-life consequences? After all, this Janice and Lisa story *really happened*, and Janice and the kids ended up *really sorrowful*. But since when did emotions prove logical direction and wisdom? Since when did someone merely feeling bad about a situation legitimize their agenda? Some murderers feel bad, not for murdering, but for getting caught and punished. Should we therefore relax the laws and punishments against murder? No? But what if that murderer had four adopted HIV babies and loved eating pecan cookies? Now don't be blinded by all those alleged religious leaders who preach against murder; they're just promoting another abstract and cloudy tradition!

Once you dispense of the Straw Man, and the Epithet, Pitts has nothing left but a sad story and a bucket-load of pity. He Appeals to it very strongly. Granted, the story *does* involve the truly sad story of a lover who has invested much of her life and emotion into another person, but strong feelings do not necessitate logical entailment. The truth does not hinge on whether the story is sad or not; it hinges on whether the relationship at the base of it is ultimately legitimate or not. The story can be sad and the relationship illegitimate at the same time.

Coulter Confronts Pitiful Logic

The Appeal to Pity has emerged as a favorite tactic of modern liberals. Conservative columnist Ann Coulter explains with characteristic acumen:

> [T]he Democrats hit on an ingenious strategy: They would choose only messengers whom we're not allowed to reply to. That's why all Democratic spokesmen these days are sobbing, hysterical women. You can't respond to them because that would be questioning the authenticity of their suffering. Liberals haven't changed the message, just the messenger. All the most prominent liberal spokesmen are people with "absolute moral authority"—Democrats with a dead husband, a dead child, a wife who works at the CIA, a war record, a terminal illness.... Liberals prey on people at a time of extreme emotional vulnerability and offer them fame and fortune to be that month's purveyor of hate. Victory goes to the most hysterical....

[O]ver the last few years the Democrats have used:

- a grieving Carolyn McCarthy, whose husband was murdered by a lunatic on the Long Island Rail Road, to lobby for gun control

- a paralyzed, dying Christopher Reeve to argue for embryonic stem-cell research

- a gaggle of weeping widows to blame [then] President Bush for 9/11

- a disabled Vietnam veteran, Max Cleland, to attack the Iraq war and call Bush, Cheney, and every other human who ever disagreed with him a "chicken hawk"

- a rare Democratic Purple Heart recipient, Congressman John Murtha, to argue for surrender in Iraq....[59]

Similarly, "Former *New Republic* editor and gay marriage advocate Andrew Sullivan brandished the openly gay chaplain to New York

City's firemen, who himself died at the World Trade Center on 9/11, in his ongoing, nonstop argument for gay priests. The chaplain died on 9/11, therefore the Pope should back off."[60] Coulter exposes the faulty logic behind Appeals to Pity, and what she explains also applies to Mr. Pitts' pitiful story above. Peeling away all the layers of emotion involved, Pitts' argument amounts to this: "Janice's lesbian lover died, Janice felt bad about it, and therefore we should legalize gay marriage."

Liberals (and others) who have no winning substance to their arguments love to resort to emotional appeals, and the more pitiful the case they can present, the more their opposition will look heartless for merely questioning them. But good judgment, questioning, and critical thinking should make up the true heart of social policy and legislation. Injecting emotions into the issue reduces both the possibility and effectiveness of reasoned discourse, and thus damages the effort of arriving at truth and justice. Squelching these virtues with Appeals to Pity indicates greater concern for a personal agenda than for truth.

The Man of Ultimate Sorrow

One question may arise here which I should address. The Bible itself contains some strongly emotive words and images which is uses to describe, for example, the sacrifice of Christ. Psalm 22 graphically describes the suffering Messiah:

> *But I am a worm and not a man, A reproach of men and despised by the people. All who see me sneer at me; They separate with the lip, they wag the head, saying, "Commit yourself to the Lord; let Him deliver him; Let Him rescue him, because He delights in him." Yet You are He who brought me forth from the womb; You made me trust when upon my mother's breasts. Upon You I was cast from birth; You have been my God from my mother's womb. Be not far from me, for trouble is near; For there is none to help. Many bulls have surrounded me; Strong bulls of Bashan have encircled me. They open wide their mouth at me, As a ravening and a roaring lion. I am poured out like water, And all my bones are out of joint; My heart is like wax; It is melted within me. My strength is dried up like a potsherd, And my tongue cleaves to my jaws; And You lay me in the dust of death. For dogs have surrounded me; A*

> *band of evildoers has encompassed me; They pierced my hands and my feet. I can count all my bones. They look, they stare at me; They divide my garments among them, And for my clothing they cast lots* (Ps. 22:6–18).

Other passages such as Isaiah 52:13–53:12 come to mind as well. Passages such as these help us to discern the proper role of emotions in literature and communication: identifying with other people and knowing our Creator. Jesus, after all, took on human flesh for that very purpose: to identify with mankind, and to reveal the Father to us. *For we do not have a high priest who cannot sympathize with our weaknesses, but One who has been tempted in all things as we are, yet without sin* (Heb. 4:15). An important difference arises between the "pity" of Jesus' sacrifice and the fallacious Appeals heard so often today: Jesus and the disciples did not appeal to pity in order to get *you* to sacrifice something (more taxes, your gun rights, parental rights, free speech rights, etc.), rather Jesus Himself *willingly accepted* the burden of pain and suffering *without complaining*. In fact, Peter teaches that Jesus' suffering serves as an example we should follow: not as a devious tool for persuading others so we can get what we want, but as a means of committing ourselves to God and helping others in their needs. The apostle writes,

> *For this finds favor, if for the sake of conscience toward God a person bears up under sorrows when suffering unjustly.... For you have been called for this purpose, since Christ also suffered for you, leaving you an example for you to follow in His steps, who committed no sin, nor was any deceit found in his mouth; and while being reviled, He did not revile in return; while suffering, He uttered no threats, but kept entrusting Himself to Him who judges righteously; and He Himself bore our sins in His body on the cross, so that we might die to sin and live to righteousness; for by His wounds you were healed* (1 Pet. 2:19–24).

Jesus entrusted himself *to Him who judges righteously*. In other words, He did not attempt to prove his message based on the enormity of His plight—even though He did suffer beyond imagination—but rather overcame the temptation to persuade through emotions. The psalms, prophets, and Gospels all use graphic descriptions in order to help us identify with the suffering Messiah. But *only since Jesus' cause was just and*

His handling of it noble to begin with is this emotive appeal *legitimate* (and then only as a means of communication, not as a justification or proof). The problem arises when, as in some of the examples above, someone hijacks the power of a legitimate emotional identification in order to promote an illegitimate goal. This commits the fallacy of Appeal to Pity, and in the interest of honesty and integrity, the student should avoid it. In fact, following the example of Christ in suffering through evil, the student must forebear the temptation to take the easy way out in promoting such fallacies in place of truth.

NOTES

1. Quoted by Jake Tapper, comment on "Bobby Rush: Senators Blocking Burris from Senate Would Be Like Bull Connor and Other Infamous Racists of Yore," Political Punch Blog, December 31, 2008; available at http://blogs.abcnews.com/politicalpunch/2008/12/bobby-rush-sena.html, accessed January 6, 2009.

2. See S. Morris Engel, *With Good Reason: An Introduction to Informal Fallacies*, Fifth Ed. (New York: St. Martin's Press, 1994), 230.

3. David Hackett Fischer, *Historians' Fallacies: Toward a Logic of Historical Thought* (New York: Harper Torchbooks, 1970), 295.

4. David Hackett Fischer, *Historians' Fallacies: Toward a Logic of Historical Thought*, 295.

5. David Hackett Fischer, *Historians' Fallacies: Toward a Logic of Historical Thought*, 295.

6. Unfortunately, two of the finest books on fallacies commit this error: Irving M. Copi, *Introduction to Logic*, 7th Ed. (New York: Macmillan; and London: Collier-Macmillan, 1986), 106; and David Hackett Fischer, *Historians' Fallacies: Toward a Logic of Historical Thought*, 294.

7. See Austin Cline, "Appeal to Force/Fear (Argumentum Ad Baculum)"; available at http://atheism.about.com/library/FAQs/skepticism/blfaq_fall_force.htm, accessed January 2, 2009.

8. David Hackett Fischer, *Historians' Fallacies: Toward a Logic of Historical Thought*, 294–295.

9. See Alfred de Grazia, ed. *The Velikovsky Affair: The Warfare of Science and Scientism* (Hyde Park, NY: University Books, 1966).

10. Robert Nisbet, "Inquisitions," *Prejudices: A Philosophical Dictionary* (Cambridge, MA and London: Harvard University Press, 1982), 195–196.

11. Eve Fairbanks, "A hot paper muzzles academia," *Los Angeles Times*, May 14, 2006;

available at http://articles.latimes.com/2006/may/14/opinion/op-fairbanks14, accessed January 5, 2009.

12. Kevin MacDonald, "Heidi Does Long Beach: The SPLC vs. Academic Freedom," *VDARE.com*, November 14, 2006; available at http://www.vdare.com/macdonald/061114_splc.htm, accessed January 5, 2009.

13. See the account by Tom Wolfe, *Hooking Up* (New York: Picadour, 2000), 80–82.

14. See, for example, the Wikipedia article, http://en.wikipedia.org/wiki/Holocaust_denial, accessed January 5, 2009.

15. David Klinghoffer, "The Branding of a Heretic: Are religious scientists unwelcome at the Smithsonian?" *Wall Street Journal*, January 28, 2005; available at http://www.opinionjournal.com/taste/?id=110006220, accessed January 5, 2009.

16. See the movie *Expelled: No Intelligence Allowed* (Premise Media Corp., 2008); and John Ankerberg and John Weldon, *Darwin's Leap of Faith: Exposing the False Religion of Evolution* (Eugene, OR: Harvest House Publishers, 1998), 93–111.

17. *The Criterion: Religious Discrimination in America* (Richfield, MN: Onesimus Publishing, 1984).

18. Bergman, *The Criterion*, xi; cited in Ankerberg and Weldon, *Darwin's Leap of Faith*, 104.

19. Bergman, *The Criterion*, 28; cited in Ankerberg and Weldon, *Darwin's Leap of Faith*, 110.

20. *Slaughter of the Dissidents, Volume I* (Southworth, WA: Leafcutter Press, 2008).

21. David Hackett Fischer, *Historians' Fallacies: Toward a Logic of Historical Thought*, 295.

22. Norman L. Geisler and Ronald M. Brooks, *Come Let Us Reason: An Introduction to Logical Thinking* (Grand Rapids: Baker Book House, 1990), 97.

23. E. Morris Engel, *With Good Reason: An Introduction to Informal Fallacies*, 5th Ed. (New York: St. Martin's Press, 1994), 211.

24. Available at http://historymatters.gmu.edu/d/5354/, accessed January 6, 2009.

25. See George Boas, *Vox populi; Essays in the History of an Idea* (Baltimore, MD: Johns Hopkins Press, 1969), 9; also quoted at http://en.wikipedia.org/wiki/Vox_populi, accessed January 6, 2009.

26. Again, this is my translation, which I think is more faithful to the Hebrew. Compare the Geneva Bible, "Thou shalt not follow a multitude to do evil, neither agree in a controversy to decline after many and overthrow the truth." The New King James says, "You shall not follow a crowd to do evil; nor shall you testify in a dispute so as to turn aside after many to pervert justice" (Ex. 23:2).

27. John Gill, *Exposition of the Old and New Testaments*, 9 Vols. (Paris, AR: The Baptist Standard Bearer, 1989), 452.

28. Norman L. Geisler and Ronald M. Brooks, *Come Let Us Reason: An Introduction to Logical Thinking*, 97.

29. Ross S. Olson, "Peer pressure and truth," *Creation*, June 1995, 17(3):24–25; available at http://www.answersingenesis.org/creation/v17/i3/peer_pressure.asp, accessed January 6, 2009.

30. Eve Fairbanks, "A hot paper muzzles academia," *Los Angeles Times*, May 14, 2006; available at http://articles.latimes.com/2006/may/14/opinion/op-fairbanks14, accessed January 8, 2009.

31. Eve Fairbanks, "A hot paper muzzles academia," *Los Angeles Times*, May 14, 2006; available at http://articles.latimes.com/2006/may/14/opinion/op-fairbanks14, accessed January 8, 2009.

32. As Dr. Hoover notes in *Don't You Believe It* (Chicago: Moody Press, 1982), 63.

33. John Henry Cardinal Newman, *Apologia Pro Vita Sua: Being a History of His Religious Opinions* (London: Longmans, Green, and Co., 1908), xv.

34. John Henry Cardinal Newman, *Apologia Pro Vita Sua: Being a History of His Religious Opinions*, xv–xvi. This example is referenced by Albury Castell, "Analyzing a Fallacy," in *Readings in Speech*, ed. Haig Bosmajian (New York: Harper and Row, 1965); also by S. Morris Engel, *With Good Reason: An Introduction to Informal Fallacies*, 5th Ed. (New York: St. Martin's Press, 1994), 207.

35. John Henry Cardinal Newman, *Apologia Pro Vita Sua: Being a History of His Religious Opinions*, xvi–xvii.

36. John Henry Cardinal Newman, *Apologia Pro Vita Sua: Being a History of His Religious Opinions*, xvi.

37. John Calvin, *Institutes of the Christian Religion*, 2 Vols., ed. John T. McNeill, trans. Ford Lewis Battles (Philadelphia: The Westminster Press, 1960), (2.8.47) 1:412.

38. John Calvin, *Institutes of the Christian Religion*, (2.8.47) 1:412.

39. John Calvin, *Institutes of the Christian Religion*, (2.8.48) 1:412.

40. Fred Schwarz, *You can Trust the Communists (...to do exactly as they say)* (Englewood Cliffs, NJ: Prentice-Hall, Inc., 1960), 1.

41. V. I. Lenin to Maxim Gorky, November 1913, in *V. I. Lenin: Collected Works, Volume 35, Letters February 1912—December 1922*, ed. Robert Daglish, trans. Andrew Rothstein (Moscow: Progress Publishers, 1973), 121–122; available at http://www.marxists.org/archive/lenin/works/1913/nov/00mg.htm (accessed January 12, 2009). Also partially quoted in David Aikman, *The Delusion of Disbelief* (Carol Stream, IL: SaltRiver, 2008), 94, 109.

42. Karl Marx, "Economic and Philosophic Manuscripts of 1844," in *Karl Marx Frederick Engels Collected Works, Volume 3: Marx and Engels 1843–44* (New York: International Publishers, 1975), 297; available at http://www.marxists.org/archive/marx/works/1844/manuscripts/comm.htm (accessed January 12, 2009).

43. See William F. Arndt and F. Wilbur Gingrich, *A Greek-English Lexicon of the New Testament and Other Early Christian Literature* (Chicago: The University of Chicago Press,

1957), 769. See also, Greg L. Bahnsen, *Always Ready: Direction for Defending the Faith*, ed. Robert R. Booth (Powder Springs, GA: American Vision, and Texarkana, AR: Covenant Media Foundation, 1996), 246.

44. Leo Strauss, *Natural Right and History* (Chicago: University of Chicago Press, 1953); quoted at http://en.wikipedia.org/wiki/Reductio_ad_Hitlerum (accessed January 13, 2009).

45. Thomas Fleming, "Reduction ad Hitlerum," *The Journal of Historical Review* 19, no. 5 (Sept.–Oct. 2000):24; available at http://www.ihr.org/jhr/v19/v19n5p24_reductio.html (accessed January 13, 2009).

46. Dinae McWhorter, "Family Values and the K.K.K.," *New York Times*, September 1, 1992.

47. Barry E. Horner, *Future Israel: Why Christian Anti-Judaism Must Be Challenged*, NAC Studies in Bible and Theology, ed. E. Ray Clendenen (Nashville, TN: B and H Academic, 2004), xviii.

48. Barry E. Horner, *Future Israel: Why Christian Anti-Judaism Must Be Challenged*, xviii.

49. *Scientific American*, August 19, 1999.

50. *Scientific American*, December 16, 2008.

51. Quoted in Eugenie C. Scott, *Evolution Vs. Creationism: An Introduction* (Berkeley, CA: University of California Press, 2005), 240–241. The actual quotation comes from Rush Holt, Conference Report on H.R. 1, No Child Left Behind Act of 2001, December 13, 2001, *The Congressional Record—Extensions of Remarks*, December 20, 2001, E2365. Available online through http://www.gpoaccess.gov/crecord/retrieve.html (must select "2001 Congressional Record, Vol. 147," and enter page number).

52. Ron Sider, *Rich Christians in an Age of Hunger: A Biblical Study* (Downers Grove, IL: InterVarsity Press, 1977), 14, 58, 207, 209.

53. Ron Sider, *Rich Christians in an Age of Hunger: A Biblical Study*, 83.

54. Thankfully, in later editions, Sider softens his appeal from "we must demand," to "could demand" and "could insist." He later reverts to old form, however, when he says, "We must end the outrage…." See Ronald J. Sider, *Rich Christian in an Age of Hunger: Moving from Affluence to Generosity*, 5th Ed. (Nashville, TN: W Publishing Group, 1997), 225, 230. It may well be that David Chilton has noticed these same revivions, at least, if Sider made them as early as the 2nd edition. Chilton provided such a critique in *Productive Christians in an Age of Guilt Manipulators: A Biblical Response to Ronald J. Sider*, 3rd Ed. (Tyler, TX: Institute for Christian Economics, 1990), 249–319. I have not taken the time to trace Sider's 2nd edition, nor compared Chilton's critique of it closely.

55. Ron Sider, *Rich Christians in an Age of Hunger: A Biblical Study*, 225.

56. Ron Sider, *Rich Christians in an Age of Hunger: A Biblical Study*, 14–16.

57. Leonard Pitts, "Nothing abstract about gay hatred," *The Atlanta Journal-Constitution*, Feb. 18, 2009, A9.

58. Leonard Pitts, "Nothing abstract about gay hatred," A9.

59. Ann Coulter, *Godless: The Church of Liberalism* (New York: Crown Forum, 2006), 101–102.

60. Ann Coulter, *Godless: The Church of Liberalism*, 102.

CHAPTER 14

"WRONG ROAD": FALLACIES OF DIVERSION

Getting from "Point A" to "Point B" requires that you stay on the right path. This applies to travel or logical reasoning. Any diversion along the way will end you up in the wrong place. Fallacies of Diversion place their audience on a path other than that which leads to truth, or that leads to the relevant truth at hand (in such a case, even a *different* truth leads to a fallacy). Any argument that avoids the main issue classifies as a fallacious diversion. The Christian must discern such deviations and reject them as the "Wrong Road."

ARGUMENT AGAINST THE PERSON (AD HOMINEM)

The Fallacy of Argument Against the Person follows a wrong road by launching attacks against the person making an argument instead of the argument itself. They attack the person arguing instead of the arguments of the person. The core of the fallacy lies in the fact that the truth of an argument does not depend upon the person giving that argument. By focusing on the person instead of the statements, the fallacy diverts attention away from the real issue. However successfully the fallacy diverts attention from the argument itself, it cannot serve as proof for or refutation of any argument because it never really addresses the argument.

Even if the fallacy's claims Against the Person hold some truth, they still do not substantially affect the truth or falsity of the argument. As I noted under Poisoning the Well, the argument "two plus two equals four" retains its validity and soundness even if uttered by Adolf Hitler. You could not rightfully argue for the falsity of the argument on the basis that Hitler was the most evil person who ever lived. This particular example helps by pairing the obviously true deductive argument, "2+2=4," with perhaps the vilest example of human character (at least in modern history), Adolf Hitler.[1] Based on such extremes, we can easily accept that the truth of a statement does not necessarily depend on the character of the person making it. The next step is learning to discern such instances where the proposition is not so clearly true, and the person's character is not so clearly irrelevant to the subject. Several such examples that involve greater obscurity between person and proposition appear below.

The Fallacy of argument Against the Person comes in many variations—Abusive Ad Hominem, Circumstantial Ad Hominem, Tu Quoque, and more—all of which we can discuss. The single thread that runs through each, remember, will be that they all direct their claims against the person arguing rather than the arguments of the person. Thus, for those who do not care to memorize the fine distinctions between types of this fallacy, it will suffice to remember the core of the fallacy as it applies to any scenario. Nevertheless, learning the distinctive types will add finesse and accuracy to you analysis of your own and other people's arguments.

The Abusive Ad Hominem simply ignores the issue completely and attempts some insult, cut-down, or joke directly at the person. This is perhaps the crudest form of Argument Against the Person. By directly denigrating the person, the abuser of the fallacy creates two diversions. First, the shift of focus from the argument to the person creates and *intellectual* diversion. Secondly, the shift from serious dialogue to ridicule or humor creates an *emotional* diversion. The fallacious arguer who can malign his opponent with a successful joke or a sour enough image thus creates a doubly powerful distraction from the real issue. Nevertheless, such an effort may succeed in stealing an audience, but it also doubly transgresses the integrity of Truth. God judges by the latter standard.

Ad Hominem in the Bible

One example of Abusive Ad Hominem comes from the biblical account of the Day of Pentecost after Jesus' resurrection. When the Holy Spirit fell on the group of disciples and they began to speak in various foreign languages, some people in the crowd dismissed their Spirit-filled utterances as foolishness. These mockers pronounced that the disciples were drunken, *full of sweet wine* (Acts 2:13). Peter responded, *These men are not drunk, as you suppose,* and went on to show this supernatural event as a fulfillment of prophecy (compare Acts 2:16–21; Joel 2:28–32). In this situation, the mockers simply dismissed what they did not understand by ridiculing the persons of disciples who spoke.

Similarly, the Pharisees answered Jesus by ignoring His teaching and instead simply insulting Him. A discussion arose after Jesus said, *If you continue in My word ... you will know the truth, and the truth will make you free* (John 8:31–32). The Pharisees argued that they had *never yet been enslaved to anyone* (8:33), and therefore Jesus teaching about *becoming free* had no point. They had misunderstood the spiritual and ethical nature of freedom. In the discussion that followed, Jesus bluntly rebuked them: *Why do you not understand what I am saying? It is because you cannot hear My word.... He who is of God hears the words of God; for this reason you do not hear them, because you are not of God* (8:43, 47). Rather than respond to Jesus' charge with reason (had it not been true it would have been easy to refute), the Pharisees resorted to Abusive Ad Hominem: *Do we not say rightly that You are a Samaritan and have a demon?* (8:48). By the end of this discussion, they had removed themselves so far from disciplined discussion that they attempted literal abuse and *picked up stones to throw at Him, but Jesus hid himself and went out of the temple* (8:59). An Argument Against the Person often covers deeper sin and hatred, and can easily devolve into an Appeal to Force. If we do not first address the spiritual and ethical side of our argumentation, we will all be slaves of such vices.

Hitchens' Abusive Ad Hominem

A nearly disgusting example of Abusive Ad Hominem occurred in 2007 upon the death of the well-known Evangelical leader Jerry Falwell. His passing had garnered national media attention. Amidst the reports and memorials, atheist Christopher Hitchens graced CNN with his judgment on Falwell: "I think it's a pity there isn't a hell for him to go to."[2] He continued by referring to Falwell as an "ugly little charlatan" who was "giggling and sniggering all the time with what he was getting away with." Hitchens snorted at the idea that Falwell actually believed what he preached, charging that the Reverend only used religion as a means of extorting money from "gullible" and "credulous" people: "He woke up every morning pinching his chubby little flanks, thinking, 'I've got away with it again.' ... I think he was a conscious charlatan and fraud."

When confronted for his hatefulness on Fox News' "Hannity and Colmes," Hitchens refused to show the slightest pity even toward the *grieving family*, saying, "I don't care whether his family's feelings are hurt or not."[3] Such is the well of abusive personal attacks: they reveal more about the person making them than about the person at whom they are directed. If Hitchens, along with other atheists, makes the complaint that atheists are unduly outcast in American society, well, perhaps he can at least understand *why* they are disliked. He makes it quite easy for us to do so.

Hitchens' attack on Falwell also serves as an example of a second form of the fallacy, the Circumstantial Ad Hominem. This version does not necessarily insult or abuse the person directly, but rather accuses the person of advancing a position only because of some vested interest or personal benefit. The fallacy still applies in such a case: even if the accusation contains some truth, even if the person only advances his position due to personal gain, this fact does not address the position itself, and cannot in itself negate the truth of the position. As Hitchens dismissed Falwell's personal faith as a fraudulent scheme profitable for extorting money from credulous people, the atheist clearly engaged in this Circumstantial form of the fallacy, on top of the Abusive type.

Ehrman's Error

We find another good example in a recent debate between apologist James White and Bible critic Bart Ehrman. Despite both men possessing scholarly credentials and reputations, during the course of their debate over the integrity of Biblical manuscripts, each resorted at times to Ad Hominem appeals. For example, James White argued that God has preserved His word in the multiplicity of fragmented manuscripts (5000+ to date), even though many of those manuscripts contain differences. Though in many pieces, the "tenacity" of the word remains. "It's like having a 1,010 pieces for a 1,000pc jigsaw puzzle. It's all there, we just have more than we need," he illustrated. Amidst his rebuttals of this claim, Dr. Ehrman complained that only Evangelical Christian scholars continue to make this "tenacity" argument (against the vast weight of international scholarly opinion), and Evangelicals do so because they must defend their underlying doctrine of inspiration.

You can see how Dr. Ehrman's rebuttal at this point commits the classic Circumstantial Ad Hominem: he dismisses Dr. White's "tenacity" argument essentially by saying, "You only believe that because you have a vested interest in doing so: your evangelical religious tenets require you to do so at the expense of truth." But this dismissal only attacks Dr. White and does not address the issue itself. Even if Dr. Ehrman's claim were true, it would not disprove, or even weaken, the "tenacity of the text" argument.

At several points, however, Dr. White treats Dr. Ehrman in a similar manner. Part of our studies in this book includes showing how even devout believers do not escape the human frailty for fallacious arguments, and here we have another case in point. Dr. Ehrman argued that since the manuscripts of the Bible exist in multiple fragments which contain many discrepancies, therefore they in fact do *not* preserve God's word. In addressing this claim, Dr. White more than once pointed out that Dr. Ehrman elsewhere in his writings and interviews denies the orthodox doctrine of inspiration. This charge implies that we should dismiss Dr. Ehrman's argument as biased liberal propaganda. But this does not *necessarily* follow. Even though Dr. Ehrman's argument does not prove the extent of what he claims (for other reasons), Dr. White's emphasis on Dr. Ehrman's personal denial of inspiration does not address the points of the actual argument. Even if Dr. Ehrman loved to draw Satanic symbols and burn Bibles for fun, these facts would have no necessary logical connection to his argument about the texts. At best they could motivate his argument, but they could not serve as a logical refutation.

Believers have no special immunity from logical fallacies just because we believe, or because we have a superior worldview. In fact, God calls us to a higher standard of integrity and veracity. We have the word and commandments of God; and we must study to apply godly principles to our thinking. We must fight against personal hypocrisy, but we must also discipline our reasoning as well.

You Too!

A third variation of Argument Against the Person bears the Latin name *Tu Quoque*, which simply means "and you, too." The abuser of this form side-steps the main issue by alleging hypocritical behavior by his opponent. As a common example, a critic might argue, "Preachers are always preaching against adultery; but a bunch of those guys have had affairs themselves!" This is unfortunate where it is true, but even cases of hypocrisy on the part of preachers do not prove their message false. Adultery remains a damnable sin even if those who preach against it should happen to fail in that area. Such behavior provides a horrible witness to Christ, but not a logical refutation of His Truth.

A good example of the You Too Fallacy occurs in the lyrics of a popular 1980s song by the Beastie Boys. They sing,

> Your pops caught you smoking man he said, "No way!"
> That hypocrite smokes two packs a day!⁴

The You Too Fallacy basically accuses its victim of hypocrisy, and thus is as logically irrelevant as other Arguments Against the Person because it attacks the person instead of their argument. Maybe Pops is a chain-smoker, but that fact does not invalidate the truth that smoking is harmful and illegal for minors, nor does it invalidate the fact that Pops has authority over his children to tell them what they can and can't do, even if he himself does it.

Of the More Vulgar Variety

A clear example of the kind of Ad Hominem that can occur in everyday discourse comes from a comment posted on an apologetical video on YouTube. The video, which provided a satirical critique of atheism, drew the ire and fire of thousands of atheists. Despite their boasts about reason and logic, nearly every response involved Straw Men, Ad Hominem, Red Herrings, and other fallacies. This choice example represents one of over 2,500 comments:

> More people have been killed because of your fictional book than any other REASON. It's so ridiculously stupid it makes my brain hemorrhage. If you had an ounce

of the critical thinking ability that [Richard] Dawkins possesses you too would be an atheist. Many others like myself are tired of the nonsense, the war has begun between reason and infantile foolishness. The sheer reason you are religious is your obvious inability to comprehend the brilliant elegance of modern sciences.[5]

Among the multiple fallacies in this comment stands most prominently the consistent Ad Hominem. He calls the video's argument "ridiculously stupid," assails the producer as without even an ounce of critical thinking ability, and sets the effort as "infantile foolishness" over against "reason," all of which merely attacks the person instead of the argument. To round out his stone-throwing he claims that our faith stems from our "obvious inability to comprehend" science. In short, believers are stupid, or at best, mentally slow. Of course, the video says very little about science, so how he could even begin to judge our "inability" escapes me.

Nevertheless, even if all of his comments were true, they would still commit the fallacy of Argument Against the Person, because they ignore the issues at hand and instead attack the person. Let's assume, for sake of example, that the author of the video actually did not comprehend the sciences, had no critical thinking ability, and always ran around spouting infantile foolishness; he could *still get the argument right*, because truth does not necessarily depend on the person's reputation, I.Q., education, credentials, virtues, or vices. The old saying that "even a blind squirrel finds a nut once in a while," should remind the abusive writer that Ad Hominem remains fallacious *even if the attacks are true*.

More of Lindsey's Logic

A final example comes from one of the most popular prophecy teachers in the twentieth century. Hal Lindsey, in his best-selling *The Late Great Planet Earth*, scoffed, "No self-respecting scholar who looks at the world conditions and the accelerating decline of Christian influence today is a 'postmillennialist.'"[6] This quip is nothing short of an Abusive Argument Against the Person. Instead of proving his point with evidence and reason, or a Biblical teaching, he resorts to ridicule. The comment implies that anyone who *does*, in fact, hold the postmillennial position is therefore *not* a self-respecting scholar.

Not only is Lindsey's quip insulting and fallacious, but it is (and was even at the time he wrote) simply false. Some well respected, able, sincere, certainly self-respecting, and Bible-believing scholars accepted the postmillennial position then and now. One need only mention Loraine Boettner and J. Marcelus Kik—both professors at Westminster Theological Seminary in Philadelphia, PA—to disprove Lindsey's claim. The number of postmillennialists has grown tremendously since (and Lindsey's failed predictions of the return of Christ have certainly helped the exodus from his premillennial camp). This example illustrates how Ad Hominem often masks the fact that a baseless argument must resort to emotional appeals to sustain itself.

"Red Herring"

Has someone ever tried to change the subject on you in the middle of an argument? If so, you have experienced the "Red Herring" fallacy. What constitutes a "Red Herring," and why such a funny name?

In a Red Herring the arguer attempts to divert attention from the issue at hand by pointing to an unrelated yet strongly compelling line of thought. This tactic will tempt an unwitting victim to follow the new subject with passion while neglecting to press for an answer to the original question. The diversion can take the form of a caricature of the opponent's position (see Straw Man), a related-sounding issue, or an entirely separate issue that may be equally or even more important than the point in question. Whatever the degree of diversion may be, if the new line of thought does not deal with the original point, then that line of thought is arbitrary and irrelevant.

Several stories, most of which emphasize the same elements, try to account for the strange name. In the previous centuries when countrymen fox-hunted regularly, hunters would train their dogs to track the scent of a fox. To teach them to stay on the proper trail, they would first drag a pungent dead fish (perhaps a herring) across the trail of the fox. When the dog reached the fishy crossing point, the new odor tempted it to follow the fish trail instead of the fox. (This also accounts for the saying, "Something smells fishy about this!") If the dog fell for the setup, the trainer would have to jerk it back to the right trail.

The person today who tries to avoid a question by raising some other point is therefore "dragging" or "throwing" a red herring into the discussion. Perhaps an acquaintance or even a friend or spouse has subjected you to such a trail. The hope is that the newly introduced subject will occupy your mind strongly enough to make you forget your original pursuit in some way or other.

The metaphor is apt for the student who must learn to sniff out the correct issue at hand. The process of detecting red herrings demands the student's *discipline*: stay focused, determine the issue at hand, and refuse to leave that issue until it is answered satisfactorily.

A critical listener can easily, almost intuitively, detect a Red Herring; but as with all critical thinking you should not judge too hastily. The process requires some discernment. The person whom you catch throwing out a red herring may simply be pointing to a different aspect of the same argument in hopes that the importance of the new angle will outweigh that of the former. For example, a certain husband (and this story is not autobiographical!) grew angry because his wife attempted to hide an expenditure from him. When confronted, she seemed to act a little nervous and at a loss for words. She replied that all he ever talked about was her spending money while he had just bought new hiking boots, fishing tackle and a bass boat without even a word (You Too!). A few days later she handed him a surprise gift for his birthday for which he was elated. The surprise made him so happy that he forgave his wife's slight deception.

In this case the wife's defensive argument does not address the fact that she acted deceptively, but rather does two things: points to her husband's own financial extravagance, and justifies her action by revealing her good intentions. This *technically* is an example of a Red Herring. Depending, however, on particulars of that family's finances, practices concerning birthdays, the size of the expenditure, etc., her justification may be acceptable in practice. It may have been uncharitable on the husband's part to make an issue of it too quickly. The fact that he forgave her may be due to the fact that he liked the present so much, even though she broke a family rule. If so, then the gift was a successful Red Herring (the letter of the law does not always prevail). If he forgave because he realized that he forgot a usual family practice and reacted too harshly and too soon, then the explanation was less a Red Herring than a reminder! It is always important to use patience and gentleness when we think someone else has an error to confront.

Cheney Changes the Subject

These types of interactions may occur and some will have a happy ending, but more frustrating examples come in areas of debate and conflict. Wherever an adversarial relationship exists, and one party is allowed to escape a situation in which their "true colors" may be exposed, and this escape is performed by pointing away from the question at hand to some other striking but unconnected issue, there a red herring has prevailed. Politicians have famously used this tactic for all of history, especially in the modern era of televised debates and interviews. In a setting where the interviewer has only a brief period of time to extract an answer, the speaker can point to as many different subjects as he or she wants, all the while carefully dancing around the original question, until the time is up.

Just such a clever evasion by diversion appeared in an interview with former Vice President Dick Cheney. Late MSNBC host Tim Russert pushed Cheney on the issue of phony evidence for weapons of mass destruction. The exchange went as follows:

> *Russert:* This is what concerns people, that the administration hyped the intelligence, misled the American people. This article from The Washington Post about pressuring from Cheney visits: "Vice President Cheney and his most senior aide made multiple trips to the CIA over the past year to question analysts studying Iraq's weapons programs and alleged links to al Qaeda, creating an environment in which some analysts felt they were being pressured to make their assessments fit with the Bush administration's policy objectives, according to senior intelligence officials. With Cheney taking the lead in the administration last August in advocating military action against Iraq by claiming it had weapons of mass destruction, the visits by the vice president and his chief of staff 'sent signals, intended or otherwise, that a certain output was desired from here,' one senior agency official said."
>
> *Cheney:* In terms of asking questions, I plead guilty.... That's my job. I've had an interest in the intelligence area since I worked for Gerry Ford 30 years ago, served on the Intel Committee in the House for years in the

'80s, ran a big part of the intelligence community when I was secretary of Defense in the early '90s. This is a very important area. It's one the president's asked me to work on, and I ask questions all the time. I think if you're going to provide the intelligence and advice to the president of the United States to make life and death decisions, you need to be able to defend your conclusions, go into an arena where you can make the arguments about why you believe what you do based on the intelligence we've got.

Russert: No pressure?

Cheney: Shouldn't be any pressure. I can't think of a single instance. Maybe somebody can produce one. I'm unaware of any where the community changed a judgment that they made because I asked questions.[7]

However much interesting information former V. P. Cheney's responses may include, they completely dodge the main issue of the question. Instead of responding to the accusation that he and the administration pressured a certain individual to produce a certain type of intelligence, he diverts the discussion to a series of more narrow and very mildly related points—namely, that it is his job to ask questions, how much he values that job, how much experience he has at that job, how important that job is, etc. All of this captures the listener's attention, but none of it comes to the point. When the interviewer pulls back to the original path—the subject of "pressure"—Cheney uses his prior response as a reference point to qualify the issue of "pressure" in such a way as to avoid the force of the accusation again. Instead of addressing "*was* there any pressure," he responded that there "*shouldn't be*" and that he couldn't think of any pressuring that occurred *because he asked questions*. Thus, by taking very clever angles, the Vice President avoided addressing the core accusation that was brought against him.

Typical Red Herrings

When such time constraints do not play a role, however, the success of the Red Herring then lies in the persuasiveness or allure of the irrelevant claim. This will hold true in the majority of cases. Just as the odor of the herring could succeed because it overpowered the scent of the fox trail, so the mental trail provided by the person committing the fallacy will succeed to the degree it overwhelms or interests the listener. This fallacy engages in seduction as much as irrelevance. The conclusion arrived at may very well be a true conclusion, and it may deserve serious attention in its own right. Such a point may carry great weight, and it may be such a powerful issue as to evoke an immediate emotional response from a whole group. The fact, however, that it may do so is the power of the fallacy: it provides a strong deterrent from the desired path of inquiry.

Atheists and critics of the faith employ many diversion tactics amidst their arguments. You will often hear something like this: "Christian faith doesn't improve morality. Just look at the Crusades! That kind of slaughter exposes Christianity for the tyranny that it really is." Christians, especially those engaged in apologetics, hear this argument all the time from critics of the Christian faith. Amidst the many fallacies it employs lingers the stench of the red herring. How so? Because the behavior of some professing Christians does not establish or disestablish, and thus is irrelevant to, the truth or efficacy of the Christian faith itself. Even if the vast majority of Christians at a given time in history turned war-like and bloodthirsty (this has never been the case—even during the Crusades), this would still not discredit the faith itself. It would more likely exemplify a *departure* from Christian morals, and thus cry out the need for more Christian faith.

This argument and its many variations persuade many people because of its shock factor. Our innate reaction at being "guilty by association" with acts of terror and violence splits us from the trail of the core issue. Once you see that our behavior does not judge the faith, but rather the faith judges our behavior, then you can detect the irrelevance of the argument. We should not hold God responsible for what evil men do in His name.

Hypocrisy is a terrible thing, but it does not render devotion to the Laws of Love (Matt. 27:37–40) and the Ten Commandments (Ex. 20:1–17) worthless. It may seem to reflect poorly on the faith, and turn away many from wanting to associate with it, but it cannot falsify it. This argument would only work if Christianity claimed that the Christian Faith produces no hypocrites; and Christendom has never claimed such an absurdity, especially since it would contradict to the words of Christ (Matt. 7:21–23).

Christians, of course, can commit the same fallacy in their own way. Many retort something like, "Christianity must be true, just look at all the good it does. Life without Christ would be cold and heartless!" This example—as widely heard as the previous claim—illustrates that Christians often engage in the same logical fallacies as our critics. How does this drag in a red herring (two actually)? Because neither good works nor a positive state of mind about life ultimately determine the truth or falsity of supernatural claims. After all, Muslims or Buddhists can also point to their works of charity and attribute them to Allah or Enlightenment, all the while denying Christ's resurrection (Muslims do not dispute the virgin birth, by the way). Moreover, the mafia legendarily has run soup kitchens to feed the poor as a front while running their black market from the back door. Terrorist organizations have likewise used charity stores to filter money to Hezbollah and other violent groups. "All the good they do" does not provide the final word on any given belief system; in fact, it could provide cover for just the opposite.

A more sophisticated apologist, however, may reply that "goodness" itself requires an ultimate standard of good and evil: an ultimate "Good." This "Good" points in many ways to the necessity that God exist. Therefore, the fact that *any* good exists at all—whether carried out by Christians, Muslims, pagans or atheists—points to the Good God Who created us all and Whose Image we all bear. While different people may attribute their good works to different sources, "goodness," or "love," in general points beyond us to our Creator. Armed with the unique religious claim that "God is love" (1 John 4:8), the Christian faith will stand alone in this discussion.

Another Red Herring occurs when someone ignores the logical aspect of an argument and focuses only on the practical effects of holding it (which the two most recent examples above both essentially do). This "pragmatic" maneuver essentially argues, "The best test for the truth of any intellectual system is, 'Does it *work*?' When ideas work in the real world, then truth has been established." Dr. Geisler helpfully addresses this point. In our American culture pragmatism rules as the unspoken philosophy of the day. This line of thought is purely results driven: whatever *works* or produces the desired results is deemed "good" and/or "true." Of course, this line of thinking conflates two very different things: truth and results. It should stand out as an elementary fact of life that just because something turns out the way an individual wants it does not mean that the results are true or good. Were it not for the fact that so much of modern culture revolves around "what works," this point would hardly merit consideration. Besides, it is only a short step from "what works" to "what works *for me*"—which completes the step from social relativism to lawlessness. Once the student understands that results are entirely irrelevant to truth, he will avoid the Red Herring of an entire culture.[8]

A Lifeless Red Herring

Nevertheless, Red Herrings pop up everywhere and in many forms. You must always remain alert for claims and arguments that have no direct bearing on the main point. For example, the following argument by liberal Catholic author Garry Wills pulls a classic Red Herring:

> Defenders of the fetus say that life begins only after the semen fertilizes the egg, producing an embryo. But, in fact, two-thirds of the embryos produced this way fail to live on because they do not embed in the womb wall.[9]

If he intends to address the argument, "*Life begins* only after the semen fertilizes the egg, producing an embryo," then the response should say something about *when life begins*. Wills' response addresses the issue of what often happens to the fertilized egg *after* life begins in this way. Instead of contradicting the argument, Wills complains that the fact included in the argument sometimes has negative consequences. This is a Red Herring. Wills has taken a wrong road. True, two-thirds of fertilized embryos may indeed never implant in the womb and thus die, but this is irrelevant to question of whether or not life begins at that embryo's conception. Wills even implicitly admits his error by saying that embryos which fail to implant "fail to live on." If they "fail to live on," then they were apparently living things, and thus life must have begun already.

Dawkins' Fishy Diversion

In another public exchange, scientist and host of the PBS program *Nova*, Neil deGrasse Tyson, confronted atheist Richard Dawkins for his harshness in attacking religion. The exchange went as follows:

Tyson: Your commentary had a sharpness of teeth that I had not even projected for you.... I felt you more than I heard you.... You're "Professor of the Public *Understanding* of Science," not "Professor of Delivering Truth to the Public," and these are two different exercises. One of them is, you put the truth out there and, like you said, they either buy your book or they don't. Well that's not being an educator, that's just putting it out there; being an educator is not only getting the truth right, but ... an act of persuasion in there as well. Persuasion isn't always "Here's the facts: you're either an idiot or you're not." It's, "Here are the facts and ... here is a sensitivity to your state of mind;" and it's the facts plus the sensitivity when convolved together, creates impact. And I worry that your methods, and ... how articulately barbed you can be, ends up simply being ineffective, when you have much more power of influence than what is currently reflected in your output."

Dawkins: I gratefully accept the rebuke [laughter]. Just one anecdote to show that I'm not the worst in this league [laughter]: a former and highly successful editor of *New Scientist* magazine ... was asked, "What is your philosophy at *New Scientist?*" He said, "Our philosophy at *New Scientist* is this: Science is interesting, and if you don't agree you can [expletive removed] off" [roar of laughter].[10]

Dawkins actually uses a combination of diversion tactics and fallacies here—he appeals to a "highly successful" authority (see Appeal to Authority), he uses humor (laughter is a great emotional distraction), he uses shock (by employing an unexpected curse word Dawkins evoked the audience's laughter and mentally jerked them from the topic)—but his overall response creates a Red Herring. Instead of addressing the charge that he communicates abusively, he appealed that someone else commits the same fault worse than he. Maybe so, but this other person's behavior does not justify Dawkins' actions, even if the other offends more greatly. But once the shock of the statement drove everyone involved to a roar in laughter, the moderator moved on and Dr. Tyson never received an appropriate response to his "rebuke." Dawkins got off the hook—the purpose of the Red Herring.

Red Herrings in A Reformed Critique

Sometimes entire articles can commit Red Herrings by spending most of their time on a tangential subject. Greg Bahnsen summarizes one such tangetial article:

> Theonomists are usually postmillennialists, and I've got these problems with postmillennialism. [Therefore theonomy is a problematic position].[11]

Bahnsen summarizes Richard Gaffin's critique of Bahnsen's book *Theonomy and Christian Ethics*. It is a fair summary, though Gaffin never explicitly added the "Therefore." Nevertheless, published as part of an overarching effort in a book designed to critique theonomy, it stands as one great big red herring. Bahnsen explains that theonomy does not require one to hold any particular millennial position, and says, "If you've got problems with postmillennialism, let's have a day somewhere else, Dick, where we can talk about that; but now, let's get back to theonomy, what about that?" Disappointed with Gaffin's scholarly interaction, Bahnsen concludes, "Dr. Gaffin has written what is basically an irrelevant millennial discussion."

The red herring this time employs a very frequently associated idea to the one at hand, thus increasing its draw. It is true that most theonomists are postmils, but there is no necessary connection between the two doctrines. Therefore, even a devastating critique of postmillennialism would say little at all about the theonomic viewpoint. Dr. Gaffin's twenty-seven page article may disturb some theonomists because they happen to be postmils, but it should not disturb their theonomic beliefs. The article may, however, have a reassuring effect to uncritical nontheonomists who do not discern the fallacy.

Red Herrings in the Bible

In the Bible, Jesus faces many people who wish to evade the weight of truth, and who therefore use Red Herrings. The woman at the well tried this tactic:

> *Jesus said to her, "Go, call your husband, and come here." The woman answered and said, "I have no husband." Jesus said to her, "You have well said, 'I have no husband,' for you have had five husbands, and the one whom you now have is not your husband; in that you spoke truly." The woman said to Him, "Sir, I perceive that You are a prophet. Our fathers worshiped on this mountain, and you Jews say that in Jerusalem is the place where one ought to worship." Jesus said to her, "Woman, believe Me, the hour is coming when you will neither on this mountain, nor in Jerusalem, worship the Father. You worship what you do not know; we know what we worship, for salvation is of the Jews. But the hour is coming, and now is, when the true worshipers will worship the Father in spirit and truth; for the Father is seeking such to worship Him. God is Spirit, and those who worship Him must worship in spirit and truth." The woman said to Him, "I know that Messiah is coming" (who is called Christ). "When He comes, He will tell us all things." Jesus said to her, "I who speak to you am He"* (John 4:16–26).

Where does a red herring appear in this encounter? It comes in a very obvious way when the woman abruptly changes the subject. After Jesus confronts her about her lifestyle of numerous adulteries, she begins talking about prophets and worship. It is not uncommon for sinners, when in the presence of someone they deem to be a holy man, to change the subject from their own spiritual life to some theological debate. As much as I love theological discussions which engage the intellect and often the emotions as well, they can be ways of avoiding more pressing issues; they can be ways of suppressing the truth in unrighteousness (Rom. 1:18). The woman in the story pulls exactly this maneuver: using the smokescreen of an argument about worship (Jewish versus Samaritan) she tries to dodge a call to repentance.

In this case, Jesus actually follows the new line of thought. Using patience and wisdom, he led the discussion back to the original point: that He was the Messiah, the living water Who could satisfy the unrealized spiritual thirst she which she was suppressing.

The issue of suppressed truth—a phenomenon resulting from the fallen condition of man—appears again later in the Gospel of John:

> *Pilate therefore said to Him, "Are You a king then?" Jesus answered, "You say rightly that I am a king. For this cause I was*

> *born, and for this cause I have come into the world, that I should bear witness to the truth. Everyone who is of the truth hears My voice." Pilate said to Him, "What is truth?" And when he had said this, he went out again to the Jews, and said to them, "I find no fault in Him at all"* (John 18:37–38).

Pilate does not address Jesus' claim to be the truth, but responds with skepticism—a purposeful and diversionary suspense of belief. The proposition Jesus put forth was that anyone of the truth would hear his voice. Pilate may simply not have believed him, but his response evades the issue under the clever disguise of a philosopher—as if he earnestly engaged in the pursuit of truth. In the light of Jesus' claim, Pilate's refusal to "hear" Christ unwittingly proves his own spiritual depravity. The combination of pride and trust in human philosophizing can easily put us in Pilate's position: looking Truth right in the face and not seeing it. In trying to devise intellectual stratagems to outwit others, we may drag a red herring across our own path, and end up fooling ourselves. This is the height of humanistic wisdom: *Professing to be wise, they became fools* (Rom. 1:22). Pilate afterward wished to acquit Jesus, yet did not wish to engage His message either.

Paul used a Red Herring justly to distract his persecutors in one instance:

> *The next day, because he wanted to know for certain why he was accused by the Jews, he released him from his bonds, and commanded the chief priests and all their council to appear, and brought Paul down and set him before them.... But when Paul perceived that one part were Sadducees and the other Pharisees, he cried out in the council, "Men and brethren, I am a Pharisee, the son of a Pharisee; concerning the hope and resurrection of the dead I am being judged!" And when he had said this, a dissension arose between the Pharisees and the Sadducees; and the assembly was divided. For Sadducees say that there is no resurrection—and no angel or spirit; but the Pharisees confess both. Then there arose a loud outcry. And the scribes of the Pharisees' party arose and protested, saying, "We find no evil in this man; but if a spirit or an angel has spoken to him, let us not fight against God." Now when there arose a great dissension, the commander, fearing lest Paul might be pulled to pieces by them, commanded the soldiers to go*

down and take him by force from among them, and bring him into the barracks (Acts 22:30–23:10).

This story actually begins way back in Acts 21:27 and ends up here, where Paul plants something of a red herring into the discussion and distracts the assembly from its purpose. A group of Jewish leaders had accosted Paul after the apostle had given his testimony to a large crowd of people. This led to his imprisonment until a centurion learned that Paul was a Roman citizen. At this point, the commander called a hearing to determine the actual charge the Jews wanted to bring against Paul.

During the confused session the opponents tried to intimidate and bully Paul, but had yet to give any real accusations. Paul noticed that the assembly had representatives from both major parties, the Sadducees and the Pharisees, and these groups lay very strongly divided on a heated issue: the reality of bodily resurrection. So, Paul seized the opportunity to announce his own charges: that they were calling him into question on the issue of the hope and resurrection of the dead. Once the issue hit the air, the two sides erupted in debate. Paul knew exactly what he was doing: using a passionate issue to create a digression. He was not being dishonest—he *had* given his testimony about his encounter with the risen Jesus—he merely saw an opportunity to avoid the inevitable "charges" that the Jews would have trumped up. The crowd grew so violent that the commander had Paul removed and placed in protective custody. The red herring worked. In this case, we may feel that the tactic was justified. No real "original point" had been stated other than to determine the charges against Paul. Sometimes, if your opponents show no interest in reasoning honestly, a red herring could be a way to move things along. After all, if the subject at hand is unacceptable, it needs to be changed anyway.

NOTES

1. I will not object if someone wishes to give this appellation to Stalin or Mao who each murdered far more millions than Hitler, but who are simply less publicized.

2. Christopher Hitchens interviewed by Anderson Cooper, "Jerry Falwell's Legacy," CNN's "Anderson Cooper 360 Degrees," May 15, 2007; available at http://transcripts.cnn.com/TRANSCRIPTS/0705/15/acd.01.html (accessed January 27, 2009).

3. Christopher Hitchens interviewed by Sean Hannity and Alan Colmes, "Christopher Hitchens and Ralph Reed Square Off over Late Leader's Influence; the Christian Right," FOX News' "Hannity and Colmes," May 16, 2007"; available at http://www.foxnews.com/story/0,2933,273295,00.html (accessed January 27, 2009).

4. The Beastie Boys, "Fight for Your Right," from the album *Licensed to Ill* (Def Jam/Columbia Records, 1986). S. Morris Engel uses the example of a smoker giving advice in his *With Good Reason: An Introduction to Informal Fallacies*, 5th Edition (New York: St. Martin's Press, 1994), 204–205.

5. Comment left by "matcotech," December 4, 2008, at http://www.youtube.com/watch?v=Lm1JYYIk-pI&feature=email, accessed December 26, 2008.

6. Hal Lindsey, *The Late Great Planet Earth* (Grand Rapids: Zondervan, 1970), 176.

7. Dick Cheney interviewed by Tim Russert on MSNBC's "Meet the Press," September 14, 2003; http://www.msnbc.msn.com/id/3080244/ (accessed March 13, 2009).

8. See Norm L. Geisler and Ronald M. Brooks, *Come Let Us Reason: An Introduction to Logical Thinking* (Grand Rapids: Baker Book House, 1990), 103–104.

9. Garry Wills, "Abortion isn't a religious issue," *Los Angeles Times*, November 4, 2007; available at http://www.latimes.com/features/religion/la-op-wills-4nov04,0,2121538.story?track=mostviewed-storylevel; accessed August 14, 2008. See also the critical blog article at http://www.principledpolicy.com/?p=108.

10. Panel discussion including Neil deGrasse Tyson and Richard Dawkins after Dawkins' lecture at "Beyond Belief: Science, Religion, Reason and Survival," Conference held November 5–7, 2006; http://thesciencenetwork.org/programs/beyond-belief-science-religion-reason-and-survival/ (accessed March 13, 2008).

11. Greg bahnsen, "Has Westminster Found a Critique of Theonomy Yet?" (audio lecture series available at www.cmfnow.org. For the actual book references involved see: William S. Barker and W. Robert Godfrey, eds., *Theonomy: A Reformed Critique* (Grand Rapids, MI: Academie Books, 1990), 197–224; and Greg L. Bahnsen, *No Other Standard: Theonomy and Its Critics* (Tyler, TX: Institute for Christian Economics, 1991), 52.

Fallacies of Continuity

CHAPTER 15

"OUT OF TOUCH": FALLACIES OF TIME

Events occur at objective points in time. Despite the continuous flow of time, what we remember or record as "history" consists of discreet and finite "snapshots" (versus the comprehensive and omniscient viewpoint of God). Our understanding increases as our number of consecutive snapshots increases (and we approach a video, or a very closely spaced series of snapshots—thirty frames per second, or so), but we will never approach the omniscient view of past and future that God possesses.

As a result, man's lust to persuade drives him sometimes to present unconnected events as actually connected in history, or to present possibilities as probabilities or inevitabilities. In essence this endeavor attempts to fuse two unconnected snapshots of history. In such cases, man witnesses falsely because he has no guarantee of his claim, and oftentimes the connection does not exist at all. Such Fallacies of Time hide the fact that they are simply "out of touch" with historical facts, or that historical facts are "out of touch" with the future. The discerning Christian will avoid these mistakes.

FALLACIES OF CAUSE

Under the heading of "Fallacies of Cause" I will discuss two primary fallacies, specifically two that relate to *time*. Some writers identify others.

Whatever differing lists you may find, all Fallacies of Cause fall under the general heading of the Fallacy *Non Causa Pro Causa*, which means confusing "Non-Cause, for Cause." You can also call it simply the Fallacy of False Cause. If you cannot prove a direct historical link between two events, then you risk some fallacy in claiming one to cause the other.

Post Hoc Propter Hoc

The first of our two bears the daunting Latin name *Post Hoc Propter Hoc*, which means "After this, because of this." After-This-Because-of-This describes the mistake of claiming something as a cause simply because it precedes another event in time. We can refer to it in abbreviated form as *Post Hoc* for convenience, or just the After This Fallacy. The error of this fallacy lies in assuming that priority in time necessarily indicates causation. But nearly every event in history occurs after a seemingly infinite number of prior events, among which only a few could act as primary causes. The pool of possible false causes is large. Precedence in time does not, therefore, guarantee a causal connection.[1]

I like to remember this fallacy also as it the Rooster Fallacy. This is because an often used illustration for it is the story of a naïve farmer who believed his rooster made the sun rise every morning. "How's that?" someone asked. "Simple," he answered, "First thing every morning my rooster crows, and then the sun comes up!"[2] The poor guy had mistakenly assumed that "happening after" means "happening because of."

Of course, by the same fallacious logic you could "prove" a causal link between any two arbitrary events simply due to their order in history. What caused the great oil fire on the Cuyahoga River in Cleveland, Ohio on July 22, 1969? Well, that's easy. It was because of the *Apollo* moon landing on July 21, 1969! Why not? The fire happened the day *after* the moon landing. Is it not clear? Of course this is absurd.[3]

The Armada that Turned the World

The same fallacy does not sound so absurd, however, when the two events lack obvious separation in location or other relation. For example, many historians at one time credited the defeat of the Spanish Armada in 1588 with tremendous causal links.[4] Famous historians Will and Ariel Durant write, "The defeat of the Armada affected almost everything in modern European civilization,"[5] and then go on to list everything from naval tactics (almost certainly true) to determining the future philosophy and theology of the English people (highly speculative and hardly demonstrable).[6]

Historian David Hackett Fischer notes that writers have claimed the famous defeat of the Armada as the cause of many various things: the decline of the Spanish empire, the rise of the British empire, the loss of control of the seas by Spain, the loss of Spanish contact with the Americas and thus New World gold, and even the rise of the Elizabethan Renaissance in literature with Shakespeare, etc.[7] Using the thorough work of Garrett Mattingly, *The Armada*, Fischer dispels each of these allegations as not only speculative, but falsified by the facts. As just one example, more American gold reached Spain during the fifteen years *after* the Armada's defeat that at any similar period before.[8]

The defeat of the Armada seems to have caused more hype than actual historical effect. Fischer concludes, "Its defeat may have caused very little, except the disruption of the Spanish strategy that sent it on its way."[9] The historians and teachers, therefore, who claim great historical outcomes based on the defeat should take great caution: they risk running ashore of a fallacy, namely, the After This fallacy. Just because many tumultuous and monumental events occurred in the related nations immediately after the defeat of the Spanish Armada does not entail that the naval defeat caused those events.

History involves so many complex and interwoven causes and effects that oftentimes we do not clearly and obviously see the links between them at first. Discerning genuine lines of causation will require us to reject many and only sometimes find the correct story. Just remember that it is better to admit, "I don't know the cause," than to assert a fallacious cause where none exists.

The Leaven of Fallacy

Jesus' disciples committed an After This fallacy at least once in the Gospels. In Matthew 16:5–12, Jesus had just finished rebuking the Pharisees for their hypocrisy when He and the disciples left by boat. When they reached the other shore, the disciples realized they had forgotten to bring bread for the trip. After this, Jesus said, *Watch out and beware of the leaven of the Pharisees and Sadducees* (Matt. 16:6). Since leaven often refers to bread, the disciples somehow thought He chided them: *They began* to discuss this among themselves, saying, *"He said that because we did not bring any bread"* (16:7). You can spot the beginnings of a causal fallacy here: they wrongly reasoned that Jesus mentioned leaven *because* they forgot to bring bread.

The disciples' forgetting and Jesus' comment, however, only relate at two points: 1) "leaven" plays a part in each, and 2) Jesus' comment came *after* the disciples' realization that they forgot bread. The "leaven" part confused the disciples. Even though Jesus had used "leaven" illustratively in a previous parable (Matt. 13:33), the disciples here took it literally. This also commits the fallacy of Equivocation, and it led the disciples also to claim a False Cause. Jesus confronted their misunderstanding by taking away their literalism: even if he had meant literal bread, had the disciples forgotten that He fed multitudes with a miracle, creating an abundance of literal bread? Obviously, Jesus had no worry about their lack of literal bread, so he must have meant something else. By forcing them to realize that their worry betrayed a lack of faith in Him, he made the true cause of his comments more apparent: *Then they understood that He did not say to beware of the leaven of bread, but of the teaching of the Pharisees and Sadducees* (Matt. 16:12). Note also that the disciples did not claim "because" here solely because Jesus' comments came *after* their error, but the time sequence did factor into their claim, and thus their error partakes of the *Post Hoc* fallacy nonetheless.

Primary and Secondary Causes

We could also label something as a *Post Hoc* Fallacy if the alleged cause is actually only a subsidiary, consequent, or secondary cause, and not the primary cause. For example, a man could not prove himself innocent of murder by blaming the death of his victim on the gun or the bullet. "I didn't kill him. The bullet did," does not work in a court of law because the weapon is only a tool of the real cause. The primary cause lies in the person who pulled the trigger. True, in this case the effect (death) came after the alleged cause (bullet), and the alleged cause is also *a* genuine cause, but it is not the primary cause. To fully avoid the fallacy here you must trace the chain of causes back to the relevant origin.[10]

Another analogy may help: if a house unexpectedly collapsed we might ask, "What caused this?" Someone inspecting the rubble may conclude that the wood was weak, rotten, and thus simply gave out. Case closed. Yet for years prior, termites had eaten away undetected, thus proving to be the primary cause. The compromised wood did cause the house to fall, but only as itself an effect of termite damage.

Depressing Logic

A great example of this last form of the fallacy comes in the standard popular explanation for America's Great Depression.[11] Historian Paul Johnson sums up the "received view" for us:

> The received view is that [President Herbert] Hoover, because of his ideological attachment to *laissez-faire* [unregulated free-market economics], refused to use government money to reflate the economy and so prolonged and deepened the Depression until the election of Roosevelt, who then promptly reversed official policy, introducing the New Deal, a form of Keynesianism, and pulled America out of the trough. Hoover is presented as the symbol of the dead, discredited past, Roosevelt as the harbinger of the future, and 1932–3 the watershed between old-style free market economics and the benevolent new managed economics and social welfare of Keynes.[12]

Economist Thomas Woods seconds the account of the popular misconception:

> Hoover sank the United States into the Depression, we're told, by his callous, ideologically blinkered fidelity to the laissez-faire economics favored by big-business. FDR rescued us through massive government spending, public works, and regulation that saved capitalism from itself.[13]

Much like our current times, popular lore looked only at surface appearances and saw wild speculation on Wall Street and poor lending practices by investment firms and banks. The immediate cry—fueled and fanned by certain vested politicians and naïve journalists—was that all this radical stock market activity drove the economy artificially high, President Hoover did nothing about it, and thus precipitated the crash.

Johnson, following some key economists, notes the thinness of the common explanation: "This most durable of historical myths has very little truth in it. The reality is much more complex and interesting."[14] Woods states even more strongly, "None of this is even slightly true."[15] Indeed, looking beyond the surface causes, you will learn some fundamental economic blunders made by the *government* actually caused the crash to occur.

What gets left out of most popular discussion is the Federal Reserve's creation and injections of vast amounts of new credit into the economy during the *decade before* the stock market crash. Over that time period the supply of credit in the economy nearly doubled as banks borrowed and began to innovate risky types of investment (easy-come easy-go money!).[16] The debt-driven demand drove prices of stocks much higher than warranted by actual earnings of those businesses. Such an artificial increase creates a stock market "bubble." Where in ordinary circumstances, some businesses succeed and others fail, the ones that fail usually go gradually or go quietly. In the "bubble" scenario, however, bad businesses get upheld for too long and at much higher prices than normal, so that when inevitable corrections come, the fall is great, the crash loud, and the effects widespread.

A few astute economists of the time foresaw what would happen. Ludwig von Mises, for example, understood that the skyrocketing "values" of stocks was an illusion based on infusions of artificial credit. While nearly everyone else hailed the "roaring 20s," and before the crash occurred in October 1929, Mises warned in 1928:

> It is clear that the crisis must come sooner or later. It is also clear that the crisis must always be *caused* [our subject, after all], primarily and directly, by the change in the conduct of the banks [lending]. If we speak of error on the part of the banks, however, we must point to the wrong they do in encouraging the upswing.[17]

So, in short, while it is true that radical *laissez-faire* economics and "speculators" did play a role in the Depression, the primary cause came from the creation of artificial money and credit *first*. After all, where did this huge wave of investors *get* all their money to invest? Exactly, the Federal Reserve and member banks foolishly lent it to them too cheaply, for too long, and for dubious investments. And when Hoover and FDR attempted to use government programs and money to reverse the course, they had to borrow the money for that, too, and from the same Fed. The results only extenuated the Depression for longer than it should have lingered. Woods notes that FDR fell for the fallacy: "He mistakenly believed falling prices had been a *cause* of the Depression (they were a consequence, not a cause)...."[18] The same lingering effect will probably occur with the current downturn today, as the government perpetuates the same mistaken view.[19]

So, the popularized view watches the economic house collapse and points to the stock market as the rotten splintered wood. True, but a closer look reveals the termites of credit that had eaten away at the substructure for years prior. The common view—taught in public schools and promoted by politicians when in power—simply foists a type of *Post Hoc* fallacy on the public. It suppresses evidence and claims something as a cause which was not the primary cause.

Fallacies from Venting to Voodoo

The After This Fallacy pops up nearly everywhere, apparently because (dare I speculate on a cause?) people like to find the cause of things, and happening *after* something provides a convenient enough connection for most. One guy wrote into a newspaper opinion column listing seemingly every bad thing that had happened in the nation and blaming it on the election of George W. Bush: the bankruptcy of Montgomery Ward, rises in postal and shipping rates, layoffs in the retail sector, "dot-com" bankruptcies, etc—and all because the Republican Party filled the White House![20] (Conservatives should take care not to make similarly fallacious claims about Obama or others.)

In another story, a pro-choice, ACLU "reproductive rights lawyer" received a timely grant that saved her newly-opened foundation from debt. The article reported, "She calls it 'fortuitous' that grant came at the same time she founded the center, adding, 'God must love choice'"[21]—a totally after-the-fact assessment on her part. I wonder if her foundation went bankrupt, would she then decide God disapproved?

On a similar subject, when a Ripley's museum in Orlando acquired two statues of fertility gods, several women associated with the office turned up pregnant.²² Word got out, dozens of calls came in, and people began to visit just to touch the statues in hopes of getting pregnant. This basest form of the After This Fallacy expresses nothing more than superstition in tribal magic: rub this and get that, drink this and receive that, dance like this and it will rain. Yet examples like all of these appear all around us.

The After This Fallacy sounds rather simple and easy to avoid, but it has appeared in crucial places with smart people and had disastrous effects in history. A medical journal recalls an account from 1897, when doctors believed that "bloodletting" (controlled draining of blood) could help cure particular diseases. The alleged proof of the benefits of such practice overtly committed the After This Fallacy. A young child afflicted by Scarlet Fever consequently developed a severe kidney infection which progressed to convulsions. The physician knew of nothing better to do than drain blood. *After* he did so, the child began to recover:

> About 100cc. of blood were withdrawn from the right median cephalic vein. The result was more striking than any the observer had ever noticed following therapeutic intervention.... [T]en days later the albumin [blood and tissue, in this case] was no longer found in the urine; the edema [swelling with excess fluid] of the eyelids disappeared and the improvement in the general condition was rapid.²³

How does this commit the fallacy? The physician believed that the improvement resulted from the bloodletting. However, doctors today know that, despite its severity, this condition regresses and abates on its own slowly but steadily. The bloodletting did not cause the improvement, it only appeared so since the improvement came afterwards. In reality, the bleeding might have endangered the child further, and thus the healing effect attributed to it committed the *Post Hoc* Fallacy big time.

This last example, as well as the Depression example and others, remind us once again that fallacies are not trivial matters. The student may get the impression from the examples in many books on the subject that fallacies generally pertain to comedy and silliness, but serious examples with serious consequences occur every day. Proper judgment enables prosperity in all ways; poor logic can endanger lives, ruin economies, perpetuate unhelpful ideas, and even weaken faith. This applies for the seemingly obvious After This Fallacy as well.

Cum Hoc Propter Hoc

A second Fallacy of Cause confuses simultaneity for causation. In other words, just because two things occur at or near the same time, someone may fallaciously assume that one caused the other. We call this *Cum Hoc Propter Hoc*, which is Latin for "*With* this, because of this." The same exposure of folly as the After This Fallacy applies here to the With This Fallacy: a myriad of possible causes exist—many we may not even see or know of—for every given occurrence. This creates a high probability for false causes, even for events that seem to concur in time. Correlation in time cannot guarantee a causal link.

Statistics Don't Lie, But Liars Use Statistics

In his book *Letter to a Christian Nation*, atheist Sam Harris cites statistical studies in order to popularize the following correlation:

> The United States is unique among wealthy democracies in its level of religious adherence; it is also uniquely beleaguered by high rates of homicide, abortion, teen pregnancy, sexually transmitted disease, and infant mortality.[24]

Sam bases his claim on a scholarly study done in 2005 which many atheists have since used to attack religion. The study itself explicitly admitted that merely correlated events do not prove causality: "because potential causal factors for rates of societal function are complex … it is not the purpose of this initial study to definitively demonstrate a causal link between religion and social conditions."[25] Sam himself carefully avoids claiming causation, though he wryly suggests that some causal link must exist: "Of course, correlational data of this sort do not resolve questions of causality—belief in God may lead to societal dysfunction; societal dysfunction may foster a belief in God; each factor may enable the other; or both may spring from some deeper source of mischief."[26]

All of this said, however, at least one journalist completely ignored Sam's carefully calyptopygian rhetoric and swallowed his hint in all its deceptiveness. She bluntly announced the stats in as classically fallacious form as possible: "Religious belief can cause damage to a society, contributing towards high murder rates, abortion, sexual promiscuity and suicide, according to research published today."[27] The allegation of a direct cause between religious belief and societal dysfunction overtly commits the fallacy of With This Because of This. Just because a scholar can present the two phenomena side-by-side in no way implies a causal link between them. Many factors exist—some we may not even know of—which could explain if and why the two things currently appear together. Even if we could find no other factors (though we do, as you will see momentarily), this would still not justify the journalist's claim (or Sam's suggestion of it) simply based on the phenomena of religion and crime occurring in society *at the same time*.

Despite anticipating that many would draw and promulgate this illogical conclusion based on his work, Sam goes on to present many similar statistics together, all claiming a correlation between religion and high crime rates, and thus suggesting a causal link to the reader. In order to do this Sam references the famous election map of "red" (Republican) and "blue" (Democratic) states (made famous by the 2000 presidential election, and used since). He compares the colors of relevant states with lists of cities ranked for high crime levels, and then reports that the conservative (and thus assumedly more "Christian") red states contain more high-crime cities than do blue (more secularist) states. The data do seem to back Sam's main conclusion that "widespread belief in God does not ensure a society's health."[28]

It does not take much investigation, however, to expose the weaknesses of these "correlational" claims. In fact, a professor of physics at Michigan University who specializes in "complex systems" has provided very helpful analyses of the election maps to which Sam refers.[29] The more detailed studies reveal a striking feature that Sam leaves out. When observed at the more detailed level of individual *counties* within the states, in almost every case of a high-crime city in a red state, that city's county itself was blue.[30] This holds true for most large cities in general—they almost all appear in blue counties, indicating that secularist thought predominates in urban areas. Only two obvious exceptions—Dallas and Houston—out of dozens appear. Even in those two cases, though, further maps modified for percentages of partisan voting showed their respective counties much closer to blue than the surrounding jurisdictions.[31] In other words, those two particular counties had a majority of conservatives, but leaned more strongly toward secularism than other red counties.

This fact correlates directly to the level of crime reported in each state, and yet does not comport with Sam's correlation of Christian conservatism with crime. The vast majority of the crime in these red states (in all states, actually) occurs in the metropolitan areas where secularist thought prevails and Christian conservatism forms a minority. In further support of this, FBI statistics show that for all types of violent crime, without exception, rural areas have much lower rates than metropolitan or urban areas.[32] And this means that centers of secular thought and liberal politics correspond to high crime rates, even when these cities fall within the state-lines of red states. Anyone who looks beyond the surface appearances that Sam identifies will therefore see the fallacy of his presentation of the statistics.

In summary, then, it appears that the statistics belie Sam's suggestion. In areas where conservative Christians have "overwhelming political influence," crimes rates tend to be much lower. These facts show how many factors go into determining causes. Discerning these factors requires careful and tenacious study. In this case, Sam's focus on large geographical boundaries hides other realities which turn out to be more detailed and complex, and yet crucially important. Careful and disciplined students will not draw—let alone publish—such claims before they first look for all the data.

The fallacy of With This appears commonly when people work with statistics. One reporter looks at a government study that "ranks jobs by rates of depression," and apparently concludes that certain jobs more likely cause clinical depression. The article concludes that "working full-time would appear to be beneficial in preventing depression. The overall rate of depression for full-time workers, 7%, compares with the 12.7% rate registered by those who are unemployed."[33] But does this correlation between certain jobs and depression mean that those occupations cause the depression? Is it true that certain work environments, full-time for example, benefit and help prevent depression? To state it this way commits the With This fallacy. The truth may prove the opposite: that people more susceptible to depression tend to seek out certain types of jobs.[34] Further causes may underlie each phenomenon, or the higher rates may merely coincide by chance. Correlations like this simply require further study to determine the causes more exactly.

Hot Air Pushes Global Warming

A more concerning example comes from Al Gore's crusade against global warming. In his video *An Inconvenient Truth*, he uses correlational data to back his points: "If you look at a thousand years worth of temperature, and compare it to a thousand years of CO2, you can see how well they fit together." He admits that the relationship between carbon dioxide in the atmosphere and temperature is very complicated, but states that the most important relationship is this: "when there is more Carbon Dioxide, the temperature gets warmer, because it traps more heat from the sun inside." Gore, famously now, presents pictures of melted glaciers and icecaps, along with warnings of increases in hurricanes and storms, flooded port cities due to rising ocean levels, and other climate catastrophes should we not immediately begin to reduce carbon emissions and our use of hydrocarbons (a scare-tactic, or Appeal to Fear). More importantly, he correlates modern human activity with the increase in carbon dioxide levels, implying that since humans cause global warming we must take drastic measures to reduce it.

Of course, all of this abuses the "With This" correlational fallacy many times over. To begin with, CO2 is not the primary cause of the "greenhouse effect" that results in higher temperatures. At least two other factors greatly outweigh it: solar activity and another more important greenhouse gas, water vapor. The Oregon Institute of Science and Medicine argues in a detailed paper, "Atmospheric temperature is regulated by the sun, which fluctuates in activity ... by the greenhouse effect, largely caused by atmospheric water vapor (H_2O); and by other phenomena that are more poorly understood."[35] Changes in solar radiation correlate more closely and for a longer period of history with temperature changes than do Gore's graphs of CO2. As well, "While major greenhouse gas H_2O substantially warms the Earth, minor greenhouse gases such as CO_2 have little effect."[36]

On top of this, while global temperatures have indeed risen in recent decades, proponents of Gore's scare-tactics rarely mention that temperatures for centuries prior cooled considerably. The current rise merely corrects the previous "Little Ice Age." The warming trend has occurred for much longer than Gore emphasizes, and has created effects that belie more of his claims:

> [M]easurements show that the trend of 7 inches per century increase in sea level and the shortening trend in av-

erage glacier length both began *a century before* 1940, yet 84% of total annual human hydrocarbon use occurred only *after* 1940. Moreover, neither of these trends has accelerated during the period between 1940 and 2007, while hydrocarbon use increased 6 fold.[37]

This scientific paper, which stands behind a petition signed by over 31,000 American scientists, concludes,

> There are no experimental data to support the hypothesis that increases in human hydrocarbon use or in atmospheric carbon dioxide and other greenhouse gases are causing or can be expected to cause unfavorable changes in global temperature, weather, or landscape. There is no reason to limit human production of CO_2, CH_4, or other minor greenhouse gases as has been proposed.[38]

So it seems that—despite Al Gore's claims about having a "scientific consensus" (a fallacious Appeal to Authority)—other obvious, more relevant, and powerful causes exist to explain global temperature changes other than those claimed by Al Gore (as well as the United Nations, and those who follow it). Al's *An Inconvenient Truth* contains little more than one big craftily presented With This Because of This Fallacy (packaged with a few other fallacies).

So why would Gore and others present the story this way? Note how he and other liberals intend to "solve" the problem: they propose a tax on carbon emissions as well as a global system of "cap-and-trade" on hydrocarbon usage. In plain language, these measures amount to a redistribution of wealth where more prosperous people and nations that use more fuel end up paying tons of money to third-world nations that do not. "Global Warming" simply acts as a mask and a fear factor for advancing the leftist political agenda, and increasing global government control of free and prosperous nations like the United States. Global warming is not an "inconvenient truth," it is a convenient lie.[39]

Suffering and Providence

False causes come in many ways, some of which the Bible captures. One of the worst religious abuses of this fallacy comes when people attribute individual suffering to particular sins or sinfulness. We find an example of such in Luke 13:1–5. The people came to Jesus to tell him about some recent tragedy—Pilate's murder and desecration of some Galileans. Christ preempted their thoughts:

> *Do you suppose that these Galileans were greater sinners than all other Galileans because they suffered this fate? I tell you, no, but unless you repent, you will all likewise perish. Or do you suppose that those eighteen on whom the tower in Siloam fell and killed them were worse culprits than all the men who live in Jerusalem? I tell you, no, but unless you repent, you will all likewise perish.*

It pertains to the popular fallen reasoning of man to assume that calamity or suffering results from individual sin. While suffering does result from sin, this means sin in general and not necessarily individual sins. Scripture clearly states that God does send poverty, invasion, slavery, debt and sickness as a result of sin (Deut 28:15–68), but these curses apply to God's people corporately if they disobey the covenant. This way of understanding sin and punishment does factor into the Luke 13 context, as Christ warned the people of the imminent destruction of the Jewish nation for not bearing fruit (Luke 12:54–59; 13:6–9). But to apply it to individuals in individual situations misses the point of God's covenantal faithfulness and His absolute sovereignty.

The book of Job clearly dispels the fallacious idea that personal suffering results directly from personal sin. God tells us that Job *was blameless, upright, fearing God and turning away from evil* (1:1). Even after his afflictions *Job did not sin nor did he blame God* (1:22). Nevertheless, his three friends—Eliphaz, Bildad, and Zophar—arrived and charged him unanimously with suffering affliction because of his personal sins. Eliphaz argued, *Remember now, who ever perished being innocent? Or where were the upright destroyed? According to what I have seen, those who plow iniquity And those who sow trouble harvest it* (4:7–8). Bildad concurred, *Lo, God will not reject a man of integrity, Nor will He support the evildoers* (8:20). Zophar even argued that God punished Job *less* than He should have (11:6), and asked Job, *Do you know this from of old, From the establishment of man on earth, That the triumphing of the wicked is short, And the joy of the godless momentary?* (20:4–5). Yet despite all of their wonderful rhetoric, in the end God absolves Job and condemns the three friends for false witness: *the Lord said to Eliphaz the Temanite, My wrath is kindled against you and against your two friends, because you have not spoken of Me what is right as My servant Job has* (42:7).

Jesus makes the same point in John 9:1–3. The man born blind did not suffer as a result of sin, but that God's glory might appear in his healing. We simply cannot state sin as the cause of any individual's suffering. To do so commits a False Cause Fallacy and therefore bears false witness.

A final example exhibits the tenacity of the human mind to cling to its fallacies. In Acts 28:1–6, when Paul helps collect firewood, a snake emerges from a bundle of sticks and bites his hand. The people immediately jumped to the conclusion that Paul suffered from vengeance for sin. They said, *Undoubtedly this man is a murderer, and though he has been saved from the sea, justice has not allowed him to live* (28:4). Paul shook the serpent loose from his hand, and the people expected to see his hand swell, or him drop dead. *But after they had waited a long time and had seen nothing unusual happen to him, they changed their minds and began to say that he was a god* (28:6). They changed their minds—a good start. But they did not change their minds about their fallacious belief—that tragedy results from personal sin, or that Paul committed some heinous sin in his past—rather, they changed their belief that Paul was mortal! "He's a god!" they said.

People stubbornly, sometimes, hold onto their presuppositions and beliefs, even when evidence or reason clearly refute those ideas. But this stubbornness results in other, often more foolish, superstitions. People often prefer to look foolish than admit that their main points commit errors. Such is the fallacy-making power of *pride*—a genuine cause of shame, contention, and destruction (Prov. 11:2; 13:10; 15:25; 16:8). *The tongue of the wise makes knowledge acceptable, But the mouth of fools spouts folly. Do you see a man wise in his own eyes? There is more hope for a fool than for him* (Prov. 15:2; 26:12).

The Gambler's Fallacy

The Gambler's Fallacy occurs when an event involves more than one possible outcome, and makes the mistake of assuming a particular outcome will occur based on the results of past experience. It appears in different varieties. A common example involves a "Gambler" who assumes that since every pull of the slot machine lever has resulted in nothing so far, therefore the next pull should win big. When someone watches a lucky streak or sequence of "beating the odds," and assumes that the streak must soon end, they also commit the fallacy. This version you could call the "It's Due" Fallacy.

The fallacy can occur in the converse as well: if the gambler assumes that since he has had success rolling the dice so far, therefore he will have success on the next roll. We could also call this the "One More Time" Fallacy. The individual thinks that a lucky streak will continue "one more time" simply because it has so far. But probability simply does not work this way.[40] The odds reset for *every individual* pull of the lever or flip of the coin—50/50 means 50/50 in each instance. Even if the last twenty coin flips landed "heads," this would not mean anything for the twenty-first flip; the odds would remain 50/50 for the next flip, and could therefore just as likely land heads or tails.

The fact that the fallacy can appear in either form—assuming the continuation of a streak, or the end of one—testifies to the fallaciousness of the idea in general. Either outcome remains just as possible, and thus to assume either way based on past outcomes commits the fallacy.

The classic incident occurred at a casino in Monte Carlo in 1913. On August 18 the roulette wheel landed "black" a record twenty-six straight times. The odds of such an occurrence calculate to roughly 1 in 273,708,560. Gamblers began to gather round on the fifteenth straight black. "This has got to end soon!" they believed as they doubled and tripled their bets. The streak of blacks continued for eleven more rounds. Many foolish people lost lots of money that day, and the casino cashed in on their fallacious reasoning.[41]

Sporting Superstitions

The Gambler's Fallacy can occur in tandem with the "With This" fallacy which attributes a false cause to the occurrence. It then leads people to do many strange things when placed in a position of multiple possible outcomes. Sports figures legendarily perform "lucky" routines which they believe essential to their performance. A local newspaper reported on such superstitions among college baseball players.[42] Georgia University third baseman Ryan Peisel batted 0-for-2 in his first two attempts against Ole Miss, then removed one of his batting gloves. He then had three straight hits. From then on he only used one glove. Did it really improve his batting? He did bat a not-to-shabby .304 after the change, but had actually batted .331

before, yet continued repeating his one-gloved batting superstition—thus showing the power of the mind to override facts with fallacies.

The same newspaper reported numerous such instances just among the local teams: one player eats the same meal before every game, even though he does not particularly like it, another rubs pine tar on everything including his helmet, another precisely repeats the same ritual in the on-deck circle every time. In almost every case, the player bases their expectation of future success on past successes during which they performed the ritual. While the players may revel in their superstitions, Georgia coach David Perno addressed the fallacy appropriately: "I am one to go the other way.... I will do little subtle things opposite just to verify that it is not because of these superstitions." By eliminating superstitious elements a player may identify the *actual* causes that influence his play, and thus truly improve.

Playing the Market? Or Letting the Market Play You?

Unfortunately, most examples given of the Gambler's Fallacy tend to include just that—gambling. Lottery tickets, dice rolling, horse racing, etc., all commonly appear where books and websites cover the idea. But the Gambler's Fallacy can lead to serious problems in everyday life. One of the most problematic areas involves investing in the stock market. People have a strong tendency to buy apparent "winners," or stocks that have consistently increased in price over time.[43] Nevertheless, a stock's successful performance in the past does not and cannot necessarily guarantee future success. Many people ignore this, wrongly assuming that past growth will continue, and thus risk potential losses by ignorance and fallacy.

Brokerage firms understand the psychology of average buyers who have little or no investing experience. The firms help fuel the fallacious behavior: "Marketers of mutual funds, stocks, and similar financial products exploit this practice of consumers by aggressively advertising the past positive performance of their offerings."[44] This is not to blame the firms, but to warn those who may fall prey to fallacious ideas promoted in the marketing literature. People tend to let the delusion of continued growth blind them to all facts and warnings: "Ads of stocks and mutual funds typically tout their past performance, despite a disclosure that past performance does not guarantee future returns."[45]

Unfortunately for such buyers, many factors play a role in the success or failure of a company. Past performance can indicate whether the company's past growth occurred because of proper factors. If the company shows signs of continuing good business policies amidst favorable markets, then success will likely continue. But these multiple other factors play the key role, *not the past performance itself* which has no necessary causal connection to the future. To make an investment decision on past performance alone, therefore, amounts literally to gambling, and is thus foolish.

The fallacy occurs with investors in many scenarios.[46] First, a trader may feel inclined to sell a stock they own after consecutive days of growth, believing that such growth simply cannot continue. This is the least risky scenario, as wisdom might say to sell simply for the profits. Nevertheless, his reason for selling—simply because he believes a reversal is "due"—commits the Gambler's Fallacy. Secondly, someone may watch a stock price increase for several days, and decide to buy simply believing the trend will continue. Many, many people have lost money with such thinking. The great "dot-com bubble" (1995-2000) led investors to ignore business fundamentals and feverishly pour money into internet "tech stocks" based on the hype that internet-based technology would continue to grow rapidly as in past years. The "bubble" eventually burst, and the crash came in March, 2000, as millions of investors lost trillions of dollars. Thirdly, an investor may decide to sell a stock based on several days of losses, but making that decision based solely on the belief that the fall will continue commits the fallacy just as in the first scenario. Lastly (although this does not exhaust the possibilities), an investor may try to beat the odds by assuming a reversal in a falling stock. Assuming that the fall will turn into a gain, he may buy *more*, hoping to catch the stock at a lower price before it goes back up. But what happens if the stock continues to fall? Many investors continue to bet against a falling stock and keep buying more as it falls. Wise investors avoid such fallacious behavior, which they call "catching a falling knife."

The Gambler's Fallacy applies to markets and finance in many other scenarios.[47] Whatever charts or graphs may indicate about the past, they cannot determine or guarantee future ups or downs. Students will find it wise to study the fundamentals of stock value and performance before trying to interpret what benefit charts and graphs actually provide.

Many Gambles in Life

The Gambler's fallacy affects other areas of life as well. Project managers must actively work to correct changes and deviations in scheduling and work performance. Believing that a positive change will naturally occur to correct a string of accidents commits the fallacy and may have costly or even fatal results.[48] Doctors and nurses must avoid poor diagnoses that can result from seeing similar cases over and over.[49] Also, multiple problems can strike the same individual. Especially in cases where a patient routinely receives treatment for a chronic ailment and yet suffers from further complications. Studies have shown that in such scenarios the effort given to the chronic disorder can cause a distraction from detecting and treating others.[50] Criminologists consider whether punishing drunk drivers may encourage their crime because once they get out of jail they might think "I certainly won't be unlucky enough to get caught again!"[51] Although, it appears that criminals who never get caught or who go unpunished also tend to think they will therefore get away next time as well.[52] (It seems that criminals employ both versions of the fallacy in their self-delusions!)

In yet another related real-life situation, one psychology study assessed people's evaluations of risk and their willingness to buy insurance. It concluded that "people tend to feel that once a low-probability even [such as a 100-year flood or drought] occurrs, they are 'inoculated' against such a repetition in the coming year."[53] As people feel secure that such an event will not happen again, they buy less insurance for the current year. The same effect "may explain why many residents in flood-prone areas are willing to move back, without insurance, following a major flood."[54] In short, the Gambler's Fallacy affects even life and livelihood. That so many people refuse even to buy insurance partially due to such thinking demonstrates the power of the human mind to cling to fallacies. Like the gambler betting on an unlikely number, we often put our property, money, and even lives at risk over unreasonable assumptions.

The Gambler's Fallacy can apply to so many areas because it applies to *all* areas of life than involve uncertainty or probability.

Risk and Faithful Living

Unfortunately, uncertainty factors into nearly every human endeavor, and thus we must deal with it wisely. We can approach the uncertain future in only three ways, only one of which God has prescribed: as a gambler, a dictator, or a businessman.[55] The gambler acts according to the fallacy, basing his actions on the patterns in past outcomes. The dictator (or "social engineer") attempts to eliminate uncertainty by imposing his will on as many factors of uncertainty as possible. This creates two problems: first, it eliminates human freedom for those whom the dictator oppresses. They lose their will because of his. Secondly, it faces an impossibility: no one has the omnipotence to control everyone else, let alone to control all other factors of the environment. Likewise, no one has the omniscience to know all the necessary factors of uncertainty that need addressing, or how best to address the ones we do know of. Dictatorships, therefore, routinely end in both mass oppression and failure.

The third way derives from biblical wisdom, and we can call it the way of the businessman, or the steward. This way addresses uncertainty in a way that includes knowledge, love for neighbor, and faith in God. It preserves society, freedom, and forms the only path to prosperity. Economist Ludwig von Mises contrasts this path with the gambler: "The card player wins money by outsmarting his antagonist. The businessman makes money by supplying customers with goods they want to acquire."[56] In other words, in a gambler's world, human behavior acts with no care for other people and no trust in purpose in the future. Thus it quickly devolves into antagonism between man and God, and between man and man. "Only luck exists," and "Get the other guy before he gets you," form the basic ground rules. In a godly society, however, individuals work to understand each others' needs and desires, and form products and services to meet those parameters. Mises explains,

> The characteristic feature of business in a society, i.e., within an order based on the division of labor, is concord in the endeavors of its members. As soon as they begin to antagonize one another, a tendency toward social disintegration emerges.[57]

The businessman or steward faces the future with knowledge and understanding of fellow man, and with others' interests involved in his own profit. This diffuses uncertainty in a faithful and peaceful way in which all people can remain free from oppression. This model simply reflects the commandments God gave us to live by. God's covenant with man promises to bless him with prosperity if he obeys (Deut. 28:1–14). The covenant, in summary form, simply calls for the love of God and the love of neighbor (Matt. 22:37–40). We must live and work in faith that by respecting this godly way of life, God will control the uncertain matters that lay beyond our control. He has the omniscience and omnipotence to bring it to pass—to bless and to curse. We must confront uncertainty with faith and not attempt to deny or escape God's providence. Christ made this point clear with His parable of the talents (Matt. 25:14–30).

SLIPPERY SLOPE

The Fallacy of Slippery Slope involves the claim that if a particular action is taken it will inevitably lead to another particular and undesirable event. The idea imagines, for example, that a person who takes a first step onto a steep slope will slide all the way to the bottom. Therefore, it argues, it is better to avoid that first step altogether. But this assumes a number of things (keeping with the metaphor): 1) that the slope actually exists; 2) that the slope is steep enough to cause someone to slip; 3) that the person stepping has not prepared some means of adequate footing, for example, special boots or ropes; and 4) that the slope actually leads exactly where the arguer claims it does. All of these assumptions, and probably more, expose Slippery Slope thinking as fallacious without lots of supporting qualifications.

Some writers call this the Domino Fallacy[58] because it assumes that taking that first action will cause a chain reaction, and all the dominos will fall to the end of the line. Again, this assumes that the events described actually align (in the grand scheme of things) like dominos waiting to fall, and that touching the first will indeed set them all tumbling. Anyone engaging in such reasoning must first prove that each individual link in the chain necessarily and causally connects before they can rightly even begin to assert the overall claim.

This Fallacy of Slippery Slope sounds very similar to the Continuum Fallacy or Fallacy of the Beard. While both fallacies do involve claims based on continuums, the difference lies in the role which the continuum plays. The Fallacy of the Beard leverages the indistinguishable nature of the increments of the continuum in order to wrongly deny the extremes or the importance of differing degrees. It is, therefore, a fallacy of *representation*. Slippery Slope, however, is a fallacy of *prediction* which involves cause and time. It contends that since position A lies on the same continuum as another (usually undesirable) position B, then therefore position A will inevitably lead to position B in due time. In effect, the Fallacy of Slippery Slope denies that the "space" between the two positions, or any outside factor for that matter, will prevent the one from eventually causing the other.

"The Root of All Evil"

A good example of Slippery Slope thinking appears (like so many fallacies do!) in the works of atheist Richard Dawkins. Although, to his credit, he did not author this particular argument, he just quoted it (of course, he did *choose* to quote it). As an example of "real extremists" that he could have exposed in his work, Dawkins quotes from "an American colleague":

> Europeans need to know there is a traveling theo-freak show which actually advocates reinstatement of Old Testament law—killing of homosexuals—and the right to hold office, or even to vote, for Christians only. Middle class crowds cheer to this rhetoric. If secularists are not vigilant, Dominionists and Reconstructionists will soon be mainstream in a true American theocracy![59]

This quotation provides multiple fallacies. For one, it erects a Straw Man. Few if any Reconstructionists actually desire to kill homosexuals, or limit voting only to Christians. Even less truly do "crowds" cheer to such rhetoric. Reconstruction—a tiny minority position—has hardly ever drawn a "crowd" to speak of! Much less even should anyone worry that the group is well on its way to taking over the country! Those serious about Christian Reconstruction actually advocate persuasion and freedom instead of violent or even sudden overthrow.

That aside, the last sentence of Dawkins' quotation simply stirs up fear by appealing to a Slippery Slope: if secularists remain complacent, these horrible theocrats will *soon* take over! Nothing could fall further from the truth, given the tiny influence of this group; yet more importantly, the argument of "will soon be" simply ignores the many causes and factors that stand between point A and the allegedly inevitable point B. Even if secularism completely vanished from the earth, other factors could—and likely would—prevent such a harsh violent theocracy from coming to pass. In fact, Reconstructionists, being fans of freedom and free enterprise, would lead the forefront of such preventative factors!

That Dawkins overlooks a fallacy here comes as no surprise. An irony, however, arises from the fact that he openly rejects "Slippery Slope" arguments elsewhere in his best-selling book.[60] Nevertheless, Dawkins allows such thought later when attacking Reconstructions, thereby also partaking of a Double Standard. His motivation seems clear: he wields the Epithet "the American Taliban," which he intends to describe "American religious leaders and faith-based politicians ... of recent years."[61] He complains that the radical activism of pro-lifer Randall Terry of Operation Rescue represents an "ambition to achieve what can only be called a Christian fascist state," and that this horrible image "is entirely typical of the American Taliban," and "an almost exact mirror image of the Islamic fascist states so ardently sought by many people in other parts of the world."[62] You can hear the fallacies piling up—Double Standard, Epithet, Straw Man, False Analogy, etc. Then Dawkins dabbles in Slippery Slope himself: "Randall Terry is not—*yet*—in political power."[63] *Yet*, he says, imposing the fear of sliding down that slope should we not dare banish God from political discourse! This hateful theocrat is not ruling—*yet*—"But no observer of the American political scene at the time of writing (2006) can afford to be sanguine."[64]

From this angle, Slippery Slopes often have a built-in Appeal to Fear, arguing that some dreaded consequence awaits should we not take some proposed action. Dawkins' now well-known "Religion is the Root of All Evil" message simply promotes a presupposed False Cause. Other atheists have adopted this course as well, such as Christopher Hitchens, whose book bears the subtitle *How Religion Poisons Everything*. The fear these propagandists spread about religion and a dreaded future merely projects their original presumed fallacy into the future. It in reality mimics the "doom and gloom" apocalyptic end-times scenarios popular among many Christians—using fear of inevitable consequences to drive people to a certain decision. Whether promoted by Christians or atheists, the tactic is fallacious. God controls the future, usually beyond all human prediction. God also controls the present, and He commands us now to reason truthfully, not project baseless fears into the future.

Fallacious Doom and Gloom

Al Gore creates a gross Slippery Slope argument with his claims about increasing greenhouse gases in the future (see above under *Cum Hoc Propter*

Hoc). The largely debunked graph that his film *An Inconvenient Truth* popularized earned the nickname "the hockey stick" because it shows only mild fluctuations in the amount of CO_2 until the last few decades, and then drastically shoots upward—thus forming the shape of a hockey stick. Even if his graph contained accurate data (many argue it does not), this would still not warrant the conclusion that Gore draws from it. In order to make his rhetorical point he mounts a man-lift and elevates it several feet high. He then points to the top of a big screen where the spike on his graph goes "off the charts." Such is the radical future we face if we do not cut CO_2 emission!

Of course this unwarranted extrapolation commits classically the Fallacy of Slippery Slope. Anyone could make any kind of radical prediction like this by simply extending the last upswing or down-tick of data indefinitely. The real question remains, "Is such an extrapolation warranted?" (Remember the books *DOW 36,000*, *DOW 36,000*, and *DOW 40,000*, all predicting wild extrapolations for the stock market?) And still then, even if the data warrant such a speculation, we still do not have proof, simply because many factors could yet affect the future.

Peter corrected a reverse application of "Slippery Slope to doomsday" thinking in his day. Instead, God's judgment did loom very near on the Jewish people as Jesus had predicted. Critics of the promised return of Christ argued that since Christ had not returned then for sometime (probably nearing 40 years), therefore the promise was a hoax and Christ would never return (a Slippery Slope and a Gambler's Fallacy). Peter relates their fallacy:

> *Know this first of all, that in the last days mockers will come with their mocking, following after their own lusts, and saying, "Where is the promise of His coming? For ever since the fathers fell asleep, all continues just as it was from the beginning of creation"* (2 Pet. 3:3–4).

Peter corrects their fallacy by reminding us who actually controls the slope of history:

> *But do not let this one fact escape your notice, beloved, that with the Lord one day is as a thousand years, and a thousand years as one day. The Lord is not slow about His promise, as some count slowness, but is patient toward you, not wishing for any to perish but for all to come to repentance* (2 Pet. 3:8–9).

Like so many fallacies that people commit, the rememdy lies in the fact that God reigns supreme, and His word shall come to pass. Any human reasoning that deviates from this standard risks all manner of fallacy.

NOTES

1. See also S. Morris Engel, *With Good Reason: An Introduction to Logical Fallacies*, 5th Ed. (New York: St. Martin's Press, 1994, 165.

2. I first heard this example listening to the excellent teaching series *Ideas Have Consequences* by R. C. Sproul.

3. See Loretta Neal, "The Cuyahoga River Fires," *Balanced Living Magazine* (July-Aug. 2005); available at http://www.balancedlivingmag.com/2005/July%20-%20August%202005/The%20Cuyahoga%20River%20Fires.htm (accessed January 28, 2009). The river in question had actually ignited many times in previous decades due to oil pollution and various available sources of spark or flame.

4. David Hackett Fischer notes this in *Historians' Fallacies: Toward a Logic of Historical Thought* (New York: Harper TorchBooks, 1970), 166–167. Fischer relies partly on Garrett Mattingly, *The Armada* (Boston: Houghton Mifflin Co., 1959), 397–402.

5. Will and Ariel Durant, *The Age of Reason Begins: A history of European Civilization in the Period of Shakespeare, Bacon, Montaigne, Rembrandt, Galileo, and Descrates: 1558–1648*, The Story of Civilization: Part VII (New York: Simon and Schuster, 1961), 37–38.

6. See this example noted also under the Speculative Fallacy.

7. Fischer, *Historians' Fallacies*, 166–167.

8. Fischer, *Historians' Fallacies*, 167; Mattingly, *The Armada*, 398.

9. Fischer, *Historians' Fallacies*, 167.

10. This scenario technically differs from a standard *Post Hoc* in that it does not designate a non-cause as a cause, but yet it qualifies as the fallacy since it designates a different type of cause as the true cause, and for that reason I include it here.

11. Arlie J. Hoover also mentions explanations of the Depression as an example of *post hoc*. See *Don't You Believe It: Poking Holes in faulty Logic* (Chicago, IL: Moody Press, 1982), 93. I have expanded what he mentions briefly.

12. Paul Johnson, *Modern Times: The World from the Twenties to the Nineties*, revised ed. (New York: HarperPerennial, 1991), 241. "Keynes" here refers to John Maynard Keynes, the economist who promoted public works projects funded by Massive government debt as a way of spurring the economy. The debts, however, made the situation worse in the long run. "Keynesianism" refers to Keynes' ideas.

13. Thomas E. Woods, Jr., *Meltdown: A Free-Market Look at Why the Stock Market Collapsed, the Economy Tanked, and Government Bailouts Will Make Things Worse* (Washington, D.C.: Regnery Publishing, Inc., 2009), 87.

14. Paul Johnson, *Modern Times: The World from the Twenties to the Nineties*, 241.

15. Thomas E. Woods, Jr., *Meltdown*, 88.

16. Paul Johnson, *Modern Times: The World from the Twenties to the Nineties*, 233, 239.

17. Quoted in Thomas E. Woods, Jr., *Meltdown*, 97. Emphases mine.

18. Thomas E. Woods, Jr., *Meltdown*, 100. Emphasis his.

19. For further reading, I refer the reader to Thomas E. Woods, Jr., *Meltdown*, 87–107, and to Paul Johnson, *Modern Times*, 230–260.

20. Leo Morris, "We're off to a bad start," *The Atlanta Journal-Constitution*, January 3, 2001, A10.

21. Desda Moss, "MacArthur surprise," *USA Today*, June 16, 1992, 2A.

22. Katy Kelly, "Ripley's great expectations," *USA Today*, January 17, 1996, 1D.

23. T. E. C., Jr. "The Therapeutic Value of Bloodletting in a Child Suffering from Severe Complications of Postscarlatina Glomerulonephritis in 1897: The Fallacy of Post Hoc, Ergo Propter Hoc Reasoning," *Pediatrics* 60:6 (Dec. 1977):907.

24. Sam Harris, *Letter to a Christian Nation* (New York: Alfred A. Knopf, 2006), 44.

25. Gregory S. Paul, "Cross-National Correlations of Quantifiable Religiosity and Secularism in the Prosperous Democracies: A First Look," *Journal of Religion and Society* 7 (2005):5; available at http://moses.creighton.edu/JRS/pdf/2005-11.pdf (accessed February 5, 2009).

26. Sam Harris, *Letter to a Christian Nation* (New York: Alfred A. Knopf, 2006), 45.

27. Ruth Gledhill, "Societies worse off 'when they have God on their side,'" *TimesOnline.co.uk*, September 27, 2005; available at http://www.timesonline.co.uk/tol/news/uk/article571206.ece (accessed February 5, 2009).

28. Sam Harris, *Letter to a Christian Nation* (New York: Alfred A. Knopf, 2006), 45.

29. See http://www-personal.umich.edu/~mejn/election/2004/ (accessed February 5, 2009).

30. See http://www-personal.umich.edu/~mejn/election/2004/countymapredbluelarge.png (accessed February 5, 2009).

31. See http://www-personal.umich.edu/~mejn/election/2004/countymaplinearlarge.png (accessed February 5, 2009).

32. "Table 2: Crime in the United States by Community Type," *Crime in the United States, 2007*; http://www.fbi.gov/ucr/cius2007/data/table_02.html (accessed February 5, 2009). The data per state illustrates this as well. See "Table 5: Crime in the United States by State," *Crime in the United States, 2007*; http://www.fbi.gov/ucr/cius2007/data/table_05.html (accessed February 5, 2009).

33. "Report ranks jobs by rates of depression," *USA Today*, October 14, 2007; http://www.usatoday.com/news/health/2007-10-14-jobs-depression_N.htm?csp=34# (ac-

cessed February 10, 2009).

34. Dr. Joy Bliss, comment on "Cum Hoc," Maggie's Farm Blog, October 24, 2007; http://maggiesfarm.anotherdotcom.com/archives/6589-Cum-hoc.html (accessed February 10, 2009).

35. Arthur B. Robinson, Noah E. Robinson and Willie Soon, "Environmental Effects of Increased Atmospheric Carbon Dioxide," *Journal of American Physicians and Surgeons* 12:3 (Fall 2007):79. Available at http://www.jpands.org/vol12no3/robinson.pdf (accessed February 11, 2009).

36. Arthur B. Robinson, et al, "Environmental Effects of Increased Atmospheric Carbon Dioxide," 79.

37. Arthur B. Robinson, et al, "Environmental Effects of Increased Atmospheric Carbon Dioxide," 82. Emphasis mine.

38. Arthur B. Robinson, et al, "Environmental Effects of Increased Atmospheric Carbon Dioxide," 89.

39. See also Christopher C. Horner, *The Politically Incorrect Guide to Global Warming and Environmentalism* (Washington, D.C.: Regnery Publishing, Inc., 2007).

40. Fischer, *Historians' Fallacies*, 118.

41. Darrel Huff and Irving Geis, *How to Take a Chance* (New York: W. W. Norton and Co. Inc., 1959), 28–29. See also http://www.fallacyfiles.org/gamblers.html (accessed February 9, 2009).

42. Carter Strickland and Mike Knobler, "Mind Games," *The Atlanta Journal-Constitution*, May 28, 2008, D1, D5; http://www.ajc.com/sports/content/printedition/2008/05/28/superstitions.html?cxntlid=inform_sr (accessed February 9, 2009).

43. Joseph Johnson, Gerard J. Tellis, and Deborah J. MacInnis, "Losers, Winners, and Biased Trades," *Journal of Consumer Research*, 32 (Sept. 2005):324.

44. Joseph Johnson and Gerard J. Tellis, "Blowing Bubbles: Heuristics and biases in the run-up of stock prices," *Journal of the Academy of Market Sciences*, 33:4 (Sept. 2005):486.

45. Joseph Johnson and Gerard J. Tellis, "Blowing Bubbles: Heuristics and biases in the run-up of stock prices," *Journal of the Academy of Market Sciences*, 33:4 (Sept. 2005):486(abstract).

46. Albert Phung, "Behavioral Finance: Key Concepts—Gambler's Fallacy"; http://www.investopedia.com/university/behavioral_finance/behavioral7.asp (accessed February 9, 2009).

47. For one other example, see James Montier, "The Gambler's Fallacy," *Global Equity Strategy*, January 23, 2003; http://gamblers-fallacy.behaviouralfinance.net/Montier2003.pdf (accessed February 9, 2009).

48. See Russell L. Purvis, Gordon E. McCrary, and Tom L. Roberts, "Heuristics and Biases in Information Systems Project Management," *Engineering Management Journal*,

16:2 (June 2004):21.

49. See Pat Croskerry, *et al*, *Patient Safety in Emergency Medicine* (Philadelphia: Wolters Kluwer Health/Lippincott, Williams, and Wilkins, 2008), 221, 409.

50. Donald L. Redelmeier, Siew H. Tan, and Gillian L. Booth, "The Treatment of Unrelated Disorder in Patients with Unrelated Medical Diseases," *The New England Journal of Medicine*, 338:21 (May 21, 1998):1516–1520.

51. Greg Pogarsky and Alex R. Piquero, "Can Punishment Encourage Offending? Investigating the 'Resetting' Effect," *Journal of Research in Crime and Delinquency*, 40:1 (Feb. 2003):95–120.

52. Alex R. Piquero and Greg Pogarsky, "Beyond Stafford and Warr's Reconceptualization of Deterrence: Personal and Vicarious Experiences, Impulsivity, and Offending Behavior," *Journal of Research in Crime and Delinquency*, 39:2 (May 2002):153–186.

53. James Shanteau and M. L. Ngui, "Decision Making Under Risk: The Psychology of Crop Insurance Decisions" (paper presented at the Colloquium at the University of Pennsylvania, September 1989): 7.

54. James Shanteau and M. L. Ngui, "Decision Making Under Risk: The Psychology of Crop Insurance Decisions" (paper presented at the Colloquium at the University of Pennsylvania, September 1989): 8.

55. I have adapted the three categories of Ludwig von Mises to more accessible terms. See *Human Action: A Treatise on Economics* (New Haven, CT: Yale University Press, 1949), 112–113. He termed them "gambling, engineering, and speculating," but employed these word in qualified terms which he explained. I convey the same ideas with more common terms.

56. Mises, *Human Action*, 116.

57. Mises, *Human Action*, 116–117.

58. T. Edward Damer, *Attacking Faulty Reasoning: A Practical Guide to Fallacy-Free Arguments*, 3rd Ed. (Belmont, CA: Wadsworth publishing Co., 1995), 135.

59. Quoted in Richard Dawkins, *The God Delusion* (Boston and New York: Houghton Mifflin Co., 2006), 319.

60. Richard Dawkins, *The God Delusion*, 293.

61. Richard Dawkins, *The God Delusion*, 288.

62. Richard Dawkins, *The God Delusion*, 292–293.

63. Richard Dawkins, *The God Delusion*, 293. Emphasis mine.

64. Richard Dawkins, *The God Delusion*, 293.

CHAPTER 16

"ANCIENTS VS. MODERNS": FALLACIES OF THE AGE

Another group of Fallacies of Time pertains to man's pronouncement of judgment upon a given period of time. Again, man's word does not create truth; rather, God calls man to witness His truth in His courtroom. When man exalts new things or old things simply because of their newness or oldness, he presents a falsehood based on time. Whether something survives from old or arises as a fresh prospect, died a long time ago or first sweeps the dreams of today's restless youth—none of this constitutes a standard for truth.

The Christian critical thinker will not fall for appeals to things old or new, progressive and modern, or old, tried and true. He will know that the "ancients versus moderns" argument occurs ultimately on the level of autonomous human reason—it is essentially a humanistic debate. Age or development does not impute truth, God does. Man must think God's thoughts after Him, and in turn impute God's judgment of good or evil onto history irrespective of the newness or oldness of any given thing.

APPEAL TO PROGRESS

The Fallacy of Appeal to Progress labels something as "bad" because it is somehow old, and labels something "good" because it represents "change" or something new. We can also call this fallacy "Progressivism," minding that we do not confuse it with the mere political label. This "Progressive" fallacy fails in the fact that just because something appeared long ago does not necessarily imply truth or falsity. Even if society appears to have "moved on," and unanimously agrees that the "old" thing in consideration is unquestionably "outdated," society's consent still cannot prove something true or false based on age.

G. K. Chesterton provides a classic refutation of "the boast of certain writers that they are merely recent."[1] He writes,

> It is incomprehensible to me that any thinker can calmly call himself a modernist; he might as well call himself a Thursdayite. But apart altogether from that particular disturbance, I am conscious of a general irritation expressed against the people who boast of their advancement and modernity in the discussion of religion. But I never succeeded in saying the quite clear and obvious thing that is really the matter with modernism. The real objection to modernism is simply that it is a form of snobbishness. It is an attempt to crush a rational opponent not by reason, but by some mystery of superiority, by hinting that one is specially up to date or particularly "in the know." To flaunt the fact that we have had all the last books from Germany is simply vulgar; like flaunting the fact that we have had all the last bonnets from Paris. To introduce into philosophical discussions a sneer at a creed's antiquity is like introducing a sneer at a lady's age. It is caddish because it is irrelevant. The pure modernist is merely a snob; he cannot bear to be a month behind the fashion.[2]

Chesterton characteristically nails the problem: snobbery, which is to say, prejudice void of logic. C. S. Lewis has since termed this type of fallacy "Chronological Snobbery." He defines it as "the uncritical acceptance of the intellectual climate common to our own age and the assumption that whatever has gone out of date is on that account discredited."[3] The key word here is "uncritical"—this indicates, as I have discussed, "without judgment," "without wisdom," or "without understanding." You may possibly reach a right belief uncritically, or possibly a wrong belief through criticism poorly applied, but the possibility for each of these scenarios remains low. The uncritical—in this case, snobbish—mind will almost certainly find itself mired in some fallacy, likely many.

Discerning his own foolishness during youth, Lewis helps us dissect the fallaciousness of an Appeal to Progress. Looking back on his younger days, Lewis explained how he reacted negatively to his best friend joining a cult. Instead of refuting the cultic beliefs specifically, Lewis simply scoffed at the "gods, spirits, after-life and pre-existence" and such things as "*medieval.*" He goes on to explain the fallacy of letting his "modern" mentality lead him to "use the names of earlier periods as terms of abuse."[4] He teaches us how to confront this "uncritical ... assumption": "You must find out *why* it went out of date. Was it ever refuted (and if so, by whom, where, and how conclusively) or did it die away as fashions do. If the latter, this tells us nothing about its truth or falsehood."[5] In other words, where an idea appears in history alone cannot determine its truth or falsity. Some vitally true things remain from time immemorial; some dangerously false things emerged into popularity in modern times, and *vice versa*. Labels like "medieval" cannot diminish the value of a good principle; the label "modern" cannot redeem a harmful idea.

Lewis finds a secondary motive at work in such "snobbery." From the same uncritical spirit grows a passivity—an apathy, a lulled indifference—which simply accepts the illusions of one's own time by living in a kind of mental bubble, never questioning or *seeking wisdom*. Lewis describes the effects of realizing how "the times" have no logical effect on truth or falsity:

> From seeing this, one passes to the realization that our own age is also "a period," and certainly has, like all periods, its own characteristic illusions. They are likeliest to lurk in those widespread assumptions which are so ingrained in the age that no one dares to attack or feels it necessary to defend them.[6]

In many ways, Appeals to Progress partake of Peer Pressure in that they create fear of bucking trends, going against the spirit of the times, or defying popularity. In addition, when we give uncritical respect to the trends of a particular era we commit an Appeal to Authority. These fallacies apply to both Appeals to Progress and to the next fallacy of Appeal to Antiquity.

Paul confronted this fallacy with the Athenian philosophers, who particularly sinned in this regard: *Now all the Athenians and the strangers visiting there used to spend their time in nothing other than telling or hearing something new* (Acts 17:21). They took interest in Paul because they thought he offered some *new teaching* (17:19). The apostle, however, confronted their ways by addressing them as *superstitious* (17:22), and by calling them back from "new" speculations to an ancient principle, the Creator God (17:23–31).

Evolution and The Shifting Moral Zeitgeist

The Fallacy of Progressivism gains great strength today from the doctrines of evolution. The specific idea that things evolve to adapt to their environment fuels the false notion that whatever exists now is generally better than what existed previously. Even many evolutionists deny this application of Darwin's theory, yet it seems to permeate the popular mind, and for good reason: secularists have worked very hard to push Darwinism in every venue of public education and knowledge. The mental mistake comes easily, and pervasive propaganda spreads it without correcting it. Evolution implies for many people that things inevitably get better as time goes on.

In his best-selling book, *The God Delusion*, Richard Dawkins spread this idea blatantly. He blasts the idea that morality requires God as its basis and refers to something he calls the shifting "moral *zeitgeist*"—a fancy word for "spirit of the times." Dawkins, who specializes in evolutionary theory, argues for ten pages that in societies the consensus of morals necessarily improves over time, but it does so naturally and without the aid of religion. To prove his point he quotes from century-old sources that use racist or sexist slurs which society accepted at the time but which we find appalling today. See? The morals *have* gradually changed over time—so he argues.

What drives this invisible force, and why does it always seem to move in direction of improvement? Dawkins has no answer. For him, "it is enough that, as a matter of observed fact, it *does* move, and it is not driven by religion—and certainly not by scripture."[7] He tinkers with an answer: leaders who are "ahead of their time," as well as "improved education" both aid the advance of the *zeitgeist*. Of course, these points are irrelevant because neither can *determine* the advance of morals, for how does one judge if a leader is "ahead" or rather "behind" his time? The "Joker," the great villain of the most recent Batman movie *The Dark Knight*, justified his terrorism and murder by labeling himself "ahead" of the social curve. How could Dawkins argue against this? By what standard do we judge an "advance" versus a "decline"? Is it if everyone applauds, versus if everyone boos? If so, then morals come by democratic decision, and whatever the majority says, goes. But this standard justifies Hitler's Nazi Germany as a good thing due to popular German vote. Likewise, exactly how do we determine if education is "improved"? If the kiddies all smile and get As when they're taught about their ape-like ancestors? And what of this when Darwin's theory turns out false? Or when pre-teen and early teenage children abandon discipline and learning for sex and mindless gratification—in other words, begin to act like animals? Again, by what standard, and who says?

Dawkins can't answer these questions and says that for his purposes of bashing God, he does not have to. But he cannot help take a stab at religion whenever he sees an opportunity. So he says, by "improved education," particularly meaning "the increased understanding that each of us shares a common humanity with members of other races and with the other sex—both deeply unbiblical ideas...."[8] I had to laugh when reading this. "Deeply unbiblical ideas"?!

Now put this in perspective. Dawkins has master's and doctorate degrees from Oxford. He is a Fellow of the Royal Society, no small accolade. He is a Fellow of the Royal Society of *Literature*, again, quite an honor. He has written nine or so major books, the most recent explicitly attacking God. He has lectured around the world and held a Professorate at Oxford for years. All of this, and yet, apparently, he has not read *the first page of the Bible*; for that first page informs us that "God created *man in His own image*, in the image of God He created him; *male and female* He created them" (Gen. 1:27). After telling us that both *sexes* bear the image of God and are thus part of a "common humanity," the next verse reveals God's command to multiply and fill the earth (Gen. 1:28). The accounts following make it clear that all of humanity, including its races and every other genetic distinction, come from one common ancestral family, and thus share a "common humanity." The New Testament develops this theme as well (Acts 17:24–27).

Now perhaps you can see the fallacious Appeal to Progress—among other fallacies—in Dawkins' idea. The delusion that the ideas of a shared humanity between races and sexes developed in modern times as a result of modern education blinds Dawkins (and his followers) to the fact that these ideas actually stem from *ancient* biblical wisdom. Of course, even had they not, emphasizing them as recent would not ensure their truth or falsity anyway. Nevertheless, Dawkins argues strongly—and ignorantly—that we've moved on.

I cover this point for no other reason than to expose the fallacies of Dawkins' educated ignorance about the religion he pretends to abolish. Like many atheists, he either pretends that the main features of Biblical religion do not exist or argues that modern science has accounted for them naturally, and that thus religious thought perpetuates outdated ideas. Along this line Dawkins quotes Ralph Waldo Emerson: "The religion of one age is the literary amusement of the next."[9] This fallacy fuels Dawkins' concept of the shifting "moral *zeitgeist*" as well. He pretends that "advances" in morals take place naturally—he has no idea what compels this invisible force, but he's certain it must be natural. Whatever it is, it isn't God—that *can't be true*, because God doesn't exist, so Dawkins must reason.

Dawkins further fails to mention that his very idea of a moral "spirit of the age" entered philosophy long before recent times as well. The idea dominated the philosophical world due to the massive influence of Hegel (writing around 1800), who believed in something like the spiritual evolution of mankind worked out gradually in history.[10] He derived this theory after reading similar ideas in Jakob Böhme, a Christian mystic who wrote 200 years earlier.[11] Whether Dawkins would admit it, Hegel thought he worked out his philosophy as a conscious justification of Christianity in history. Many Christians rightfully object to much of Hegel's thinking, but Hegel did correctly attain the idea that *history and morals do not change on their own, or merely because of the times*. Behind movement and change in history stands some kind of *reason*, a divine personality. C. S. Lewis likewsie concluded his discussion of chronological snobbery describing how he confessed that "the whole universe was, in the last resort, mental; that our logic was participation in a cosmic *Logos*."[12] As usual, the atheists have to steal Christian ideas in order to support their atheism.

A more sane view of the moral *zeitgeist* comes from the noted Church historian Philip Schaff. In discussing the Roman Emperor Constantine (just one example), Schaff lays down what he calls "the great historical principle," placing historical change in its rightful perspective:

> [A]ll representative characters act, consciously or unconsciously, as the free and responsible organs of the *spirit of their age*, which moulds them first before they can mold it in turn, and that *the spirit of the age itself*, whether good or bad or mixed, *is but an instrument in the hands of divine Providence*, which rules and overrules all the actions and motives of men.[13]

Delusions and Insults

The fast pace and great output of science and technology in the past two centuries has perhaps fueled the Fallacy of Progressivism more than anything. Everything seems "up-and-up," nothing appears unattainable, and "progress" looks inevitable. Of course the fallacy here lies in the fact that technological change only advances our *tools*, not to our ethics and values. It may improve the quality and length of human life in the advances of modern medicine, but it cannot change the truth of that to which we impute worth and worship. Unfortunately, the people tend to let this fact get buried by dozens of everyday cares and the fast pace of life. Technological change begins to stand as a symbol of *all human* progress. Human Life 1.0 is old and out-of-date as soon as Human Life 2.0 hits the shelves of the latest computer store, despite the fact that this metaphor defies facts and logic (it's a False Analogy!). Dawkins partakes of this False Analogy as well in his Appeal to Progress. Arguing that morals improve over time, and yet at a loss to explain why, he guesses it probably involves "a complex interplay of disparate forces like the one that propels Moore's Law, describing the exponential increase in computer power."[14] The analogy may hold strictly concerning the interplay of forces involved, but even here the association of human moral progress with technological progress (computer chips, in this case) transgresses the boundary between fact and fallacy. Dawkins simply does not have the evidence or logic to support this claim.

Like other fallacies, Appeals to Progress show up everywhere, from best-selling works like Dawkins' to your everyday newspaper. A final example come from the latter, as I noticed an old newspaper clipping about the Southern Baptist Convention's 2000 decision that Scripture does not allow women to act as pastors. A syndicated columnist condemned this decision as "retrograde," and pronounced his opinion of the Convention: "They are going backward."[15] Such a claim tastes of chronological snobbery—an attempt by the columnist at maligning a male-only clergy as undesirable because it belongs to a by-gone age. Jeers like "stepping backward," or "turning back the clock," ring as classic insults from liberals. If they only realized that the type of leftist religion and politics they themselves preach has roots in Plato,[16] 2400 years ago, they might realize the fallaciously idiotic nature of this tactic.

APPEAL TO ANTIQUITY

A fallacious Appeal to Antiquity argues the opposite of an Appeal to Progress. Appeal to Antiquity claims that something deserves respect because it is ancient or long-trusted, and that we should avoid "new" things until they have withstood the test of time. We can also call this the fallacy of Conservatism, again maintaining a distinction between the broader logical error and the limited political sense of "conservative." This Appeal fails by the same standard that Appeals to Progress fail: neither chronology nor age determine truth. Some truths have emerged as "new" in modern times (at least as far as modern knowledge can discern), and some tragically false ideas existed and have continued through antiquity. In either case "withstanding the test of time" does not factor into the truth of the idea, but rather contradicts it.

History exposes this fallacy in the fact that *everything* was new or novel at some point in history. One of the first of the more modern writers on fallacies, Jeremy Bentham, made this point: "To say that all new things are bad is as much as to say that all things are bad, or in any event that all were bad at their commencement. For of all the old things ever seen or heard of, there is not a single one that was not once new."[17]

Christianity itself confronted the people of Christ's time with some completely new ideas. Christ argued that some old ways of doing things needed reform and that He refused to impose some old traditions on his disciples: *No one puts new wine into old wineskins; otherwise the wine will burst the skins, and the wine is lost and the skins as well; but one puts new wine into fresh wineskins* (Mark 2:22; Matt. 9:17). In fact, by the Appealer to Antiquity's logic, God should never have created, for *that* introduced an innovation and changed the ancient *status quo*![18]

Some people, it seems, simply hate change in general. I've personally known of churches that fought and *split* because the pastor changed the color of the carpeting to their dislike. Along these lines an elderly preacher once told me a story:

> Every church has a "Brother 'Gain'-it"; no matter what change someone proposes, even if the church badly needs it, he opposes, "I'm a-gain' it!" When someone proposed that the church needed new chandeliers, he spoke up vehemently, "I'm a-gain' it." When asked why, he huffed, "Three reasons: we don't need 'em; we can't afford 'em; and we don't have anyone who knows how to play 'em!"

While the first and second reasons may have some plausibility, the third shows that ol' Brother 'Gain'-it had no real idea what he was talking about. He just didn't want *change*.

Unlike this stubborn brother, the Appeal to Antiquity does not try to hide its prejudice behind reasons; it puts the sentiment clearly into words. "We must reject X because we have never used X before, X is an unproven program, no one has ever heard of X before, our forefathers never required X, etc." Despite how sound biblical teaching logically applied might properly reform old ways, many people forcefully cling to old ways. As Fischer puts it, "There is scarcely a corner of the world in which men do not, in some degree, bow down before absurdities inherited from their ancestors."[19]

Of course, the human proclivity for venerating "the fathers" leads nearly everyone—even progressives—to adopt Appeals to Antiquity. Fischer helps us again:

> In our own time, it is a rare political proposal which is not, in some fashion, legitimized by an out-of-context quotation from the Founding Fathers. Consider, for instance, the rhetorical raids which have been made upon the writings of Thomas Jefferson. His works have been ransacked by Democrats and Republicans, liberals and conservatives, radicals and reactionaries, New Englanders and Southerners, to sustain elitism and equality, capitalism and social-

ism, states' rights and interventionism, isolationism and internationalism, rationalism and romanticism, atheism and Christianity, agrarianism and urban development. He has been quoted at length by Earl Browder in defense of Communism, and by Ezra Pound in the cause of Fascism; by Sukarno in the interest of "guided democracy," and even by Ho Chi Minh in the name of Vietnamese nationalism.[20]

Of course, such quotations commit an Appeal to Authority as much as they merely venerate old wisdom, but the chronological snobbery remains. An appeal to an old dead dignitary persuades some people more than appeals to modern celebrities or academics, and for good reason: the Appeal to Antiquity resonates with our sense for established wisdom.

The Law of Unintended Consequences

Many instances of this fallacy additionally refer to the "law of unintended consequences" as an added Appeal to Fear when condemning proposed changes. Not that we should ignore the phenomenon: unintended consequences should indeed factor heavily into judging such propositions. As economist Thomas Sowell remarks,

> Fallacies are not simply crazy ideas. They are usually both plausible and logical—but with something missing. Their plausibility gains them political support. Only after that political support is strong enough to cause fallacious ideas to become government policies and programs are the missing or ignored factors likely to lead to "unintended consequences," a phrase often heard in the wake of economic or social policy disasters.[21]

In too many instances fallacious ideas form the basis of government, business, family, church, or institutional programs, only to have disastrous results down the line. Such effects do happen, often due to incomplete or improper planning on the front end. Henry Hazlitt explains in his classic work on the subject, about the

> persistent tendency of men to see only the immediate effects of a given policy, or its effects only on a special

group, and to neglect to inquire what the long-run effects of that policy will be not only on that special group but on all groups. It is the fallacy of overlooking secondary consequences.

In this lies the whole difference between good economics and bad.[22]

In Hazlitt's comments we should take special note of the phrases "neglect to inquire," and "overlooking." Herein lies the root of this fallacy: uncritical application of change. Men should rightly fear legislation or ideas that have evaded criticism or testing.

Nevertheless, any reference to such a problem ahead of time should include reasons and arguments spotting real unintended consequences. Apart from actually doing the work of thinking through such consequences (as much as we can anyway), the "unintended consequences" claim verges on an empty Appeal to Fear, a Slippery Slope, a Gambler's Fallacy, an Appeal to Ignorance, or a handful other fallacies.

Instead, in most instances, we discern the unintended consequences after the fact, due to experience. Such is the case with the many examples that Sowell, for example, writes about.[23] If resorted to outside of such experience, and in order merely to impede change, the argument, "We shouldn't accept this change because we don't know what adverse effects it will have," simply stirs up Fear based on no evidence. The refutation is simple: by the same standard of "we don't know" we can equally argue that *positive* changes may arise from the change. Without any evidence or indication either way, negative or positive results stand equally likely. So the argument really solves nothing, it just returns us to the point in question.

Of course, the fear of unintended consequences serves as just one tool for those who use Appeals to Antiquity. The fallacy does not depend on this tool and often appears without it.

Puritan Progress

One of the clearest examples of Appeals to Antiquity occurred in widespread fashion during the rise of Puritan influence in England, roughly 1620 to 1680. The enigmatic figure of Francis Bacon spurred dramatic changes in science and technology, as well as in philosophy.

New ideas in these areas as well as in civil government clashed with ancient and accepted ways, especially in the institutions of government and academia. Thus ensued a battle between "ancients" and "moderns."

Bacon and his followers simply desired to learn and apply new knowledge to trade, industry, and the improvement of human life. But they faced a world in which an entrenched view of knowledge dominated learning and science. Two major beliefs ruled this world: 1) that the world inevitably decayed, taking with it knowledge and society, and therefore 2) the best of all knowledge and learning had already occurred in ancient times. Both filled men with pessimism, despair, and discouragement. As a result, traditionalists of the time

> faced backward rather than forward in the quest for truth, and prepared themselves for scientific investigation by mastering the Greek and Latin languages. The natural result was an ardent worship of the great classical minds, and a submission to their authority which is hard for us to appreciate.[24]

Without question the "ancients" revered ancient Aristotle above all. So fiercely did they defend his authority that they instituted him by law: Oxford University decreed "that Bachelors and Masters who did not follow Aristotle faithfully were liable to a fine of five shillings [about $125 today][25] for every point of divergence, and for every fault committed against the logic of [Aristotle's work,] the Organon."[26] In addition to Aristotle, the work of Galen ruled medicine, and Ptolemy astronomy—both over a millennium and a half old!

To make any advancement at all, Bacon had to confront this chronological snobbery of his day: "the most significant obstacle to the advancement of science was reverence for antiquity, and in combating this evil Bacon helped to establish an essential attitude of the new science...."[27] Bacon refuted the fallacies of Authority and Antiquity, dared to critique Aristotle and dependence on him, and established an optimistic mindset that fueled science. In the same generation the famous poet and tractarian John Milton would express such optimism:

> The end, then, of learning is to repair the ruins of our first parents by regaining to know God aright, and out of that knowledge to love him, to imitate him, to be like

him, as we may the nearest by possessing our souls of true virtue, which being united to the heavenly grace of faith makes up the highest perfection.[28]

It takes courage to overcome fallacies, especially when society and institutions of authority have entrenched themselves in the uncritical reverence of antiquity. When fallacies become incarnate in such ways, they require momentous figures and events to overturn them, even though their illogic stands evident.

The Bible versus Tradition

The Pharisees attempted to confront Jesus using an Appeal to Antiquity. They inquired, *Why do Your disciples break the tradition of the elders? For they do not wash their hands when they eat bread* (Matt. 15:2). Notice their concern: "tradition of the elders," not "law of Moses." Jesus responded by simply pointing out that their traditions have no genuine authority in God's eyes. God's word demands no such ritual hand-washing. In fact, Jesus pointed out, parts of their tradition itself transgressed the word of God by allowing young people to abandon care of their mother and father through giving a gift of money to the temple (Matt. 15:3–6).

Christ here shows the corrective to the fallacious Appeal to Antiquity: the Word of God is the only absolute authority. Nothing else can bind the conscience of men, despite even great age. All else that pretends authority can at best approximate some level of authority *relative* to the Word, and often has none at all. So Paul warns, *See to it that no one takes you captive through philosophy and empty deception, according to the tradition of men,… rather than according to Christ* (Col. 2:8). He himself had lived though this problem:

> *I was advancing in Judaism beyond many of my contemporaries among my countrymen, being more extremely zealous for my ancestral traditions. But when God, who had set me apart even from my mother's womb and called me through His grace, was pleased to reveal His Son in me so that I might preach Him among the Gentiles, I did not immediately consult with flesh and blood, nor did I go up to Jerusalem to those who were apostles before me; but I went away to Arabia, and returned once more to Damascus* (Gal. 1:14–17).

Paul argues that it took a work of God to break him away from the Pharisaical traditions, and in order to maintain the integrity of his Gospel message he argues that he did not receive it by tradition: *For I would have you know, brethren, that the gospel which was preached by me is not according to man. For I neither received it from man, nor was I taught it, but I received it through a revelation of Jesus Christ* (Gal. 1:11–12). Paul rightly learned that Appeal to Antiquity holds no genuine authority, only revelation from God does. Peter teaches the same lesson, that truth does not depend on tradition: *[Y]ou were not redeemed with perishable things like silver or gold from your futile way of life inherited from your forefathers, but with precious blood, as of a lamb unblemished and spotless, the blood of Christ* (1 Pet. 1:18–19).

Confronting traditions with the Word of God shows the fallaciousness of the Appeal. Tradition cannot guarantee truth, and thus must fall under the judgment of a higher standard. God's word will determine whether traditions are good, bad, or just ugly. Many of the traditions handed down from our fathers may actually dishonor God. Jeremiah confronted this problem already in his time:

> *The Lord said, "Because they have forsaken My law which I set before them, and have not obeyed My voice nor walked according to it, but have walked after the stubbornness of their heart and after the Baals, as their fathers taught them," therefore thus says the Lord of hosts, the God of Israel, "behold, I will feed them, this people, with wormwood and give them poisoned water to drink. I will scatter them among the nations, whom neither they nor their fathers have known; and I will send the sword after them until I have annihilated them"* (Jer. 9:13–16).

Notice the fallacy here described as "stubbornness of their hearts." Notice God's punishment against these men who uncritically followed what their "fathers" taught them instead of seeking God's law: He would "scatter" them, and they would live disconnected amidst foreign nations where *they would have no traditions except heathen traditions*. God abandoned them to their fallacy.

In the New Testament, the desire to perpetuate old traditions like circumcision caused considerable confusion and strife (Acts 15). Paul later said that such old practices profit nothing: *For neither is circumcision anything, nor uncircumcision, but a new creation* (Gal. 5:16). Sadly, Appeals to Antiquity often cause great harm in the name of ancient wisdom. Truth demands that we have supple enough hearts to let unnecessary things pass on, holding only to that which is truly eternal and of godly profit.

TIMELESS WISDOM

The biblical correction of both of these fallacies—Appeals to Progress and to Antiquity—rests in its doctrine of "wisdom." Wisdom is precious—more valuable than gold, silver, and rubies (Prov. 3:14–15)—not because it is new or ancient, not because it has either evolved afresh or withstood the tests of time, but because *it is wisdom*, and because *it is the gift of knowledge and understanding from God* (Prov. 2:6). Biblical wisdom by its very nature allows it to both withstand the tests of time and apply afresh to new challenges.

To argue for something because it is new or because it is old places age above God's Word. It places a temporal attribute above an eternal one. But all temporal things (all of creation) changes over time. Only the Triune God and His Word do not change (Ps. 102:25–27; Is. 40:8; Mal. 3:6; Matt. 5:18; Luke 16:16–17; Heb. 1:10–12; 13:8; James 1:17; 1 Peter 1:23–25). God's Wisdom, therefore, is both changeless and timeless: it endures from ancient times and yet remains vitally relevant to every modern circumstance. It never changes in content nor fades in relevance. It defies both Progressivism and Conservatism; it exposes both chronological snobberies as fallacies, and corrects both with proper biblical balance.

Solomon, in God's wisdom, elucidated this biblical view of new and old: both occur inevitably. He writes,

> *"Vanity or vanities," says the Preacher," Vanity of vanities! All is vanity."… A generation goes and a generation comes, But the earth remains forever. Also, the sun rises and the sun sets; And hastening to its place it rises there again. Blowing toward the south, Then turning toward the north, The wind continues swirling along; And on its circular courses the wind returns. All the rivers flow into the sea, Yet the sea is not full. To the place where the rivers flow, There they flow again. All things are wearisome; Man is not able to tell it. The eye is not satisfied with seeing, Nor is the ear filled with hearing. That which has been is that which will be, And that which has been done is that which will be done. So there is nothing new under the sun. Is there anything of which one might say, "See*

> *this, it is new"? Already it has existed for ages Which were before us. There is no remembrance of earlier things; And also of the later things which will occur, There will be for them no remembrance Among those who will come later still* (Eccl. 1:2, 4–11).

All things change, and yet nothing really changes. There is nothing new under the sun, and yet each sunrise begins a uniquely new day. The Lord's compassions are *new every morning* (Lam. 3:23). Ideas alleged as "new" have actually all occurred in the past, and almost all get lost again in the wastebasket of history. The human propensity to forget history makes it seem as if new things arise all the time; yet nothing truly does. With this in mind, the person who attempts to base goodness or truth on the newness or antiquity of an idea simply embraces the *Vanity* that Solomon warned against.

To confront these fallacies, merely remind their abusers of a burden of proof that they have assumed. "Progress" implies movement, which raises the question of direction and purpose. When someone begins touting "progress" simply require them to explain exactly "where" they intend to progress to. The answer to this will reveal 1) whether or not the individual has any idea what they're talking about, and 2) the worldview from which they argue. Likewise, with the opposite error of Conservatism inquire as to what exactly the party intends to "conserve" and what not. The answer will reveal if they have at all thought their position through and what worldview presuppositions lurk behind their thinking.

In some places Scripture tells us to respect the aged, specifically because of age: *You shall rise up before the grayheaded and honor the aged* (Lev. 19:31). This applies, of course, to people, and not necessarily to their ideas, however. Elders can and do sometimes promote bad ideas, and even fallacies. We must also balance such respect for age in light of other Scriptural ideas. God's people sing a "new" song (Ps. 33:3; 40:3; 96:1; 98:1; 144:9; 149:1; Rev. 5:9; 14:3). The lovers in Solomon's Song share *choice fruit, both new and old* (Song 7:13), which as sacred poetry has many implications. Jesus taught, *Therefore every scribe who has become a disciple of the kingdom of heaven is like a head of a household, who brings out of his treasure things new and old* (Matt. 13:52). The disciple of Christ must learn to value both old thing and new things, and use both as the Word values them. The key lies in studying the Word first.

I always ask, "Where are progressives progressing?" and "What are conservatives conserving?" If the answers to these questions do not reveal biblical values behind their goals, then the progress is not true progress, and what is conserved is not worth conserving.

NOTES

1. G. K. Chesterton, *All Things Considered* (Project Gutenburg Edition, 2004 [Original 1915]); http://www.cse.dmu.ac.uk/~mward/gkc/books/11505-h.htm#THE_CASE_FOR_THE_EPHEMERAL (accessed February 16, 2009).

2. G. K. Chesterton, *All Things Considered* (Project Gutenburg Ed., 2004 [Original 1915]); http://www.cse.dmu.ac.uk/~mward/gkc/books/11505-h.htm#THE_CASE_FOR_THE_EPHEMERAL (accessed February 16, 2009). Partially quoted in A. J. Hoover, *Don't You Believe It* (Chicago: Moody Press, 1982), 54.

3. C. S. Lewis, *Surprised By Joy: The Shape of My Early Life* (New York: Harcourt, Brace and Co., 1955), 207.

4. Lewis, *Surprised By Joy*, 206.

5. Lewis, *Surprised By Joy*, 207–208. Emphasis mine.

6. Lewis, *Surprised By Joy*, 208.

7. Richard Dawkins, *The God Delusion* (Boston: Houghton Mifflin Co., 2006), 272.

8. Dawkins, *The God Delusion*, 271.

9. Dawkins, *The God Delusion*, 29.

10. Good introductions are R. G. Collingwood, *The Idea of History* (New York: Oxford University Press, 1956), 113–126; and Karl Löwith, *Meaning in History* (Chicago: The University of Chicago Press, 1949). For a Biblical view, see Rousas John Rushdoony, *The Biblical Philosophy of History* (Vallecito, CA: Ross House Books, 1997).

11. See Glenn Alexander Magee, *Hegel and the Hermetic Tradition* (Ithaca, NY: Cornell University Press, 2001).

12. Lewis, *Surprised By Joy*, 209.

13. Philip Schaff, *History of the Christian Church: Volume 3: Nicene and Post-Nicene Christianity From Constantine to Gregory the Great, A.D. 311-590*, 8 vols. (Peabody, MA: Hendrickson Publishers, 1996 [1867]), 13. Emphasis mine.

14. Dawkins, *The God Delusion*, 273.

15. Tom Teepen, "Southern Baptists step backward with policy," *Atlanta Constitution*, June 20, 2000, A9.

16. See Karl Popper, *The Open Society and Its Enemies: Vol. 1: The Spell of Plato* (Princeton, NJ: Princeton University Press, 1971).

17. Jeremy Bentham, *Bentham's Handbook of Political Fallacies*, ed. Harold A. Larrabee (Baltimore, MD: The Johns Hopkins Press, 1952 [1824]), 94.

18. Of course this is absurd. Before creation, time did not exist; there is no "new" or "old" in eternity, technically. But Scripture does describe the Lord as the "ancient of days" (Daniel 7:9, 13, 22), so the metaphor works.

19. David Hackett Fischer, *Historians' Fallacies: Toward a Logic of Historical Thought* (New York: Harper Torchbooks, 1970), 297.

20. David Hackett Fischer, *Historians' Fallacies*, 298–299.

21. Thomas Sowell, *Economic Facts and Fallacies* (New York: Basic Books, 2008), 1.

22. Henry Hazlitt, *Economics in One Lesson* (New Rochelle, NY: Arlington House Publishers, 1979 [1946]), 15–16.

23. Thomas Sowell, *Economic Facts and Fallacies*.

24. Richard Foster Jones, *Ancients and Moderns: A Study of the Rise of the Scientific Movement in Seventeenth-Century England* (New York: Dover Publications, Inc., 1961), 4.

25. Assuming that a Shilling was 1/20 of a Sovereign, which was roughly 1/2 ounce of gold. With gold near $1000/ounce, this makes quite a punishment!

26. Quoted in Richard Foster Jones, *Ancients and Moderns*, 4.

27. Richard Foster Jones, *Ancients and Moderns*, 43.

28. John Milton, "Of Education," *John Milton Complete Poems and Major Prose*, ed. Merritt Y. Hughes (Indianapolis, IN: The Odyssey Press, 1957 [Original 1644, 1673]), 631.

APPENDIX

AUGUSTINE AND CALVIN VS. RATIONALISM

The Bible—as I have shown throughout this book, particularly in the early chapters—commands us to think critically (using discernment) and faithfully (admitting the facts), and equates breaking of this commandment with idolatry. Such idolatry when expressed in humanistic theories of knowledge usually adopts one of a few approaches: rationalism, empiricism, or some combination of the two. We credit Cornelius Van Til with reforming apologetics and Christian philosophy in such a way as to deny the primacy of all human autonomy, and instead restore God's Revelation as the source of all human being and activity (Acts 17:28). But even before Van Til, Christian thinkers defended against humanistic theories of knowledge, at least partially, by relying on biblical Revelation about creation, etc. This brief and piecemeal essay includes some of that defense as coming from Augustine and Calvin.

The following essay relates some of the thoughts of these great men against forms of rationalism, and does not attempt to address empiricism or its antecedents, or combined forms. Perhaps I can get to an attempt at these in the future. As the following addresses limited issues and draws from limited resources for each of the writers involved, the reader should expect the results to necessarily provide only a *flavor* of the attitude these writers had towards Plato, rationalism etc. Nevertheless, Augustine's anticipation of Descartes, and Calvin direct rejection of Platonic doctrines need highlighting, and thus I offer the studies below. Additionally, the comments by Dr. Clark (perhaps the last of the Christian rationalists?) need wider exposure as well, if for nothing else than carrying on the important discussion of a Christian theory of knowledge.

A Brief Introduction to Rationalism

Rationalism is the belief that unaided human reason forms the basis of at least part of human knowledge, if not all of it. While appearing in many forms and degrees, the consistent belief throughout all of rationalism is that some human knowledge exists apart from sense experience. This *a priori* (before experience) knowledge forms the basis, according to rationalism, for a further portion of *a priori* knowledge made up of deductions from basic principles and laws (such as the laws of logic, which are also innately held).

For example, human beings innately know that the number three is a prime number, and also that the number three is greater than the number two. Both of these ideas constitute basic innate ideas. From these ideas (combining them in conjunction) one could deduce that there exists a prime number that is greater that the number two.[1] We have no need to count physical objects, etc., in order to arrive at this conclusion, and thus we have no need of prior experience to make such deductions.

At least two problems arise with rationalism at this point (and we have not even arrived yet at the most objectionable form of rationalism!). First, how does the innate and immaterial portion of our knowledge (that includes universal ideas and laws) relate to the particular facts about the physical universe? If ultimately reality is immaterial, then why do we expect the material world to behave according to reason, or any order at all? Rationalism can give us no guarantee of correspondence between the two. As so, rationalism fails as a foundation for science, which requires an orderly and predictable *physical* universe.

Secondly, how do we know what portions of our knowledge are innate and which are not? There seems to be no good criteria by which to draw the line. Philosophers hold widely varied opinions on the matter: "Some rationalists take mathematics to be knowable by intuition and deduction. Some place ethical truths in this category. Some include metaphysical claims, such as that God exists, we have free will, and our mind and body are distinct substances."[2]

Most philosophical rationalists will admit that parts of the universe may lie beyond the ability of human reason to comprehend. These will admit, "Some aspects of the world may even be beyond the limits of our thought, so that we cannot form intelligible descriptions of them, let alone know that a particular description is true."[3] Among the broader range of philosophers involved with the discussion of rationalism you will find many varying degrees of opinion and perspective. Most thinkers will recognize at least the possibility of the limits of human knowledge and its implications for beliefs about reality, science, and even faith.

The worldview fallacy of Rationalism primarily (though not only) pertains to a more radical version of rationalism that refuses to recognize *any* limits to the power of human reason. These would argue that human reason alone can comprehend the nature of all reality, and that no part of reality lies outside the powers of human reason to comprehend. In other words, rationalism claims that no knowledge exists beyond human reason, and that human reason is the only tool needed to learn the truth of everything in the universe.

Skeptic Antony Flew defined rationalism as having four main characteristics: "(a) the belief that it is possible to obtain by reason alone a knowledge of the nature of what exists; (b) the view that nature forms a single system, which (c) is deductive in character; and (d) the belief that everything is explicable, that is, that everything can in principle be brought under the single system."[4]

A Brief Pedigree of Rationalism

You will hardly find a thoroughly consistent proponent of these views today except for a very few remaining idealists in philosophy and perhaps implicitly in the thought of some Hindus or Theosophists. Historically in philosophy, however, pure rationalism has quite a pedigree. Among the earliest Greek philosophers, the "father" of the rationalist viewpoint, Parmenides, said, "Thinking and the thought that it is are the same; for you will not find thought apart from what is, in relation to which it is uttered";[5] and more clearly, "thought and being are the same."[6]

Picking up and developing similar ideas, the most famous of the Greek rationalists was Plato. Plato believed that all of reality was immaterial, and that the particulars that we sense are merely images and perceptions of the underlying true objects which he called "forms."

Consequently, we do not comprehend reality through our senses, but only truly apprehend reality through reason. And, consistent with his beliefs about reason and a reason-discerned reality, he believed that all of reality together with the human intellect coheres into one single unity.

Further, Plato (along with his predecessor and literary mouthpiece Socrates) argued that the immaterial human soul possesses immortality, has existed from ages past, and has experienced reincarnation many times. And since the human soul/intellect partakes of the unified immaterial reality throughout its many lives, therefore it already possesses all knowledge. Based on this, Plato taught, we do not learn new things; rather, all acquiring of knowledge actually expresses "remembering" or "recollection" of what the soul already knows. Hear Socrates himself explain their rationalism:

> Seeing then that the soul is immortal and has been born many times, and has beheld all things both in this world and in the nether realms, she has acquired knowledge of all and everything; so that it is no wonder that she should be able to recollect all that she knew before about virtue and other things. For as all nature is akin, and the soul has learned all things, there is no reason why we should not, by remembering but one single thing—an act which men call learning—discover everything else, if we have courage and faint not in the search; since, it would seem, research and learning are wholly recollection. So we must not hearken to that captious argument: it would make us idle, and is pleasing only to the indolent ear, whereas the other makes us energetic and inquiring.[7]

From our modern perspective—dominated by science and "observation"—we can easily demur from Plato's view that from a single recollection we can deduce or intuit all further knowledge. We demand more than just thinking by itself, and those who would hold such a position as the key to discovering *"everything* else" we would quickly leave to the playground of their imaginations, and regard their conclusions as little more than fables or fiction—that is, as long as we could not further corroborate such conclusions by evidence or revelation (of course, such a standard simultaneously denies their rationalism).

Nevertheless, many subsequent philosophers have promoted the pure rationalism of Plato and Socrates earnestly right down to modern times. In fact, modern philosophy begins with the rationalist Descartes, runs through the rationalists Spinoza and Leibniz, continues through the twentieth century with many thinkers, notably Christian philosopher Gordon Clark, and perhaps R. G. Collingwood and A. N. Whitehead.

For example, in constructing his defense of Christianity Gordon Clark argued from a rationalistic view of truth. He writes,

> [I]f a man knows, he must know something.... Knowledge therefore requires an existing object, and that object is truth—truth that always has and always will exist.... [T]ruth must be unchangeable.... [T]ruth is also mental or spiritual.... Not only does it defy time; it defies space as well.... Truth is not individual, but universal; truth did not begin when we were born, it has always existed.
>
> Is all this any more than the assertion that there is an immutable Mind, a supreme Reason, a personal, living God?[8]

Clark goes on to approximate not only Plato's view of knowledge, but his deification of it:

> The truths or propositions that may be known are the thoughts of God, the eternal thought of God. And insofar as man knows anything he is in contact with God's mind. Since, further, God's mind is God, we may legitimately borrow the figurative language, if not the precise meaning, of the mystics and say, we have a vision of God.[9]

The position of this book wholeheartedly agrees that the truths that we can know are the thoughts of God, yet I would add this caveat: the truths we know are the thoughts of God as God has revealed them to *creatures, on the level of creation,* and *as man thinking God's thoughts after Him.* The knowledge we have does not approach *identity* with God's knowledge which is exhaustive, eternal, and perfect—all things which man cannot attain to. Furthermore, I reject the notion that in thinking God's thoughts after Him we thereby attain to a "vision of God," for such a claim equates God's own knowledge of creation (which we cannot attain anyway) with God Himself—an obscuring of the line between Creator and creation. Rationalism, even when raked over and sown with Christian language by the most fertile of Christian minds (of which Dr. Clark's was one), still keeps autonomous human reason at its root, and thus the fruit ultimately appears in the form of idolatry or compromised faith in the Creator.

RATIONALISM SELF-DEFEATING

The basic fallacy inherent in all of rationalist thinking is that of dogmatism, or arbitrariness: it assumes up front that nothing exists which human reason cannot comprehend. In philosophical terms, rationalism is a metaphysic driven by an epistemology—a theory of reality driven by a man-centered, theory of man's knowledge. Thus, it must logically conclude, without rational proof (ironically) or any other kind of demonstration, that no incomprehensible God exists, no mysterious supernatural realm exists, no miracles occur, no otherwise unattainable revelation from God exists, etc. It operates on the assumption that human reason represents the highest form of knowledge and communication in the universe. But how can the rationalism prove such a claim? To remain consistent with the claim itself, the rationalist must demonstrate that reason itself can account for all reasoning. Thus rationalism ultimately rests on an arbitrary, unfounded assumption, namely, that human reason can account for all of reality. In truth, human reason cannot explain the order inherent with the laws of reasoning themselves, and thus human reason cannot even account for its own reasoning. Based on the rationalist's standard of proof, not only can reason not comprehend all of reality, it cannot prove that it can comprehend *any* of reality.

AUGUSTINE VERSUS PLATO (AND DESCARTES!)

Augustine understood Platonic rationalism and its subsequent philosophical variants. In addressing these, Augustine thought so thoroughly and presciently as to anticipate the rationalism of Descartes (over 1,200 years prior!) who began his method by removing any object of knowledge which he could possibly bring into doubt. Effectively, this method rests on *doubt* as the tool for discerning true knowledge—only that is true which is indubitable. Thus rationalism actually finds its roots in skepticism, or systematic unbelief. As an effect, therefore, this method rules out all knowledge gained by the senses, because the senses can easily and often fall under deceptions. Augustine allows that the senses may deceive us, yet we are not left to doubt everything and run into a radical skepticism. He writes,

> For to pass by those things that come into the mind from the bodily senses, among which so many are otherwise than they seem to be, that he who is overmuch pressed down by their resemblance to truth, seems sane to himself, but really is not sane;—whence it is that the Academic philosophy has so prevailed as to be still more wretchedly insane by doubting all things.... In regard to this, indeed, we are absolutely without any fear lest perchance we are being deceived by some resemblance of the truth; since it is certain that he who is deceived, yet lives.[10]

Skeptics have only succeeded in denying sensory knowledge, not all knowledge:

> For whereas there are two kinds of knowable things,—one, of those things which the mind perceives by the bodily sense; the other, of those which it perceives by itself,—these philosophers have babbled much against the bodily senses, but have never been able to throw doubt upon those certain perceptions of things true, which the mind knows by itself, such as is that which I have mentioned, I know that I am alive.[11]

Such knowledge is possible, not because of reason alone, but because God has created us and the universe so that all can both know and be known. Augustine reveals this as he subsequently rejects Platonic (and preemptively, Cartesian) rationalism simply through understanding the doctrines of Creation and of the Trinity.[12] He writes,

> But far be it from us to doubt the truth of what we have learned by the bodily senses; since by them we have

learned to know the heaven and the earth, and those things in them which are known to us, so far as He who created both us and them has willed them to be within our knowledge.[13]

This standard of knowledge, Augustine argued, extends to what we learn from the testimony of other people's sensory experiences, for "not only our own senses, but those of other persons also, have added very much indeed to our knowledge."[14] For him, this biblical point of view opposes "Academic philosophy," which for him meant the Platonic and more so the Neo-Platonic schools. In Augustine's view, God plays the primary and central role in human knowledge. Without His prior existence, His creation of man and the universe, and His sustaining of both every fact in the universe *and* every unifying and ordering law of nature and logic in the universe, human knowledge would be impossible altogether.

CALVIN ON PLATO

John Calvin also rejected Plato's rationalism by countering it with a consistent Biblical view of both creation (reality) and man (fallen human nature).

In discussing the effects of the fall of man on the rational faculties, Calvin begins by summarizing Plato's rationalistic view:

> The philosophers (obviously with substantial agreement) imagine that the reason is located in the mind, which like a lamp illumines all counsels, and like a queen governs the will. For they suppose that it is suffused with divine light to take the most effective counsel; and that it excels in power to wield the most effective command. On the other hand, they imagine that sense perception is gripped by torpor and dimness of sight; so that it always creeps along the ground, is entangled in baser things, and never rises up to true discernment.[15]

Calvin thoroughly understood the Platonic view of things, and he subsequently criticized the rationalist's view of learning as "remembering": "There are at hand energy and ability not only to learn but also to devise something new in each art or to perfect and polish what one has learned from a predecessor. This prompted Plato to teach wrongly that such apprehension is nothing but recollection."[16]

Having described Plato's rationalism as an error, Calvin proceeds in places to contrast biblical teaching with various implications of Platonic philosophy. For example, Calvin teaches the biblical doctrine that God's revelation of Himself and His law reaches man clearly through his conscience, and thus stands as a just condemnation of the natural man as "inexcusable" for his sin. For Plato, however, when the rational man acquires true knowledge he will naturally act in accordance with it; therefore, anyone committing error must not yet have acquired the truth. Calvin disagrees: men act ignorantly in regard to the truth not out of genuine ignorance of it, but hoping to hide their guilt. He writes,

> Man is so indulgent toward himself that when he commits evil he readily averts his mind, as much as he can, from the feeling of sin. This is why Plato seems to have been compelled to consider (in his *Protagoras*) that we sin only out of ignorance. This might have been an appropriate statement if only human hypocrisy had covered up vices with sufficient skill to prevent the mind from being recognized as evil in God's sight. The sinner tries to evade his innate power to judge between good and evil. Still, he is continually drawn back to it.... It is falsely said, therefore, that man sins out of ignorance alone.[17]

Calvin continues to contrast biblical teaching with that of Plato regarding the view of the body. Whereas Plato saw the body as an impediment to knowledge and something desirable to escape from, Calvin saw it as corrupted but redeemable:

> Accordingly, so long as we dwell in the prison house of our body we must continually contend with the defects of our corrupt nature, indeed with our own natural soul. Plato sometimes says that the life of a philosopher is a meditation upon death; but we may more truly say that the life of a Christian man is a continual effort and exercise in the mortification of the flesh, till it is utterly slain, and God's Spirit reigns in us.[18]

In other words, since he hoped to escape the body, Plato summarized this life as merely waiting to die, meditating upon what glory will attend the molting of the earthly weight of this body. Calvin, following the Bible, argued that escape is not the key, but repentance, redemption, and sanctification by the Spirit in order to overcome the flesh *in this life*. In this way we do not meditate upon future death, but "die daily." Clearly, this effort will involve the Christian accepting the body as (1) real, and (2) worth redemption by God. Furthering such a positive view of the physical body, Calvin later adds,

> It is difficult to believe that bodies, when consumed with rottenness, will at length be raised up in their season. Therefore, although many of the philosophers declared souls immortal, few approved of the resurrection of the flesh. Even though there was no excuse for this point of view, we are nevertheless reminded by it that it is something too hard for men's minds to apprehend. Scripture provides two helps by which faith may overcome this great obstacle: one in the parallel of Christ's resurrection; the other in the omnipotence of God.[19]

REFORMATION VERSUS RATIONALISM

Looking through the lenses of Augustine and Calvin, we can see how biblical faith contrasts with a rationalistic outlook. Rationalism encounters great difficulties from a biblical perspective. As it argues that only the immaterial (rational) world is ultimately real and that the material world forms only a series of illusions for the senses, it runs counter to several biblical doctrines, including the doctrines of God, Creation, Man, Law, and aspects of Redemption and Salvation.

This holds substantial consequences for the life of the mind. God has created the physical world and He pronounced his physical creation "very good" (Gen 1:31). He created man and gave him senses with which to interact with ("witness") that very good creation. He commands us to bear a true witness based on our sensory experience (Ex. 20:16). After the fall of man, God sent his own Son *in the flesh* (John 1:14) to partake of the physical creation in order to save it. The end of salvation will involve the resurrection of the body, and a creation of a new heavens *and new earth*. From beginning to end the Bible affirms the reality, goodness, general reliability, worthiness, and future preservation of the empirical world and the reality of our sensory experience.

From this we can conclude that, while some parts of our knowledge may not depend on sensory experience, nevertheless some of them do, and we will be held accountable for such knowledge that we both receive and communicate. This refutes the pure rationalism of Plato, Descartes, and their followers.

It is worth noting that the worldview of Rationalism, despite all of its technical permutations (many carried out by believing Christians), has devolved generally into a synonym for any anti-faith position. Dr. Flew defines rationalism in the "most popular sense" as, "(a) the rejection of religious belief as being without rational foundation, or (b) more generally, a commitment to reason as opposed to faith, prejudice, habit, or any other source of conviction considered to be irrational."[20]

This popular species of rationalism lies at the root of modern atheism. Although varied in the many expressions and attendant beliefs, all modern atheists detest any supernatural explanation for reality or ethics, and instead attempt to develop a worldview based on "reason." While "reason" plays a central role in this worldview, equally fundamental aspects appear as well: "evidence," and moral assumptions, for example. Since these factors all adhere together in modern skepticism, I have considered them under Worldview Fallacies and under Naturalistic Fallacies in earlier chapters.

The logical problem with this worldview rests in the root attempt to measure all of reality, and all of what *can be* reality, by merely human standards. The Christian rationalist's generic argument that "God gave us reason, and therefore we should use reason to determine the truths of theology," commits multiple errors. For one, it succeeds no better than an empiricist's own narrow argument (should he make it) that, "God gave us five senses, and therefore we should use our senses to determine truth." Nor does it surpass the weakest of such arguments that could whine, "God gave us *feelings*, and therefore we should just rely on our feelings to determine truth." This latter, of course, sounds absurd until we remember that the mantra from *Star Wars*, "Search your feelings, Luke, you know it's true," encouraged two generations of youth to abandon facts for dreams. And what happens when someone confuses a rumbling in their bowels for a "feeling"? Could Vader's journey to the Dark Side have begun simply by skipping breakfast one morning?

In all seriousness, these errors expose the rationalist's folly as well as each others'—the fallacy underlying each of them is the ignoring of what each of them presupposes: "God gave us..." For each scenario, God must exist prior to giving the particular gifts. In addition, this God must be the type of God who communicates to his creatures via creaturely reason, sense, and feeling. Further reasoning will show that only the Christian Trinity fills all of the requirements of human experience, and thus this Trinitarian God must exist before human experience can mean anything (as others have shown).[21] Given this, the ultimate source of human knowledge abides in this God's Revelation to mankind—a revelation of Himself found generally in nature and man himself, and *specially* in Scripture. To reduce "truth" to any of the narrow parts or outlets of general revelation misses the proverbial forest for the trees, in fact, for the dead leaves on the forest floor.

NOTES

1. "Rationalism vs. Empiricism," *Stanford Encyclopedia of Philosophy*; http://plato.stanford.edu/entries/rationalism-empiricism/ (accessed March 16, 2009).

2. "Rationalism vs. Empiricism," *Stanford Encyclopedia of Philosophy*; http://plato.stanford.edu/entries/rationalism-empiricism/ (accessed March 16, 2009).

3. "Rationalism vs. Empiricism," *Stanford Encyclopedia of Philosophy*; http://plato.stanford.edu/entries/rationalism-empiricism/ (accessed March 16, 2009).

4. Antony Flew, "rationalism, 1." *A Dictionary of Philosophy*, 2nd Ed. (New York: Gramercy Books, 1979), 298–299.

5. Parmenides (28 B 8:34–36); compare the translation in Jonathan Barnes, *Early Greek Philosophy* (London and New York: Penguin Books, 1987), 135.

6. Parmenides (28 B 3); compare the translation in Jonathan Barnes, *Early Greek Philosophy*, 132.

7. Plato, "Meno," 81, *Plato in Twelve Volumes*, 12 Vol., trans. W. R. M. Lamb (Cambridge, MA: Harvard University Press; London: William Heinemann Ltd. 1967); http://www.perseus.tufts.edu/hopper/text.jsp?doc=Plat.+Meno+81&fromdoc=Perseus%3Atext%3A1999.01.0178 (accessed March 17, 2009). See the full discussion of "recollection" between Socrates and Meno in "Meno," 81–84.

8. Gordon H. Clark, *A Christian View of Men and Things* (Grand Rapids: Eerdmans, 1952), 318–321.

9. Gordon H. Clark, *A Christian View of Men and Things*, 321.

10. Aurelius Augustine, "On the Trinity," 15.12, *The Nicene and Post Nicene Fathers, First Series*, 14 vol., ed. Philip Schaff, trans. Arthur West Haddan (Grand Rapids: Eerdmans, 1980), 3:210–211.

11. Augustine, "On the Trinity," 15.12, *The Nicene and Post Nicene Fathers, First Series*, 3:211.

12. For more on Augustine and rationalism, see Dewey J. Hoitenga, *Faith and Reason from Plato to Plantinga: An Introduction to Reformed Epistemology* (Albany, NY: SUNY Press, 1991), 62–65.

13. Augustine, "On the Trinity," 15.12, *The Nicene and Post Nicene Fathers, First Series*, 3:211–212.

14. Augustine, "On the Trinity," 15.12, *The Nicene and Post Nicene Fathers, First Series*, 3:212.

15. John Calvin, *Institutes of the Christian Religion*, 2 vol., ed. John T. McNeill, trans. Ford Lewis Battles (Philadelphia: The Westminster Press, 1960), [2.2.2] 1:257.

16. John Calvin, *Institutes of the Christian Religion*, [2.2.14] 1:273.

17. John Calvin, *Institutes of the Christian Religion*, [2.2.22] 1:282.

18. John Calvin, *Institutes of the Christian Religion*, [3.3.20] 1:614–615.

19. John Calvin, *Institutes of the Christian Religion*, [3.25.3] 2:990.

20. Antony Flew, "rationalism, 3." *A Dictionary of Philosophy*, 2nd Ed. (New York: Gramercy Books, 1979), 299.

21. See Cornelius Van Til, *The Defense of the Faith*, 4th Ed., ed. K. Scott Oliphint (Phillipsburg, NJ: Presbyterian and Reformed Publishing, 2008).

Subject & Person Index

A

accent 138–146
   French Foreign Minister and 142–143
   Hebrew text and 144–145
   Huldah the prophetess 144–145
   Jerry Falwell misquoted 143
   Olivet Discourse and 140
   Peter and 139–140
   Roman Catholic Church and 139–140
Adam 4, 10, 38, 46, 78, 79
adultery 45
"after this" fallacy. *See* post hoc propter hoc
Alcuin of York 287
Allah 94
American Humanist Association 86
   Humanist Manifesto II 86–87
amphiboly 123–126
   Greek: net fallacy 124–125
   Israeli Defense Forces and 125
   Jay Leno and 124
   John Madden and 126
   Ludwig Wittgenstein and 125
Apollo moon landing 338
appeal to antiquity 374–379
   David hackett Fischer on 375–376
   Francis Bacon confronts 377–378
   Henry Hazlitt on 376
   Jeremy Bentham on 374–375
   Jesus confronts 374
   law of unintended consequences and 376–378
   Oxford University and 378
   Pharisees and 379–381
   Thomas Sowell on 376–377
   wisdom corrects 381–383

appeal to authority 133, 245–257
   Argumentum Ad Verecundiam 247
   Council of Trent 254
   embryonic stem cell research and 251–252
   legitimate authority versus 248–250
   Leon Trotsky and 257–259
   Mao Tse-Tung and 257–258
   Marxist tradition and 256–258
   Roman Catholic Church and 252–254
   Tombstone and 246
   Victor J. Stenger and 255–256
appeal to fear (or force) 271–283
   Bible examples 279
   Bobby Rush and 273
   Darwinism ans 281–282
   Edward O. Wilson 281
   Immanuel Velikovsky victim of 279–280
   intelligent design victim of 282
   Israel Lobby and U. S. Foreign Policy 280–281
   Kevin MacDonald 281
   legitimate fear 273–278
   Pascal's Wager 278
appeal to ignorance 258–267
   appeal to silence
    Jesus-mythicists 264–266
   appeal to silence as 264
   black squirrel and 258
   David A. Noebel on Dewey 261
   Humanist Manifesto II and 262
   John Dewey and 260–261
   Ronald H. Nash on Dewey 261
   Victor J. Stenger 263–264
appeal to peer pressure 283–289
   Aaron, golden calf and 288

Subject & Person Index

Alcuin of York on 287–288
Ambrose Bierce on 287–288
Bible teaching on 288–290
Darwinists and 290
Democratic National Convention, 1896 and 285
John Gill on 288
King Saul and 288
marketing and 285
Peter's denial 289
Pharisees and 289–290
Pontius Pilate and 289–290
William Jennings Bryan and 285–286
appeal to pity 302–310
   Ann Coulter on 307–309
   Christian mercy versus 302–305
   gay marriageand 304–306
   Leonard Pitts and 304–306
   Messiah and legitimate pity 309–310
   Ron Sider and 303–305
appeal to progress 367–374
   C. S. Lewis defines 368–369
   evolutionism and 370–373
   G. K. Chesterton defines 368–369
   "moral zeitgeist" and 370–373
   Paul confronts 370
   Philip Schaff confronts 372
   Plato and 374
   Ralph Waldo Emerson and 372
   Richard Dawkins and 370–373
   Southern Baptist Convention victim of 374
   technology and 373–374
   wisdom corrects 381–383
appeal to silence 264–266
   Brian Flemming 265
   Jesus-mythicists 264–266
Aquinas, Thomas 11, 136
argument against the person 315–322
   atheists and 320–321
   Bart Ehrman and 318–319
   Beastie Boys and 320
   Bible examples 317
   Christopher Hitchens 317–318
   Hal Lindsey and 321–322
   James White and 318–319
   Jerry Falwell victim of 317
   postmillennialists victim of 321–322
argument to the stick. *See* appeal to fear (or force)
argumentum ad baculum. *See* appeal to fear (or force)
argumentum ad hominem. *See* argument against the person
argumentum ad verecundiam. *See* appeal to authority
Aristotle 20, 57, 65, 67, 70, 145, 147, 378
   accent and 138
   fallacies as dishonesty 62
   fallacies happen 61
   fallacies pay 62
   Homer and 138
   ignoratio elenchi 64
   refutation and 65
   Sophistical Refutations 64
   sophistry and 64
artificial intelligence 95, 189–191
Augustine 69, 78, 133
   creation and knowledge 391–392
   Descartes, anticipates 390–391
   Plato, on 390–392
   rationalism, on 390–392
autonomy 78–80
Ayer, A. J.
   "is"-"ought" fallacy 233

B

Bavinck, Herman 36, 40, 54
begging the question 149
   fossils and rocks and 151
   J. E. O'Rourke and 151
   Jim Wallis and 152
   petitio principii 151
Bentham, Jeremy
   appeal to antiquity, on 374–375
Bergman, Jerry 282
Berra, Tim

evolution of the Corvette 129–130
Bierce, Ambrose 287–288
"big if" 175–181
   Al Gore and 177–178
   Darwinism 178–180
   Larry Moran and 178–180
   Newton named in 178–180
   Spanish Armada and 176–177
   Thomas Paine and 180
   Will and Ariel Durant and 176
   William Dembski confronts 179
bin Laden, Osama 105
biology 109
black swan 114
Blagojevich, Rod
   scandal 273
Boettner, Loraine 11, 17, 210, 322
Böhme, Jakob 372
Bono 248
boundaries 14, 46–49, 48, 49, 175, 197, 223, 225, 347
   laws of logic and 47–48
   naming and 46–47
   of logic (set by God) 33
Buddhism 80
Burris, Roland 273
Bush, George W. 105

C

Calvinism 120
Calvin, John 159, 170, 181, 252, 267, 294, 312
   Plato, on 392–394
Carrier, Richard 86
Carroll, Lewis
   Alice's Adventures in Wonderland 70
Carter, Jimmy 211
category mistakes 233–240
   creator-creation distinction and 237–239
   G. E. Moore and 235–236
   materialism, naturalism and 235–237
   probability and 239–240
   Richard Dawkins and 234–241

Charlemagne 287
Cheney, Dick
   red herring 324–325
Chesterton, G. K.
   appeal to progress, on 368
Christ
   completes man 24
Clark, Gordon 69–70
   equivocation and 132–133
   rationalism, on 389–390
Clinton, Bill
   complex question 165
   false dilemma 105
Community 28
complex question 162–167
   Bill Clinton and 165
   interrogation and 166
   Jesus confronts 164–165
   Pope, Alexander and 163
composition (and division) 198–203
   distinguishing 202–203
   families as democracies and 201
   John Rosemond 201
   Solidarity and the Church 199–201
computer
   binary language and 23
Confucianism 80
consequences 49
conservatism, fallacy of. *See* appeal to antiquity
continuum fallacy. *See* fallacy of the beard
Council of Trent 254
courtroom
   God's 23, 50, 51, 57
cranes
   definition 82
   versus skyhooks 82–86
critical thinking 53–59
   biblical words 53
   God and 54
   Isaiah and 56
   Jesus and 54
   Paul and 56

training in 55–56
cum hoc propter hoc 345–352
    Al Gore and 348
    global warming and 348–350
    Jesus confronts 350–351
    Oregon Institute of Science and Medicine confronts 348–350
    Sam Harris and 345–348
    societal dysfunction (crime) and 345–347
    statistics and 345–348
    suffering and sin 350–351
Cuyahoga River 338

D

Dark Knight, The
    appeal to progress 371
Darwinism 86
David
    and Goliath, story of 115–116
Dawkins, Richard 84–86
    appeal to progress 370–373
    category mistakes 234
    fallacy of the beard 216–217
    red herring 328–329
    skyhooks versus cranes 84–86
    slippery slope 358–360
    straw man 205–207
Dembski, William 179
Dennett, Daniel 82–86
    hypostasization 136
    "is"-"ought" fallacy 230–231
    skyhooks versus cranes 82–86
Dewey, John 260–261
division. *See* composition (and division)
domino fallacy 357. *See also* slippery slope
double standard 167–175
    feminism and 172–175
    Obama campaign ad and 168
    Sam Harris, atheism and 170–171

E

Ehrman, Bart
    argument against the person 318–319
Emerson, Ralph Waldo
    appeal to progress 372
Engel, E. Morris 285
epistemology 31
epithet (and euphemism) 153–162
    Charles Spurgeon and 156
    Civil War and 155
    John Calvin and 159–161
    Norman Geisler and 156–159
equivocation 126–133
    abortion and 130–132
    crucifixion and 127–128
    evolution and 129–130
    Gordon Clark and 132–134
    Sam Harris and 130–132
    Tim Berra and 129–130
    World Series and 134
euphemism. *See* epithet (and euphemism)
Eve
    deception of 44
evolution and jihad 93
    Darwin 93
    Heraclitus 93–94
    Islam 94
    Marxism 93
    struggle and 93
Evolution of the Corvette 128–129

F

fallacies 68–70. *See also* each fallacy by name
    accent 138–146
    amphiboly 123–126
    appeal to antiquity 374
    appeal to authority 245–257
    appeal to fear (or force) 271–283
    appeal to ignorance 258–267
    appeal to peer pressure 283
    appeal to pity 302

appeal to progress 367
begging the question 149–152
"big if" 175
books on, trivial 69–70
category mistakes 48, 132, 233
complex question 162–167
composition (and division) 198–203
cum hoc propter hoc 345
definition of 68
double standard 167
epithet and euphemism 153–162
equivocation 126–133
fallacy of the beard 213–216
false analogy 185–198
gambler's fallacy 351
hypostasization 134–138
"Is"-"Ought" 48
"is"-"ought" fallacy 224–233
poisoning the well 290
post hoc propter hoc 338
red herring 322
slippery slope 357
straw man 203
Fallacies of Ambiguity 123–146
Fallacies of Cause 337
Fallacies of Relevance 14
Fallacies of Representation 13
Fallacies of Time 15
fallacy
  argument against the person 315
fallacy of the beard 213–216
  Loki and 214
  Richard Dawkins and 216–217
  tax brackets and 215–216
false analogy 185–198
  artificial intelligence 189–191
  Betty Friedan and 192–194
  box of chocolates and 187
  David Hume and 188
  feminism and 192–195
  Francis Bacon and 188–189
  Marxism and 195–198
  Nazi camps and 192–194
  Southern Baptist Convention victim

of 194–195
  Stanley L. Jaki confronts 191
  Victor J. Stenger and 189–191
false dilemma 103–111
  Bill Clinton and 105
  George W. Bush and 105
  Jesus confronts 105
  Justin Raimondo and 108
  Sam Harris and 109
  tax policies and 107
FBI
  false dilemma 108
Fictional Questions. *See* "big if"
Fischer, David Hackett 276, 339
  appeal to antiquity, on 375
five points 9, 41–51
Flemming, Brian
  appeal to silence 265
Flew, Antony 12, 15, 17, 99
  leaky buckets 91
  rationalism 387
  rationalism, on 395
Flying Spaghetti Monster
  fallacy of the beard 216
Fox, Michael J. 248
Friedan, Betty 192–194

G

gambler's fallacy 351–360
  all of life and 354–355
  insurance and 355–356
  sports superstitions and 352
  stock market and 353–355
  three ways to approach 355–356
  uncertainty and risk, dealing with 355–356
garbage collecting
  Fallacies and 19
Garden of Eden 30
Geisler, Norman 181
  appeal to peer pressure, on 288
  epithet 156
Gill, John 288
global warming 348

403

God
    self-authoritative 28, 30
    self-consistent 27, 30, 32
    self-identity 28, 33
    self-naming 28
Gore, Al
    cum hoc propter hoc 348–350
    slippery slope 359–360
Grizzly Adams 214

H

hairless dog
    Mexican and Peruvian 113
Harris, Sam 219, 227, 232, 241, 250, 267, 345, 362
    equivocation by 130–132
    false dilemma and 109–110
    "is"-"ought" fallacy 227–228
    poisoning the well 299
    straw man 207–209
hasty generalization 111–113
    Paul on 112
Hazlitt, Henry 376
Hegel, G. W. F. 372
Heraclitus 93–94
Hitchens, Christopher
    argument against the person 317–318
    slippery slope 359
Holm, Ian 292
Homer 138
Humanist Manifesto II 86–87, 262
human nature
    fallen 77–80
Hume, David 188
    "is"-"ought" fallacy 224–226
hypostasization 134–138
    Daniel Dennett and 136
    Hilary Putnam and 136
    Jacques Monod and 135–136
    M. Mitchell Waldrop 136
    natural selection and 135–136
    science and 136–137

"Word of Faith" movement and 137–138
hypothesis contrary to fact. *See* "big if"

I

idolatry 45
    adultery as 45–46
Image of God 10, 44
    human order and 29–31
incremental fallacy. *See* fallacy of the beard
intelligent design 109, 115, 282
"is"-"ought" fallacy 224–233
    A. J. Ayer and 233
    Daniel Dennett and 230–231
    David Hume and 224–226
    G. E. Moore and 226–228
    Marquis de Sade 228–230
    Sam Harris and 227–230

J

Jaki, Stanley L. 191
Johnson, Paul
    Great Depression debunked 341–343
judgment 49–50

K

Keynes, John Maynard 235
Kuyper, Abraham 231

L

law of unintended consequences 376–378
leaky buckets 15, 91
leaven 98, 339
Lewis, C. S. 11, 17, 169, 383
    appeal to progress, on 368–369, 372
liar's paradox 113
Lindsey, Hal

argument against the person 321–322
straw man 209–210
Little Ice Age 348
Locke, John 20, 26
logic
   Bible and 22–24
   Christian faith and 20
   Christ/Incarnation and 37–40
   Creation and 30–32
   definition of 22, 39
   fall of man and 77–80
   imputed from without 28
   laws of 14, 29, 33, 47–48, 386
    law of excluded middle 48
    law of identity 33, 47
    law of non-contradiction 32, 48
   limited to limits of creation 33–35
   logos and 37
    equivocation on 132–134
   objective reality and 27–28
   redemptiion/repentance and 35–36
   Revelation and 32–36
   Ten Commandments and 41–51
Loki
   fallacy of the beard 214

M

MacDonald, Kevin
   appeal to fear (or force) 281
Marquis de Sade 228–230
Marx. Karl
   reductionism by 120–121
Mencken, H. L. 95
metaphysics 31
Mises, Ludwig von 122, 342, 342–343, 356, 364
   money, on 118–119
   simplification vs reductionism 118
Monod, Jacques 135
Moore, G. E.
   category mistakes 235
   "is"-"ought" fallacy 226–228

Mttingly, Garrett 339
Münster 160–162
murder 22, 43, 44–45, 49, 130, 131, 160, 166, 170, 171, 229, 232, 236, 275, 306, 340, 346, 350, 371

N

Napoleon 97
Nash, Ronald H. 261
naturalism 79–88
   Jesus on 81
   "negative" concept 80, 83
   problems with 80–82
   skyhooks versus cranes 82–86
   subjectivism and 88
   supernaturalism versus 80
   uniformitarianism and 80
Nehru, Jawaharlal 208
New Age 80
Newman, John Henry Cardinal
   Apologia Pro Vita Sua 291
Nietzsche, Friedrich 95–97
   war and 96
nihilism 92–93
   chaos and 93
ninth commandment 22, 30, 41, 49, 55, 149
Nisbet, Robert
   appeal to fear (or force), on 280
Noebel, David A. 261
nothing-buttery fallacy 115

O

obscurantism 118
Olympics, Moscow 1980 200
O'Rourke, J. E. 151

P

Paine, Thomas
   "big if" 180–181

straw man 203–204
Parmenides 387
Pascal's Wager 278
petitio principii 151
Pitts, Leonard
   appeal to pity 304–306
Plato 374
   Calvin on 392–394
   immaterial soul 388
poisoning the well 290–299
   "anti-Semitism" and 300
   Barry Horner and 300
   character, reputation and 294–295
   Charles Kingsley and 291–294
   Christopher Hitchens and 299
   Darwinists and 301–302
   Emperor's New Clothes and 292
   Eugenie Scott and 301–302
   Family Values and K.K.K 299
   Fred Schwarz on 295
   John Calvin on 294
   John Henry Cardinal Newman victim of 291–294
   liberal agenda and 299
   Marxism and 295–296
   Paul versus 297
   Pharisees and 296
   reductio ad Hitlerum 298
    dispensationalism and 300–301
   Rush D. Holt 301–302
   Vladimir Lenin and 295
Pontius Pilate 266
   appeal to peer pressure 289–290
   Christ and 9–10
   red herring 332
Pope
   John Paul II 200
post hoc propter hoc 338–345
   America's Great Depression and 341–343
   Apollo moon landing 338
   Cuyahoga River fire 338
   G. W. Bush victim of 343
   Jesus confronts 339
   medicine and 344–345
   Paul Johnson on 341–343
   reproductive rights and 343
   Ripley's museum, fertility gods and 343
   rooster 338
   Spanish Armada and 338
   Thomas Woods on 341–343
   Will and Ariel Durant and 338
postmillennialism 210–211, 321–322, 330
Powell, Colin 165
pride 11, 155, 169, 177, 208, 252, 332, 351
progressivism. *See* appeal to progress
Putnam, Hillary
   hypostasization 136

R

Raimondo, Justin
   false dilemma 108
rationalism
   Antony Flew on 387, 395
   atheism and 395
   Augustine on 390–392
   basic fallacy of 390
   bible versus 394–396
   Calvin on 392–394
   creation versus 394–395
   definitions of 386–387
   Gordon Clark on 389–390
   history of 387–390
   Parmenides on 387–388
   Plato on 387–388
   problems with 386–387
reason
   Isaiah 1:18 and 56
redemptive truth 35–36
red herring 322–334
   abortion and 328
   Crusades and 326
   Dick Cheney and 324–325
   Garry Wills and 328
   Greg Bahnsen confronts 330

history of name 322
Neil deGrasse Tyson victim of 328–329
Paul and 332–333
Pontius Pilate and 332
pragmatism and 327–328
Richard Dawkins and 328–329
Richard Gaffin and 330
theonomy victim of 330
typical examples 325–327
woman at the well and 330
reductio ad Hitlerum 298
reductionism 114–120
advertisement and 119–120
"big fly" theory 117–118
Calvinism victim of 120
David and Goliath 115
evolution and 116–118
Karl Marx and 120–121
"nothing-buttery" 115
obscurantism and 118
Timothy, youthfulness and 115
Reeve, Christopher 248
refutation 63–68
Aristotle and 65
biblical view of 65–68
Holy Spirit and 66–68
reification. *See* hypostasization
representation 10, 45–46
revelation
anthropomorphic 34
Rushdoony, R. J. 229
Russell, Bertrand 208
Tea Pot 234

S

Sabbath 49
Sadoleto, Jacopo
appeal to authority 252–254
Schaff, Philip 372
Schwarz, Fred 295
Scott, Eugenie
poisoning the well 301–302
Sider, Ron

appeal to pity 303–304
Silvas, Christina
false dilemma and 106
skyhooks
definition 82–83
versus cranes 82–86
slippery slope
Al Gore and 359
Christopher Hitchens and 359
fallacy of the beard compared 357
Peter confronts 360
Reconstructionism victim of 358
Richard Dawkins and 358–360
Slippery Slope 357–361
Smith, Morton H. 31
Sophistry 63
Sowell, Thomas 376–377
speculative fallacy. *See* "big if"
Spurgeon, Charles 156
squirrel, black 258
Star Wars 395
Stenger, Victor J. 263–264
appeal to authority 255–256
false analogy 189–191
Stradivarius 111–112
straw man 203–213
dealing with 212–213
Hal Lindsey and 209–210
homosexuality, the Bible and 211–212
India and Pakistan and 207–209
Jimmy Carter and 211
Merrill Unger and 210
postmillennialism 210–211
Richard Dawkins and 205–207
Sam Harris and 207–209
Thomas Paine and 203–204
struggle 93–94
Darwin and 93
Heraclitus and 93
Islam and 94
Marxism and 93
subjectivism 89–92
empiricism and 90

rationalism and 89
reason and evidence and 89–91
relativism and 92
superman 94
  Nietzsche and 95–97
supernaturalism 80
Sutton, Ray 17, 42, 44, 51
sweeping generalization 113–114
  black swan 114

T

Taoism 80
Ten Commandments 41–51
  two tablets 41
Tertullian
  On Idolatry 45
Tyson, Neil deGrasse
  red herring 328–329

U

uniformitarianism 80

V

Van Til, Cornelius 31, 40, 59, 99, 385, 397
Velikovsky, Immanuel 279–280, 283

W

Waldrop, M. Mitchell 136
Wallis, Jim
  begging the question 152
  false dilemma 107
Wall Street Journal 149
war 105
  "War on Terror" 105
Westminster Confession of Faith 254
Wills, Gary
  equivocation 130
  red herring 328
Wilson, Edward O.
  appeal to fear (or force) 281
wisdom
  vs. fallacies of time 381–383
"with this" fallacy. *See* cum hoc propter hoc
Wittgenstein, Ludwig 125, 146, 235
Wojtyla, Karol 200
Woods, Thomas
  Great Depression debunked 341–343
Worldview Fallacies 10, 77–98

Y

"yes" and "no" 22–23
  computers and 23